SCHNAUFER

Major *Heinz Wolfgang*
Schnaufer

SCHNAUFER

ACE OF DIAMONDS

The Biography of Heinz Wolfgang Schnaufer:
Germany's Top-Scoring Night Fighter
of World War II

Peter Hinchliffe

TEMPUS

First published 1999

PUBLISHED IN THE UNITED KINGDOM BY:

Tempus Publishing Ltd
The Mill, Brimscombe Port
Stroud, Gloucestershire GL5 2QG

PUBLISHED IN THE UNITED STATES OF AMERICA BY:

Tempus Publishing Inc.
2A Cumberland Street
Charleston, SC 29401

Tempus books are available in France, Germany and Belgium from the following addresses:

Tempus Publishing Group	Tempus Publishing Group	Tempus Publishing Group
21 Avenue de la République	Gustav-Adolf-Straße 3	Place de L'Alma 4/5
37300 Joué-lès-Tours	99084 Erfurt	1200 Brussels
FRANCE	GERMANY	BELGIUM

British Library Cataloguing in Publication Data.
A catalogue record for this book is available from the British Library.

ISBN 0 7524 1690 1

Typesetting and origination by Ace Filmsetting Ltd, Frome, Somerset.
Printed and bound by Butler and Tanner Ltd, Frome, Somerset.

A saying was coined during the American Civil War, but it is no longer remembered by whom:

'Poor is the nation that has no heroes, but beggared is the nation that has, and forgets them.'

This book is dedicated to the heroes of all nations who flew in the Second World War. May we never forget them.

Contents

Acknowledgements

Many persons, all of whom I look upon as friends – and that includes, I am happy to say, former enemies – have willingly and unstintingly helped me with information, material and advice during the writing of this book, and I am deeply grateful to them. Then there are official sources such as the Public Record Office, the Imperial War Museum, the *Bundesarchiv/Militärarchiv* in Freiburg, the *Gemeinschaft der Jagdflieger e.V.*, and so on, to whom I am also indebted. Background reading was, of course, necessary – and enjoyable – and where I have quoted from other writers I have inserted an appropriate footnote. I have also compiled a list of titles selected from the many books that bear on my subject.

I should like to name everyone who has helped me but I fear that, try as I might, human fallibility will mean that I will omit some. To them, my apologies – it was not intentional! Some, of course, helped more than others, because their background, experiences and insight better fitted them to do so, as will be clear from the text. All were indispensable, and it would be invidious, I think, to pick out anyone for special mention. I will list them, therefore, in alphabetical order, and I will omit ranks, decorations and so on: Gebhard Aders; Robert Bansfield; Heinrich Becker; Martin Becker; Heinz Bönsch; Lewis Brandon; Stan Bridgman; Charles W Brister; Phil Butler; John Chaloner; David Cheetham; Bill R Chorley; Eddy Coward; Stephen Darlow; Horst Diener; Martin Drewes; Wulfhild Drewes; John Elsom; Fritz Engau; Wolfgang Falck; Georg Fengler; Waltraud Fengler; Neville Franklin; Otto Fries; Sidney Goldberg; Georg Hermann Greiner; Ernst Güse; Steve Hague; Peter Harris; Hajo Herrmann; Werner Hoffmann; Hans-Joachim Jabs; Ken James; Wim Johnen; Erich Jung; Chris van Kerckhoven; Peggy Langdown; Mark Langdown; Gunther Lauser; Eugen Lebzelter; Peter Loncke; Dick Lord; Allan McRae; Ludwig Meister; Kurt Meyer; Johannes Mohn; Bob Orzel; Paul Rathgeber; Jean-Louis Roba; Alain Rosseels; Fritz Rumpelhardt; Jill Rutter; Manfred Schnaufer; Harry Shinkfield; Peter Spoden; Herbert Thomas; Ton Weulink; Paul Zorner.

Foreword

By Oberstleutnant a.D. Hans-Joachim Jabs,
former Kommodore of Nachtjagdgeschwader 1

I am delighted to accept the invitation by the successful author Peter Hinchliffe to write a foreword to his new book on the life of Heinz Schnaufer. Peter is well known in Britain and abroad for his objective presentation of historical events, and he is also very highly respected by former members of the German night-fighter force because of the unbiased reporting in his book *The Other Battle*.

Today, sadly, it would be virtually impossible for a German author to write a book for publication in Germany about Heinz Schnaufer, the most successful of night fighters. That sad fact makes us all the more grateful that a former enemy, who himself flew by night as a navigator in the Bomber Command offensive, should take the trouble to preserve Schnaufer's life and achievements for posterity.

In his steadfastness of character and his personal integrity Schnaufer bears comparison with Manfred *Freiherr* von Richthofen, the 'Red Baron' of the First World War. He commanded a *Staffel* in my *Gruppe* and later, when I took over the command of NJG 1 from *Oberstleutnant* Werner Streib, he was my successor as *Kommandeur* of the highly successful night-fighter *Gruppe* IV./NJG 1.

Towards the end of 1944, on the basis of his ability to motivate his subordinates to high achievement, he was appointed *Kommodore* of NJG 4. Despite all his successes and his high decorations he remained a true comrade, always ready to help where he could, a man upon whom everyone could rely.

It is greatly to Peter Hinchliffe's credit that as a result of this book the name of Heinz Schnaufer will never be forgotten, either at home or abroad.

Achim Jabs,
Lüdenscheid,
Germany,
June 1997.

Introduction

If either chance or design should take you to the Black Forest township of Calw in the *Land* of Baden-Württemberg, picturesque with its half-timbered buildings and set in a fold of tree-covered hills, and if you should find yourself on the main road north in the direction of Pforzheim, a small town that was devastated in an attack by Bomber Command in the final months of the Second World War, you might notice a cemetery lying back from the road on the right-hand side as you leave. It is an old cemetery, its close-set headstones arranged in orderly rows parallel to the road and rising, auditorium-like, up the steep slope. Well-tended graves and fresh flowers testify to the lasting love and reverence in which those buried there are held and to the Germans' innate attachment to orderliness and tradition.

I first visited the cemetery at Calw in October 1995, looking for the grave of Heinz Wolfgang Schnaufer. I began my search at the bottom tier of graves, climbing zigzag as inspection of each row proved fruitless. In my search I came across a number of gravestones inscribed 'Schnaufer' or 'Schnauffer', but it was not until I reached the topmost row that I found what I was looking for. The gravestone was modestly impressive, unostentatious. Beneath the outline of an eagle in flight, wings widespread, was inscribed,

> *Hier ruht der beste u. niebesiegte Nachtjäger des 2. Weltkrieges, Major u.*
> *Geschwaderkommodore Heinz Wolfgang Schnaufer, 1922–1950,*

and below that was a short piece of verse. Translated, the inscription reads, 'Here rests the best and never-conquered night fighter of the Second World War, *Major* and *GeschwaderKommodore* Heinz Wolfgang Schnaufer, 1922 to 1950'. Schnaufer had lived for just five years after the end of the war, and had been only twenty-eight years of age when Death, from which he had miraculously escaped during years of uninterrupted operational combat, claimed him at last.

The verse extract beneath the dedication is harder to translate effectively, because it is impossible to reproduce in English the harsh, sweeping, vibrant onomatopoeia of the German original. Nor is it possible to translate it so that the thyme pattern is preserved. But there is a feeling about the stanza, when one reads it in German, of being left up in the air, as if there should be another line to complete it:

'Thee would I salute in the threshing of thy wings,
My heart foretells me triumph in thy name.
Onward, proud eagle, to thee the cloud must yield.'[1]

That Schnaufer was the most successful night-fighter pilot of World War Two is indisputable: in all probability he will take his place in history as the most successful night fighter of all time, because it is unlikely that there will ever again be another vast and sustained aerial battle like the one in which he achieved his distinction. From his first operational victory on 1 June 1942 to his final one on 7 March 1945 he and his crew shot down a confirmed total of 121 British bombers by night: they had other victories that remained unconfirmed because they did not meet the exacting requirements set by the *Luftwaffe* before a victory could be officially accredited. Whether he was the <u>best</u> night fighter is open to debate. Other Germans achieved very high scores but then lost their life before they could fulfil their potential – *Oberleutnant* Helmut Woltersdorf, for instance, who died in June 1942 with a score of 24 four short days after Schnaufer had had his first success; *Hauptmann* Ludwig Becker, the so-called '*Professor der Nachtjagd*', killed in action in February 1943 with a score of 44 when Schnaufer had shot down a mere seven; the charismatic and legendary *Major* Heinrich *Prinz* zu Sayn-Wittgenstein, who, with 83 kills, about twice the number that Schnaufer had reached, was the leading night-fighter pilot when he was killed in action in January 1944; *Oberst* Helmut Lent, who died in a flying accident on 7 October 1944 when his tally stood at 110 and Schnaufer's at 98; and others who might, had they survived, also have achieved very high scores. And can one compare the capabilities and qualities of German defensive night fighters with those of their British counterparts, whose tallies were so much lower? The RAF men had far fewer opportunities to amass high scores because they had far fewer bombers to shoot at. The Germans did not attack Britain by night in anything like the enormous numbers in which Bomber Command struck at targets in the Third Reich and in the territories they occupied, so that direct comparison, RAF versus *Luftwaffe*, is impossible. But there can be no doubt that Schnaufer was an outstanding pilot: his achievements render debate on that point superfluous.

In attempting to put the effect that Schnaufer alone had on Bomber Command's efforts between mid-1942 and the end of the war in Europe into context and into perspective, there are several ways in which one might look at his achievements. Firstly, all but seven of Schnaufer's kills were four-engined bombers, Stirlings, Halifaxes and Lancasters. Each of these machines normally carried a crew of seven, but this was sometimes brought up to eight by the inclusion of a second pilot, usually under training, or other 'spare bod'. The seven twin-engined machines that Schnaufer also shot down comprised six

---

[1] Translated from *Der preußische Grenzadler* (The Prussian Border-Eagle) by Theodor Körner, 1791–1813.

Wellingtons and one Whitley, each probably carrying five men. A fair average complement of the aircraft that Schnaufer destroyed might, therefore, be seven. It follows that Schnaufer was directly responsible for putting out of action something like 850 British, Commonwealth and Allied aircrew. Of these, statistically, 700 would have been killed, 125 would have been taken prisoner and 25 would have evaded capture and returned to Britain. Many of those who survived attacks by Schnaufer, either as prisoners or as passengers in a damaged bomber that made it back home, would have suffered injuries that ranged from the superficial to the near-fatal.

Or one might look at Schnaufer's performance in terms of the aircraft he shot down rather than in terms of the men he eliminated. The establishment of a Bomber Command squadron in wartime varied between twenty and thirty aircraft, with an average of perhaps twenty-four. Hence the German ace and his crew alone destroyed the equivalent of five complete squadrons. More imaginatively, one might attempt to visualise 121 Lancasters, Halifaxes or Stirlings lined up wing tip to wing tip. Each 'heavy' had a wingspan of about 100 feet, so that the imaginary line of bombers would extend a distance of over two and a quarter miles!

Almost as remarkable as Schnaufer's achievements in destroying enemy bombers is the fact that in the course of the many aerial combats from which his victories came he was never once shot down, never had to make a crash-landing or take to his parachute, nor were he or members of his crew ever injured other than superficially. The majority of aircrew of the *Nachtjagd*, the German night-fighter force, were shot down, wounded or forced to bale out at some time during their career, many several times, so that those who came through unscathed were the exceptions rather than the norm. No doubt luck played its part, but there can also be little doubt that Schnaufer's skills as a pilot and tactician contributed greatly to his apparent immunity.

Night-fighter crewmen who knew Schnaufer during his operational career, including the one most qualified to comment, his former radar-man, Fritz Rumpelhardt, bear testimony to Schnaufer's marksmanship. It has often been claimed, quite fairly, that the installation of so-called *Schräge Musik* into the German night-fighter aircraft in the second half of 1943 made the task of hitting a target aircraft much easier. *Schräge Musik* was the code-name for upward-firing cannon set in the fuselage of the night fighters, so that a pilot who could manoeuvre his fighter below a bomber had a simple, non-deflection shot at his target. In addition, he aimed from a position in which he could not be seen by the bomber's crew, so he could take his time and ensure that his aim was true. Some German pilots became so attached to this form of attack that they almost completely neglected the more traditional, and more difficult, *von hinten unten* (from astern and below) approach, while others – notable among whom was the formidable Hans-Joachim Jabs, *Kommodore* of NJG 1, who ended the war with an overall total of fifty victories to his credit – never came to terms with it. But then Jabs was a former *Zerstörer* pilot, and he had served his apprenticeship in daylight operations on the Bf 110[1] twin-engined escort fighter, on which he had earned nineteen of his victories, so that he was a master of the art of aiming off for a moving target. So averse was Jabs to the innovation, *Schräge Musik*, that he had it removed from his personal aircraft.

That Schnaufer, on the other hand, was at home with both his forward-firing guns and his *Schräge Musik* cannon is testified to by the fact that he had already scored about 30 night victories before his Bf 110 was fitted with vertically firing guns. After that, according again to Rumpelhardt, he would, on approaching a bomber, simply decide which weapon system was appropriate to that particular target and then make his attack, and he was equally deadly with either. But we will consider *Schräge Musik* in depth later on.

The end of the war saw Heinz Schnaufer the Commanding Officer of a night-fighter *Geschwader*, NJG 4, with the rank of *Major*. He was just 23 years of age, and he was the youngest German officer to have reached a position of such responsibility. The extent of that responsibility may be judged by recalling that each fighter *Geschwader* normally comprised three or four *Gruppen*, each made up of three *Staffeln* of from nine to twelve aircraft. The *Staffel* was the basic fighting unit. At *Gruppe* and *Geschwader* level there were Staff (*Stab*) flights, usually of three aircraft each. When Schnaufer commanded NJG 4 it had three *Gruppen*, so that its establishment strength was between 90 and 120 aircraft. Many authors attempt to simplify the reading of their works on the German Air Force by translating, for example, '*Staffel*' as 'Flight', '*Gruppe*' as 'Squadron' and so on, but that is misleading. There is no real equivalence, because the operational structure of the *Luftwaffe*, like its tactical and strategical doctrine, differed considerably from that of the RAF. But it is interesting to try to compare the responsibility shouldered by the young Schnaufer with that exercised by his equivalent in rank in Bomber Command. *Major* equates to the Royal Air Force rank of Squadron Leader, and a Squadron Leader in the RAF would probably hold no higher command position than that of Flight Commander, with a Wing Commander having command of a squadron. There were usually three flights to a squadron. So whereas Schnaufer exercised direct command over at least 100 aircraft, their crews, their ground crews and all their support staff, his British equivalent in rank might have had nominal command of perhaps eight to ten machines.

After the hostilities in Europe were over Schnaufer returned to Calw. There he took over from his mother the reins of the family wine-distribution business, which she had assumed when her husband, Heinz's father, had died of a heart attack early in the war. Not surprisingly, given the rigours of wartime, the business was moribund. Schnaufer brought to bear the same energy, the same organisational and leader-

---

[1] So frequently referred to as the Me (Messerschmitt) 110 that the two designations may be considered to be interchangeable. The former, and strictly correct, version (Bf) will generally be used in this book.

ship qualities that he had amply demonstrated during the war, and by 1950 the firm was prospering. Then tragedy struck. In July that year Heinz Schnaufer was on a wine-buying visit to Southern France when the car he was driving was in collision with a lorry that emerged from a side-road without yielding right of way. In itself the accident would probably have been nothing more than an unpleasant incident, and Schnaufer might only have incurred minor injuries. But Fate decreed otherwise. Schnaufer was driving an open car, and the lorry was carrying heavy gas cylinders. The two vehicles struck broadside on and slid to the side of the road, tilting as they skidded into a ditch. One or more of the gas bottles, insecurely fixed, fell off the lorry and struck Schnaufer on the back of the head, injuring him so severely that he died in hospital the following day.

Seldom had the saying 'Whom the Gods love die young' seemed more appropriate. A life of outstanding achievement and high promise had been cut off abruptly, apparently perfunctorily. There are few who would now claim that the regime that Schnaufer flew for and fought for was not corrupt: many, on the other hand, even – or, rather, particularly – among his wartime enemies, would agree that he was a great hero and that he had achieved his high distinction in the direct defence of his fellow-citizens.

Since Schnaufer's untimely death a large number of stories about him have been circulated, many of them in print: to a large degree they can be categorised as legend and myth, but they persist. This book will attempt to expose and correct such distortions of history.

It is unlikely that Schnaufer will ever achieve the romanticised status or attract the undiscriminating admiration that now attach to many of the fighter aces of the First World War such as McCudden, Mannock, Guynemer, Ball, Udet, von Richthofen, or even, if possibly to a somewhat lesser degree, to those of World War Two like Bader, Johnson, Finucane, Clostermann, Cunningham, Braham, Hartmann, Galland and so on. Literature on the war in the air between 1939 and 1945 has, to a considerable extent, neglected the night fighters of the *Luftwaffe*, what they were called upon to do and what they accomplished in conditions and circumstances that always demanded very high standards of bravery, ability and tenacity. There are a number of reasons for this. On one level, night fighting lacked the glamour of aerial combat by day, the stylised image of the cut-and-thrust of man and machine in mortal combat against man and machine. The task of the night-fighter crews was, on the face of it, more pedestrian and less swashbuckling, and it was harder to write about in the sort of easily-absorbed, stimulating hyperbole that so often sells books.

But there are deeper, more fundamental reasons for the neglect of the German night fighters in written works. The initiative for writing authoritatively about them first lay in the hands of those who had themselves flown with the *Nachtjagd*, the pilots, radio and radar operators, mechanics and gunners who flew in the Messerschmitt 110s, the Junkers 88s, the Heinkel 219s and the other machines that formed the force.

And very few chose to record their experiences. This is easy to understand. The bomber offensive against the Fatherland had been unimaginably and indescribably brutal and devastating, and Germany had suffered a shattering defeat, to which the bombing had contributed hugely. It had affected, very deeply, all those who had experienced it, either on the ground or in the air. It was something they would ideally have liked to forget but could not, but still something they did not want reminding of. In Britain and in America after the end of hostilities the pride and glorification in victory triggered off a flood of books – many historically irresponsible – about the war and how the west had won it, but for the Germans the idea of going into print was not as attractive: they had been comprehensively beaten and they had been disgraced as a nation, and there is nothing to crow about in defeat and disgrace. And so the night-fighter aircrew had little incentive to write about their experiences, and the German public did not want to read about them. And in any case the German nation was subjected by the victors to a period of 're-education', in which, particularly in East Germany, the part played by the German armed forces was at best a subject not talked about, at worst the object of bitter criticism.

All history, including that of war, is multi-faceted and deserves to be observed and recorded objectively from as many viewpoints as possible. Men and women are at the very core of history. It is by looking closely at individuals against the background of contemporary happenings that history reveals its many dimensions. Schnaufer was not only a man of unique talents but also a man of his time and a man, it might be said, in the right place at the right time. He was born in 1922, which meant that in his formative years he was exposed to and conditioned by the burgeoning nationalism of the Third Reich. His age meant, too, that he was destined to find himself, voluntarily or involuntarily, in the German armed forces and to fight in the Second World War. In common with so many other German youths he was attracted at an early age by the state-sponsored propaganda devoted to the glamour and the challenge of flying in the period following the emergence of the *Luftwaffe* from clandestinity in 1935, so that a career in the German Air Force was a natural path for him to follow. Once he was in that service his innate qualities, which some might say amounted to genius, ensured that he became an outstanding pilot and leader, while the way in which the battle between the British night bombers and the German night fighters developed provided him with an arena in which his education, training and talents could realise their potential.

This is the first serious and responsible biography of Heinz Schnaufer to reach publication, but it is also a belated attempt. Sadly, the length of time that has passed since his death means that many primary human sources who would ideally have been consulted are no longer with us. And equally regrettably there are wide gaps in the documentary material still available. Lastly, human memory fades and perspectives alter. It follows that many questions that arise will have to remain unanswered.

Glossary of German Words and Phrases

I trust that the meaning of the German words and phrases used in the text of this book will be readily apparent from the context in which they appear. Nevertheless, I give below a table of meanings that I hope will be useful to those who feel that they need further guidance. It must be born in mind that the form of German words, particularly adjectives and verbs, varies to some extent in relation to their grammatical function.

Abitur	The public university-entrance examination, equivalent (pre-war) to Matriculation.
Abzeichen	Badge.
Achtung!	Attention! Look out!
Adler	Eagle. '*Adler 133*' was a callsign used by Heinz Schnaufer.
Alt	(Adjective) – old.
Altdeutsch	(Adjective) - Old German.
Alte Hasen	Literally 'Old Hares'. German equivalent of 'Old stagers'. 'Old lags,' Old timers,' etc.
Andere	(Adjective) – other.
Arbeitdienst	Labour Service.
Arbeiter	Worker.
Archiv	Archives, library.
Areopag	Areopagus. A *Luftwaffe* conference held in Berlin in Autumn 1944.
Ausbildung	Training.
Befehl	Order, command.
Beobachter	Observer. Can be used in the sense of either 'navigator' or 'look-out'.
Bereitschaft	Readiness, stand-by.
Berühren	(Verb) – to touch, to make contact. '*Ich berühre*,' – 'I am in contact with the enemy.'
Berührung	Contact.
Bewaffnung	Armament.
Blindflug	Blind flying (on instruments only).

Blindflugschule	Blind Flying School.
Bodenplatte	Floor tile, paving stone etc. Operation mounted by the *Luftwaffe* against Allied airfields in France and Belgium on New Year's Day 1945.
Bordbuch	Flying Log Book.
Bordfunker	Air radio and/or radar operator.
Bordmechaniker	Air mechanic. A crew-member in some night fighters.
Bordschützer	Air gunner.
Brillanten	The Diamonds. The third higher grade of the *Ritterkreuz*. This was effectively the highest order of the Knight's Cross, and the nearest equivalent to the Victoria Cross.
Brillantenträger	Holder of the *Brillanten*.
Buch	Book
Bucht	Bay.
Bundesarchiv	The Federal Record Office.
Calwer Tagblatt	The 'Calw Daily'.
Christbaum	Christmas tree.
Deutschlandhalle	A large exhibition hall in Berlin.
Dienst	Service.
Diktat	A dictate, ultimatum etc. The Versailles Treaty was widely known in Germany as the '*Versailler Diktat*'.
Division	Division.
Donnerkeil	Thunderbolt. Codeword for the successful operation in early 1942 to move the capital ships *Scharnhorst*, *Gneisenau* and *Prinz Eugen* through the English Channel.
Dritter Mann	Third Man. An extra man carried in some night fighters to keep a careful look-out in the darkness.
Dudelsack	Bagpipes. Vernacular name given by night-fighter aircrew to a form of aural jamming practised by the RAF.
Dunaja	Abbr. for *dunkle Nachtjagd*, q.v.
Dunkel	Dark.
Dunkle Nachtjagd	Literally 'dark night fighting'. Close-controlled interception. Abbreviated *Dunaja*.
Düppel	German codeword for strips of aluminium-coated paper dropped to jam enemy radars. (British 'Window').
Eichenlaub	The Oak Leaves. The first higher grade of the *Ritterkreuz*.

Eisbär	Polar bear – codeword for *Himmelbett* control area.
Eisern	(Adjective) – iron.
Eisernes Kreuz	Iron Cross.
EK	Abbr. for *Eizernes Kreuz* (q.v.).
EKI, EKII	Iron Cross First Class and Second Class respectively.
Eliteschule	School for the élite.
Emil-Emil	Codeword meaning, 'I have *Lichtenstein* contact.'
Europa	Europe.
Fahnenjunker	Officer Cadet.
Fähnrich	German rank roughly equivalent to Warrant Officer (RAF).
Fasan	Pheasant: codeword meaning 'enemy activity expected immediately' .
Feind	Enemy.
Feindberührung	Contact with the enemy.
Feindfriedhof	A cemetery for members of the hostile forces.
Feldmarschall	Field Marshal.
Feldpostnummer	Field Post Office Number.
Feldwebel	German rank equivalent to Sergeant (RAF).
Festung	Fortress.
Feuersee	'Sea of flames' (Codeword).
Flensburg	A German AI equipment that homed on British radar transmissions.
Flieger	An airman, a flier.
Fliegerausbildung	Flying Training.
Fliegerdivision	Air Division.
Fliegerkorps	Air Corps.
Fliegerzug	(At *Napola*) – Trainee Aircrew Platoon.
Flugzeug	Aircraft, aeroplane etc.
Flugzeugführer	Pilot.
Flugzeugführerabzeichen	Pilot's badge (wings).
Friedhof	Cemetery.
Führer	Leader. Not only the Reichs *Führer*, Adolf Hitler.
Führerprinzip	A basic tenet of the Nazi Party, the 'Leader Principle' or 'Leadership Principle', which said that there should be competent and responsible decision-talking leaders at all organisational levels.
Führung	Leadership.
Funker	Radio operator, wireless operator, radar operator, etc.
Gefechtsstand	Operations Room, Operational Control

	Headquarters etc.
Gefreiter	German rank equivalent to Aircraftman (RAF).
Gegenwehr	Enemy defensive action.
Gemeinschaft	Group, association etc.
Gemse	Chamois. Codeword for *Himmelbett* control area.
Generalmajor	Major-General. Equivalent to Air Vice-Marshal (RAF).
Gerät	Piece of equipment, set (radio, radar etc.).
Geschichte	History.
Geschwader	An operational unit comprising, usually, three or more *Gruppen*.
Geschwaderkommodore	The officer commanding a *Geschwader*.
Geschwaderstab	*Geschwader* Staff.
Gespenst	Ghost.
Gisela	Girl's name. Codeword for an intruder operation carried out by the German night-fighter force in the closing stages of the war.
Grenzadler	Border Eagle (Title of poem).
Grenze	Border.
Gross	Large, big, great etc.
Grossraum	Large (control) area.
Grossraumgefechtsstand	The control centre of a *Grossraum* (q.v.)
Gruppe	An operational unit comprising, usually, three *Staffeln*.
Gruppenkommandeur	The officer commanding a *Gruppe*.
Gymnasium	Grammar school.
Halle	Hall, hangar.
Halsschmerzen	Sore throat. Aircrew aspiring to the Knight's Cross (a neck decoration) were said to suffer from the condition.
Hauptmann	German rank equivalent to Flight Lieutenant (RAF) or Captain (Army).
Haus	House, building.
Heer	The German Army.
Heimat	Home, homeland.
Hell	(Adjective) – light, bright.
Helle Nachtjagd	Literally 'light night fighting.' Interception with the aid of searchlights.
Henaja	Abbr. for *helle Nachtjagd*, q.v.
Himmelbett	Four-poster bed. Codeword for a system of close-control night fighting.
Himmelbettraum	*Himmelbett* close-control area.
Hinten	(Adverb). Behind, astern.
Hitlerjugend	Hitler Youth.
Horchdienst	The German radio-monitoring service.

Horrido!	Used originally by day fighters, later by night fighters as well, to announce a 'kill'.
Hundertschaft	(Archaic) A military body of one hundred men.
Husar	Hussar.
Jagd	Hunt. Interception.
Jagddivision	Fighter division.
Jagdflieger	Fighter aircrew.
Jäger	Fighter (aircraft or pilot). Literally 'Hunter'.
Jägerleitoffizier	Fighter control officer.
JLO	(Pronounced 'Eelo'). Abbreviation for *Jägerleitoffizier*, q.v.
Jungmann	(Archaic) Young man. A *Jungmann* was an aspirant knight who had not gained his spurs. At *Napola* (q.v.) the term was used for a pupil.
Jungvolk	Broadly equivalent to the Scout Cubs. The junior division of the *Hitlerjugend*.
Jungvolkführer	A *Jungvolk* leader.
Kadettenanstalt	Cadet Training Centre.
Kamerad	Comrade.
Kandidat	Candidate.
Kapitän	Captain – but not an army or air force rank. A *Kapitän* was the officer commanding a *Staffel* (q.v.)
KG	Abbr. for *Kampfgeschwader* – Bomber *Geschwader*.
KG	Kommanditgesellschaft or limited partnership company.
Klau	(Vernacular) – theft.
Kolibri	Humming Bird (Codeword).
Kommandeur	Commander. The officer commanding a *Gruppe*.
Kommodore	Commodore. The officer commanding a *Geschwader*.
Korps	Corps.
Krieg	War, warfare.
Kriegsabitur	The wartime matriculation examination, in which it was not necessary to take written tests.
Kumpel	A good friend, a mate.
Kumpeltyp	A matey person.
Kurier	Courier. Codeword for heavy bomber.
Land	The approximate equivalent of a County (England) or a State (USA).
Landser	The German equivalent of the British 'Tommy'.

Ledergasse	Leather Lane, Leather Alley.
Leichentuch	Shroud (codeword).
Leistung	Performance, achievement.
Leistungsbuch	Achievements Book.
Leutnant	German rank equivalent to Pilot Officer (RAF).
Lichtenstein	An early air intercept radar used by the German night-fighter force.
Li-Gerät	Short for *Lichtenstein-Gerät*.
Luftflotte	Air Fleet.
Luftkriegsschule	Air Warfare Academy.
Luftnachrichten	Air Signals.
Luftnachrichtenregiment	Air Signals Regiment.
Luftwaffe	The German Air Force. Unlike the RAF it was not an independent force, but was one of the three arms that made up the *Wehrmacht* (q.v.)
Lurch	Amphibian. Codeword for *Himmelbett* control area.
Major	German rank equivalent to Squadron Leader (RAF).
Mammut	Mammoth – a German long-range surveillance radar.
Marine	The German Navy.
Maschine	Machine, aircraft.
Meise	Titmouse. Codeword for *Himmelbett* control area.
Militärarchiv	Military Archives.
Moskito	Mosquito.
Murmeltier	Marmot. Codeword for *Himmelbett* control area.
Nachtgespenst	Night Ghost.
Nachtjagd	Literally 'night hunting'. Night fighting. The name by which the German night-fighter force was known.
Nachtjagddivision	Night-Fighter Division.
Nachtjagdgeschwader	Night-fighter *Geschwader*.
Nachtjagdgruppe	Night-fighter *Gruppe*.
Nachtjäger	Night fighter (either pilot or aircraft).
Napola	Abbr. for *Nationalpolitische Lehranstalt* – National Political Teaching Institute. One of the several types of Party-run school for the elite set up in the Nazi era. See also NPEA.
NJG	Abbr. for *Nachtjagdgeschwader*.
NPEA	Abbr. for *Nationalpolitische Erziehungsanstalt* – National Political Educational Establishment.

	Synonymous with *Napola* (q.v.).
NS-Führungsoffizier	National Socialist Leadership Officer. Introduced late in the war to monitor and report on the political reliability of the troops.
Oberfeldwebel	German rank equivalent to Flight Sergeant (RAF).
Obergefreiter	German rank equivalent to Leading Aircraftman (RAF).
Oberleutnant	German rank equivalent to Flying Officer (RAF).
Oberschule	Secondary school.
Oberst	Colonel. Equivalent to Group Captain, RAF.
Oberstleutnant	Lieutenant-Colonel. Equivalent to Wing Commander (RAF).
Offen	(Adjective) – open.
Offizier	Officer.
Ordensburg	'Castle of the Knightly Order'. One of the Nazi elite schools.
Ordentlichkeit	Orderliness, tidiness etc.
Planquadrat	A grid reference square for navigation.
Plq	Sometimes used as an abbreviation of the above
Preussich or *Preußich*	(Adjective) – Prussian. (using the double 's' in German Gothic letters.)
Rassenkunde	Racial studies; ethnology.
Rattenkaster	(Vernacular) – old banger.
Raum	Area, e.g. *Himmelbett* control area. Plural; *Räume*.
Reichsarbeitdienst	Reich Labour Service.
Reichsmarschall	Reich Marshal. Hermann Göring was the only officer to hold the rank.
Richtfest	Topping-out ceremony.
Riese	Giant.
Ritterkreuz	The Knight's Cross to the Iron Cross.
Ritterkreuzträger	A holder of the Knight's Cross.
Rundfunk	Radio
Rundfunksender	Radio station.
Salamander	Salamander (codeword).
Sau	Sow, but can be translated as 'boar'.
Sauerkraut	Night-fighter vernacular for a type of British radar jamming that produced a 'mushy' effect on the screen.
Schädelspalter	(Vernacular) – skull-splitter.

Schein	Certificate, licence.
Schlecht	(Adjective) – bad.
Schräg	(Adjective) – slanting, sloping, oblique etc.
Schräge Musik	(Vernacular) – jazz. Codeword for upward-firing cannon in the roof of a nightfighter's fuselage.
Schwarm	A small flight of aircraft, usually no more than three in number.
Schwerter	The Swords. The second higher grade of the *Ritterkreuz*.
Seele	Soul.
Seelenbohrer	Literally 'Soul-borer'. Night-fighter vernacular for a type of aural jamming of a penetrating nature.
Sender	Transmitter, radio station.
Siebenmal	(Adverb) – seven times.
Sieg Heil!	Used by night-fighter pilots do announce a 'kill'. See *Horrido*!
Sieg	Victory.
Sitzbereitschaft	Cockpit readiness.
Soldat	Soldier. Also a simple private.
Soldatensender	Forces Radio Station.
Stab	Staff.
Stabsschwarm	Staff Flight.
Staffel	The basic operational flying unit of the *Luftwaffe*. A fighter *Staffel* usually comprised nine aircraft.
Staffelkapitän	Commanding officer of a *Staffel* (q.v.)
Stark	(Adjective) - strong.
Start	Take-off.
Startbereitschaft	Immediate readiness.
Sterne	Stars.
Stieglitz	Goldfinch. The name of a pre-war biplane training aircraft.
Stuka	A dive-bomber. This term was not used exclusively for the Ju 87, as is commonly believed.
Tagblatt	Daily newspaper.
Technische Offizier	Technical Officer. Abbreviated TO.
Teerose	Tea-rose. Codename of a *Grossraumgefechtsstand* (q.v.) at Deelen in Holland.
Terrorflieger	Terror fliers. Germans' name for RAF Bomber Command.
TO	Abbreviation for *Technischer Offizier*, Technical Officer.
Tod	Death.
Todeskandidat	Death candidate.

Unmöglich	(Adjective, adverb) – impossible, impossibly.
Unten	(Adverb). Beneath, below.
Unteroffizier	German rank equivalent to Corporal (RAF).
Vaterland	The Fatherland.
Verfahren	System, procedure.
Viermot	(Vernacular) – four-engined aircraft.
Viermotorig	(Adjective) – four-engined.
Viktor	R/T equivalent of 'Roger!' ('Your message received and understood.')
Visier	Sight(s).
Volksschule	Primary school.
Volkssturm	Territorial Army. Old, unfit and young men and boys conscripted by the Nazis for the defence of the homeland in the closing stages of the war.
Von hinten unten	From behind and below. Traditional form of night-fighter attack.
Vorfeld	Territory in front of the main battle-line.
Wassermann	Aquarius – a German long-range radar.
Wehrmacht	The combined German armed forces (*Heer, Marine, Luftwaffe*).
Weltkrieg	World War.
Werk	Factory.
Werknummer	Factory number (aircraft).
Westfälisch	(Adjective) – Westphalian.
Wild	(Adjective) – wild.
Wilde Sau	Wild Boar. Codeword for freelance interception, generally in the target area.
Wildvogel	Game-bird (Codeword).
Wirbel	Eddy, turmoil (Codeword).
Wolken	Clouds.
Würzburg	Type of control radar used originally by German searchlights and anti-aircraft units.
Würzburg Riese	Würzburg Giant. Improved version of the *Würzburg* control radar used in the *Himmelbett* control system.
Ypsilon	The letter 'Y'. Codeword for a system of VHF fixing and control.
Zahm	(Adjective) – Tame.
Zahme Sau	Tame Boar. Codeword for freelance interception within the bomber stream.
Zeremonienmeister	Master of Ceremonies. German misnomer for the RAF Master Bomber.
Zerstörer	Destroyer. A long-range escort and ground-

	attack fighter. Not only the Messerschmitt Bf 110.
Ziel	Target, objective, radar return.
Zieldarstellung	Literally 'target representation'. Practice interceptions.
Ziele decken sich	'Returns overlap.' Said by the Fighter Controller to inform the pilot that the returns from bomber and fighter respectively were indistinguishable – i.e. that the fighter was in the immediate vicinity of his target.
Zug	In a military context, a section or platoon.
Zweiter	(Adjective) – Second.

CHAPTER ONE

Before 1939

Family background, childhood and early youth. Formative years in an evolving Germany.

Schnaufer is a word that has its origins in old Swabian dialect and means, variously, a person who gasps or puffs or pants, or it can mean, by extension, a breather or a short pause to get one's breath back. It is also an old Swabian name, and it seems likely that the first man to be called that was someone who suffered from shortness of breath, possibly an asthmatic. There are on record a number of spelling variations through the years – Schnauffer, Schnupfer, Schnupper, Schnapper, and so on. Fragmentary records exist of people in the area around Schnaufer's home town, Calw, bearing the name as far back as the 14th Century. It might well be that there were Schnaufers in Calw itself as early as that period, but most of the parish records were destroyed in disastrous fires in the 16th Century. The first substantive traces in Calw of the Schnaufer family we are interested in date back to 1523: they seem mainly to have been butchers and were clearly prosperous and respected members of the community. They were also prolific: a Hans Schnaufer lost his wife Katharina in 1612, by which time she had born him thirteen children. Despite the complexity introduced into the family tree by so many offspring, it is possible to trace Heinz Schnaufer's ancestry, with some degree of probability, back to this Hans and Katharina.

By the end of the end of the 17th Century, it seems, the Schnaufer family were no longer primarily butchers but had diversified into an allied trade and were tanning hides and dealing in leather. Members of the family were also innkeepers. During this century the Schnaufer family purchased a share of an imposing four-storey house on the *Ledergasse*, the Leather Alley, above the Nagold, the river that runs through Calw. Today this tall, imposing half-timbered building still stands and is known as the *Altdeutsches Haus* or, colloquially, as the '*Schnaufer Haus*'. Schnaufers remained in the leather business until the twentieth century, when, in 1919, one Hermann Schnaufer, then 62 years of age, and his son Alfred broke with tradition and founded a wine-dealing business with its headquarters in the *Altdeutsches Haus*, the huge cellars of which were ideally suited to the storage of wine. Alfred Schnaufer, the son,

The 'Schnaufer Haus' on the Ledergasse *in Calw, Heinz Schnaufer's home town, in the nineteen-twenties. This building was the original base of the Schnaufer family wine business.* (Calw Town Archives)

was a qualified mechanical engineer. He had been working in England at the beginning of the First World War and had been interned on the Isle of Man as an enemy alien 'for the duration'. When he returned to his homeland he was unable, in the economic conditions of the post-war slump, to find work in his profession and so, apparently reluctantly at the time, he went into partnership with his father Hermann. Despite his reservations his change of direction from engineer to dealer in wines marked the beginning of considerable prosperity.

At first sight Calw would seem to have been an unlikely location in which to set up business trading in wine, because there were no vine-yards of any size in the immediate vicinity, but there were sound his-torical factors that made the venture one likely to succeed. In the

Middle Ages Calw had been an important trading post, exporting cloths, salt, wood and other goods to a large part of Europe. On the way back home from delivering their wares the horse-drawn wagons would load up with wine, and in this way Calw had developed into the main wine-distribution centre for the adjacent area of the Black Forest.

When the Schnaufer wine business first began it operated in a manner founded in long-established traditions and practices: wagons drawn by teams of two or four horses would collect wine in large wooden barrels from vineyards in the Württemberg wine-growing area centred on Heilbronn, some fifty miles away. The collection took place mainly in autumn, after the wine harvest, and the horse-drawn carts returned to Calw abundantly decorated in the autumn colours of straw, flowers and leaves. The barrels were then stored in the cellars of the Schnaufer premises in, adjacent to and behind the *Altdeutsches Haus* until the wine was either sold locally or conveyed, still in its barrels, to the inns and hotels in the surrounding countryside. There it was dispensed to customers directly from the barrel into traditionally decorated glazed earthenware jugs.

In April 1921 Alfred married Martha Frey, and their first child was born in a hospital in nearby Stuttgart on the 16th of February 1922. He was christened Heinz Wolfgang. Alfred and Martha were later to have three more children, Manfred, Waltraut and Eckart, born in 1925, 1927 and 1928 respectively,

Hermann Schnaufer died in 1928 when his grandson, Heinz, the future night-fighter ace, was six years of age, and Heinz's father Alfred

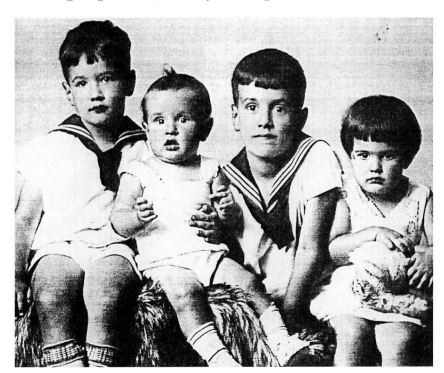

The Schnaufer children in about 1930. Left to right: *Manfred, Eckart, Heinz and Waltraut.* (Schnaufer)

took over full control of the business, which continued to prosper, to expand and to change with the times. By the nineteen-thirties, for example, the wine was no longer being distributed in barrels, but was bottled in Calw before being sold to customers. The internal combustion engine was taking over from the horse, and more modern business methods were gradually ousting many of the traditional local and regional conventions that the firm observed. But despite its now considerable prosperity the Schnaufer enterprise remained deeply rooted in the tradition of the family business, as indeed it does to this day.

Heinz Schnaufer, it will be seen, was born into a family that was stable and financially secure. Snapshots dating from the nineteen-twenties and -thirties amply testify to the closeness of the family and the comfortable circumstances in which they lived. Alfred was a strict but fair-minded and well-loved father and Martha, although also strict, a loving mother. It was a family based on clearly defined but not oppressive discipline and *Ordentlichkeit*, a family in which the children unquestioningly accepted and took for granted that there were rules to be obeyed but that those rules were necessary to ensure family harmony.

*   *   *

The Germany into which Heinz Schnaufer was born was not as stable as the family of which he was the eldest child. Four turbulent years earlier the Great War – widely seen in the West as the 'war to end all wars' – had ended in Germany's surrender. But the majority of the German citizens – not to mention her generals and her politicians – could not accept that Germany had suffered a military defeat. In the earlier months of 1918 Germany had seemed to be heading for a certain victory, so that the announcement in October that she was seeking peace terms came as a devastating blow. Germany, most of its citizens maintained, had been betrayed on the home front: her armies in the field had not been defeated. There was a saying that summed it up: '*Wir siegten uns zum Tod*' – 'We conquered ourselves to death'. And so the dream of one united, German-speaking nation, one of the primary factors that had triggered off the war, was not extinguished: if anything it burned more brightly in adversity.

In 1920, under the ill-starred Treaty of Versailles, the League of Nations was formed in an attempt to create a forum in which international disagreements might be settled without recourse to arms. But under the same Treaty Germany was disarmed and required to surrender her colonies overseas and considerable areas of territory at home – Alsace Lorraine to France, large areas in the east to Poland and smaller areas to Czechoslovakia, Lithuania, Belgium and Denmark. As a direct result of these latter provisions of the Treaty – which was generally referred to among Germans as the Versailles '*Diktat*' – Germany lost nearly fifteen percent of her arable land, twenty-five percent of her coal resources, sixty-eight percent of her zinc and almost seventy-five percent of her iron ore. The Rhineland was demilitarised and German rearmament comprehensively restricted; extremely harsh war-damage reparations were imposed on a country ill-equipped, as a result of the sacrifices and economic demands of war, not to speak of the loss under the Treaty of a large percentage of her wealth-generating potential, to meet them. The establishment of the League of Nations had been suggested by American President Woodrow Wilson in 1917 as one aspect of an eventual peace settlement with Germany: the high level of reparations when the war was over was set largely at the insistence of France, who had suffered grievously in a war fought largely on her territory.

The Allies' intense desire for revenge on Germany following the enormous bloodshed and indescribable suffering that resulted from a world-wide conflict that they saw as having been caused by that country is entirely understandable. There was a well-nigh incredible naiveté and lack of foresight implicit in the imposition of a treaty that on the one hand established a talking-shop for the furtherance of peace while on the other it dictated conditions likely to lead to economic, social and nationalistic tensions capable themselves of generating bitter internal disorder, international dispute and the danger of another war. While sponsoring peace among nations the Versailles Treaty set the preconditions for renewed conflict. It had also created a lasting resentment, a focal point for future determination to re-establish itself, in the German military class, who said that the Treaty had left them '*heerlos, wehrlos und ehrlos*'[1].

When Heinz Schnaufer was born inflation, triggered by the impossible economic situation into which Germany had been forced, was burgeoning. The mark, normally standing at about four to the US dollar, had fallen in value to less than half a cent. By January the following year the dollar would buy almost 20,000 marks, and by November the mark was literally worth less than the paper it was printed on, with the exchange rate – if anyone could be found who wished to buy German currency – peaking at a theoretical 4,200,000,000 marks to the dollar, figures easy to quote but hard to visualise. It was a period of intense deprivation and suffering for much of the German population, particularly for small traders and wage-earners, but the Schnaufer business seems to have survived without difficulty, possibly because wine was a commodity always in demand and convenient to use for barter. When inflation came to an end in 1924 as a result of huge American loans, a period of increasing prosperity began in Germany. The economic, and hence the social, prospects seemed much brighter. But in the post-war turmoil within Germany the seeds of further conflict had already been sewn, and roots were taking hold.

In September 1919, when Hermann and Alfred Schnaufer were founding their wine business, a low-level veteran of the Great War, virtually unknown but with political aspirations, had joined one of the many small groups that were then spawning in post-war Germany, the

---

[1] 'Without an army, without defences and without honour.'

Deutsche Arbeiterpartei or German Workers' Party. When he joined it was an apparently insignificant group with only just over fifty members. His name was Adolf Hitler. He soon became the seventh member of the party's committee, and in July 1921, just a few months before Heinz Schnaufer's birth, he was elected its President. In the meanwhile the group's membership had grown to 3,000 and the word '*Nationalsozialistische*' – 'National Socialist' – had been added in front of its name. It was now the National Socialist German Workers' Party, abbreviated NSDAP but more generally, and more ominously, known as the Nazi Party. There were few people in Europe – indeed, throughout the world – whose lives would not be affected, directly or indirectly, by this one man. The young Schnaufer's life had begun with every prospect of prosperity and security, even modest wealth. He had had a good start in life. But he had also been born into a Germany that was already in its way towards a war even more costly than the one that had ended in her defeat just a few years earlier.

This seems to be a convenient moment to clear up one of the common errors that constantly recur when Schnaufer is written about: as often as not he is referred to as either 'Heinz Wolfgang' or 'Heinz-Wolfgang'. The former form, without a hyphen, is the correct one, but to his family and to his friends and, later, his colleagues in the *Luftwaffe* he was simply 'Heinz', as Martin Drewes, himself a highly successful night-fighter pilot, emphasises:

> As you know, a godfather's name is often entered on a birth certificate: in my opinion that is something of a nonsense. I knew my great friend <u>only</u> as Heinz Schnaufer. I wish to make that point clear from the very beginning. You will find that in the notice of his funeral, which was written by his family, his name is given simply as 'Heinz Schnaufer'. Among the many pieces that have been written about him I have even seen 'Wolfgang Schnaufer'. That is a clear indication that the writer never knew him and has never been in touch with his family.

Heinz began his schooling, as was customary, at the age of six by entering the local *Volksschule*. It was already apparent to his parents that their first child was gifted, and his early promise was fulfilled when he began school. He was clearly of very high intelligence and regularly came at, or near to, the top of his class in virtually every subject. He was also a very good-natured and amenable child, never seeming to make enemies. Learning came easily to him and he demonstrated, in addition to academic excellence, athletic ability and musical talent, and he could play the piano and the accordion quite early in life. A fellow pupil, Eugen Lebzelter, remembers him:

> Concerning my friend and contemporary Heinz Schnaufer: our parents' homes on the *Ledergasse* in Calw were not far apart, so Heinz and I got to know each other before we went to elementary school. After so long a time I can no longer recall details of the days before we started school – it is, after all, nearly seventy years ago. But one thing I know for cer-

tain, and the few school-comrades who are still alive confirm it: Heinz was not only one of the most intelligent pupils, but he was also one of the most liked. What we particularly remember is that he as good as never took part in quarrels – which quite often became very violent – but tried, whenever possible, to mediate and to make the peace. This served to make him very popular, not only with the other pupils but also with the teachers, and we were very sad when, after three years at school together, Heinz left us to go to a higher school. There is one thing I must add: Heinz was among the best in the class, not only in academic subjects but also in school sports.

Although Eugen Lebzelter's comments are short, he seems almost to paint an idealised picture of the young Schnaufer. He is, however, also clearly aware that human nature is fallible, and one is bound ask oneself whether his memory has perhaps been conditioned by both the passage of time and his perception, which is shared by many, of Schnaufer as a great national hero. This is a question that recurs virtually each time someone who was near to Heinz Schnaufer speaks of him today, and it will come out even more strongly as other witnesses are recorded and comments made. Not all, however, see Schnaufer as a paragon as unquestioningly as many do. One former night-fighting ace did not know Schnaufer personally, nor did he know his family and educational background, although, of course, he knew of his outstanding reputation as a night fighter. When told, fifty years after the end of the war, that Schnaufer had attended a *Napola* as a youth, he dismissed him in one word – 'Nazi!' What was a *Napola*, and why was the former night-fighter pilot's reaction so unequivocal?

'*Napola*' is an abbreviated form of '*Nationalpolitische Lehranstalt*', some-

At the age of sixteen Heinz Schnaufer entered a 'Napola', a National Socialist boarding school for specially selected pupils destined mainly for a career in the armed forces. This photograph shows some of Schnaufer's classmates and clearly demonstrates the military nature of the training: Schnaufer himself took the photo. (Meyer)

One of the training staff at the Backnang Napola in 1938. (Meyer)

times also referred to as an 'NPEA'[1], which translates as 'National-Political Educational Establishment'. Immediately after assuming power in 1933 Hitler began the transformation of the democracy of the Weimar Republic into a dictatorship, while at the same time, as part of that process, remodelling the educational system, formerly looked upon by other western countries as an example of excellence, in ways consistent with his aim of propagating the ideology of National Socialism. The changes to the educational system, which were introduced progressively from the moment of the assumption of power by the NSDAP, were designed to eradicate the 'decadent' culture inherited from Weimar. 'Those who have youth on their side,' announced Hans Schemm, leader of the Nazi Teachers' League, 'control the future.'

---

[1] NPEA is the abbreviation of *Nationalpolitische Erziehungsanstalt*, which was the original name of the schools but which translates similarly.

Emphasis within all school curricula was on Germanic studies, for example, great weight being placed on *Rassenkunde* – Racial Study – at the heart of which was the principle of the superiority of the Aryan race and the inferiority of other ethnic groups, particularly of the Jews, and biology was distorted to support that thesis. Pupils were rehearsed in the correctness and infallibility of the *Führer* State and the necessity for obedience to it, history was rewritten to justify the existence and rightness of such a dictatorship, and the personality of Adolf Hitler as the leader and the saviour of Germany was glorified. There was a significant reduction in religious education, examinations in religious knowledge were discontinued, and attendance at school prayers was made optional.

Not content with changing the fundamental nature of the educational system in all schools and universities from one in which pupils were trained to think for themselves to one of political and sociological indoctrination, the Nazis also saw a need for special Party-controlled establishments in which the elite of German youth could be educated and trained as dedicated National Socialists and future leaders of the nation, and three types of '*Eliteschulen*', or 'Schools for the Elite', were created. They were the *Ordensburgen*, the *Adolf Hitler Schulen*, and the *Napola*s.

The *Ordensburgen* (Order Castles) which took their name from the fortresses of the orders of medieval Teutonic knights, might be described as Party universities and were designed to qualify carefully selected students as future Party leaders. The *Adolf Hitler Schulen* recruited cadets directly from the Hitler Youth, also for service in the Party. Selection was made when the candidates were still members of the *Jungvolk*, in which boys served between the ages of ten and fourteen before moving up to the *Hitlerjugend*, and the training was largely military in character, although at the age of eighteen successful pupils qual-

The Director of Studies at Backnang, Dr Gräter. For obvious reasons he was nicknamed 'Mussolini'. (Meyer)

In 1938 large-scale manoeuvres, in which all the Napolas participated, were held in Mecklenburg. This was the field kitchen, nicknamed the 'Gulaschkanone' - the 'Stew Cannon'. (Meyer)

The manoeuvres were attended by the Minister of Education, Dr Bernhard Rust, seen here addressing the Jungmannen.

Visits to agricultural and industrial centres featured on the Napola syllabus. Here Schnaufer's class visits a coal-mine in the Ruhr region in 1938. Heinz Schnaufer is second from the right in the back row. (Meyer)

Stress was placed on physical fitness. Here Jungmannen, *who are carrying gasmasks, on an obstacle course at Backnang in 1938. Schnaufer is at the rear of the centre pole. (Meyer)*

Jungmannen at another stage of the obstacle course. (Meyer)

From Backnang Schnaufer transferred to the Napola at Potsdam. This is the Hundertschaft *(Company) building in which he lived.* (Meyer)

Summer 1939, just before the outbreak of war. Schnaufer took this photograph of Kurt Meyer during the boating excursion on the Berlin lakes described in the main text. (Meyer)

ified for entrance to university, sometimes to *Ordensburgen*. The *Napola*s, one might say, came somewhere in between the two.

The first three *Napola*s, which were boarding schools supposedly providing an education in very broad terms similar to that of a traditional *Gymnasium*, or Grammar School, were set up in 1933 at Potsdam, Plön and Köslin, and by the end of the war there were approximately twenty to thirty of them spread throughout the country. There was a certain SS interest in these institutes, which was to become much stronger

The Fliegerzug (Flying Platoon) at Potsdam. Of these Jungmannen, nine out of ten were destined to die in the war. Schnaufer is second from the left in the front row. (Meyer)

Gliding was a popular subject on the curriculum. Schnaufer excelled. (Meyer)

Skiing in the Allgäu,
Winter 1938/1939.
Schnaufer is second from
the left, with Kurt Meyer
to the right. (Meyer)

from 1940 onwards, but it would be wrong to categorise them as being a component of, or being under the control of, the SS at any time. The original *Napola*s had previously been Cadet Schools, and the military tradition established there was to some extent continued in the new institutes. Whereas, however, military instruction at the *Kadettenanstalten* had predominated and the cadets had been destined for an officer career in the armed forces, with the instructional staff being mostly serving officers and NCOs, the pupils at the *Napola*s, called '*Jungmannen*', were not trained for any specific career and the class teachers were all State-qualified civilian pedagogues. It goes without saying that both pupils and instructional staff had to be ethnically 'pure' and to have Party approval, but Party membership was not a prerequisite for either the teachers or for the parents of the pupils. Interestingly enough, the Germans' admiration of the British public-school system played a strong part in the *Napola* concept, and the institutes were, in part at least, modelled along those lines. The word '*Jungmann*', in common with the word '*Ordensburg*', mentioned earlier, has its origins in old Teutonic lore, and both names reflected the Nazi preoccupation with and emphasis on Germanic tradition. A *Jungmann* was, originally, a young man destined to become a knight but who had yet to earn his spurs.

The annual selection of candidates for entry to a *Napola* took the form of a week's attachment to one of the institutes, during which rigorous tests had to be taken and passed. The parents' social standing was not taken into account, although of course their political reliability – perhaps, better, the absence of any record of political unreliability – was, and the boys had to be of pure Aryan blood. The main criteria for selection, assuming them to be racially 'pure', were outstanding academic achievement at school, unsullied character and physical excellence. Of every four hundred who were recommended by their school to take

A GÖ 4 twin-seater glider used by the Fliegerzug *at Potsdam for training.* (Meyer)

Kurt Meyer in front of the Klemm KL 25 used for glider-towing. Potsdam, Summer 1939. (Meyer)

*A Napola class at work.
Heinz Schnaufer is fourth
from the right.* (Meyer)

the entrance examination to a *Napola*, only about forty successfully passed the rigorous selection procedure.

In addition to studying a normal – for that period – *Gymnasium* curriculum, great attention was paid to physical exercise and the teaching of military leadership and 'officer qualities'. Life at a *Napola* was regimented and strenuous, discipline was strict, and the instruction, particularly in sports, games, physical training and quasi-military exercises, was of a high standard. The *Jungmannen* wore uniform and were organised along military lines and with strong regard to the *Führerprinzip*, the 'Leader-Principle': each class was a *Zug*, or platoon, and there were various grades of military-type seniority among the pupils within each *Napola*. A typical day's programme included four hours academic study in the morning and outside work in the afternoon with gymnastics, games, swimming, light athletics, obstacle courses and cross-country exercises. There were exchange visits with other schools and, on occasion, with educational establishments abroad, including English public schools – although the latter had ceased by the time Schnaufer entered his *Napola* – and there were educational and work-experience detachments to, for example, the farms, coal-mines and iron foundries within Germany.

The *Jungmannen* enjoyed a life which, although strictly regimented and demanding, was active and challenging, a form of education tailor-made to appeal to healthy, imaginative and ambitious youth. To be selected to attend a *Napola* was a dream entertained by many but achieved by few. A large number of those lucky enough to be accepted went there with thoughts of eventual entry into the *Wehrmacht*, the German armed forces. Included among them was Heinz Schnaufer, who went to the *Napola* at Backnang in early 1938, when he was just sixteen. In June 1943, when he was a *Leutnant* in the *Luftwaffe*, Schnaufer

Another classroom at a Napola. Hitler's portrait is on the wall. (Meyer)

summed up the attraction of a *Napola* career in short *curriculum vitae* he wrote for official purposes while serving with a Night-Fighter *Gruppe*[1]:

> At six years of age I went to *Volksschule* and, after the Fourth Form, to the Upper School (*Oberschule*) in Calw. Very soon I became deeply interested in joining a youth organisation of military character and so, at the beginning of 1933, when I was ten years of age, I joined the *Jungvolk*[2]. The basic ideals of this youth movement – selection and the principle of leadership deriving from achievement – formed in me a philosophy that has to a very large extent guided me during my career. From these thoughts there developed my ambition to become a member of a National Political Educational Establishment.
>
> Following the Sixth Form at Upper School in Calw, and after taking the selection examination, I succeeded in being accepted for the NPEA at Backnang in Württemberg. Education at this school was conducted in the old German military spirit: the same year I volunteered for an aircrew career as an officer-cadet. I spent my final school year, until Autumn 1939, in the Aircrew Class at the NPEA at Potsdam. Here we *Jungmannen* received our first flying instruction.

Another German youth whose *Napola* career ran parallel to that of Schnaufer was Kurt Meyer. His recollections today of life in a National-Socialist selective school not only contribute to a picture of Schnaufer but also give a good feeling of the sort of routine that pupils experi-

---

[1] Schnaufer's unit at the time was II./NJG 1, located at Saint-Trond in Belgium. See later.

[2] German boys joined the *Jungvolk* (Young People) at ten years of age and transferred to the *Hitler Jugend* at the age of fourteen.

enced there and of the atmosphere in Germany during the pre-war period:

Heinz Schnaufer was my friend when we were young, and we sat next to each other at both boarding schools. I first got to know him at Backnang in Württemberg at the beginning of 1938 when we were just sixteen and seventeen years old respectively.

He had passed the very difficult entrance exam as a future *Jungmann* at an NPEA with distinction and was put into my *Zug* (Class). Heinz rapidly adapted himself to the hard but interesting work at the Institute. He very soon stood out by reason of high achievement in scientific subjects, and he was a good and well-liked comrade. We gave him the nickname of 'Schnoffer' – pronouncing his name like a French verb – which

Kurt Meyer as a 'new boy' at Rottweil NPEA 'Napola' in 1936. (Meyer)

he quite liked because he was fond of the French language.

During the day, for our class-work and practical experiments in Chemistry and Physics, we used to wear our official school clothes, a sort of overall made of hard-wearing moleskin material. We looked like moles, but were happy that we didn't need to iron these uniforms.

For outdoor work and military exercises (obstacle course, scaling walls and so on) we wore special suits comprising corduroy breeches, jackboots, olive-green battledress blouse with epaulettes in the colour of our particular *Napola* (Backnang was red with white piping, Potsdam red without piping), and an olive-green forage cap with the Imperial Eagle.

For functions and events that we carried out together with the local *Hitler Jugend* (HJ) we wore the complete HJ uniform, with black shorts in summer and black breeches and brown shirts in winter, together with all the usual badges and so on. For formal occasions (dancing lessons, balls, the theatre and so on) we wore a special uniform consisting of black long trousers with gold braid at the side, a brown uniform jacket and white linen, a black tie, white gloves and a peaked cap. We had a green-brown cape we could wear over our uniform when it was raining. For the winter there were two greatcoats, one in the *Hitler Jugend* style and one that matched our outdoor uniform. It goes without saying that we had special clothing for sports.

Back, then, to Heinz Schnaufer. Not only was he an 'ace' in scientific subjects, but he also outstripped the rest of us in small-bore shooting and, later, in glider flying. In sports however he was, one might say, 'average'. Nevertheless he was, without giving himself any airs and graces, '*primus inter pares*'.

In 1939 Heinz and I were the only two from our Class to be posted to the NPEA at Potsdam. There was a so-called '*Fliegerzug*'[1] into which all *Jungmannen* [destined for a flying career] from all the NPEAs in Germany were placed. At that time there were fifteen *Napola*s, as they were colloquially known, in Germany, and thirty-five *Jungmannen* from all the districts who had volunteered as aircrew officer-cadets were brought together.

At Potsdam Heinz and I now began our flying training on gliders and also workshop lessons in aircraft construction. In addition we still had instruction in scientific subjects, sport and outdoor activities (practice alarms, night marches and so on). We even had time to learn sailing, because the school had a number of Olympic-Class dinghies, and there were also a number of sculling-boats there for our use.

In one of these boats (a two-seater without helm) Heinz and I made a weekend excursion on the Havel Lakes. It was a hot summer's day. We had taken a few pieces of canvas, our eating utensils and a spirit cooker with us, and we planned to set up camp for the night on one of the islands. Very stupidly we didn't wear anything on our head, because we thought it was unbecoming for sailors to wear a forage cap. Because of the fresh breeze over the lake we didn't notice that we were very soon suffering from sunburn, not to mention sunstroke. When we landed in the evening we were feeling very unhappy. We both had a headache and didn't want to talk. Our morale was zero. When, next morning, Heinz

---

[1] *Fliegerzug* – 'Flying Section', 'Flying Platoon' or 'Flying Class'. As already indicated, each class at a *Napola* was, in military tradition, called a '*Zug*', translated as either 'platoon' or 'section'.

wanted to make a bet with me, things began to get quite out of hand!

Heinz, my best friend, maintained unequivocally that officers of the German Navy wore their medal-clasp on their greatcoat, while I said that they only wore it on their tunic. Both of us, because of the effects of the sun, which we hadn't noticed, became so angry with each other that we climbed into the boat without saying a word and rowed on for hour after hour until we reached our mooring at the school.

Both of us collapsed when we got out of the boat and had to be taken to sick-quarters. There we spent a few days quite restfully and in perfect harmony. When we were recovered a former officer of the *Marine*, who worked at the school as an instructor, told us that we were both right (or wrong): the medal-clasp was worn on the half-length jacket but not on either the tunic or the greatcoat.

So Heinz and I stayed friends, and in the holidays I went with him to Calw and met his parents and his brothers and sister. In Potsdam at that time the producer Karl Ritter was making a UFA film entitled 'Cadets'. As we counted as 'brown cadets' in those days two companies (*Hundertschaften*) from our institute were detached for work on the film. I myself played the rôle of a Prussian corporal-cadet, but I can't remember what part Heinz had.

We carried out our glider training on the Güterfelde Hills near Potsdam. First of all we practised short hops on the SG 38 school glider, which we christened the 'Skull-splitter' (*Schädelspalter*). The average time that we of our *Zug* managed to stay in the air at our first attempt was twelve seconds, but Heinz Schnaufer didn't land until he had been up eighteen or nineteen seconds. From the very beginning he was gifted pilot, and he was always well ahead of the rest of us.

Later we had a sports machine, a Klemm KL 25, to act as tow for us, and with this aircraft we were towed aloft in the two-seater Gö 4, a high-performance glider. Heinz also excelled in thermal gliding.

On 20 April 1939 Adolf Hitler celebrated his fiftieth birthday with a very great parade – possibly the biggest in the world – on the East-West Axis[1] in Berlin. Special seats next to the main grandstand were allocated to us *Jungmannen* from the NPEA Potsdam, but because we, not being very tall, couldn't see very well because of the SS-men lining the route, we moved to the trees nearby. I still remember how Heinz and I climbed to the very top of a lime tree, from where we had what was certainly the best view among all the spectators, including the many foreign military attachés.

As the many aeroplanes thundered overhead in formation I saw Heinz staring fascinated at the machines, almost as if he were saying, 'One day soon I'll be in one of those!' And as it happened he was one of the first to enrol as a volunteer, and after getting his *Kriegsabitur* (Wartime Matriculation), for which we didn't have to sit an examination, he was called up for flying training on 15th November 1939.

From then on, because I joined up on the same day, Heinz and I lost touch with each other. Of the thirty-five *Jungmannen* from the *Fliegerzug* at Potsdam only five survived the war.

---

[1] The East-West Axis, part of the Hitler/Speer plan for a triumphal city of Berlin, stretched in a straight line across Berlin from *Unter den Linden*, through the Brandenburg Gate, past the Victory Column (*Siegessäule*) and *Adolf Hitler Platz*, a distance of about six miles. It was handed over to Hitler by Speer in its completed state on the very day that Kurt Meyer recalls here.

Heinz Schnaufer, in common with so many young men of his time, had maturity forced upon him by the outbreak of the Second World War. When, just after attaining the age of seventeen, the young Schnaufer had, from his perch in the lime tree, seen the triumphal birthday procession of his idol, Adolf Hitler – for virtually all German youth idolised their *Führer* – through Berlin with the massed bombers and fighters overhead, Hitler was already planning the final aggression which would loosen the flood-tides that would submerge first Europe, and later most of the world, in warfare. It was a war that would cost countless of thousands of young men their lives: and older men, too, and women, and children, all in numbers and in agonies undreamed of on that fine April day.

We have no way now of knowing with any certainty how Schnaufer felt inside himself when war came, but we can hazard a good guess, because there are still many still alive today who, like him, were young and convinced of the rightness of their country's cause. Anti-war voices in Germany were few. For German youth – as well as for many, possible the majority of, older citizens – the first years of Nazi rule were a golden age, and it was to defend the way of life that the régime had promised them and already seemed to be giving to them that they willingly took up arms. Schnaufer was trained in soldierly ways and in leadership, and, above all, he had tasted the joys of flying. Flying was the key to future warfare, and he with the best air force and the best men would win: and who could doubt the superiority of Hitler's men and Hitler's machines? A glittering prospect of blue skies, of thrilling duelling and skirmishing in aerial combat and of glory called. There were many young men in Great Britain and the Commonwealth to whom the same prospect beckoned: comparatively few of them would find glory, but tragically the majority would find an early grave, and as often as not that grave would be unmarked.

CHAPTER TWO

November 1939 to November 1941

Basic Luftwaffe training and move to the Nachtjagd.
Meeting with Fritz Rumpelhardt.

On the 15th November 1939 Schnaufer was called to the colours. His first posting as an officer-cadet was to *Fliegerausbildungsregiment* (Aircrew Training Regiment) No. 42 at Salzwedel in Northern Germany, roughly between Berlin and Hamburg. It was just over two months since the German invasion of Poland had been followed by the declaration of war by Britain and France, and the *Luftwaffe*, which had spearheaded the invasion, was riding high. Warsaw had surrendered after only three weeks of fighting and Polish troops, faced not only by the overwhelming superiority of the German forces in the west but also with the opportunistic invasion by Russia in the east, had finally given up the unequal struggle in early October.

The first few weeks of the Second World War had emphasised what had been very clear since the latter stages of the 1914–1918 conflict, namely that in any future war air power was likely to be the key to victory, and Hermann Göring's *Luftwaffe* had, it seemed, proved that proposition beyond any reasonable doubt, even allowing for the fact that the opposition they encountered on the part of the Polish Air Force was only slight. The German air arm, adding to its propaganda-generated reputation of invincibility, had operated in close tactical support of the ground forces in the front line and struck with precision at targets behind the lines. Included among their targets had been the city of Warsaw, which, rejecting calls for surrender, had been bombed by over a thousand German aircraft on 24 September and had surrendered the same day. To young men who, like Schnaufer, were just on the point of entering the air force, the fear was that the war would end before they had a chance to prove themselves in action and share in the glory that was there to be won. No doubt they took some slight comfort from the knowledge that there were still other enemies to be faced in the form of the Western Allies, Britain and France, but realistically the likelihood seemed to be that the war would not persist and some sort of accommodation would be reached between Berlin on the one hand and London and Paris on the other. There was an air of unreality abroad on both sides in Europe, a feeling that the war was nominal rather than actual. Now began what came to be known in Britain as the 'Phoney War', an uneasy period of seven months during which neither side initiated decisively aggressive action but in which, nevertheless, both sides took advantage of the lull to build up their forces and plan for future military contingencies.

To a young German embarking on a flying career in the *Luftwaffe* in 1939 there were various options. If he wanted to be a commissioned officer and had passed the necessary strict tests of suitability he would look forward to becoming a pilot or an observer, preferably the former. Other aircrew trades such as signaller, gunner and flight mechanic would normally be filled from the ranks. After initial flying training, assuming that he was confirmed for further training as a pilot, a decision would be made as to whether he was more suited to single-engined or multi-engined aircraft, and the direction of his future training would depend on that decision. He would of course be asked to state his personal wishes, but these would be secondary to the results of his aptitude assessments and the requirements of the *Luftwaffe* at the time. In parallel with his flying training the cadet would be rigorously trained as an officer. Throughout the war, and particularly in the earlier stages, much greater weight was given in the *Luftwaffe* to training officers for command responsibilities than was the case in the Royal Air Force.

The Schnaufer family in about 1940, when Heinz was still under training. Father Alfred is standing at the rear: then, left to right, Mother Martha, Heinz, Manfred, Eckart, Waltraut. (Schnaufer)

*Heinz Schnaufer in flying
kit during his training.*
(Schnaufer)

Trainees selected to fly single-engined machines were, in broad terms, destined to operate on day fighters or on dive-bombers such as the Ju 87 'Stuka', while those selected for multi-engined training would expect to go on to bombers, reconnaissance aircraft, transport machines and so on. Training for the latter categories lasted, understandably, much longer. When Heinz Schnaufer began his training – and, indeed, until his training was well advanced – there was no night-fighter arm in the *Luftwaffe*, despite the fact that Royal Air Force bombers had been flying over Germany by night since the very beginning of the war. But at that stage the Germans saw the RAF incursions as an irritant rather than a serious threat: first Whitleys, later Wellingtons and Hampdens as well, were dropping not bombs but millions of propaganda leaflets, most of which missed their allocated target area by many miles. Some attempts were made by single-engined Bf 109s of the *Luftwaffe* to intercept the British machines, but there is no confirmed record of success, and the probability is that the proportionately few bombers that failed to come home were victims of either anti-aircraft fire or of flying accidents.

We have only very superficial details of Schnaufer's early training, but we can describe the usual pattern of instruction that applied at that time to trainee cadets destined to pilot multi-engined aircraft. Commonly the training lasted in the region of two years, sometimes considerably more. The various courses, particularly after the pupil obtained his pilot's badge[1], did not necessarily follow a standard sequence, and sometimes extra short courses were included, usually to occupy time when awaiting the next stage in the training programme. Schnaufer did not join an operational unit until late 1941, roughly on the second anniversary of his call-up, by which time the war had taken on a far grimmer aspect than it had presented in the first heady months.

The basic recruit's training that the officer cadet underwent lasted from two to four months, at the end of which time he was posted for a period to *Luftkriegsschule* (Air Warfare School) where, in addition to theoretical and academic subjects, his practical flying training began. Then would follow a course equivalent, in British terms, to elementary and advanced flying training, designated in the *Luftwaffe* as 'A' and 'B' respectively. This part of Schnaufer's career took place at A/B *Schule* No. 3 at Guben, on the Polish border, beginning on 1 November 1939 and finishing on 20 August 1940. On this course he would have flown in a wide variety of machines such as the elementary training Focke-Wulf 44 'Stieglitz', Fw 58 'Weihe' and Bücker 131 biplanes and possibly in more powerful machines like the Heinkel 50, also a biplane but one that had seen operational service as a dive-bomber. He might have flown such single-engined monoplanes as the Klemm 35 and the Arado 96, perhaps the Messerschmitt Bf 108 or the Bücker 181. At the end of the course he was awarded his pilot's badge and the A/B Certificate, showing him to be qualified on elementary and advanced single-engined machines.

Heinz Schnaufer would have entered the *Luftwaffe* with the rank of *Fahnenjunker* (officer-cadet), but by this time he would have passed rapidly through the grades of *Fahnenjunker-Gefreiter* and *Fahnenjunker-Unteroffizier*, roughly equivalent to Lance-Corporal Cadet and Corporal Cadet respectively, and have been promoted to *Fähnrich* (Warrant Officer) and possibly to *Oberfähnrich* (Senior Warrant Officer).

For those destined to fly single-engined fighters the next stage in a pilot's career would take him to an operational unit via a specialist training course, but there was further basic training to be undergone if one was to fly multi-engined machines, when the newly-qualified pilot would go on to a *C-Schule*. On completion of this course the student would be awarded his *C-Schein*[2] (C-Certificate) and he would probably be promoted to *Leutnant*. Heinz Schnaufer carried out his multi-engined

---

[1] *Flugzeugführer-Abzeichen*, more frequently written as one word (*Flugzeugführerabzeichen*).
[2] The *C-Schein* was formally known as the '*ELF-Schein*' (*Erweiteter Luftwaffenflugzeugführer-Schein*) or 'Advanced Air Force Pilot's Certificate'.

A studio portrait of Heinz Schnaufer, newly commissioned as Leutnant, *April 1941.*

training at the *C-Schule* at Alt-Lönnewitz, where he was promoted to *Leutnant* on 1 April 1941. There he flew a number of twin-engined machines – the Do 17, the He 111, the Ju 88 and the Ju 86 – as well as the three-engined Ju 52.

Fritz Engau, a contemporary of Heinz Schnaufer, recalls details of life at Alt-Lönnewitz[1]. The trainees were accommodated in primitive barrack-blocks on the main airfield or at the satellite fields at Alteno and Pretsch, huts so profusely surrounded by air-raid trenches that to go out at night without a torch was to risk falling into one. The food was poor, fog was frequent, and the thin-walled, draughty living blocks made the nights miserably cold. Fritz Engau goes on:

The accommodation block at Altenau had a special place in our memory, as did its location about three kilometres distant from the air traffic

[1] As related in his book, *Nachtjäger, Bomber, Wolken und Sterne*, published 1993 by Hoppe, Graz.

control and kitchen building, which was exactly opposite on the other side of the airfield. Every morning at 0530 hours, bare-footed and clad only in gym shorts, we had to run at high speed through the wet grass to this air traffic control building, where the duty officer of the *Gruppe* had the task of putting us through the usual morning PT. Then we had to go the whole way back, again at high speed. Then, in rapid sequence, it was a matter of washing, cleaning teeth and so on, after which we had to face the same stretch – which by now was quite daunting – once more in order to be at the kitchen for our breakfast punctually at 0640 hours. It goes without saying that by that time our outward appearance had to be impeccable.

Another aircraft also flown at Alt-Lönnewitz was the Dornier 23, one of the original bombers that equipped the *Luftwaffe* when it emerged from clandestinity in 1935. It was a high-winged, square-fuselage monoplane with a fixed undercarriage, twin motors and an open pilot's cockpit, and Engau refers to it as a '*Ratterkasten*' – an old banger. He recalls with amusement the occasion when a student-pilot 'beat up' a local township and a part of an exhaust fell off into the market place, narrowly missing a local inhabitant. But there were also tragedies: one day a Ju 52 crashed on take-off killing the pupil pilot, Kontny, and severely injuring the instructor. French prisoners of war were the first on the scene and dragged the two men out of the burning aircraft, but too late to save them. It was Engau's birthday and it was he who should have been at the controls of the Ju 52 – Kontny had taken his place so that Engau could have a celebratory drink.

Perhaps surprisingly, pilot's training so far would have included comparatively little night flying. The next course, therefore, would at Blind-Flying School (*Blindflugschule*), which usually lasted about eight weeks. The aircraft used were principally the Do 217 and the Ju 52. The Blind-Flying School that Schnaufer attended was at Schwäbisch Hall in Bavaria, from where he was posted for ten weeks to a *Zerstörer-Schule*, or 'Destroyer School' at Wunstorf near Hanover.

It is often thought that '*Zerstörer*' was a name used exclusively for the Bf 110, but that belief is mistaken. The term applied to a whole class of combat aircraft, the strategic fighter. Just as in the Navy a destroyer was a fast and manoeuvrable vessel employed, among other things, to escort and protect capital ships, so the *Zerstörer* was primarily conceived as a long-range, heavily armed fighter aircraft to escort day bombers and to be used for standing patrols, deep-penetration offensive sorties into enemy territory and ground attack. The Bf 110 was the main machine of this class, but not the only one. Although outclassed in the Battle of Britain when it came up against the faster and more nimble Hurricanes and Spitfires of the Royal Air Force, it performed well in a fighter-bomber and ground-attack rôle in other theatres. It was, however, in a different guise that it was to enjoy perhaps its greatest success, becoming as it did the first effective and the most widely used night fighter flown by the *Luftwaffe* in the Second World War, and many German night-fighter pilots would claim that it was also the best. In terms of the number of enemy bombers that it shot down, that claim is certainly justified.

The crew of a Bf 110 when it was flown as a *Zerstörer* and when it was first used as a night fighter comprised two men, the pilot (*Flugzeugführer*) and the radio operator (*Funker* or *Bordfunker*). In addition to being responsible for radio communications and, to a large extent, for the navigation of the aircraft, the *Funker* also manned a rearward-facing flexible 7.9 mm. MG 15 machine gun. In later versions of the Bf 110, twin machine-guns were fitted. It was usual practice for pilots arriving on the *Zerstörer* course to come already 'crewed-up' with a *Funker* whom they had been paired with at Blind Flying School and who, in normal circumstances, would go on with them to an operational unit on successful completion of the course. History does not record who Schnaufer's first *Funker* was: he fell by the wayside and was replaced by Fritz Rumpelhardt.

Fritz Rumpelhardt, born in Nordhalden near Konstanz on the 19th of June 1920, was almost two years older than Heinz Schnaufer, twenty-one years old to Schnaufer's nineteen, when they met at Wunstorf. He was one of three sons born to Rosa Rumpelhardt, the wife of Emil, a senior primary school teacher: his twin brothers also joined the *Luftwaffe* and were commissioned as pilots, and both were killed in action. After primary school Rumpelhardt attended the *Gymnasium* in Singen where, at the end of 1938, he applied to join the *Luftwaffe*, nominating the Flak as his preferred speciality. The normal course of events, which applied in the case of Rumpelhardt, was that a young man would volunteer in advance of taking his *Abitur*, the equivalent of Higher School Certificate, and would eventually be called up some time after successfully passing that examination. Fritz Rumpelhardt sat and passed his *Abitur* in 1939 and then, while his application to join the Air Force was still pending, was called up for national service with the Reich Labour Service, the *Reichsarbeitdienst*. On the outbreak of war he was immediately drafted into a *Wehrmacht* construction company, from which, in February 1940, he was transferred to the *Luftwaffe* on the basis of his earlier voluntary application. As the Anti-Aircraft Service was already oversubscribed, he found himself allocated to the Signals Service, the *Nachrichtentruppe*.

From February to July 1940 Rumpelhardt carried out his basic training at Cottbus, on completion of which he was posted to *Bordfunkerschule* (Aircrew Signallers' School) at Nordhausen. His rank was *Gefreiter*, the equivalent of a senior private (PFC in the American Army) or Lance Corporal. In the Royal Air Force all aircrew were volunteers, but that nicety did not apply in the German Air Force. The radio operator's course at Nordhausen lasted seven months, until February 1941, when he was posted to Blind-Flying School No. 4 at Vienna-Aspern. The pilot to whom Rumpelhardt had been allocated was then 'washed-out' – withdrawn from flying – and Rumpelhardt found himself with time on his hands. It was not until July 1941 that he was posted to Wunstorf, where he met Schnaufer. Rumpelhardt himself takes up the story:

At Wunstorf I was crewed up with Heinz Schnaufer on 3 July 1941. He
was *Leutnant*, I was *Gefreiter*. I was allocated to Schnaufer because his previous *Funker* had proved unable to cope with aerobatics. So that he
wouldn't have the same thing happen yet again, Schnaufer first of all
gave me a very thorough test of my ability to cope – aerobatics, first of
all in a Bücker 131 and then in an Me 110. Outcome – 'Let's try working together.'

It was at Wunstorf that Schnaufer decided, in consultation with
Rumpelhardt, that they would volunteer to fly as night fighters. Early
resistance to joining the new arm, which had been endemic among
pilots and radio operators, had by this time diminished. Successes were
being reported and the official propaganda machine was extolling the
night-fighter men, and there was a vigorous recruitment campaign for
crews to fly in the ever-increasing number of machines that were being

*Fritz Rumpelhardt in
front of a Bf 110 in
1942, probably at Stade.
He 'crewed-up' with
Heinz Schnaufer in July
1941 and was destined
to share 100 victories
with him.*
(Rumpelhardt)

produced. Leading night-fighter pilots were sent to visit training centres such as Wunstorf and give lectures to drum up recruitment. We do not know precisely what it was that motivated Schnaufer to switch from *Zerstörer* to *Nachtjäger*, but we do have Fritz Rumpelhardt's comment:

> Towards the end of our training at Wunstorf volunteers for the night-fighter arm – the *Nachtjagd* – were called for, and after talking it over with me Schnaufer volunteered, together with two other crews. And so we went to Schleissheim, where we only had to do our night-flying training. Schnaufer believed that flying night fighters would be a greater professional challenge for him, that there would be greater opportunities for success, and that with Comrade Night on his side his chances of survival would be greater. (This is my personal opinion).
>
> Schnaufer made a very good impression on me as both an officer and a pilot, and I quickly came to trust him entirely. It was on the 12th of July 1941 that I flew with him for the first time.

By the time Schnaufer completed his *Zerstörer* course at Wunstorf the war, which many had thought, and hoped, would be over in a few months, was entering its third year and had escalated into a major European conflict. To all outward appearances Germany was winning it. Following his unprecedented victories in the west in 1940 Hitler had loosed his forces on the Soviet Union in June 1941, envisaging another rapid victory there, and as yet there was little reason to believe that he would not achieve that aim. Elsewhere German arms had enjoyed, and were on the whole still enjoying, consistent success. America, although committed to supporting the Anti-Nazi cause and supplying Britain with war material, was not yet an active participant in the conflict. There was, however, one dark cloud on the Germans' horizon: RAF bomber operations against the Third Reich, originally more a nuisance than a menace, had by this time become the major problem that had necessitated the introduction by the *Luftwaffe* of a specialist night-fighter force.

Let us look at the new arena of warfare in which night fighter and night bomber confronted each other in mortal combat, and into which Schnaufer was about to enter. From the beginning of the war until the German offensive in the west in May 1940 RAF Bomber Command had not attempted to hit land targets within Germany. Such few offensive operations as were carried out were mainly by day and against naval targets at sea, when German fighters, Bf 109s and Bf 110s, had inflicted prohibitively high losses on the Wellingtons and Blenheims that came within their range. Night-time leaflet raids, mainly by Armstrong-Whitworth Whitleys, had been mounted from the first night of the war, but the only significant bombing attack by darkness, carried out in March 1940 by thirty Whitleys and twenty Hampdens against the German seaplane base at Hörnum on the island of Sylt, had been a complete failure. In April, after the German invasion of Norway and Denmark, the RAF had begun to extend its night offensive by sending heavy bombers, mainly Whitleys and Wellingtons, to strike at airfields in those two countries. It was during this period, while Heinz Schnaufer was still learning to fly, that the first tentative steps were taken towards the forming of a German night-fighter force.

One of the German-occupied airfields frequently attacked by Bomber Command was at Aalborg in Denmark: stationed there was I./ZG1, under the command of *Hauptmann* Wolfgang Falck and equipped with the Bf 110. Working in conjunction with an anti-shipping radar unit on the coast, Falck found that with early warning from the radar operators he could scramble his aircraft with some chance of intercepting the incoming bombers. Although success in the form of the destruction of enemy machines eluded him, the promise shown by his experiments led him to write a paper on the feasibility of night interception and to forward it to Berlin.

Following the invasion of the Low Countries and France Bomber Command began to send aircraft to strike at road and rail targets behind the front. Some of their targets were in Germany, although at first the bombers were restricted for political reasons to the area west of the Rhine. Bombers flew individually, the pilots themselves deciding the tactics for each attack: there was no attempt to plan concentration in time. Navigational difficulties meant that designated targets were only rarely hit. Then, on 15 May 1940, the Germans bombed Rotterdam by day, inflicting heavy casualties among the civilian population. In response the British War Cabinet permitted Bomber Command to strike at industrial targets within Germany that night, and 99 bombers headed for the Ruhr industrial area. Damage to the targets there was negligible, but historically these were very significant operations: the bomber offensive proper against the Third Reich had begun. And still the *Luftwaffe* had no night-fighter force to defend against it.

In the course of the campaign in the west Falck's Bf 110 *Gruppe* was

Major *Wolfgang Falck* (second right), *NJG 1's first* Kommodore, *with* Hauptmann *Werner Streib (*first right) Kommandeur I./*NJG 1.*

moved from Denmark to an airfield near Le Havre in readiness to take part in the planned assault on the British Isles. On the 22nd June it was summarily withdrawn from the front line and Falck was ordered, on the basis of the paper he had submitted from Aalborg some weeks previously, to set up a night-fighter organisation using his *Gruppe* as a nucleus. Falck and his crews were less than pleased. The forthcoming assault on Great Britain promised action, decorations, possibly accelerated promotion. Now, suddenly, these alluring prospects were no longer there: instead there was the uncertainty of a completely new, untried form of warfare in an element – darkness – for which they were not fully trained and which had no appeal to their natural instincts as aggressive air-warriors.

From such small beginnings grew two of the most powerful aerial forces in the Second World War, on the one hand the night-time bomber armada of the Royal Air Force that pounded Germany with escalating savagery and increasing accuracy to the very end of hostilities, and on the other the *Nachtjagd*, the night-fighter force that opposed it tenaciously and to a degree that came, on occasions, very close to being decisive. By the time that Heinz Schnaufer began his specialist night-fighter training on 1 September 1941 both Bomber Command and the *Nachtjagd* had expanded significantly. Bomber Command had begun the war with a total of 209 nominally heavy and medium bombers suitable for use at night, made up of 77 Wellingtons, 61 Whitleys, and 71 Hampdens, although without sufficient crews to man them all. By September 1941 the total night-bomber strength of the Command stood at approximately 500 with crews for about 400 of them. Wellingtons, Hampdens and Whitleys, in that order, still made up the bulk of the force, but a new generation of heavy bombers – four-engined Stirlings and Halifaxes and two-engined Manchesters – was beginning to appear in small numbers. The German night-fighter force, less than eighteen months in being, now comprised over 250 machines, mostly Bf 110s. Just as it was in the Royal Air Force, manning was a problem, and there were crews for only about 120 of the available aircraft.

The pattern of Bomber Command's offensive against Germany was changing, slowly but relentlessly. After the Battle of Britain, during which much of Bomber Command's strength was deployed against the barges that the Germans were concentrating along the Channel coast in preparation for their planned invasion of England, and following the German bombing of targets in London and other British cities, the RAF had gradually begun to turn its attention to targets in mainland Germany. The War Cabinet was, at this period, attempting to define a rôle for Bomber Command, seemingly not realising – or, ostrich-like, not willing to accept – that the Command was incapable of performing with any degree of effectiveness the rôle that was its *raison d'être*. Directives to the Commander-in-Chief of the Command specified war-related targets within the Third Reich, giving priority to those connected with the production and distribution of oil. Looking back now, there seems to have been an Alice-in-Wonderland atmosphere of unreality surrounding such prognostications. Bomber Command crews, as those writing the directives should well have known, were neither trained nor equipped to find or bomb targets with any semblance of accuracy, yet the directives were based on the assumption that they in fact possessed such capabilities. The self-deception was compounded when the crews came back claiming to have hit the targets they had been sent out to hit, when, as was later to transpire, they were in reality scattering their bombs seemingly indiscriminately over vast areas of countryside and seldom hitting even the cities in which their targets were located. Yet despite – and partly because of – the fact that the specified targets were not being hit, the threat facing the Germans was becoming more real, because now it was bombs that were being dropped, not leaflets, and even badly-aimed bombs were capable of causing death and destruction, and they were doing so.

Bombing tactics were changing, too. No longer were pilots planning their own route and altitude and time on target: now they were being given planned routes to fly and specific periods of time within which to bomb. As yet Bomber Command was not sending large forces against individual targets, nor was it planning the tight concentration in time that would emerge as the war progressed, but it was spreading its effort by attacking a number of targets in widely separated areas of Germany more or less simultaneously.

The tactics of the night-fighter force and its deployment had been developing step by step in response to the threat that the bombers presented. When Falck began to set up his defences his first action was to create belts of searchlights across the routes most frequently followed by the RAF machines, and the night fighters – black-painted Bf 110 *Zerstörer* – would lie in wait in the hope of catching sight of a bomber in a searchlight beam and being able to pursue it until within firing range. Early warning was provided by *Freya* radars ahead of the searchlight belt, and the method was christened '*Helle Nachtjagd*'[1]. These searchlight belts were the extended, and in increasing numbers the searchlights were equipped with primitive radars with the name '*Würzburg*' to enable them to focus on their targets, and a logical next step was that the radars should be used to show controllers on the ground the position of the enemy bombers so that they could bring the fighters directly into their proximity, thus dispensing with the need for searchlights to help the fighter pilots to find their targets. It would, however, take some little time before a night-fighting system based on this concept (*Himmelbett*) could be introduced. By this time the strength of the *Nachtjagd* had been increased to that of a *Division*, Falck had been superseded as Commander by *General* Joseph Kammhuber and the searchlight barrier initiated by Falck had been christened by the bomber crews of the RAF as the 'Kammhuber Line'.

---

[1] '*Helle Nachtjagd*' – literally 'bright night-fighting', or 'illuminated night-fighting'. Sometimes abbreviated to '*Henaja*'

Kammhuber now introduced a system that was called '*Dunkle Nachtjagd*'[1], and the first kills by this method took place in mid-1941. The radars used were the early-warning *Freyas*. It was found that one *Freya* could be used to pick up two aircraft, an enemy bomber and a friendly fighter, simultaneously and that with practice and no little skill a controller on the ground, using R/T and working directly from the cathode-ray tube, could direct the fighter towards the bomber. The system, primitive but not without its successes, was known as the '*AN-Verfahren*', or 'AN Method'.

At the same time, in and around the searchlight belt were being set up an ever-increasing number of overlapping circular areas (*Räume*) with a radius corresponding to that of a more advanced *Würzburg* radar, the '*Würzburg Riese*' (Würzburg Giant). There were two of these radars in each circular area, one of which was used to acquire the incoming bomber, the other to pick up the night fighter. The position of each of the aircraft was 'told through' orally to the fighter-control post and displayed in the form of a coloured pinpoint of light (red for the bomber, blue for the fighter) on a horizontal plotting table from which fighter-control officer, or '*Jägerleitoffizier*', would speak to the fighter pilot by R/T and, by referring to the relative positions of the coloured spots of light, direct him into the proximity of the bomber. The two search radars were labelled the 'Red' and the 'Blue' *Würzburg*. The fighter pilot still had to finalise the interception visually, which meant the controller bringing him to within less than two kilometres or so of his prey, but the system was very much more effective than the original *Helle Nachtjagd* or the Freya-based *Dunkle Nachtjagd* described immediately above. This method of night fighting, code-named *Himmelbett*, still came under the general heading of *Dunkle Nachtjagd*.

In the ten months from the outbreak of war until the end of June 1940, when the *Nachtjagd* was born, Bomber Command had despatched a total of 5,391 sorties and had only lost 75 machines from all causes. From July that year until the end of August the following year, when Schnaufer was completing his *Zerstörer* training and about to move into the world of night fighting, Bomber Command losses had amounted to 749 out of 31,427 sorties despatched. In rough terms, while the number of bombers sent out had increased by a factor of under six, losses had gone up tenfold. More significantly, night fighters claimed almost exactly half of the missing bombers – 364 out of the 749. This figure is all the more remarkable when one considers that it was achieved during a period in which the German night-fighter organisation was being built up from scratch. An even clearer picture of the growing potency of the new arm is given when one considers that in the first full month of the existence of the *Nachtjagd*, July 1940, the fighters shot down eight of the 40 British bombers missing, or one in five, while in July 1941 the figures were 63 out of 97, or two-thirds.

When Falck had first been faced with the task of creating a night-fighter organisation out of nothing the majority of his pilots and radio-

---

[1] '*Dunkle Nachtjagd*' – literally 'dark night-fighting'. Sometimes abbreviated to '*Dunaja*'.

operators had been very unenthusiastic about having to change from the known world of day fighting to the unknown one of night fighting, and it had not proved easy to recruit crews voluntarily as the force began to expand. By mid-1941, however, the *Nachtjagd* was becoming a more popular option to flying personnel of the *Luftwaffe*. There were two main reasons. The first one lay in the increasing numbers in which the Royal Air Force was striking at German cities, so that there was a natural and completely understandable desire on the part of many to defend against what had already come to be known as the *Terrorflieger*: secondly, the increasing successes scored by the night fighters, well publicised in the German press – just as the feats of the RAF and Allied pilots in the Battle of Britain had been extolled in the British media – made the *Nachtjagd* more attractive to young men seeking action and glory.

It is worth considering here the term 'Terror Fliers'. From the German point of view, particularly that of the civilian population, it was an entirely justifiable epithet. No matter how much the bomber crews were given precise war-related targets to strike at, and no matter how much they deceived themselves into believing they were finding and hitting those targets, the indisputable fact – suspected in some quarters but neither generally accepted nor, indeed, fully realised at the time – is that they were quite incapable of doing so. To the Germans on the ground it seemed that the ever-growing number of bombers penetrating their airspace each night were scattering bombs indiscriminately with the intention of killing civilians. This was precisely what had happened in the First World War when the Germans had despatched Zeppelins to attack military objectives in Britain, which they regularly managed to miss by many tens of miles. And indeed the impression that Bomber Command was aiming at civilians was not completely without foundation. More and more, successive Chiefs of Staff of the RAF, in their periodic policy directives to the Commander-in-Chief of Bomber Command, were adducing the morale of the German citizens as a legitimate target. In the directive of 9 March 1941 was included the sentence: 'Priority of selection [of targets] should be given to those in Germany which lie in congested areas where the greatest moral [sic] effect is likely to result.' In a Directive dated 9 July 1941 this had hardened somewhat: 'I am directed to inform you that a comprehensive review of the enemy's political, economic and military situation discloses that the weakest points in his armour lie in the morale of his civil population and in his inland transportation system – and there are many signs that our recent attacks on industrial towns are having great effect on the morale of the civil population. I am to request that you will direct the main effort of the bomber force, until further instructions, towards dislocating the German transportation system and to destroying the morale of the civil population as a whole and of the industrial workers in particular.'[1]

---

[1] Both these quotations are from the *Official History of Bomber Command*, Section VI, Appendix 8, Pages 133–136.

Such, then, was the state of the bomber war when Heinz Schnaufer became a night fighter. The battle between the bombers and the night fighters would intensify into a bitter confrontation of attrition costing the lives of tens of thousands of men on each side, and Heinz Schnaufer was destined to play a prominent part in it.

CHAPTER THREE

November 1941 to December 1942

Becoming a night fighter: early operations and first kills. A slow start.

Heinz Schnaufer's and Fritz Rumpelhardt's 'destroyer' training at Wunstorf had concentrated almost exclusively on operational flying in daylight — there was no rôle foreseen for the Bf 110 *Zerstörer* in the hours of darkness. At the Night Fighter School at Schleissheim, on the outskirts of Munich, of course, the greater emphasis was on flying and operating by night. Some skills, notably gunnery, were practised by day, taking the form of both 'dummy' exercises using camera guns with other machines as targets, and also live air-to-air firing at drogues towed by other aircraft. Night flying was carried out on the Arado 96 (a low-wing single-seater monoplane with retractable undercarriage), the Focke-Wulf 58 (an elderly twin-engined multi-purpose monoplane) and, of course, the Bf 110. The training by night comprised night take-offs and landings, co-operation with searchlights, radio-beacon homings and cross-country flying. This was before the advent of airborne radar, so there was no training in that field, even theoretical. That would have to be learned later, 'on the job'. And the art of night-time interception would also have to be practised later on the operational unit by means of so-called '*Zieldarstellung*', or 'target simulation', in which one aircraft flew as target and one as fighter, the latter being 'talked in' by the ground controller to a position from which he could carry out an attack. The equivalent exercise in the RAF was called 'PIs', the abbreviation of 'practice interceptions'.

The airfield at Stade lay in Northern Germany, close to the River Elbe, and it was at Stade, at the end of October or the beginning of November 1941[1], that *Leutnant* Heinz Schnaufer and *Gefreiter* Fritz Rumpelhardt joined their first front-line unit, II./NJG 1, based there primarily to defend the great sea port of Hamburg lying some thirty miles to the east. They were assigned to the 5th *Staffel*, 5./NJG 1. A word here about the make-up of a night-fighter *Geschwader* would be in

---

[1] In the *curriculum vitae* that he wrote in 1943 Schnaufer said that he joined II./NJG 1 at Stade on 20 October 1941, whereas the official nominal roll of the unit gives the date of his posting as 1 November.

place. It should be noted that there were frequently variations, particularly later in the war, to the general outline now given.

The smallest sub-unit administratively was the *Staffel* and it usually comprised nine machines. Three *Staffeln* made up a *Gruppe* and three, or occasionally four, *Gruppen* made up a *Geschwader*. In addition there were so-called '*Stab*', or Staff, flights at *Geschwader* and *Gruppe* level. (A flight was a '*Schwarm*' and comprised, usually, two or three machines). A *Nachtjagd-Geschwader* (also, indeed more usually, written as one word – *Nachtjagdgeschwader* – and abbreviated as NJG) carried an Arabic numeral, and during the course of the war six of them came into being, NJG 1 to NJG 6 inclusive. These were the main night-fighter formations: in addition numerous independent and self-administrating units were formed during the course of the war. Each *Gruppe* within a *Geschwader* was designated by a Roman numeral, a full stop after it indicating that it was an ordinal number (I. meant 1st, II. meant 2nd, and so on). II./NJG 1, then, was the Second *Gruppe* of NJG 1. *Staffeln* were numbered in Arabic numbers, again with a full stop, so that 5./NJG 1 meant the 5th *Staffel*. As there were three *Staffeln* to a *Gruppe*, it will readily be seen that 5./NJG 1, Schnaufer's first *Staffel*, was part of II./NJG 1, while 2./NJG 1, for example, would form part of I./NJG 1.

The operational *Gruppe* that Schnaufer joined was a successful one: it had already shot down over 110 British bombers of the total of 397 destroyed by the whole night-fighter force. The unhappy distinction of being the one-hundredth victim of II./NJG 1 had fallen to a Vickers Wellington[1] on the 19th September 1941. One *Staffel* alone, 4./NJG 1 under its *Kapitän*, *Oberleutnant* Helmut Lent, had destroyed well over half of the *Gruppe*'s victims. Lent was destined to become, after Schnaufer, the second-highest-scoring night-fighter ace in World War Two. On the very day that Heinz Schnaufer joined II./NJG 1, Lent was appointed *Kommandeur* of a new *Gruppe* then being formed as part of the rapid build-up of the *Nachtjagd*, II./NJG 2.

The Bf 110s that Schnaufer's *Gruppe* flew were not yet equipped with airborne interception radar, but experiments were under way and *Oberleutnant* Ludwig Becker of 4./NJG 1 had already shot down five bombers using a device known as *Lichtenstein*, but some time was to pass before the front-line machines were equipped with it. By the time Schnaufer began to fly operationally *Himmelbett* had improved considerably from the first hesitant experiments in the winter of 1940/41. With continuing practice both controllers and pilots had gained in skill and, most importantly, pilots had overcome their initial mistrust of the controllers' ability to bring them close enough to the bombers to be able to see them either with the naked eye or by means of a primitive infrared device known as '*Spanner*', the precursor of airborne radar. But the system had its disadvantages.

For newly operational crews such as Schnaufer's there was one particular disadvantage that caused them considerable frustration. The

---

[1] Probably Z8344, LQ-F, of No. 405 Squadron, Pocklington.

more experienced pilots, who were usually, if not always, senior in rank, were almost invariably given priority of take-off when incoming raids were reported. They thus formed the so-called '*erste Welle*', or First Wave, and when scrambled they had to fly to a radio beacon to await the instructions of the controller. By the time it was the turn of the younger and junior crews to take to the air the bombers would usually have passed through the line of defences and there would be no more pickings. It was, of course, understandable that the crews with greater experience should be given the first 'go' at the bombers – they were, after all, more likely to bring them down – but the motives of some of the senior pilots were suspect to the frustrated junior ones, who were longing to see action. Some 'old hands' suffered, they said, from sore throats – '*Sie haben Halsschmerzen*' – an envious euphemism for a desire to earn the coveted Knight's Cross to the Iron Cross, a neck decoration awarded to those who shot down a given number – which varied during the war but seems eventually to have settled down at 25 – of enemy aircraft.

Schnaufer's early opportunities for action were, in any event, affected by the fact that he joined his front-line unit at a time when there were fewer RAF bombers coming to Germany. The fortunes of Bomber Command were at a low ebb: indeed, the future of the air offensive against Germany was very much in the balance. As a result of increasing concern in some circles as to the accuracy, and therefore the effectiveness, of the RAF bombing, an investigation had been undertaken by

Schnaufer boards his aircraft. This photo was probably taken when he was serving with II./NJG 1 at Saint-Trond.

a member of the War Cabinet Secretariat, Mr D M Butt, and his findings, published in August 1941, had been devastating, concluding that the bombers' results were far worse, even, than the most pessimistic of critics had imagined. On 13 November 1941, despite a marked reluctance among the senior echelons of the Air Staff and Bomber Command to accept Butt's findings, the Prime Minister, Winston Churchill, advised by his scientific consultant, Lord Cherwell, instructed the then Commander-in-Chief, Sir Richard Peirse, that during the coming winter months only limited operations were to be a carried out, while an in-depth reconsideration of the rôle of Bomber Command would be undertaken. From then until 15 January 1942, when II./NJG 1 transferred from Stade to Saint-Trond in Belgium, the unit only shot down two RAF bombers, *Leutnant* Ludwig Meister claiming a Halifax and a Whitley during a comparatively heavy attack on Hamburg on the evening of 30 November. It was not until April 1942 that II./NJG 1 scored its next kill, the technical and administrative difficulties associated with quitting one base and settling in a brand-new one no doubt playing their part in the lack of success.

Saint-Trond (the French-language version of the name: in Flemish it is Sint-Truiden) lies in the Province of Limburg, roughly half-way between Aachen and Brussels, which made it an ideal defensive location from which to attempt the interception of enemy bombers heading for the Ruhr Valley industrial complex and for Central Germany. In the early months of the war Saint-Trond had been a grass airfield used by the Belgian Air Force, but after the German invasion the *Luftwaffe* had taken it over for their own use. During the Battle of Britain it had been used by Dornier and Junkers bombers flying against England, and at the same time the development of the field as a major air base had begun, with particular attention being paid to camouflage, so that the hangars and administrative buildings were disguised to look from the air like houses and the newly-built concrete runways painted in drab colours to blend into the surrounding countryside. The Belgian Army Cadet School nearby was taken over as a Command Centre and two nearby country houses, the *Châteaux* Nonnen Mielen and Rochendael, were requisitioned as officers' accommodation. Work on the construction of the base was completed in March 1942, when II./NJG 1 had already been in occupation about two months.

For the first two months of 1942 bad weather, coupled with the restrictions on Bomber Command activity over Germany and the process of settling in at Saint-Trond, provided II./NJG 1 with few opportunities for action. And indeed, the entire night-fighter force of the *Luftwaffe*, with an establishment of 367 aircraft and an actual strength of 265, claimed only sixteen kills in January and a meagre five in February. Schnaufer has sometimes been described as a 'late starter', but in his defence it can be seen that his opportunities for 'breaking his duck' at that period were very limited. His first taste of action came in an unexpected way.

In February 1942 II./NJG 1, which had not yet scored a single suc-

cess from its new base, had temporarily to abandon its night-fighting duties altogether and revert to a *Zerstörer* rôle. On the 8th of the month, without any preliminary warning, the *Gruppe* was ordered to deploy to Koksijde on the Belgian coast, just over the border from Dunkirk. Fritz Rumpelhardt writes:

Schnaufer's aircraft (centre) over Norway during Operation Donnerkeil *in February 1942.*

> Take-off followed so quickly that a lot of us didn't have time to get all our things together. One of us went without his shaving kit, another without his uniform jacket. I myself didn't have any footwear apart from my fur flying-boots, which was to have unpleasant consequences for me. It was not until we went to the operations room of the airfield at Koksijde that we learned the reason for the move. On the 12th of February – favourable weather having been forecast – Operation *Donnerkeil* was due to begin. The battleships *Scharnhorst*, *Gneisenau* and *Prinz Eugen*, lying blockaded in the harbour at Brest, were to sail through the English Channel so that they could take part in the naval war again. The *Führerbefehl*[1] on the operation was read out to us in the early morning. In addition to the naval units protecting the convoy the fighter crews were ordered to intercept any attacking aircraft. 'There will be so much firing from both shores and the ships themselves that there will scarcely be room in the air for aircraft! No fighter may leave the area of operations unless he is relieved. If you run out of ammunition, you must ram the enemy aircraft. The battleships must be saved at any price, even if it means the sacrifice of the last fighter aircraft!' To our great relief we night fighters were first assigned as first-line reserves, that is that we would not be thrown into action until there were no longer sufficient single-engined fighters available. The feelings that we experienced when we were faced with the possibility of having to go into action in the imme-

[1] *Führerbefehl*: Führer's order.

February 1942.
Schnaufer first saw
action as an escort in his
Bf 110 for the German
capital ships
Scharnhorst *and*
Gneisenau, *which were*
heading north through the
English Channel.
(Jägerblatt)

diate future can only be imagined. However that might be, we had the shits!

On the day in question there was thick fog over the Channel, just as the High Command had hoped there would be. We sat in the operations room. Our nerves were taut to breaking point. Up to mid-day we were able to follow continuously the position of the warships, which was broadcast on the radio. At about 1230 hours they reached the narrowest point of the Channel. At this time there was still not the slightest reaction from the English coast. To this very day it is a miracle to me, and I still can't understand it, that the British, despite their highly-developed radar system, had still not picked up the convoy until then. There was an almost eerie silence, which was, however, abruptly interrupted shortly after 1330 hours by the code-word '*Offenes Visier*'[1], which meant that the other side had realised what was happening. From now on things became hectic. The single-seater fighters started their engines, and in no time they were airborne and heading west. By this time the fleet had long left the narrows behind and was out of range of the British coastal anti-aircraft guns and artillery. The moment of greatest danger was therefore past, and the fighters 'only' had to cope with torpedo-carrying aircraft and short-range bombers and to tangle in violent air combat with the British Spitfires and Hurricanes, in which they achieved considerable success, as they announced by means of the customary waggling of their wings when they came back to the airfield. I don't know how high our own losses were. Overall, Operation *Donnerkeil* achieved great success and – very importantly for us – the night fighters could be kept for their intended job.

But we were still not quite finished with our convoy-protection rôle. We were kept in reserve and moved that same evening to Amsterdam-Schiphol. The following afternoon we made a reconnaissance flight over the Zuider Zee and the North Sea and then, the same day, we moved

---

[1] *Offenes Visier* – 'Open sights'.

See previous page.

to Westerland on the island of Sylt. In the following few days we moved yet again, this time to Aalborg-West in Denmark. We took off from there and made an exhilarating low-level flight in close formation over the Skaggerak and landed at Stavanger-Sola. For the next few days our airfield was at Forus. Then we flew along the wildly rugged skerry coast and made short-term landing at Bergen-Hertla.

We made just two operational flights as such, but didn't come into contact with the enemy. Our task was to provide convoy protection for the battleships *Admiral Scheer* and *Prinz Eugen*. Because of the considerable difference in speed between ship and aeroplane this meant that we had to keep turning steeply in a tight circle around the 'tubs' at between two and three thousand metres altitude, and that in tight formation. While we were doing so I noticed something strange. The *Prinz Eugen* didn't have a normal, sharp stern, but looked as if it had been cut off square. It was only later that we learned that a mine had taken off the rear eight metres. That explained her relatively slow forward speed.

We were very sad when we were told that the '*Zerstörer-Intermezzo*' was finished and we had to go back to night fighting, which we were not very happy about at that time. We went back to Aalborg via Oslo-Gardemoen, and then, on the following day, via Lüneburg to Bonn-Hangelar, the 5th *Staffel*'s new base.

On 22 February 1942, while Schnaufer was still on detachment on Operation *Donnerkeil*, there was a development in London that was destined to change the nature of the bomber war: Air Chief Marshal Sir Arthur Harris was appointed to the post of Commander-in-Chief of Bomber Command. Just one week before Harris took over the job, on 14 February, the Deputy Chief of the Air Staff, Air Vice-Marshal N H Bottomley, had issued an updated directive for the Command. This document has become notorious as the 'Area Bombing Directive'.

Firstly, it lifted the restrictions placed on the bombers the previous autumn: 'You are accordingly authorised to employ your effort without restriction, until further notice.' Secondly, it contained the ominous passage: 'It has been decided that the primary object of your operations should now be focussed [sic] on the morale of the enemy civil population and in particular, of the industrial workers.'[1] Sir Charles Portal, Chief of the Air Staff, sent Bottomley a minute the following day: 'Ref. the new bombing directive: I suppose it is clear that the aiming points are to be in built-up areas, not, for instance the dockyards or aircraft factories where these are mentioned in Appendix A. This must be made quite clear if it is not already understood.'[2]

Harris, subsequently and erroneously much maligned as the originator of area bombing, entered his new job under unequivocal orders to take the war directly to the German population. He inherited a force of no more than 469 night bombers, of which only 62 were powered by four engines. But there was light in the darkness, literally as well as metaphorically, in the form of new electronic navigational aids under development and coming slowly into use, the first of which was 'Gee', which held out the promise of greater target-finding and bombing accuracy. And four-engined aircraft, Stirlings, Halifaxes and Lancasters, capable of carrying heavier loads of bombs faster, higher and further than could their twin-engined predecessors, were now being produced and delivered in steadily increasing numbers.

Harris began his term of office with a series of experimental raids, within the terms of his directive, intended largely to check the efficacy of 'Gee' – the results were disappointing by and large – and to help him to define the best way in which to use his bomber force. Significant among these operations were the raids on Lübeck on the 28th/29th of March and on Rostock on four nights in late April, concentrated attacks with a preponderance of incendiary bombs dropped in the early waves with the specific intention of setting the towns on fire so that the bombers following on would have a clearly-defined target to aim at. This was area bombing in its raw reality, and it set a basic pattern for the offensive that would persist, with many important modifications and variations, until 1944. A number of other German cities were also visited during this period, but there was no great improvement in navigational or target-finding standards, particularly when the targets were outside the range of 'Gee', which at that time was in the order of 250 to 300 miles, depending on the altitude at which the bombers were flying.

On 10 April 1942 Schnaufer was appointed Technical Officer (TO – *Technischer Offizier*) of the *Gruppe* and moved back from Bonn to Saint-Trond. Schnaufer was a so-called 'Active' officer – the equivalent of a General List Officer in the Royal Air Force, a full career officer. German officers commissioned solely for wartime service were cate-

---

[1] *Official History*, Volume IV, Page 144
[2] *Official History*, Volume 1, Page 324.

gorised as 'Officers of the Reserve'. Among aircrew, far more emphasis was placed in the *Luftwaffe* on the status and on the command and
administrative responsibilities of officers, particularly 'active' ones, than
in the Royal Air Force, and there were a number of staff posts that were
usually, if not always, occupied by career officers, such as Adjutant and
Technical Officer. There were Technical Officers on Royal Air Force
flying stations, but these were officers of the Technical Branch and not,
usually, qualified aircrew. In the *Luftwaffe* it was the responsibility of the
Technical Officer of the *Gruppe* to supervise all the technical aspects –
routine maintenance, servicing, modifications, and so on – of the aircraft on strength. As Technical Officer Schnaufer was no longer a
member of the 5.*Staffel* but a member of the Staff of the *Gruppe*,
Stab/II./NJG 1. The job was not a sinecure: there were about thirty aircraft on strength, and Schnaufer had to see that they were all properly
maintained, serviced and modified as necessary. Ludwig Meister, who
by the end of the war had 39 night-time victories to his credit and wore
the *Ritterkreuz*, recalls that period:

> Heinz Schnaufer and I first met each other in November 1941, when we
> were both members of 5./NJG 1. We got on very well with each other,
> and were soon close friends. Heinz was very gifted technically, and so he
> was soon appointed Technical Officer, first of the *Staffel* and then of the
> *Gruppe*, II./NJG 1. He was responsible for seeing that the aircraft were
> at optimal readiness for operations at all times, and he devoted himself
> to that task to an outstanding degree. If anyone was looking for him they
> only needed to go to the aircraft dispersals, and he would be there. Our
> ways parted after we returned from Operation *Donnerkeil* in February
> 1942, but despite that our friendship with each other was never broken.

From Saint-Trond the *Gruppe* shot down seven bombers during the
course of April and May. But it also had its losses, one of which Horst
Diener, the Chief Clerk of the *Gruppe*, describes:

> On 21.5.42 the *Gruppe* lost the *Staffelkapitän* of the 6th *Staffel*,
> *Oberleutnant* Gutezeit, who shot down one bomber and then picked
> another but rammed it and came down, together with the enemy
> bomber, near to the airfield at Saint-Trond. Neither he nor his
> radio operator, *Feldwebel* Januschewski, survived the crash.

And then, on the night of 30/31 May, Harris mounted the first of his
'Thousand-Bomber Raids', with Cologne as his target. Not only was
this a successful experiment in city bombing, with the city being hard
hit, but it was also a masterly and successful publicity stunt by the
Commander-in-Chief, designed to promote his Command and its methods. The venture worked.

   On the night of the mass attack on Cologne the RAF lost 41 aircraft,
of which II./NJG 1 claimed eight but were only credited with seven.
After a long period without success, the knowledge that they were back
in business was a great boost to the morale of the aircrew. Horst Diener
records the detail:

The 31st May 1942, with eight indisputable kills, gave the *Gruppe* fresh heart. *Oberleutnant* Barte scored three, *Leutnant* Brinkhaus two, *Leutnant* Niklas two and *Leutnant* Bokemeyer one. That was the night the enemy carried out its heaviest raid so far on Cologne. In this operation *Leutnant* Niklas was severely injured and had to take a break from operations. Transferred later to NJG 3, he lost his life in a daylight defensive operation over Northern Germany.

Schnaufer was not scrambled against the one-thousand-plus bombers that attacked Cologne. The *Himmelbett* fighter-control procedure was still being used, and only the most successful pilots were sent off to try to catch the bombers. As Rumpelhardt comments: 'We did not take off operationally on the night of the 30th/31st May. In *Himmelbett* only a limited number of aircraft could be used, and people like us, who had yet to make their first kill, were often overlooked.' When they were scrambled, it was most frequently in the third wave, sometimes the second, so that chances of catching a bomber were minimal. Let him comment further:

> Ten 'scrambles' without even seeing a bomber! At that period, however, our *Gruppe* was getting very few kills at all. And in addition, young, inexperienced crews like us were not as a rule put into the most favourable waves or sent to the most favourable *Räume*. On top of all this, in the first five months of the year, up to 30 May, very few bomber forces flew through our area. We had the feeling that luck was simply not on our side. Above all, morale among us was very bad. Things went so far that Schnaufer said to me that we should seriously consider applying to go back on to *Zerstörer* operations, flying by daylight. By this time I had been made up to *Obergefreiter* (Private First Class) and I had been to the Personnel Officer to see if I could be promoted to *Unteroffizier*. I should in fact have been promoted much earlier, but our *Staffelkapitän*, *Leutnant* Gresens – who, by the way, never shot a single bomber down himself – was against it, so I didn't get promoted. However, on 1 June I was made *Unteroffizier* (Corporal) at last.

In the early hours of the morning of the day following Fritz Rumpelhardt's promotion, *Leutnant* Heinz Schnaufer and he claimed their first victim, a Halifax that crashed near to the village of Grez-Doiceau, fifteen kilometres south of Louvain and so only a short distance from their base at Saint-Trond. The target that night was a prime one, the heavy-industrial centre of Essen, and it was the second of Harris's 'thousand force' raids – a thousand force in name only, because only 956 bombers set out. In contrast to the success of the Cologne raid, when a high degree of bombing concentration – for those days at least – had been achieved, the attack represented a disappointment for Bomber Command: there was haze and low cloud over the target, no concentration of bombing was achieved and bombs fell in numerous other Ruhr towns, causing more casualties there than in the target city itself. The problem of haze over Essen, generated by the many heavy industrial factories and coking ovens in the city, was a perennial one,

Heinz Schnaufer returns from making his first kill on 2 June 1942. Flying from Saint-Trond he destroyed Halifax MP-J of No. 76 Squadron. (Fengler)

and it would not be solved until the advent of the *Oboe* blind-marking device later in the war. Bomber Command lost 31 aircraft that night, 3.2% of the force despatched as compared with the 3.9% that had been lost in the attack on Cologne two nights previously. Fritz Rumpelhardt recalls this night and the first of the one hundred victories he was destined to share with Heinz Schnaufer. But, such are the whims of Fate, it could easily have been the final flight for each of them:

I had only just fixed my new shoulder-badges to my uniform when we were scrambled for our thirteenth operational take-off. The weather conditions were very good, and we were airborne for *Raum* 6C at 0104 hours. Communication with our fighter-control officer was first-class, so that all the prerequisites for a good mission were to hand. After we had been in the air for about forty minutes we made our first interception on a homeward-bound bomber at 3,500 metres right up to '*Ziele decken sich.*'[1] But we still couldn't see a victim. After we had altered course a number of times on instructions from the ground station I thought I glimpsed something suspicious on the horizon above and to the right, scarcely discernible. I directed Heinz Schnaufer spontaneously towards it, and after a few moments we could make out an enemy aircraft, which swiftly revealed itself as a four-engined Halifax.

---

[1] '*Ziele decken sich*'; Literally, 'Targets are covering each other.' The fighter controller announced this when the positions of fighter and bomber on his plotting table coincided.

Schnaufer positioned his Bf 110 slightly below the Halifax and about 150 metres to the side. He paused to steady his nerves, because his victim was continuing on its course, apparently unaware of the presence of the German night fighter. Then he went into the attack, pulling up and curving in astern of the RAF machine. He pressed on the firing button, letting the Halifax fly through the lethal concentration of cannon-shells and machine-gun bullets. At the last moment he shoved his control column forward, diving steeply away in order to avoid any return fire from the Halifax's four-gun rear turret. Then he carried out another attack:

> Immediately after our first attack a fire started in one wing, while the second caused a huge banner of flame, and the fate of the giant bird was sealed once and for all. Neither time did we experience any return fire. We stood off to one side, and we could see the RAF roundel in the light of the flames. We saw the crew baling out. We were glad that they would survive and become prisoners. Our joy at our first victory was boundless. A long, quite unintelligible scream sped through the ether to the ground station, where the joy was almost as great. The kill, after all, was theirs as well. Suddenly the Halifax tipped over and dived steeply to earth. The crash, followed by several explosions, could be seen for miles around, fifteen kilometres south of Louvain.

The unhappy distinction of being Schnaufer's first victim probably went to a Halifax from No. 76 Squadron captained by Sergeant T R A West. It had taken off from Middleton St George at 2306 hours on the 1st of June. West and one other member of the crew were killed.

The *Himmelbett* controller then put Schnaufer on to another target, but he had to tell him to break off when it transpired that a fighter from a neighbouring *Raum* was already in pursuit of it. Heinz Schnaufer and Fritz Rumpelhardt watched this bomber, too, go down in flames. Probably it was the Bristol Blenheim shot down by *Hauptmann* Ehle, the only other victory claimed by II./NJG 2 that night.

> Shortly before 0300 hours we saw action again. Even flying with the throttle lever up against the stops we only gained on our target slowly. By the time we got '*Ziele decken sich*' we were in the Ghent area and the R/T communication was very weak. Nevertheless we continued heading west, and then suddenly I was successful once more, making out what looked like a darker spot in the sky off to one side. I was lucky again, and this was the second Tommy to come within range of our guns. In our excitement we couldn't agree what type it was. In any case, it was a four-engined aircraft, and that could only have come from the other side of the Channel.
>
> The procedure was as before, but this time things didn't go as smoothly. I quote from my diary: 'We were very surprised at the high speed of the enemy, 390 to 400 kph. [About 250 mph]. Again Schnaufer positioned himself some distance below the target. We observed him for a short time, then made our first attack, aiming at the starboard wing, but without success. After our second attack we could only see a slight flame,

and then for the third attack we had first to catch up because of the high speed of the Tommy. We came in close and thought we saw hits in his wing. Then a banner of white vapour shot towards us out of his fuel tanks. Still firing all our guns, we came in as close as twenty metres. Our foolhardiness got what it deserved, and we were sprayed with heavy machine-gun fire. So nose down and away out of it! After we had pulled out of our dive we were able to assess the effect of the enemy's gunfire. Schnaufer had, as we later found out, a bullet lodged in his left calf. There was a slight fire in our port engine, which we had to close down. We couldn't use our rudders, because a bullet had severed the control cable. Our headlamp was permanently on, probably as the result of a short circuit, and we had to stagger through the air like an illuminated practice-target. We were so concerned with ourselves that we didn't see what the effect of our final attack had been.

At first it seemed to Schnaufer and Rumpelhardt that they would have to take to their parachutes, but they were only at 600 metres and baling out at such a low level would be even more hazardous than usual. The Bf 110 was not, in any case, an easy aircraft to abandon in flight. Fortunately it proved possible, after a short time, to restart the port engine, which gave an extra degree of control, but fuel was running low and it was obvious that they would have to get down soon. No pilot likes landing away, however, and they thought they might be able to make it back to Saint-Trond. Because of the distance they had flown in pursuit of the British bomber they were out of R/T contact with the fighter controller, who would normally have given them directions back to base. After flying by rule of thumb for what seemed like a long time, Rumpelhardt, with the aid of his trailing aerial, managed to get a QDM[1] from Saint-Trond, and they found base without further trouble. When they got there, however, the airfield lights were switched off, as was normal practice unless aircraft were taking off or landing, and Rumpelhardt had to fire the colours of the day twice, and a red (emergency) signal once, before they were switched on again. Rumpelhardt felt very apprehensive as Schnaufer came in to land: the rudder controls were still not working and Schnaufer had to turn on the ailerons and engine-power alone, which meant banking very steeply. Schnaufer could not hold the Bf 110 when it touched down, and it swerved violently to one side and into a ploughed field:

> Switches off and slam on the brakes! At last the aircraft came to a halt, and for some moments an almost unearthly stillness surrounded us. But that didn't stop us getting out of the crate as rapidly as possible. When we were on the approach to the airfield I had asked for emergency medical assistance, so we were able to get our wounded pilot straight into the ambulance and driven off to sick quarters. Our 'Dora-Cesar'[2] collected 19 bullet-holes, and I was the only item unscathed. But our patience had been rewarded at last, and we no longer needed to hide behind the other,

---

[1] QDM – Magnetic course to steer.
[2] 'Dora-Cesar' – Phonetic alphabet for 'DC'. The aircraft they were flying was G9+DC.

more successful, crews. At the weather briefing on the 6th June I was awarded the Iron Cross Second Class by the *Kommandeur*. Until then Schnaufer had been hoping that the bullet lodged in his calf would isolate itself so that he would be able to continue flying operationally, and he had being doing daily exercises to further the process. But this possibility had proved to be unrealistic, and on the 8th June he was admitted to hospital in Brussels. I was surplus to requirements for the moment, and I was given home leave on Lake Constance until the 26th June, with the understanding that I would probably get an extension by telegram. It goes without staying that I travelled via Brussels, where I found the patient in a very bad condition. As a result of the medication he had been given he had developed a severe allergy: his whole body, and in particular his face, was covered with a rash that made him almost unrecognisable to me. I broke my journey in Calw so that I could visit the Schnaufer family. I was greeted very warmly by Mother Schnaufer with the words, 'Here comes Heinz's other half!'

Heinz Schnaufer remained in hospital until the 25th of June, making his next operational flight the day after he was discharged: Rumpelhardt was not yet back from leave, so a certain *Feldwebel* Schulz flew as Schnaufer's *Funker*. Then it was to take two months and two further operational flights before Schnaufer and Rumpelhardt tasted success again. But they had at last made the breakthrough, and there was no further talk of leaving the *Nachtjagd* and going back to flying on *Zerstörer*. Quite astoundingly, the occasion of their first kill was the only time their aircraft was damaged in air combat or any member of the crew wounded. Most German night-fighter crewmen – at least, those who survived, because the attrition rate was high – were injured or had to abandon their aircraft several times. When their next kill came it did so in a manner that not only confirmed in their own minds that they had made the

Briefing of members of IV./NJG 1 at Leeuwarden, 1942. (Greiner)

right decision in becoming night fighters, but which also gave a first slight indication that they might be a crew of above-average potential.

By the end of June 1942, following an attack by 960 aircraft against Bremen on the night of the 25th/26th of the month, Harris's 'Thousand Force' ventures were behind him: he had rekindled faith in his Command and ensured the future of the bomber offensive. The Bremen attack had been less impressive than that on Cologne, but more so than that against Essen, but Bomber Command had suffered its heaviest losses to date, 48 machines, or 5% of those taking part. Now it was summer, and short nights limited the targets the bombers could attack in darkness to those towards the west. Harris was determined to sustain the pressure on German cities, and he sent bomber forces to the Ruhr Valley whenever possible, moon conditions and the weather influencing his selection of targets. On the night of 31 July/1 August Harris deployed what was by far the biggest 'non-thousand' force so far, and his target was Düsseldorf. 386 twin-engined bombers – Wellingtons, Hampdens and Whitleys – and 244 with four engines – Lancasters, Halifaxes and Stirlings – set out from England. Casualties among the bombers were again heavy, at 4.6% of those despatched, and bombing results were only moderate.

That night II./NJG 1, however, enjoyed morale-boosting success, claiming seven of the 29 RAF bombers lost, and of those seven Schnaufer shot down three in just an hour, a Wellington at 0247 hours, a second Wellington at 0317 hours and a Whitley at 0345 hours. This was only the third time that any crew of II.NJG 1 had scored three in a night.

Schnaufer had taken off from Saint-Trond at 0213 hours on 1 August, heading north. His first Wellington, DV439 of No. 25 OTU, had gone down at Loon op Zand, near the Dutch town of Tilburg. Following this interception Schnaufer had flown south again and his second Wellington, DV552 of No. 27 OTU, had crashed at Huldenberg, a short distance south-east of Brussels, thirty minutes later. The crew, all of whom perished, comprised one New Zealander – the pilot – and five Australians. From Huldenberg Schnaufer continued further south.

Following the precedent that Harris had set in his three 'thousand-bomber' raids, training units provided 105 of the aircraft and crews of the 630 that took part in the attack on Düsseldorf, and the training machines suffered disproportionately high losses, with No. 92 (OTU) Group losing 11 aircraft, a percentage of 10.5. Like the two Wellingtons that he destroyed, Schnaufer's third victim was also a training machine, a Whitley V from No. 24 Operational Training Unit stationed at Honeybourne. Its registration number was BD347 and it was piloted by an Australian, Pilot Officer G Silva. Silva had formerly served with No. 77 Squadron, and was now, presumably, an instructor at Honeybourne. The other men on board were the navigator, Sergeant J B R Black; the wireless operator, Sergeant A J Whicher and the air gunner, Sergeant W T Whiting. They had taken off at 2340 hours on the 30th July, and

Opposite: Schnaufer's claim for his fourth kill, on 1 August 1942, a Whitley V from No. 24 Operational Training Unit. The scribbled word 'Anerkannt' at the top of the page means 'Confirmed', and the words 'Bruch gefunden' (No. 5) mean 'wreckage found'. 'Flüchtig' (No. 6) means that the crew evaded capture. (Rumpelhardt)

Unbekannt.

II./Nachtjagdgeschwader 1   **den 2. August 1942**
(Name, Dienstgrad, Truppenteil)   (Ort)   (Datum)

R.d.L.u.Ob.d.L. Az.29 Nr. 849/44 vom 27.10.44
als 54. Luftsieg der II/1 Nachtj.   *fc.*

ϟ Abschußmeldung

1. Zeit (Tag, Stunde, Minute) und Gegend: **1.Aug.42, 03,45 Uhr, Vorfrand von
Gilly,   41539.**

   Höhe: __**2800 m**__
   Durch wen ist der Abschuß erfolgt: Lt.Schmaufer - Uffz.Rumpelhardt

2. Flugzeugtyp des abgeschossenen Flugzeuges: **Whitley V**

3. Staatsangehörigkeit des Gegners: **E n g l a n d**

   Werknummern: _ _ _ _ _   bzw. Kennzeichen: _ _ _ _ _ _

4. Art der Vernichtung:

   a) weiße Benzinfahne, dunkle Rauchfahne, helle Flammen

   b) abmontiert (Einzelteile, auseinandergeplatzt)

   c) zur Landung gezwungen (diesseits oder jenseits der Front
   glatt bzw. mit Bruch)

   b) nach Notlandung jenseits der Front am Boden in Brand geschossen

5. Art des Aufschlages:

   a) diesseits oder jenseits der Front

   b) senkrecht, flachen Winkel, Aufschlagbrand, Staubwolke

   c) nicht beobachtet, warum nicht?

   d) Bruch gefunden

6. Schicksal der Insassen (tot, mit Fallschirm abgesprungen, nicht beobachtet)   **flüchtig.**

7. Gefechtsbericht (siehe Anlage):

8. Zeugen:

   a) Luft _____ **Uffz. Rumpelhardt**

   b) Erde _____

9. Anzahl der Angriffe, die auf das feindliche Flugzeug gemacht wurden: **zwei.**

Lager-Nr. 1895. Verlag und Druck: Heß, Braunschweig-München

they were on their way back home when Fate, in the person of Heinz Schnaufer, intervened.

Schnaufer was flying under *Himmelbett* control in *Raum* 6C, and his controller for the interception was *Oberfeldwebel* Büchte. G9+DC[1], the Bf 110C that Schnaufer was flying, was still not fitted with airborne-intercept radar, so that once again the attack had to be finalised visually. As was always the case with *Himmelbett* interception, much clearly depended on the skill of the fighter controller, Büchte, and of the pilot, Schnaufer, in interpreting the information and instructions that the former broadcast.

A copy of the Fighter Control Unit's tracing of the interception survives, and it is possible roughly to reproduce the development of the action. At 0326 hours the Whitley was heading westward on its way back to England when it was picked up by the 'Red' *Würzburg* radar about thirty kilometres west of Liège. At the same time the 'Green' *Würzburg* showed Schnaufer's Messerschmitt a further twelve kilometres west, heading south-east. The two machines were flying towards each other, but if Schnaufer had not altered course he would have passed well in front of the Whitley. Büchte, the controller, ordered Schnaufer to do a left turn through about 225 degrees, so bringing him out a short distance astern of the British bomber. He then continued to control Schnaufer in a tail-chase, until, at 0335 hours, Fritz Rumpelhardt caught a glimpse of the Whitley, which was flying at 10,000 feet, 500 metres ahead. Its fate was sealed. Schnaufer carried out two attacks. In the first he saw his shells hitting home in the rear turret of the bomber, while his second burst of fire set its starboard engine and wing on fire. Trailing behind it a banner of flame and black smoke, the doomed aircraft went into a wide left-hand curve; Schnaufer followed it down and saw it crash at the village of Gilly, near to Charleroi, at 0345 hrs. Of the crew of four, one, the rear gunner, died, possibly as a result of Schnaufer's first attack. The other three succeeded in evading capture and returning safely to England.

Schnaufer's three kills had been made without the aid of radar in his aircraft, but as mentioned earlier there was in fact an intercept radar in existence, and it was being increasingly widely used by the *Nachtjagd*. It was called *Lichtenstein*. First laboratory experiments with the radar had begun as early as the autumn of 1940, but it was not until the following year that operational testing was begun by 4./NJG 1. Flying a Dornier 215B-5, a night-fighter adaptation of the Do 215 bomber, the formidable *Oberleutnant* Ludwig Becker had shot down a Vickers Wellington on 9 August 1941, directed on to his target by his *Funker, Unteroffizier* Stab, by means of *Lichtenstein*, the first German kill achieved with the aid of airborne-intercept radar. Despite this and subsequent successes by Becker, however, it was not until mid-1942

---

[1] The accepted way of referring to a German military aircraft's designation, the '+' representing the Imperial German Cross. Here, G9 = NJG 1; D = individual aircraft; C = *Stab II. Gruppe*. As already seen, 'DC' was phonetically spoken *'Dora-Cesar'*

Leeuwarden, Holland, in 1942, before Schnaufer joined IV./NJG 1. Three distinguished night fighter pilots. From left *to right, excluding the unknown officer in the background: Lippe-Weissenfeld (killed March 1944); Helmut Lent (killed October 1944); and Ludwig Becker (killed February 1943).* (Greiner)

that *Lichtenstein* began to appear on the operational units in any appreciable numbers.

The Do 215 night fighter carried a crew of three: pilot, radio operator and *Bordmechaniker*, or Flight Mechanic. Becker's regular Flight Mechanic was *Obergefreiter* Wilhelm Gänsler, destined, as will be seen, to play an important part in the Schnaufer story. Becker had 44 victories to his credit when he was killed in February 1943, ironically, for a night fighter, on a daylight mission against B-17s of the USAAF. On that occasion he was piloting a Bf 110, so that Gänsler was not flying with him.

After shooting down his three enemy bombers within a single hour in the small hours of 1 August 1942, Schnaufer did not have long to wait before he gained his first AI-controlled kill. He and Rumpelhardt had already flown practice intercepts – so-called '*Zieldarstellung*' (Target Simulation) – with other aircraft of the *Gruppe*, so they were not unfamiliar with *Lichtenstein*'s capabilities and the way in which is was used.

Harris mounted only a minor attack on the night of 5/6 August, just five days after Schnaufer's triple success. Twenty-five aircraft set out to attack the Ruhr towns of Essen and Bochum: only four pilots claimed to have bombed their target, and five bombers were lost. Schnaufer was scrambled: his Bf 110 was carrying *Lichtenstein* for the first time operationally. He did not add to his score, but Rumpelhardt comments:

We flew operationally with *Lichtenstein* for the first time on the night of 5/6 August 1942. I made an approach at 5,000 metres altitude, finding a target at a range of three kilometres. I was able to give Schnaufer continuous alterations of course, the range grew shorter and shorter, and he picked the target up visually. Probably as a result of a moment's lack of concentration on his part it disappeared again from his field of vision.

We were both very disappointed, because our first interception with the
Li-Gerät[1] had gone well yet we hadn't crowned it with a success. In any
event, the equipment made a very good impression on us.

The *Lichtenstein* display that the *Funker*, sitting back-to-back with his pilot,
used comprised three very small, greenly-fluorescent cathode-ray tubes.
The left-hand tube had a circular time-base and showed other aircraft
ahead up a range of about two-and-a-half miles as 'bumps' outward
from the circle; the centre screen showed the range of a specific target
and whether it was higher or lower than the fighter; and the right-hand
tube showed whether the target was to the left or the right of the fighter's
nose. The pick-up range was usually in the region of a mile or so, which
might at first sight seem unimpressive but which was nevertheless
incomparably better than the human eye alone, no matter how practised, could usually achieve. The equipment had made a favourable
impression on Rumpelhardt and Schnaufer, as it had on virtually all the
night-fighter crews that used it, but there were still a very few 'old lags'
who mistrusted it instinctively and never fully came to terms with it. It
was well – for the Germans, if not for Bomber Command – that the
backward-looking views one former fighter pilot did not prevail. The
flamboyant, egotistical Commander-in-Chief of the *Luftwaffe*, the fighter ace of the First World War Hermann Göring, had at first been scorn-
fully dismissive of airborne radar – 'A fighter isn't a movie show!' – and
his objections had delayed the introduction of *Lichtenstein* by an unquan-
tifiable period. In fact when it belatedly appeared on the scene, and as
the night-fighter crews became skilled in its use and confident of its
capabilities, Bomber Command losses began to increase dauntingly.
When Schnaufer was first with II./NJG 1, at the time when operational
experiments with *Lichtenstein* were being conducted, overall losses of
bombers from night fighters were rather less than one percent of sorties. By June 1942, with *Lichtenstein* being fitted into more and more
machines, that figure had increased to about three percent. In August
1942, during which month Schnaufer made his first kill using radar,
Bomber Command mounted 2,454 sorties against Germany and the
Nachtjagd claimed 100 'kills', a percentage of 4.07.

Schnaufer's fifth kill, and the first in which Rumpelhardt guided him
into contact by means of *Lichtenstein*, came at 0254 hours on the 25th of
August 1942. The unfortunate victim was a Wellington on its way to
Frankfurt, and like Schnaufer's previous victims it came down near to
Saint-Trond, at Loonbeek. With five victories to his name Schnaufer
now came officially into the category of 'ace', but he was in fact still
only a lesser ace. Helmut Lent was the leading scorer of the German
night-fighter force, with approaching fifty kills, while there were more
than twenty other night-fighter pilots in the *Nachtjagd* who could claim
more than double Schnaufer's score.

The front-line strength of Josef Kammhuber's Twelfth (Night-Fighter)

---

[1] '*Li-Gerät*: '*Li*' is short for *Lichtenstein*, while '*Gerät*' means 'equipment'.

Corps – the force had attained the status of a *Korps*, made up of three Divisions, in May 1942 – was increasing steadily, but so was that of their opponents. The dynamism, self-confidence and uncompromising realism of the new Commander-in-Chief of Bomber Command had swept aside earlier doubts as to the potential and legitimacy of the bomber offensive, and there was a new sense of purpose and self-esteem among the commanders and aircrews. And not only were there more and more bigger bombers dropping bigger and more lethal bombs on Germany almost every night, but the tactics and methods that they were using were constantly being modified and improved. Harris was aiming at greater and greater concentration of his bombers in both space and time, with a view to overwhelming the defences both in the air and on the ground. With an urgency bordering on the frantic Kammhuber was setting up more and more *Himmelbett* stations, his ultimate objective being gapless coverage of the whole of the territory he had to defend. For the time being his close-control system was enjoying success, but it was a system that lacked flexibility: the fighters had to lie in wait for the bombers to come to them, and only those pilots deployed to *Himmelbett* areas penetrated by the bomber stream had a chance of making contact with the enemy, while other fighters circled endlessly around the radio beacons waiting for a target that more often than not didn't come. Within a year the system would break down, but for now the increasing number of bombers invading German airspace meant richer pickings for the *Nachtjagd* as a whole and obscured the fundamental flaw in Kammhuber's system.

At this time, late summer 1942, there had been a development in the bomber strategy that boded ill for the Fatherland. Under the command of an officer in his own way just as determined and ruthless in the application of his duties as Harris himself, Acting Group Captain (later Air Vice-Marshal) Donald Bennett, the Pathfinder Force had been set up, its task to find and mark targets for the mass of the bombers, which later came to be known as the 'Main Force'. New electronic devices were coming into being, particularly, at that specific time, H2S[1], an airborne radar set by means of which the bomber navigators could see a primitive map of the territory over which they were flying on a cathode-ray tube. Originally used solely by the Pathfinder Force, H2S would eventually be in the majority of Bomber Command aircraft.

This is also a convenient point at which to make first mention of another outstanding electronic target-marking device that Bomber Command eventually had, *Oboe*. *Oboe* allowed high-flying Pathfinder aircraft, principally Mosquitoes, to mark aiming-points with a precision that was, for those days, well nigh incredible.

By the end of the year 1942 Schnaufer had increased his score by only two, a Halifax shot down in the early hours of the 29th August and

---

[1] There are several versions of the origin of this name. The most likely seems to be that it is a glib abbreviation of 'Height-to-Surface'. This would seem likely, in that H2S was developed from a radar device known as ASV (Air to Surface Vessels)

a Lancaster destroyed on the 21st of December: there was still no indication that he would develop from a run-of-the-mill night fighter to the
ace among aces he was destined to become: admittedly he had shot
down three in one sortie in August, but that could have been a flash in
the pan. Routinely he had been awarded the Iron Cross Second Class
(*Eisernes Kreuz 2. Klasse* – EK 2) after his first kill, and the Iron Cross
First Class (EK 1) in early September, after his seventh victory.

In August 1942 Otto Fries was a junior NCO-pilot of 5./NJG 1: he
was later commissioned and finished the war with eighteen kills to his

Opposite: A personnel
list of II./NJG 1.
Schnaufer is at the top,
No. 52. The columns
read: Leutnant *and*
Pilot; Active Officer;
Heinz Schnaufer;
Commissioned 1.4.41;
From Schleissheim
1.11.41.
(Bundesarchiv)

16

Lfd. Nr.	Dienstgrad und Dienststellung	Att. Res. Ldw. z.V.	Vor- und Zuname	Patent oder Tag der Ernennung	Zugang Datum Woher?	Abgang Datum Wohin?	Bemerkungen
52	Lt. u. Flugzfhr.	akt.	Heinz Schnaufer	1.4.41	Schleißheim 1.11.41		
53	"	"	hans Georg Birkenstock	1.2.41	Nachtjagd-schule 1	6.4.42 Erg.Gr.NJ.G1	s. Verlustliste Nr. 37
54	Oblt.-R.O. u.Flugzfhr.	Kr.O.	heinr. Petersen	1.7.41	10.11.41 Erg.St.NJG1	1.8.42 N.J.G.1	
55	Oblt. u.Flugzf. Staffelkapitän	Res.	Wilh. herget	1.8.39	15.1.42 III./N.J.G.3	1.8.42 II./N.J.G.4	
56	Lt. u. Flugzfhr.	akt.	Kurt Martinek	1.4.40	15.1.42 III./N.J.G.3	1.5.42 II./N.J.G.4	
57	"	"	Gustav Knoch		15.1.42 III./N.J.G.2	16.1.42 III./N.J.G.2	
58	"	"	Joh. Cenkier	1.7.40	16.1.42 III./N.J.G.2	† 25.3.42	
59	Oblt. u. Flugzfhr.	"	hubert Rauh	1.6.40	16.1.42 N-Sch. Schleißh.	1.5.42 II./N.J.G.4	
60	"	"	ludw. Bielmann	1.4.40	29.1.42 Erg.Gr.NJG1	11.9.42 gefallen	1.7.42 hauptmann.
61	Lt. u. Flugzfhr.	"	Fritz Gräff	1.4.41	29.1.42 Erg.Gr.NJG1	1.5.42 II./N.J.G.4	
62	"	Kr.O.	Wilh. Gehring	1.10.40	15.1.42 III./N.J.G.3	1.5.42 II./N.J.G.4	
63	hauptmann u. (Maj. b. Stabe	Res.	heinr. Ruppel	1.11.41	27.2.41 L.Sch.Jg 261	1.11.41 II./N.J.G.2	
64	Lt. u. Flugzfhr.	akt.	helmut Niklas	1.5.41	19.2.42 Erg.Gr.NJG1	25.11.42 III./N.J.G1	
65	Oblt. u. Jägerleitoffz.	Kr.O.	herbert Steinhausen	1.4.41	26.2.42 Flugzf. Sch.	1.5.42 II./N.J.G.4	
66	Oblt. u. Jägerleitoffz.	Res.	Karl Lahm	1.11.41	10.2.42 Fr.Flg-Sgr.Drd	9.7.42 Jagfü-Doll Ruhrgb.	
67	Oblt. u. Flugzeugfhr.	akt.	heinz Jhrke	1.6.40	15.4.42 6./N.J.G.1	26.4.42 1./N.J.G.2	
68	"	"	Wilh. Telge	1.10.40	15.4.42 6./N.J.G.1		
69	Lt. u. Flugzfhr.	Kr.O.	Fr. Brinkhaus	1.9.41	15.4.42 6./N.J.G.1		
70	Lt. u. Jägerleitoffz.	"	Fritz Lepenius	1.3.41	29.1.42 N.J.G.1	1.5.42 N.J.G.4	
71	"	"	paul Kühnel	1.4.40	8.4.42 I./N.J.G.1	4.11.42 N-J-Raumfor.6	
72	Reg. Insp. b.B.	a.Kr.	Karl Asche	1.5.42	1.3.42 2.N.J-division		
73	Major + Flugzfhr.	akt.	Rolf Leuchs	1.11.42	1.10.42 E/N.J.G.1	1.7.43 II./N.J.G.6	
74	Oblt. + Flugzfhr.	akt.	Werner husemann	1.4.42	1.9.42 E./N.J.G.1	1.10.42 N.J.G.1	
75	Oblt. + Flugzfhr. Staffelkapitän	akt.	K-heinz hollborn	1.10.40	16.9.42 E./N.J.G.1	1.7.43 XII.Flg.Korps	
76	hptm + Flugzfhr.	akt.	Alfons Vonnier	1.2.41	1.10.42 N.J.G.1	1.11.42	
77	Lt. + Adjut. Bordfunker	Res.	leo Baro	1.9.42	1.9.42		
78	Lt. + flugzfhr.	Res.	Otto Selig	1.12.40	29.10.42 N.J.G.2	1.4.43 U.U.Obd.L.	
79	Lt.	Res.	herbert hellwege	1.10.42	1.10.42 N.J.G.5	6.2.43 N.J.G.5	
80	Oblt. + Flugzfhr.	akt.	Fritz Engau	1.4.43	24.11.42 N.J-Schule1	3.2.44 J.G.11	

credit. On the 28th/29th August, when Heinz Schnaufer shot down the Halifax, Fries had his first clash with an RAF bomber, a Stirling. It was not, for him, an auspicious encounter. The rear gunner of the British bomber shot his port engine into flames, and Fries and his *Funker*, Staffa, had to bale out. Before the war ended they had been shot down on three more occasions, each time the victim of a Mosquito intruder. Otto Fries wrote up his wartime experiences for his family, and we are indebted to him for an evocative account of what it was like for the night-fighter men of Schnaufer's unit, II./NJG 1, as they waited the order to take off to meet the approaching bombers:

> It was still warm that summer's night, and there was the scent of drying hay over the airfield. The farmer had presumably mown some corner of the field because his herd of sheep couldn't manage to keep all the grass on the huge area of the aerodrome short.
>
> The aircraft of the crews on the battle order were set out in a row on the southerly edge of the airfield: on the extreme right were the first wave, the ones that would be the first to get airborne, then those of the second and third waves, and then, right at the left, there were the machines for the reserve crews.
>
> In the south-east corner of the airfield, close behind the first-wave aircraft, was the operations caravan. It was a sort of mobile readiness room that was parked there in the evening and then, at dawn, pushed for camouflage under the cherry trees that stood so thick round the Fifth *Staffel* dispersal that one might even call them a wood. Two months ago we had picked cherries there, lying on our backs on the wings of our Me 110s.
>
> Some of the crews were sitting in the blacked-out caravan playing cards, but most of them were lying outside on the grass, chatting and enjoying the mild night air. Permanent readiness rooms were being built on a plot of ground on the other side of the Liège Road, immediately opposite the entrance to the airfield, but as long as summer lasted we managed very well with the caravan. We did not expect to take over the new operational readiness building until the middle of September.
>
> Popular melodies were issuing from the loudspeakers: the operations personnel were clearly buying the latest creations of the German and French gramophone-record industry.
>
> He [Otto Fries writes in the third person] and his *Bordfunker* were lying in the grass with their friends from the Fifth *Staffel*, Hanne and Mäcky, who were down as first reserves for the third wave. Crews detailed as third reserve had virtually no chance of going into action. Almost every time they got their operational flying meals without flying, because the first crews of the individual waves were made up of the officers of the *Gruppe*. The first wave was basically made up of the *Kommandeur*, the officers of the *Stab* and the *Staffelkapitäne*. The second and third waves were made up of crews of the officers, and sometimes of the experienced senior NCOs, so that the only thing left for the junior crews was the reserve. So the chances of getting airborne were ten to one against.
>
> The music stopped abruptly. '*Achtung! Achtung!* First wave cockpit readiness!' It was shortly after 2100 hours.

The Halifax that Schnaufer destroyed that night was probably from No.

9 August 1942: Schnaufer (right) and Rumpelhardt examine the wreckage of a Halifax from No. 78 Squadron that they shot down near Tombeek, Belgium. (Diener)

78 Squadron. Halifax II W7809, piloted by Sgt J A B Marshall of the Royal Australian Air Force, was one of a small force sent on a secondary raid to Saarbrücken while the main attack was against Nuremberg. Marshall had taken off from Middleton St George at 1941 hours on the 28th, and Schnaufer's victory came at 0116 hours on the 29th. The Halifax was on its way back from the target, presumably having bombed. Schnaufer was operating in the second wave in *Raum* 6C.

Between 29 November and 16 December, Rumpelhardt was confined in Sick Quarters with a high fever, and *Unteroffizier* Heinz Wenning took his place as Schnaufer's *Funker*. Wenning, whose regular pilot was *Oberleutnant* Helmut Niklas, had been flying with the latter when they shot down two bombers during the thousand-bomber raid on Cologne in May, but on that occasion Niklas had been gravely injured. Wenning flew three missions with Schnaufer during this period, but without success, although, surprisingly, Schnaufer later often spoke about him to Rumpelhardt as a first-class *Funker*.

In December 1942 Fritz Engau, who had been at *C-Schule*, Alt-Lönnewitz, together with Heinz Schnaufer in 1940/1941, but whose career had followed a different course from that of his comrade, arrived at Saint-Trond on posting to II./NJG 1, and the two renewed their acquaintance.[1] On the night of 21 December Engau, as part of his initiation into the craft of night fighting, was in the Group Operations Room (*Grossraumgefechtsstand der II. Gruppe*) when Schnaufer was pursuing the Lancaster he destroyed that night, and he describes the proceedings. Schnaufer, with Rumpelhardt back in the rear seat of the Bf 110, was under the direct control of a fighter controller at a smaller control post (*Jägerleitstelle*), but the positions of fighter and bomber respectively were displayed in blue and red lights on a translucent vertical map-screen and the 'chatter' between the controller and Schnaufer was monitored in a number of cells, so that interested individuals were able to listen in. Schnaufer was in contact with a target:

> *Adler* 52 from *Salamander*, *Adler* 52 from *Salamander*, do you still have *Emil-Emil?*' ['*Salamander*' is the fighter controller, '*Adler* 52' is Schnaufer's call-sign, '*Emil-Emil*' means *Lichtenstein* contact].
>
> *Viktor*, I still have *Emil-Emil*.' [*Viktor* is the equivalent of the RAF's '*Roger*'].
>
> Pause: then: 'Target is turning tightly!' from Schnaufer. Then, 'I have no more *Emil-Emil!*'
>
> Pause: then, from the controller: 'Target has turned about! Turn on to 110 degrees!' From Schnaufer: '*Viktor!*'
>
> Controller: '*Adler* 52 from *Salamander* – vector 090 and climb to six-two!' [6,200 metres, equals 20,500 feet]. Schnaufer; '*Viktor!*'

Engau describes how the R/T exchanges continued 'blow by blow', until the two dots of light on the vertical map coincided and Schnaufer reported, '*Ich berühre!*' – 'I have (visual) contact!' and then, a short time later, at seven minutes before midnight, '*Sieg Heil!*' Schnaufer's victim was a Lancaster, its allocated target Munich, and it crashed near Poelkapelle. Of the 137 bombers despatched that night, twelve, or 8.8 percent failed to return.

It was the practice for fighter pilots to maintain not only a Flying Logbook (*Bordbuch*) but also a so-called '*Leistungsbuch*', which one might translate as 'Achievements Book'. One section of the book was specifically for combat victories. Many pilots were not as conscientious as they might have been in ensuring that this book was kept up to date, but fortunately Schnaufer was, so that a complete record of his kills survives. The confirmation of claims by fighter pilots required a strict bureaucratic procedure, and only when all the formalities were

---

[1] As related in Engau's book, *Nachtjäger, Bomber, Wolken und Sterne*. Future references to Engau are mostly based on his book.

observed was the claim allowed. Application forms had to be filled in giving full details of the claim, and two witnesses had to be provided. When there were only two crew-members, as in the case of the Bf 110, one witness could be the pilot's *Funker*, but the other had to be independent. In Schnaufer's *Leistungsbuch* flak gunners, ARP personnel, searchlight crews, other pilots and so on are named as witnesses, but against the Lancaster he destroyed that night is written, under the 'Witnesses' column: 'Interrogation of prisoner, Ft/Sgt. Leedhem (sic).' This makes a positive identification possible. Flt Sgt S P Leedham was the Bomb Aimer of Lancaster Mk.1 R5914 of No. 106 Squadron piloted by Sgt J D Brinkhurst, which had taken off from Syerston at 1710 hours bound for that night's target, Munich. Brinkhurst, Wireless Operator Sgt T Mellors and Rear Gunner Flt Sgt V Greenwood lost their lives, while the remainder of the crew – Flight Engineer Sgt H J Elsom, Navigator Flt Sgt J A Shepherd, RNZAF, Mid-Upper Gunner Sgt C Ward and Flt Sgt Leedham – were all taken prisoner. On his return to the UK at the end of the war Flt Sgt Shepherd reported that after the fighter attack it was discovered that the forward escape hatch was jammed: Sgt Brinkhurst left his pilot's seat and freed the hatch, then returned and took control of the Lancaster again, holding it steady while crew members baled out. Following this report, Sgt Brinkhurst was awarded the Distinguished Flying Medal.[1]

John Elsom survived the war and subsequently emigrated to South Africa. In 1997 he recalled the operation from which he did not return:

> As I recall, the outbound trip from base to the target area was without incident. On arrival over the target, which was still lit up by coloured markers and flares from earlier strikes, we were able to identify our aiming point with ease, and so, after a dummy run, we went round again and made a good approach and released our bomb-load as planned at the briefing. We left the area well pleased and confident that our strike had been highly successful, and we relaxed for a comfortable and uneventful return journey to base.
>
> Our complacency was shattered when we were alerted by our IFF set that enemy aircraft were following us[2]. We took evasive action by adopting 'corkscrew' flight tactics whilst climbing into scattered clouds. This seemed to be working until we again received a signal from our IFF set and our rear gunner had a visual sighting of a fighter below and to starboard of us. Our pilot then required more power in order to reach the cloud cover ahead and slightly higher, but as we reached it we were hit from below by a burst of machine-gun fire in the starboard wing between numbers three and four engine-nacelles. A fire started immediately. We continued our evasive tactics in order to avoid further contact. However the fire spread inboard between three and four engines and also into the

---

[1] There seems to be some confusion here. The Distinguished Flying Medal was not awarded posthumously. Presumably Brinkhurst had already been recommended for the award before his death.

[2] This is unclear. IFF (Identification Friend or Foe) did not have such a capability. The tail-warning devices *Monica and Boozer*, which did, were not introduced operationally until 1943

fuselage, which was now our main cause for concern. The pilot request-
ed that I operate both bulkhead fire extinguishers while he went into a
steep dive to attempt to draw the fires out of the mainplane. This seemed
to slow down the fires but on resuming straight and level flight they
spread again rapidly. The pilot called for a status report from all crew
stations, and on receiving confirmation that no injuries had been received
he advised the crew to prepare themselves for 'bale out' if the fire could
not be brought under control. My duties under these circumstances
required that I assist the pilot to gather his flight bag with all the secret
codes and documents, retrieve his parachute from storage and assist him
to fit same. I set the engine controls as required and folded down the
flight engineer's seat in order to allow for ease of crew to evacuate from
the front hatch. While this was being done the pilot gave the order to
bale out.

The rear gunner was the first one I heard confirming the order before
I disconnected my helmet. The pilot got out of the seat and was standing beside me while I checked his harness etc. He then told me to go
forward and bale out. I went to the front hatch and sat facing forward
with my feet out while I did my own checking of harness etc. As I leaned
forward to go I glanced back to see who was following me and I noticed
that the pilot had returned to his seat at the controls. I was now committed and must have blacked out on leaving. I only regained consciousness a few feet from the ground, and I was aware of the explosion
and impact of the aircraft in the adjacent field to the one in which I had
landed.

After releasing my parachute, gathering it up and trying to hide same
in a ditch, I went over to the wreckage calling various crew members'
names. After a very short time, while I was trying to gather my thoughts
together, I was surrounded by civilians and soldiers who quickly bundled
me into a transport and on to Ghent prison, where I was put into a cell
on my own for the remainder of the night.

The next morning I was interviewed by a *Luftwaffe* officer, who greeted me with these famous words: 'For you the war is over.' He offered
me cigarettes and a drink and was generally most courteous and sympa-
thetic. He also conveyed by sign language that he was the one who had
shot us down and that two other crew-members had been captured and
were 'in the bag'.

As I was the last member of the crew to leave the aircraft — as I
learned later — the reason for our pilot, Sergeant Brinkhurst, returning
to the controls was in order to try and gain height so that the remaining
crew could bale out.

It is likely that Schnaufer was also responsible for the demise of another of the eight Lancasters that failed to return that same night. Soon
after destroying Brinkhurst's machine Rumpelhardt picked up a further
return on his *Lichtenstein* and talked Schnaufer into an attacking position.
Schnaufer opened up with his cannon and both men saw their victim
catch fire and plunge earthwards. Rumpelhardt takes up the story:

The Lancaster came down near Grammont, to the west of Brussels.
According to eye-witnesses' statements and the time of the crash, this was
quite certainly our kill. We put it up for confirmation, and everything

seemed to be going smoothly. But *Hauptmann* Herget [from another unit, I./NJG 4], had also fired at a four-engined Lancaster at about the same time. At the time I wrote in my diary, 'Although none of the criteria spoke in his favour, he too claimed this victory. We were told that the *General* was unable to make up his mind to whom the kill should be awarded, and he ruled that we should decide by drawing for it. We were unlucky.'

CHAPTER FOUR

January to June 1943

British 'Main Offensive' against the Ruhr.
Rumpelhardt is absent, but successes mount.

January 1943 dawned with Heinz Schnaufer still well down in the over-all *Nachtjagd* 'league table' of kills. He had been flying operationally for something like fourteen months and had only seven confirmed victories to his credit. Nevertheless, his achievement, seen in the context of that of his own unit, was not unimpressive. He was responsible for over a tenth of the confirmed victories scored during the same period, in the course of which II./NJG 1 had a score of 67, of which its *Kommandeur*, *Hauptmann* Walter Ehle, laid claim to ten, thereby bringing his person-al tally to sixteen. Schnaufer and four other pilots, with seven kills each, were in joint second place.

By the end of 1942 the *Nachtjagd* had claimed a total of 1,108 bombers destroyed since it was first set up, of which II./NJG 1, found-ed in September 1940[1], had shot down the respectable number of 182. The leading scorer of the *Nachtjagd* at the turn of the year was *Hauptmann* Helmut Lent, *Kommandeur* of IV./NJG 1 at Leeuwarden, with the impressive personal tally of 49 night-time victories to add to the eight he had earlier claimed as a *Zerstörer* pilot.

Even at this early date in the long confrontation between the *Nachtjagd* and Bomber Command, and despite the considerable number of victories the arm had scored, there were complaints among the German crews – particularly the less successful ones – about the inher-ently inflexible nature of Kammhuber's *Himmelbett* defensive system. *Himmelbett*, in simple terms, meant that the fighters had to wait for the bombers to come to them, and the instinct of many of the pilots, par-ticularly those who had come from *Zerstörer* formations, was to go out and hunt the bombers. There is no direct German translation for the English word 'fighters' in the sphere of aerial defence: the German word is '*Jäger*' or 'hunter', and the generic term for aerial fighting is '*die Jagd*', 'the hunt', and that is what the pilots wanted to do – to seek out, stalk, chase and eliminate their enemy.

---

[1] In fact this was the third time that II./NJG 1 had been 'founded'. In the early months of the Nachtjagd new units were founded and renamed and changed identities with bewildering rapidity.

Helmut Lent

The *Himmelbett* close-control areas for which II./NJG 1 at Saint-Trond was responsible at this period were of two kinds, although functionally they all operated in the same manner – a *Würzburg Riese* radar to pick up the fighter scrambled to the specific *Raum* and another separate one to concentrate on a bomber allocated to that fighter as his target; positions 'told through' to a horizontal display in the Fighter Control Post; and a fighter controller to 'talk' the fighter crew to a position close enough to his target for the pilot to go into the attack either visually or with the aid of *Lichtenstein*. The first zones were sectors of Kammhuber's original searchlight belt, in which they had been used for *helle Nachtjagd* and which had then been adapted for close control using the *Würzburg* radars that originally controlled the lights. That section of the belt immediately to the west of Saint-Trond was numbered '6' and was divided into three sectors, 6A, 6B and 6C respectively, reading from north to south. Schnaufer had been operating in *Raum* 6C when he shot down his Lancaster on 21 December 1942. Then, set back behind Sector 6, came three of Kammhuber's custom-made circular

Himmelbett areas code-named *Kolibri*, *Gemse* and *Meise*.[1] Because Bomber Command tended, in general terms, to follow the shortest route to their target, and because such targets tended to be concentrated in specific industrial areas – for example the Ruhr Valley – certain of the areas were penetrated more frequently than others and so were favoured by the fighter pilots, because it was there that action was to be had.

The early months of the year 1943 were a sparse time for II./NJG 1. Schnaufer's next kill did not come until the 14th of May, and in the meanwhile the entire *Gruppe* scored none in January, only two in February, one in March and three in April. There was in general a comparative shortage of 'trade' for the Belgium-based fighters during this period, although their colleagues stationed in Holland were more fortunate. The long nights of winter meant that Harris was able to send his bombers on forays deeper in Germany. Berlin was attacked by large forces on four occasions – albeit not very successfully – and there were raids to such places as Stuttgart, Nuremberg, Munich and Pilsen; targets in Italy were also visited – La Spezia, Turin and Milan – as were cities in North Germany such as Hamburg, Bremen, Wilhelmshaven and Kiel, which meant only very rare penetrations of the Saint-Trond close-control areas. At this time, too, much Bomber Command attention was diverted from the attack on the Fatherland and directed

In silhouette: A Bf 110 night fighter equipped with Lichtenstein antennae. *(Hinchliffe)*

Opposite: Compare with the previous photograph. This Bf 110 is fitted with *Lichenstein* SN2, which worked on a longer wave length. The small aerial in the centre is for a wide-angle *Lichtenstein*.

---

[1] *Himmelbett Räume* were named after animals, birds and so on. These three translate as Humming Bird, Chamois and Titmouse respectively. Later '*Lurch*' (Amphibian) and '*Murmeltier*' (Marmot) would be added to II./NJG 1's areas.

against the U-boat pens in the French ports of Lorient and St-Nazaire, again taking the bomber stream well away from the Saint-Trond hunting grounds.

The *Himmelbett* areas manned by II./NJG 1 were principally there to trap bombers heading for targets in the Ruhr area, and from January to April inclusive Bomber Command mounted only ten major attacks in that direction, one to Düsseldorf and three each to Essen, Duisburg and Cologne. With one exception, all the kills made by II./NJG 1 during this period were against bombers attacking Cologne and Essen. Harris also sent out small forces to the Ruhr, principally to Essen, in operational tests of *Oboe*, in which the device already showed exciting potential.

In much simplified terms, one ground station (CAT) in England controlled a high-flying aircraft – Mosquitoes were used almost exclusively – along the arc of a circle with its centre at CAT and its radius computed to pass through the aiming point. Another ground station (MOUSE) transmitted a signal to intersect this arc at the point at which the bombs were to be dropped: the navigator of the Mosquito heard a distinctive sound, and he pressed the bomb-release. An extraordinary degree of accuracy was achieved, but the system had its limitations. To receive signals the aircraft under *Oboe* control had to fly very high, which was why the Mosquito was used: on the credit side, *Oboe* Mosquitoes, by reason of the height at which they flew and their remarkable speed, enjoyed almost complete invulnerability to enemy flak and fighters. Another disadvantage was that only one, or at the most two, *Oboe* aircraft could be controlled at any one time. For this reason *Oboe* Mosquitoes were used not to drop bombs themselves but to mark targets for a large number of following bombers to aim at.

Since the end of the war the Bomber Command offensive has retrospectively been divided neatly into a series of 'Battles' – the Battle of the Ruhr, the Battle of Hamburg, the Battle of Berlin and so on. These are generalisations: they were not clearly defined periods, and the 'Battles' tend to overlap and blur at the edges, so to speak. Thus the 'Battle of the Ruhr' is seen as lasting between March and July 1943, so that one might reasonably expect there to have been more opportunities for engagement for the Saint-Trond-based night fighters from March onward than there actually were. Harris, who himself in fact coined the phrase 'The Battle of the Ruhr', wrote[1]:

> Bomber Command's main offensive began at a precise moment, the moment of the first major attack on an objective in Germany by means of *Oboe*. That was the night of March 5-6th, 1943, when I was at last able to undertake with real hope of success the task that had been given to me when I first took over the Command a little more than a year before, the task of destroying the main cities of the Ruhr.

1 *Bomber Offensive*, by Marshal of the RAF Sir Arthur Harris GCB, OBE, AFC.

*Air Vice-Marshal Sir
Arthur Harris*

Harris also described the route his bombers took on this night: 'The force flew to Egmong [sic – in fact Egmond] on the Dutch coast, and thence directly to a point 15 miles north of Essen.' Such a route would take the bomber stream well to the north and east of the areas allocated to the Saint-Trond fighters, who had no successes to report that night, although 14 of the 386 bombers that finally headed for Essen (56 of the force that took off returned early to base with technical faults) failed to come back.

When Schnaufer shot down two Lancasters on the 14th Fritz Rumpelhardt was not in the radio operator's seat of his Bf 110. He had been recommended, and accepted, for officer training. From February, therefore, he had to undergo a so-called Officers' Selection Course after which, when he had successfully completed it, he was posted as an instructor to a Junior NCOs' Course from 1 May to 15 June. After a short break, between mid-June and mid-July 1943, he had to attend War Academy (*Kriegsschule*) until the 18th of September.

During the eight months of Rumpelhardt's absence Schnaufer flew, with considerable success, with a number of different radio operators, and by the time that Rumpelhardt next flew operationally with him, in October, he had shot down a further 21 bombers, bringing his total score to 28. Of the radio operators who were involved in successful attacks on bombers, the most prominent was *Leutnant* Dr Baro with twelve; *Unteroffizier* Erich Handke was with Schnaufer for five kills, *Oberleutnant* Freymann and *Unteroffizier* Heinz Bärwolf for two each. *Unteroffizier* Heinz Wenning had also made three operational flights with Schnaufer between 29 November and 16 December 1942 while Fritz Rumpelhardt was in hospital with a fever, but without success.

Much happened in the increasingly bitter and dynamically expanding battle between Bomber Command and the *Nachtjagd* during Rumpelhardt's absence. By the time he rejoined Schnaufer not only had the crew increased to three and the Bf 110 been equipped with more deadly armament, but also night-fighting tactics had changed considerably, in such a way that offered greater scope for success to those pilots of the *Nachtjagd* endowed with the personal abilities and qualities to grasp and exploit the opportunities presented to them. Schnaufer himself had matured from being a moderately successful night-fighter pilot to being a very successful one. From the strategic point of view the air battle had intensified and altered its character considerably: it was these changes, initiated by Harris and his subordinates in Bomber Command, that had, at last, forced the night-fighter force to abandon, to all intents and purposes, the static defence system that Kammhuber's disputed *Himmelbett* represented. But all this was for the future.

At the beginning of the period Schnaufer's rank was still *Leutnant*, the equivalent of Pilot Officer in the RAF, Sub-Lieutenant in the Royal Navy or Second Lieutenant in the Army, the lowest commissioned rank. He was not promoted to the next higher rank, *Oberleutnant*, until July 1943, two years and three months after his original commissioning. When one considers the wartime practice in the RAF, when a newly commissioned officer served only six months as Pilot Officer before being automatically promoted to Flying Officer and was then promoted, again automatically, to Flight Lieutenant (German equivalent *Hauptmann*) eighteen months afterwards, this slow promotion seems difficult to understand, even more so when one recalls that among aircrew officers in the RAF the award of acting rank was not at all unusual, many a Pilot Officer being 'made up' to Flight Lieutenant even before he was entitled, by reason of the time that he had served in the rank, to be a Flying Officer; and Flight Lieutenants not infrequently carried the acting rank of Squadron Leader, Wing Commander or even, on occasion, Group Captain. On a macabre note, such rapid promotion was a more often than not a case of 'dead men's shoes'. But the Germans had their losses too. The life-expectancy of a night-fighter pilot was little, if at all, greater than that of the enemy he pitched his wits against, the Bomber Command crewman.

Normally, Schnaufer could have expected to be promoted *Oberleutnant* on 20 April 1943: 1 April was Adolf Hitler's official birthday, and by tradition the day on which promotions were promulgated. Fritz Engau and he had been commissioned on the same day, as Engau tells in his book, and logically should have become *Oberleutnant* simultaneously. Engau was in hospital in April 1943 and it was Schnaufer who brought him news of his, Engau's, promotion. Why Schnaufer was overlooked at that time remains obscure: he already had seven kills to his credit, whereas Engau had still yet to open his account, and Schnaufer held the responsible position of Technical Officer of the *Gruppe*. It was not until 1 July that his promotion was promulgated, by which time he had shot down a further ten bombers.

From mid-May 1943, still during Harris' Battle of the Ruhr, when there began to be more bombers venturing into the areas defended by II./NJG 1, Schnaufer's successes began to mount, and that despite the absence of his regular *Funker*. On the night of 13/14 May Harris sent 432 heavies – Lancasters, Halifaxes, Stirlings and Wellingtons – plus ten Mosquitoes to strike at the Ruhr coal-mining town of Bochum, always a difficult and hazardous target. Of this force, 24 were destined not to return, and two of them went down to the guns of Schnaufer's Bf 110. Manning the radio and radar equipment and, nominally at least, the single flexible machine-gun at the rear of the cockpit, which was only rarely used, was *Leutnant Doktor* Baro. Schnaufer was scrambled that night to *Raum Lurch*, which had first come into operation the previous

In the Divisional Control Centre both target and fighter were shown on a vertical screen by coloured dots of light projected by *Lichtpunktwerfer*, or 'Light-spot projectors'.

February. In all, II./NJG 1 claimed four kills. Schnaufer's first was a Short Stirling, which he shot down at 0214 hours in the morning near to the Dutch township of Heerlen, 15 kilometres east of Maastrich, still no great distance from Saint-Trond. When Schnaufer attacked his victim it was flying at about 12,000 feet, a typical altitude for the type. The Stirling, an ungainly and underpowered aircraft, had been the first four-engined bomber to enter operational service with Bomber Command, doing so in February 1941. It did not instil confidence in the crews that flew in it. In action its principal shortcoming was its low operational ceiling, which made it comparatively easy picking for the night fighters and the Flak, and losses of the type were consistently heavier than those of the other four-engined bombers, the Halifax and the Lancaster, which could fly much higher. It is said that the crews of the Lancasters and Halifaxes were always pleased to see Stirlings on the Battle Order, because they knew that they would attract the majority of the hostile defensive attention. By the end of 1943 the Stirling had been withdrawn from front-line service against targets in Germany.

By a macabre coincidence the 214 Squadron Stirling met its fate at 2.14 a.m. BU-O, R9242, had taken off from Chedburgh one minute after midnight and was on its way to Bochum. The pilot, Sgt R M Gibney, and three other members of the crew lost their lives, while three survived to become prisoners of war.

Schnaufer's next victim, at 0307 hours, was a Halifax (JB 873, EY-J of No. 78 Squadron) and, as one would expect, it was flying much higher than the Stirling, at 15,400 feet. It crashed a short distance southeast of Louvain, having bombed Bochum about three-quarters of a hour earlier. The captain, Sergeant G Dane, and the second pilot, Sgt J H

Night-fighter operations room.

Body, died in the crash. Five other members of the crew survived and were taken prisoner but a sixth, Sergeant R G Goddard, the navigator, evaded capture and succeeded in returning to England.

Bomber Command losses to the night fighters were increasing significantly. Four-engined bombers were rapidly ousting the twin-engined machines from the force that was attacking Germany almost nightly. Hampdens and Whitleys were long gone, and only the redoubtable Wellington still carried its high-explosive load to bring destruction and death to Germany – and to inspire the night-fighter men to even greater efforts. A bomber shot down meant one more that would either not reach its target or, if it had bombed before it was destroyed, could not come back again to ravish and to kill. Ironically the night-fighters called their RAF opponents *'Die Kameraden von der anderen Feldpostnummer'* – the comrades from the other Field Post Office – and in general they had considerable respect for them, seeing them as young men, not unlike themselves and with a fascination for flying, who were carrying out orders. But by and large they killed them unhesitatingly, because that was their job, just as the Bomber Command killed German civilians unhesitatingly, because that was their job. To the Germans a Wellington shot down meant, in all probability, five enemies eliminated – probably killed – and a four-engined bomber seven. So when, for example, 25 four-engined aircraft and eight Wellingtons failed to come back from an attack on Wuppertal a fortnight later, on 29/30 May 1943, over 200 RAF aircrew were lost. The majority, statistically, would have met their death, some would be taken prisoner of war, and possibly a handful would escape capture and succeed in the hazardous enterprise of making their way back to England.

The other side of the balance sheet also gives food for thought. This was Bomber Command's most concentrated attack yet, and in the unhappy town of Wuppertal a large area of fire was generated in the Old Town, which in its turn attracted more and more bombers to unload their ghastly cargoes of high-explosive and incendiary bombs with a degree of accuracy rarely attained hitherto. There was considerable damage to industrial and domestic premises, and more than 3,000 civilians paid with their lives because they were citizens of a country that had gone to war to satisfy its dictator's territorial, nationalistic and ethnic ambitions.

That night Schnaufer shot down two Stirlings and a Halifax. The Stirlings were at 11,500 and 14,800 feet respectively, the Halifax at 21,300 feet. With *Leutnant* Dr Baro as radio/radar operator, Schnaufer was scrambled to *Raum Lurch* at 2351 hours on the 29th, returning to base at 0231 hours on the 30th. Under *Himmelbett* control, his kills came at 0048 hours, 0143 hours and 0222 hours.

Schnaufer, now one of the more experienced pilots, had been in the First Wave to take off. Fritz Engau, who was to be in the Second Wave and was waiting to be called forward, gives a vivid portrayal of front-line service as a German night fighter in 1943. His account emphasises how close to the operational airfields, sited as they were on the likely approach routes of bombers from England, many of their kills took place:

> Across the airfield at the *Staffel* dispersals an engine roars, then a second, a third. The roar grows louder, there is a rumbling and a shaking. With whistling undertones the first dark phantoms emerge from their shelters and their dispersal pans. Headlights flash on and are extinguished, warning other aircraft. Off. On. They move through the darkness as if it were not there. There is a restlessness in the darkness, it seems to waver, to be in a turmoil. The airfield perimeter and runway lamps start to light up. In their feeble shine the first aircraft creeps into take-off position, pauses as if to take breath, then races headlong, engine howling, into the darkness of the night sky. The next takes his chance, and then the next.
>
> A few minutes later the last aircraft is gone. The thunder of engines recedes, further and further away, then finally fades. The airfield lights go out. Silently the darkness sinks down upon us. I go into the ops. room to listen in to the R/T exchanges between the duty officer and the pilots in the air, but they have all left the frequency.
>
> It is not long before one can hear, to the north, a dull rumbling and thrumming. The bombers! We go into the open in case there is anything to see. As we later find out it is the main bomber stream, passing to the north of Saint-Trond and Hasselt and heading towards Cologne.
>
> We do not have long to wait. Flames glow in the northern sky. They flicker and sway and dive downward. Then comes a flashing in the firmament – fire in the sky. The horizon is aflame.
>
> Which is it – friend or foe?
>
> The spine-chilling spectacle is repeated several times. The flames are *Viermots*[1], shot down by our comrades. And Schnaufer has sent three of them plunging to earth.

It was a good night for Heinz Schnaufer, and it was also a good night for II./NJG 1 as a whole. Three Do 217s and thirteen Bf 110s went into action and made a total of eleven kills, a third of all the losses wrought on Bomber Command that night. But the *Gruppe* suffered its own casualties. A Do 217 flown by *Unteroffizier* Roscher was shot down in flames by a British intruder: his two-man crew baled out but Roscher himself was killed. A second Do 217, that of *Leutnant* Hager, came under fire from a British bomber and, with all members of the crew wounded, had to make a forced landing on the airfield at Florennes, where it caught fire on the ground. Hager managed to get out of the burning wreckage, but the *Funker* was burned to death. Two Bf 110s also came to grief, one of which was that of *Leutnant* Engau, who had duly taken off for *Raum* 6C in the Second Wave at 0126 hours and had to bale out with his crew about an hour later when his machine, too, was hit by fire from a Vickers Wellington he was attempting to shoot down. His first encounter with a British bomber had ended in disaster for him.

RAF intruders were becoming an increasing hazard to the German flyers by night, with Mosquitoes beginning to replace the Bristol

---

[1] A '*Viermot*' was a widely used term for a four-engined aircraft (*Viermotoriges Flugzeug*).

Beaufighters that had already earned the respect of the *Nachtjagd* crews. But it was not only by night that such danger lurked. Increasingly British and American fighter-bombers were making their presence felt during the daylight hours, sweeping in at low level to strike at specific objectives and targets of opportunity including, of course, any *Luftwaffe* aircraft that they came across. In late May or early June 1943 Fritz Engau flew Schnaufer to the Erla Factory in Brussels, where the latter's Bf 110 had been specially polished to give it a few extra kilometres per hour in speed and was now ready for collection. It was only a short distance – something like 40 miles – and Engau flew his Bf 110 without its glazed cockpit-canopy. Schnaufer was in the radio operator's position, sitting back-to-back with Engau, and neither was wearing intercom headphones. Engau:

> The sun was high in the sky as I took off for Brussels with Schnaufer as 'cargo'. I flew at an altitude of about 500 metres. I was a real pleasure flight – no darkness, no clouds, no radio, no oxygen masks, no operational stress. At least, it was at first. The countryside lay green and fruitful beneath us, dazzling the eye with its magic. Here and there in the fields I could see a farmer, two farmers, a farmer's wife, carts, farmhouses, gleaming in the sunlight. A deep peace seemed to lie over the land. We hadn't been in the air long when Schnaufer gave me a hefty thump on my right shoulder from behind. When I turned round and looked behind me through the small gap I saw him pointing excitedly above and to the right.

What Schnaufer had seen was four USAAF Thunderbolts flying in loose formation some three or four hundred metres above. They seemed to be turning in for an attack. Engau put his aircraft into a steep diving turn, descending until he was barely above treetop height. Fortunately for the two Germans the Americans had apparently not spotted them after all, and they were able to continue their journey to the Erla Works. There Engau asked Schnaufer if he would have been able to use the rearward-firing machine gun had they been attacked from astern. Schnaufer answered that he knew how to use it in theory, but as they weren't carrying ammunition that wouldn't really have been a lot of use.

After the successful night of 29/30 May there was a pause in operations for II./NJG 1 until the middle of the following month. This was a moon period, and Bomber Command confined its operations to mine-laying and leaflet raids. Then, on the night of 11/12 June, Harris unleashed his force again, sending nearly 800 bombers to Düsseldorf, already one of the most bombed cities in Germany, and the attackers inflicted further enormous damage there. Approaching 9,000 separate fires were started in an area of 40 square kilometres, 1,200 people were killed and more than 140,000 bombed out. Bomber losses approached 5 percent, while on a minor raid by 72 aircraft to Münster 6.9 percent failed to return. The total number of bombers lost was 43, and they again took with them in the region of 300 young men. This was the

Jabs (right) and Schnaufer in front of an American Thunderbolt that was shot down and had to land at Saint-Trond, 1944.

most devastating raid in the Battle of the Ruhr, and the attrition suffered by both sides was daunting.

II./NJG 1 scrambled twelve Bf 110s that night, and they claimed five kills, of which four were confirmed. Schnaufer, with Baro in the rear seat, patrolled in *Raum Meise* between 0202 and 0325 hours, but had no success. Nor did he get a kill under *Himmelbett* control during the night of the 16th/17th June, when 212 four-engined bombers struck at Cologne, bombing on sky-markers dropped by PFF aircraft using H2S, but achieving only very poor concentration. Either Schnaufer's shooting skills deserted him that night or another victim went unclaimed, as an extract from the Operational Diary of his unit testifies:

> 17.6.43, 0117 to 0126 hours. Contact with an inbound Lancaster at 6,500 metres altitude by *Oberleutnant* [sic – but his overdue promotion had still not been promulgated] Schnaufer / *Lt* Baro II./1 in *Raum Lurch*. Three attacks, including two with good strikes in fuselage and rear turret. A small fire in the rear turret area extinguished quickly. Contact with the enemy was lost when it entered cloud in a dive at 2,400 metres.

Five nights later, however, Schnaufer and Baro achieved a further success, shooting down a Short Stirling at 0133 hours on the morning of the 22nd June. The Ruhr town of Krefeld was the target that night, the attack was concentrated and civilian casualties, once more topping the figure of 1,000, were high: so, too, were bomber losses. Clear visibility, which enabled the Pathfinder aircraft to mark their target accurately, together with a residual moon – the moon period was coming to its end – resulted in both good marking by the Pathfinders and good hunting conditions for the night fighters. Of the 44 bombers lost, 12 were from PFF, and of those six were from No. 35 Squadron. Schnaufer's victim was from a Main Force squadron, No. 218.

Stirling HA-D, BK 712, had taken off from Downham Market at 0015 hours on the 22nd June, and she met her fate just one hour and eighteen minutes later. Captained by Pilot Officer W Shillinglaw, she was carrying Flying Officer Arne Helvard, a Dane, as second pilot. Pilots new to a squadron usually flew one or two operations as a super-numerary crew-member, designated 'Second Pilot', before venturing over Germany as captain of their own crew, so that it is likely that Helvard's first or second operation was also his last. The Stirling crashed just north-east of Aerschot, barely more than twenty miles from Schnaufer's base at Saint-Trond. This was Heinz Schnaufer's thirteenth kill, and *Leutnant* Baro was again flying with him as *Funker*.

The fighter controller who guided Schnaufer in to his kill that night was *Leutnant* Kühnel of the 13th *Gruppe* of Air Signals Regiment No. 211 (13./*Luftnachrichten-Regiment* 211) and the *Raum* in which he was working was *Meise*, to the north-east of Brussels. Schnaufer took off at 0054 hours on the 22nd and took up his position at the radio beacon. At 0120 hours Kühnel called up – he had a target, a '*Kurier*' in the *Nachtjagd* code. It was BK-712. Kühnel talked Schnaufer into radar contact with the Stirling, and then *Funker* Baro took over. The bomber was destroyed, according to the fighter controller's log, at half a minute past 0133 hours. The kill was witnessed from the Control Room of *Raum Meise* by *Unteroffizier* Schellenberg. The following day *Leutnant* Kühnel visited the scene of the crash. In his report he wrote:

> Report
> *Dunkelnachtjagd* Victory by *Lt* Schnaufer – *Lt* Baro on 22.6.43 at 0133 hours.
> I report to the *Gruppe* that at 0600 hours on 22.6.1943 I visited the crash-site of the Short Stirling Mk. I shot down by *Leutnant* Schnaufer at 0133 hours.
> The wreck is three kilometres north-east of Aerschot, map reference NK 31 b. The number of enemy crew-members is seven. They are all in the wreckage of the aircraft, some of them completely incinerated. As a result of the fire caused when it crashed the Short Stirling is almost completely destroyed. The elevator and rear turret are lying about 1,500 metres from the wreckage.

Presumably the remains of the crew were so badly burned that Kühnel failed to discover that the aircraft was carrying an eighth crew-member.

The number thirteen, superstition has it, is unlucky. For Schnaufer the opposite might be said to have applied, because his thirteenth kill marked the beginning of the phenomenal run of victories, lasting until the end of the war, that distinguished him as the most successful night-fighter pilot ever. Until then his twelve kills had taken him nineteen months to accrue. Now, however, it was if he was switching into a high-er gear. Luck surely played its part, but in the grim, unforgiving busi-ness of aerial combat by night over Europe no amount of luck alone could ensure success and survival: the odds against it were simply too great.

In two more sorties before the end of June 1943 Schnaufer added a further four kills to his score, a Wellington on the 25th, two Halifaxes and a Lancaster on the 29th. *Leutnant* Baro was still flying with him as *Funker*. On the night of the 24th/25th Wuppertal was Harris' target, on the 29th Cologne was hard-hit yet again. On both nights the toll of German dead was numbered in four figures – 2,800 in Wuppertal, 4,377 in Cologne. Bomber Command losses continued to average out at about five percent of those despatched. This Battle of the Ruhr was a battle the like of which had never been seen before, a battle in which on some nights civilian casualties outnumbered military ones by a factor of twenty or more. The attack on Cologne, for example, claimed at least 4,500 civilian lives, in that some of those gravely injured would later die, while Bomber Command lost about 175 aircrew and the *Nachtjagd* an unknown, but much smaller, number. But the Bomber Command crews and the night-fighter men of the *Luftwaffe* flew night after night, the bomber crews until they had completed a tour of thirty operations, the German crews until they died, were gravely injured or became otherwise unfit to fly, or – most unusually – were posted to a non-operational job. For a bomber crew to complete a tour at this period of the war was an unusual event. Quite clearly a tour of thirty trips, with a one-in-twenty chance of not coming back each and every time, was actuarially not a good risk. And the large majority of night-fighter men were killed even before they reached the arbitrary number of five kills that qualified them to be called an ace.

CHAPTER FIVE

June to October 1943

Overdue promotion. 'Willem' joins the crew, and Fritz comes back. The move to Leeuwarden, and a new appointment. New bomber tactics are met by new fighter tactics. Further successes.

4 July 1943. The wreckage Stirling III OJ-B of No. 149 Squadron. This was Schnaufer's 19th kill and took place at Geetbets, Belgium. His Funker *on this occasion was* Leutnant *Dr Baro.* (Fengler)

In the early hours of 29 June 1943, when Schnaufer scored his three victories – a feat he accomplished in thirty minutes – II./NJG 1 scrambled seventeen fighters, which shot down twelve bombers without loss to themselves. Their twelve victories represented almost half of Bomber Command's entire losses that night. On the night of the 3rd and 4th of July Harris struck again at Cologne, and in response II./NJG 1 put 21 fighters up and claimed fourteen of the thirty bombers that did not return to their bases. Schnaufer and Baro accounted for a Wellington and a Stirling. The growing threat presented by RAF intruders was underlined by the loss of *Oberleutnant* Fuchs, *Unteroffizier* Adami and

Oberfeldwebel Matschuck, whose Do 217 was shot down by an intruder shortly after it had taken off from Saint-Trond.

   This particular RAF attack on Cologne coincided with the introduction by the *Luftwaffe* of a new and unconventional form of night fighting. Single-seat day fighters joined in the air battle, engaging the bombers over the target. The fighters were led by *Major* Hajo Herrmann, and remarkably enough he was not a fighter pilot by background but a highly successful bomber pilot. Herrmann, who had more than three hundred bombing missions in several theatres of war to his credit, had been reluctantly posted to a desk job in 1942 and had found himself at Potsdam, near Berlin, dealing with the figures of requirements and supplies of aircraft, and he had perceived the weaknesses of Kammhuber's static *Himmelbett* night-fighter organisation. In addition he had calculated that not enough fighters, in particular night fighters, were being produced to deal with the growing threat presented by Bomber Command and the USAAF. Unauthorised, but with the support of well-placed friends, he had personally experimented by flying single-engined fighters at night against RAF bombers attacking Berlin, and he had come to the conclusion that there was a place in the scheme of things for such aircraft – Bf 109s and Fw 190s – to operate in a free-lance rôle independently of Kammhuber's force. Herrmann reasoned

Opposite: *1 June 1943. Schnaufer, still serving with II./NJG 1 at Saint-Trond, wrote his* curriculum vitae *for an unknown but official reason. Old-German script was still usual.* (Schnaufer)

Generalmajor *Josef Kammhuber,* Kommandeur *of* 1 Nachtjagddivision *until September 1943.*

Schmaucher Heinz, Leutnant   1. 6. 43.

II. / Nachrichten... 1

Lebenslauf.

Am 16. 2. 1922 wurde ich als ältester Sohn des Kaufmanns Alfred Schmaucher und seiner Ehefrau Martha Schmaucher geb. Frey in Stuttgart geboren. Mein Vater war vor dem Weltkrieg im Ausland als Kaufmann tätig und mußte 1919, da er keine passende Anstellung erhielt, die Weinkellerei seines Vaters in Calw über-nehmen. — Schon nach wenigen Tagen zog meine Mutter mit mir von Stuttgart nach Calw im Schwarzwald, meiner eigent-lichen Heimatstadt, zurück. Als wuchs ich

that the pilots should fly to the target, heading for the searchlights, the PFF markers and the fires and explosions on the ground, and engage the bombers visually. His small but potentially lethal fighters could operate without ground control. The Herrmann concept was graced with the name of '*Wilde Sau*', or 'Wild Boar', and Göring himself – Kammhuber was opposed to the idea – had given Herrmann authority to set up and operate an experimental unit, JG 300. The night of the 3rd/4th July was chosen for the first trial of the Wild Boars. But there was a complication.

Herrmann's plan for freelance interceptors over the target area included the precaution that the local Flak would be restricted to a certain level, above which the single-seaters could range without being threatened by 'friendly fire'. But those who had forecast the likely target that night had been mistaken: they had predicted that the attack would be directed against the Essen area, and the commander of the flak there had agreed to conform to Herrmann's wishes. Circling over

Hajo Herrmann is seen here later in the war, when his rank was Oberst *and he had been awarded the Oak Leaves with Swords to the Knight's Cross.*

Essen, knowing that they would not come under fire from the ground, Herrmann's irregulars – like him, they were mostly bomber men – saw the first fires on the ground as the conventional night fighters, II./NJG 1 among them, struck at the bombers stream, and they were encouraged. But the stream turned and headed for Cologne, which came under a different Flak Commander and where no height restriction had been agreed. Herrmann and his nine Wild Boar pilots pursued the stream, and over the target they shot down, they claimed, twelve bombers. But the Cologne Flak, whose record until then had been modest in the extreme, also claimed the same twelve victories. Eventually, after a period of 'horse-trading', JG 300 was credited with six of the kills and the anti-aircraft guns with the other six. It was nevertheless a clear success for Herrmann, and Göring confirmed his appointment as *Kommodore* of JG 300 and gave him until September to organise and train his command. As history shows, however, the Wild Boars were back into the front line well before that training period had expired.

Cologne attracted a smaller force of fewer than three hundred bombers on the night of the 8th/9th of July, and Schnaufer took off shortly after midnight for *Raum Lurch*. II./NJG 1 put up 24 machines that night under *Himmelbett* control, experimenting with two, and sometimes three, fighters in a *Raum* simultaneously. Weather conditions were not good. The *Gruppe* managed only three kills, one of which, a Lancaster, fell to Schnaufer's guns at 20,000 feet. The low success rate seems to have been due to the fact that the bombers were flying in over thick cloud, into which many dived for cover when attacked, so that very few interceptions could be followed through to their proper – from the German viewpoint – conclusion.

Leutnant Baro was no longer flying with Heinz Schnaufer for this, Schnaufer's twentieth kill. After participating in ten kills in a period of just eight weeks he had been replaced in the rear seat by *Oberleutnant* Freymann, Signals Officer of the *Gruppe*. Freymann was destined to share another victory with Heinz Schnaufer, but before he did so the whole character of the night battle would have changed.

An attack by Bomber Command on Aachen on 13/14 July brought the Battle of the Ruhr to its close, and Harris turned his sights on the great northern port of Hamburg, Germany's second city and without doubt a prime target. Harris' aim, as he had expressed it succinctly in late May 1943 in an operational instruction addressed to Bomber Command Group Commanders, was simply 'To destroy Hamburg', and he chose the code-name 'Gomorrah' for his plan. It was an apt pseudonym, as it turned out.

Much of the concentration of bombing that had frequently, if not always, been attained during the Battle of the Ruhr had been due to the accuracy with which *Oboe*-equipped Mosquitoes of the Pathfinder Force had marked the aiming points for the Main Force, but Hamburg was well out of *Oboe* range. On the other hand the geographical location of Hamburg, some distance inland on the River Elbe and southeast of the distinctive Wilhelmshaven/Cuxhaven/Schleswig Holstein coastline, made it an ideal subject for identification by H2S. Accurate target marking, as ever a prerequisite for concentrated bombing, would therefore, in theory, present little difficulty.

Increasing losses of bombers to night fighters were a subject of much concern to the Air Staff and, indirectly, of frustration to some, including Harris. The mounting success-rate of the *Nachtjagd* was directly attributable to the introduction of *Lichtenstein* radar into their aircraft, and the frustration of such as Harris was due to the fact that there already existed a simple method of jamming *Lichtenstein* and other radars that operated on a similar wavelength, such as the *Würzburg Riesen* on which the *Himmelbett* fighter-control system was based. Code-named '*Window*', it was a simple concept. Strips of aluminium foil cut to half the wavelength of the enemy radar and scattered in huge numbers within the field of view of that radar would each produce a return on the radar's CRT[1], so that the picture would be effectively 'jammed out' and the operator would be unable to identify genuine targets. But the powers-that-be were reluctant to authorise the introduction of 'Window': it was known that the Germans were also aware of its capabilities – they called it '*Düppel*' – and it was feared that once it was used there would be nothing to stop the Germans using it against our own radars. Ironically, it was just the same line of argument that had prevented the Germans from themselves introducing *Düppel* earlier.

Clearance was given, however, for 'Window' to be used by Bomber Command in the Battle of Hamburg, as the few eventful weeks that followed came to be known. 'Window' was an immediate, if short-lived, success. The night fighters and their controllers were effectively deprived of their ability to see the bombers, and Kammhuber's *Himmelbett* defences were rendered virtually redundant at a stroke. But, despite first reactions, the ultimate advantage probably lay with the Germans. What many night fighters had been advocating, and Kammhuber had been resisting, was forced upon him – the abandonment of the rigid *Himmelbett* close-control procedure and the introduction of more flexible, and eventually more effective, methods of hunting by night.

Hamburg not only brought about a new approach to the business of night-fighter operation, but it also demonstrated, to a degree not hitherto seen despite the terrible slaughter inflicted on the Germans during the Battle of the Ruhr, the awful potential of area bombing. In comparison, and in terms of loss of human life, not to speak of material destruction, Guernica. Warsaw, Rotterdam, London, Coventry, Essen, Düsseldorf, Cologne, all were eclipsed. Between 40,000 and 50,000 civilians were exterminated in the course of four major night attacks by the RAF and two minor day attacks by the USAAF from the 24th July until the 2nd August. It was a death toll possibly only exceeded, in Germany, in the controversial Bomber Command raid on Dresden in February 1945.

---

[1] CRT – Cathode-Ray Tube. This was the radar's visual display unit in the aircraft or on the ground.

Opposite: Schnaufer's promotion to Oberleutnant. Signed by Hermann Göring, this certificate shows the date of promotion as 1 July 1943. (Schnaufer)

IM NAMEN DES FÜHRERS
BEFÖRDERE ICH

den Leutnant in der Luftwaffe

H e i n z   S c h n a u f e r

mit Wirkung vom 1.Juli 1943 zum

O b e r l e u t n a n t

**ICH VOLLZIEHE DIESE URKUNDE IN DER ER-
WARTUNG · DASS DER GENANNTE GETREU
SEINEM DIENSTEIDE SEINE BERUFSPFLICH-
TEN GEWISSENHAFT ERFÜLLT UND DAS VER-
TRAUEN RECHTFERTIGT · DAS IHM DURCH
DIESE BEFÖRDERUNG BEWIESEN WIRD.
ZUGLEICH DARF ER DES BESONDEREN
SCHUTZES DES FÜHRERS SICHER SEIN.**

Hauptquartier des Ob.d.L., den 22.Juni 1943

**DER REICHSMINISTER DER LUFTFAHRT
UND OBERBEFEHLSHABER DER LUFTWAFFE**

The immediate reaction of the Commander-in-Chief of the *Luftwaffe*, the pragmatic *Generalfeldmarschall* Hermann Göring, shocked as he was by the news of the first attack and the laming of the night-fighter defences, was to call Hajo Herrmann's Wild Boars out of their formative training and throw them into the front line. They went into action against the second raid mounted by the RAF on the night of the 27th/28th July, and they enjoyed moderate success. But already, after the first shock of 'Window', the conventional defences were also reacting positively, and Bomber Command losses were beginning to creep up from the 1.5 percent incurred in the first raid. The second raid cost 2.2 percent of the attacking bombers, the third 3.6 percent and the final one 4.1 percent.

Some of the ground radar operators were beginning to be able to discern genuine targets among the plethora of spurious signals on their screen, while some of the night-fighter *Funker* were also developing a feeling for what was a target and what were 'Window' returns, but the main factor behind the increase in RAF losses was that many of the night-fighter crews, realising that *Himmelbett* was not longer able to lead them to an interception, were heading for the target area and freelancing there and in the vicinity. Once in the bomber stream, particularly in the well-illuminated target area, it was possible to pick up enemy bombers visually. These twin-engined fighters – Bf 110s, Ju 88s, Do 217s and so on – were, in fact, independently adopting Herrmann's Wild Boar concept. Indeed, in the immediately following months 'Wilde Sau' was to become a recognised night-fighter procedure for the conventional *Nachtjagd* as well as for Herrmann's single-engined men-at-arms.

Another officer, senior to Herrmann, had also been apprised of the strategic weakness of *Himmelbett* and had already conceived an alternative approach to the problem of intercepting the Bomber Command machines. *Oberst* Viktor von Lossberg's reasoning was uncomplicated: the British bombers were coming in streams, and if night fighters could be infiltrated into those streams there would be targets aplenty for them. If the position, height and heading of the bomber stream could be broadcast from the ground and received by the night fighters, those fighters should be able to navigate themselves into the stream. The *Funker* of a night fighter was trained in basic air navigation, even though he had had little opportunity to use the skill during the *Himmelbett* period, when he had been virtually completely relieved of the responsibility for fixing and guiding his aircraft because it was under continuous surveillance by the ground controller. It would not take much training and practice to enable him to navigate well enough to find the bomber stream, and there were various possible ways he could be helped from the ground. Von Lossberg's proposals were avidly accepted, and his method christened, by an obvious progression, '*Zahme Sau*' or 'Tame Boar'.

A problem that faced the ground controllers in *Zahme Sau* was that of determining the position of the fighters at any moment so that they could direct them towards the bomber stream and, equally important, back to base after they had been in action. In terms of the whole battle, too, it was tactically desirable for the officers in overall control to know where any specific fighter was at any moment and, if necessary, to be able to inform him of his location. There was in existence a form of VHF radio-control known as '*Ypsilon*' control that met the requirement and which was widely used by day fighters. *Ypsilon* is German for the letter Y, and the system was written '*Y-Führung*'.

As *Zahme Sau* developed, 'Window', initially intended to protect the bombers from the attentions of the German night fighters, became a useful tool for the German controllers, particularly as long-range panorama radars, which had a rotating aerial and showed an all-round picture, came more and more into operation. Then the slowly-descending 'Window' dropped by the bombers left a very clear track of their route on the screen, enabling the controllers to infiltrate their fighters more easily than they could have done otherwise.

The rapid reaction of the *Nachtjagd* to the laming of *Himmelbett* may be seen in the fact that on the night of 25/26 July, immediately after the first attack on Hamburg, the first Y-Control night-fighter sorties were flown against a major Bomber Command attack on Essen. Five aircraft from II./NJG 1, controlled from the huge Division Operations Room at Deelen, near Arnhem, callsign '*Teerose*', flew *Zahme Sau* while three other machines were deployed in the *Himmelbett* areas. The *Gruppe* scored no victories.

Schnaufer himself was not on the battle order on the night of the raid on Essen, nor when, on 30 July, II./NJG 1 was scrambled by day against USAAF daylight raiders. He was, however, in *Raum Meise* on the night of 30/31 July when Bomber Command hit at Remscheid with 273 bombers and lost fifteen, two of which were accounted for by II./NJG 1, but he personally had no success. II./NJG 1 were not in action for the final episode of Gomorrah on 2/3 August, and then Harris sent no bombers to Germany, apart from Mosquitoes on harassing raids, until the night of the 9th/10th August, when, with Mannheim the target, Schnaufer was again in *Raum Meise*, one of fourteen aircraft deployed that night without success. He as, however, successful the following night.

The Bomber Command target on the night of 10/11 August 1943 was Nuremberg, deep inside the Fatherland, and Harris' force was made up of 653 aircraft, all of which were four-engined. The sturdy Wellington, which had seen action continuously since the beginning of the war, had at last been withdrawn from the front-line force. Of the seventeen fighters put up by II./NJG, twelve went to the *Himmelbett* close-control areas while the remaining five came under the control of *Teerose* (Deelen Divisional Operations Centre), flying Tame Boar. The five were all flown by experienced pilots: *Major* Walter Ehle, the *Gruppenkommandeur*, 28 kills; *Hauptmann* Eckart-Wilhelm von Bonin, 17 kills; *Oberleutnant* Walter Barte, 10 kills; *Oberleutnant* Wilhelm Telge, 12 kills; and Heinz Schnaufer, 20 kills and belatedly promoted *Oberleutnant* at the beginning of July.

Once again *Oberleutnant* Freymann was flying as *Funker* with Heinz Schnaufer. Schnaufer took off at two minutes before midnight on the 10th, and just over thirty minutes later he shot down a Lancaster near the village of Hählein, to the south of Darmstadt, the first night victory achieved under Y-control in the entire night-fighter force. It was Schnaufer's 21st kill, and his last as a member of II./NJG 1.

For some time Schnaufer, according to Fritz Engau, had wanted to be moved from Saint-Trond to Leeuwarden in Northwest Holland, situated close to the Friesian coast north of the Zuider Zee. Leeuwarden, a non-military grass field at the beginning of the war used mainly for local flying and for a KLM feeder service to Amsterdam, had been taken over by the *Luftwaffe* when the Germans invaded Holland in May 1940. The Germans began a rapid operation to extend and develop the airfield – 7,500 workers, mostly locally employed, were engaged on the work, which eventually included the laying of concrete runways – and for a short period it housed single-engined fighters, Bf 109Es being moved up from Jever in Ostfriesland. Then, when the *Nachtjagd* came into being, it was recognised that Leeuwarden was ideally located to intercept bombers on the way to targets in Northern Germany and, for example, Berlin, and it was increasingly used by the night fighters. On 1 October 1942 a newly-formed *Gruppe*, IV./NJG 1, made Leeuwarden as its permanent home. The *Gruppe* rapidly became one of the most successful in the *Nachtjagd*. Pilots based at Leeuwarden enjoyed the advantage over their colleagues at airfields further east of being able to take off as soon as early warning of an approaching raid was received and head out over the North Sea to meet the bombers before they even crossed the Dutch coast.

Major *Walter Ehle* (Kommandeur *II./NJG 1 until he was killed 17 November 1943) being presented with the* Ritterkreuz *by* General *Kammhuber on 20 August 1943.*

Hauptmann *Eckart-Wilhelm von Bonin* (left) *who, when Ehle was killed, took over as* Kommandeur *II./NJG 1.* Hauptmann *Walter Barte* (middle) *and* Hauptmann *Wilhelm Herget* (right).

Again according to Engau, Schnaufer wanted to be at Leeuwarden so that he would have greater opportunities of adding to his score than he had at Saint-Trond. Engau tells of a conversation that Schnaufer had with *Major* Helmut Lent, who was *Kommandeur* of IV./NJG 1 at Leeuwarden and a redoubtable night fighter who already had fifty victories to his name. Lent was on a very short attachment to Saint-Trond on the night of 13/14 July 1943, when the RAF attacked Aachen, and he and Schnaufer flew in Areas *Meise* and *Lurch* respectively. After they had landed Schnaufer sought and was granted a formal conversation with Lent, in which he put a request for a transfer to Leeuwarden.

Be that as it might, on the 13th August 1943 Heinz Schnaufer was posted to IV./NJG 1, taking over command of the 12th *Staffel* to replace *Oberleutnant* Eberhard Gardiewski, who had been shot down over the North Sea on 25 July in daylight combat with B-17s of the USAAF and had been picked up from his inflatable dinghy by the RAF Air Sea Rescue Service and taken prisoner. Since his reported conversation with Schnaufer Helmut Lent, who had in the meanwhile brought his score up to 65, had been replaced as *Kommandeur* of IV./NJG 1 on his appointment as *Kommodore* NJG 3 at the beginning of August, and the leadership of the Fourth *Gruppe* had been taken over by the then *Hauptmann* Hans-Joachim Jabs. Jabs' early impressions of Schnaufer were not entirely favourable. One night, shortly after Schnaufer arrived at Leeuwarden, the *Gruppe* was scrambled. Both Jabs himself and Schnaufer were on the battle order that night, and as Jabs was taxying out Schnaufer's Bf 110 emerged from a side turning without giving way, so that Jabs was effectively forced into second place in order of take-off. After flying was over that night Jabs called Schnaufer to his office and formally reprimanded him, reminding him that he, Jabs, was the *Kommandeur* and Schnaufer one of his subordinates, and pointing out in no uncertain terms that junior officers did not 'cut up' their commanding officer. 'He was a very arrogant young man,' comments Jabs. Very quickly, however, Jabs came to appreciate Schnaufer's many positive qualities as a pilot and an officer.

Schnaufer's first operational flight from Leeuwarden took place only four days after his arrival there to take over the 12th *Staffel*. On the night of the 17/18 August 1943 Bomber Command flew one of the most important raids of the war, with almost six-hundred four-engined bombers attacking the German research establishment at Peenemünde on the Baltic coast, where the V1 pilotless aircraft and the V2 long-range rocket were under development. The two revolutionary weapons were being constructed and tested in separate areas within the Peenemünde complex, and the bombers' target was the area dedicated to the V2. So secret was fact that the Germans were making such missiles that the Bomber Command crews were not told the true nature of their target. They were, however, warned that if the target were not hit they would have to go back there again.

There were a number of distinctive features about the raid. Firstly, it was not the customary area raid but a precision attack by night, and bombing was to be carried out from comparatively low level. To enable the Pathfinders and Main Force crews to find and hit their target a moonlight night was chosen. Lastly, the bombing was controlled by a 'Master of Ceremonies'.[1]

The name 'Master of Ceremonies' was soon afterwards changed to 'Master Bomber', although in enemy circles the German version, '*Zeremonienmeister*' persisted throughout the war: indeed, it persists to this day in German accounts of the bomber offensive. Following the assault on Peenemünde Master Bombers became a recognised part of the tactics of Bomber Command, and most major attacks from that time on were directed by specially selected Pathfinder pilots who circled above the target and broadcast bombing instructions to the Main Force. The Master Bomber usually flew in a Lancaster, but later in the war the same technique was sometimes used by Mosquito pilots, such as, for example, Group Captain Leonard Cheshire, VC, who flew at low level, actually under the falling bombs, in order to ensure that they hit the target.

Basing their forecast on intercepted radio and radar signals emanating from bombers as they were being tested and prepared in England, the Germans had concluded that a major attack would be mounted that night, and that the probability was that it would be directed against Northern Germany. The defences had been put on the alert.

Just after eleven o'clock in the evening local time, which was an hour

---

[1] Group Captain J H Searby, DSO, DFC, of No. 83 Squadron, PFF. This was not the first time that this officer had acted in that capacity – he had experimentally directed a raid on Turin the previous week.

ahead of British time, the coastal radars picked up the first British air-craft approaching from the west. Four Bf 110s were scrambled from Leeuwarden. The crews were briefed to fly *Zahme Sau*, but a modification had been introduced. The leader of the Messerschmitts, navigating by 'Y', was intermittently to broadcast a homing signal so that by tuning in to that signal the others could follow him into the bomber stream.

Schnaufer had been chosen to lead this experimental sortie. It is not known for certain who was flying with him as *Funker*, but it seems probable that it was Erich Handke. The other pilots were *Oberfeldwebel* Karl-Heinz Scherfling; *Feldwebel* Heinz Vinke; and *Unteroffizier* Georg Kraft. The German radars showed the approaching enemy aircraft heading eastward to the north of the coast, and Schnaufer's group of night fighters headed north to intercept. Not long after take-off, however, both Schnaufer's aircraft and that of Scherfling developed engine trouble and they had to abort the mission. Schnaufer headed for the airfield at Wittmundhafen, and came under fire from 'friendly' flak on the approach.

The radar returns that had been picked up were not, however, from British bombers but from Beaufighter intruders from No. 141 Squadron, RAF, sent out – clearly successfully – to tempt the German

W/Cdr J R D 'Bob' Braham achieved 19 of his 29 victories by night. Pictured here on the right, with his navigator D S 'Sticks' Gregory, Braham ended the war as a PoW.

night-fighter force into the air. One of them was flown by Wing
Commander Bob Braham, DSO, DFC, and he shot down both Vinke
and Kraft. Vinke survived, as did Kraft's *Bordfunker, Unteroffizier* Rudi
Dunger. Both were picked up by the *Luftwaffe* Rescue Service, Dunger
two hours after parachuting from his Bf 110 and Vinke after spending
eighteen hours in a small inflatable dinghy. For Schnaufer, this was an
inauspicious beginning to his new appointment.

One of Schnaufer's first tasks as *Kapitän* of 12./NJG 1 – a task he
would later be called upon repeat many, many times – was to write a
letter of sympathy to the parents of a comrade killed in action. Twenty-
year-old *Leutnant* Gerhard Dittmann was a new arrival at Leeuwarden,
but he died on the night of the Peenemünde raid, probably also shot
down by an intruder. It had been his first night operation, but he had
flown twice against American daylight attacks, on the 25th and 26th July
respectively, and had claimed two B-17s, one of which was confirmed.

Schnaufer's *Leistungsbuch* shows a victory recorded for 0009 hours on
the morning of 24 August 1943, but it is out of sequence, appearing as
it does after the 31st of the month. The kill is however confirmed by the
historian Martin Middlebrook in *The Berlin Raids*. Middlebrook interviewed Erich Handke, who has since died, when researching for his
work. Handke, incidentally, was for a long time the radar operator of
Martin Drewes. Schnaufer and Handke were flying *Wilde Sau*:

> Firstly we searched for half an hour east of the Zuider Zee and north of
> the Ruhr. We saw three single-engined fighters, between Münster and
> Hanover; they were flying with their tail lights showing. Then, suddenly,
> Schnaufer saw four exhaust flames to the left and above us. The exhausts
> belonged to a Halifax. Schnaufer opened fire *von unten hinten*[1] a short burst
> in the left wing, and then dived quickly away. The wing burned – at first
> only a small fire – but after two minutes there was a white stream of
> burning petrol twenty metres long. Shortly afterwards we saw three men
> leave the underside and open their parachutes. The bomber turned over
> on to its back suddenly, reared up, then went into a spin and, still burn-
> ing, went into the cloud which was at 2,000 metres. There was a red
> glow and then a bright flash.
>
>   Next day we flew to Celle because the crash had been seen by Flying
> Control there, so we had an eyewitness.

In Schnaufer's *Leistungsbuch* the location of the shooting-down is logged
as '20 kilometres north-north-east of Celle'. It was Schnaufer's first kill
from Leeuwarden.

The aircraft was a Halifax Mark II from No. 77 Squadron, and it
had taken off from Elvington in Yorkshire at 2019 hours local time,
captained by Pilot Officer A Massie. It crashed at Queloh, to the north
of Celle, after four of the seven-man crew had managed to escape by
parachute. The mid-upper gunner was Sergeant Charles W Brister,
who recalls:

---

[1] '*Von unten hinten*' (more usually '*von hinten unten*') – from astern and below.

We were briefed to attack Berlin. All went well across the North Sea, Holland and into Germany. We were picked up by night fighters, our rear gunner informed our skipper and he started weaving not too violently and we kept a good look-out. I was about to ask my skipper to bank the aircraft first to one side then to the other so that I could have a downward search, which was our normal practice. Without warning we were hit with two good bursts from below, which hit the port wing tanks. The fire burnt slowly at first and the skipper put the nose down to try and put the flames out, but it only got worse.

My rear gunner and I had an understanding, which was to help each other if we ever were in trouble, so I tried to make my way to the rear turret. When I was almost there the aircraft's nose dropped and I was thrown back to the cross-beam just aft of the mid-upper turret. The aircraft was spinning by now and I could not get back to the tail turret. I managed to get my parachute on and after a struggle reached the rear entrance hatch, which I had opened on my way down to the tail turret. Sitting on the floor I got my feet out, and the slipstream seemed to pull me out. I noticed the whole of the tailplane was burning as I went out and the port side was almost gone. I landed in the treetops of a wood somewhere north-east of Celle.

Heinz Schnaufer's second kill as a member of IV./NJG 1 took place at 0358 hours on the morning of 28 August 1943. Fritz Rumpelhardt was still not back from *Kriegsschule* and Schnaufer again had Erich Handke with him as *Funker*. Their victim was a Lancaster on its way to Nuremberg, which he intercepted and shot down near Darmstadt. In an article published in *Jägerblatt*[1] in 1962 Handke recalled that night: a radio operator with considerable operational experience, he was apparently not very favourably impressed by the way in which Heinz Schnaufer handled his first attack:

On 27 August 1943 we took off after bombers flying over Belgium on the way back from Nuremberg. We were scrambled under Ypsilon control. We were soon given a target at a height of 6,000 metres, which I picked up on my radar at a range of 3.5 kilometres. We approached it slowly, and then we saw a Lancaster about 200 metres away. It was flying straight ahead. Schnaufer managed to fire at it from fifty metres and miss. He pulled up far too steeply, corrected too late and therefore fired too late. In doing this we showed our entire belly to the rear gunner. Luckily, however, he must have been sleeping. Then the Lancaster altered course away from us, and we lost him. After being given a few more targets without result, Schnaufer suddenly saw a Halifax above us, flying straight and level. He fired into the port wing from below and behind at a range of between eighty and a hundred metres. It did not catch fire at once, and we continued to fire, until we were sitting beneath him and astern. His rear gunner and his mid-upper gunner opened heavy fire at us. As if by a miracle only our right fin was damaged. At last the wing began to burn brightly, and we pulled away in a dive. Three men baled out. The Halifax went down like a torch and came down about 15 kilometres to the west of Namur.

[1] *Jägerblatt* is the magazine of the *Gemeinschaft der Jagdflieger e.V.*, the Association of Fighter Crewmen.

Erich Handke was sick two nights later when Schnaufer shot down a Halifax in the course of a Bomber Command raid on the neighbouring towns of Mönchengladbach and Rheydt, and the *Funker*'s position in Schnaufer's Bf 110 was taken by *Unteroffizier* Heinz Bärwolf, a Berliner who already showed signs of having a charmed life. Bärwolf had been flying with one *Unteroffizier* Alfred Naumann in March 1943 when they had shot down a B-17 by day but had to make a crash-landing, with an engine on fire, on the beach on the Friesian island of Ameland. On their very next take-off their Bf 110 swung off the runway, Naumann tried to brake and the machine ended up in a ditch. Bärwolf suffered a broken nose and concussion in the crash, and when he came out of hospital Naumann had been posted away and Bärwolf was crewed up with *Oberleutnant* Eberhard Gardiewski[1], whom Schnaufer subsequently replaced as *Staffelkapitän* of 12./NJG 1. On his first operation with the new pilot their Messerschmitt came to grief. It is possible that they were caught by a marauding intruder, but post-accident investigations suggested the possibility of sabotage. Bärwolf is convinced that the latter is the correct explanation:

> When I lost my pilot I flew with Gardiewski, and on my very first operation with him we had got up to three hundred metres when the machine exploded. It was the result of sabotage. We managed to bale out, and I was caught up a tree. It was night-time and I was in a farmyard. I broke into the farmhouse – I had lost my boots – and I telephoned the local police. I had broken my arm, but I didn't feel any pain.

Bärwolf was more fortunate with Heinz Schnaufer. The Halifax they shot down crashed at 0353 hours on the morning of 31 August.

As dusk approached that same evening 622 heavy bombers began to take off from their bases in England to attack Berlin in the second raid of Harris' assault on the capital city of Germany that came to be known as the Battle of Berlin. The night fighters were alerted in good time and Schnaufer and Bärwolf claimed a Vickers Wellington at 2241 hours, locating the shooting-down at Kuinre, just off the north-east corner of the Zuider Zee. Heinz Bärwolf: 'The Wellington caught fire, and it burned like a torch. I was very, very shocked. After all, they were human beings just like ourselves.'

We are faced with a problem here. There were no Wellingtons going to Berlin that night. Yet the time and place fit well with the outward route taken by the bombers. The distinctive recognition feature of the Wellington, particularly in silhouette, was its tall single fin, while the Lancaster and Halifax had twin fins. But the Stirling also had a similar single fin and, despite the fact that the Wellington had two engines and the Stirling four, misidentification was possible. Yet even that solution will not do. That night 106 Stirlings took part in the raid, and seventeen failed to return. Closer investigation suggests a different solution.

---

[1] As earlier related, Gardiewski was subsequently shot down by Braham on the night of the Peenemünde raid.

W R Chorley has published a series of meticulously researched books, each covering a year, entitled *Royal Air Force Bomber Command Losses of the Second World War*, in which he records, wherever they are available, details of the fate of each bomber. None of the Stirlings missing would seem to fit the time and place of Schnaufer's victim, but a Halifax does:

> Halifax II, HR878, TL-J [No. 35 Pathfinder Squadron]. Took off 2010 Gravely. Outbound at about 16,000 feet, crippled either as a result of the photo flash flare igniting, or from an unseen night-fighter attack. Crashed at Kuinre (Overijssel), 10 km SE of Lemmer, Holland. Those who died are buried at Kuinre General Cemetery.

This possibility is considerably strengthened by the researches of that excellent and reliable historian, Martin Middlebrook. In his book *The Berlin Raids* he says,

> ...the bomber force was easily tracked on its approach flight over Holland and Germany, and more of the twin-engined fighters were able to make contact with the bombers before the target area was reached. A Pathfinder Halifax of 35 Squadron went down near the Zuider Zee, and thereafter the Germans scored steadily...

In 1943 the Commander of the Luftwaffe, *Hermann Göring, inspected night fighters stationed in Holland at Deelen. Here he is being saluted by Heinz Schnaufer, who by this time was with IV./NJG 1 at Leeuwarden: Hans-Joachim Jabs is on Schnaufer's right and Martin Drewes on his left. This event took place before Schnaufer or Drewes received the* Ritterkreuz. *(Diener)*

It seems certain that Schnaufer's 'Wellington' was in fact a Halifax.

Schnaufer had to return to base early after despatching his victim. Heinz Bärwolf was suffering from shortage of breath, even with the oxygen supply turned full on, and he blacked out: 'When I recovered consciousness I got a radio bearing and we got back to base. The Medical Officer saw me, and he sent me to a specialist, who found out that I had a hole in the lung and was suffering from tuberculosis. That was the end of my flying career for the time being.'

This was a busy period for Schnaufer. If he had sought a posting to IV./NJG 1 in order to see more action, his efforts were being repaid. He was also experiencing the administrative responsibilities that went with being a junior commander. On 10 and 11 September 1943 IV./NJG 1, including Schnaufer's 12.*Staffel*, began an attachment at Quakenbrück, which lies between Oldenburg and Münster. With the nights growing longer, and on the basis of the three heavy raids that Harris had already made against Berlin, the Germans had calculated that longer-range raids were to be expected, that the capital was likely to be the further object of Bomber Command's attentions, and that therefore defence in depth was needed. There was also another, tactical, reason for the decision to move IV./NJG 1 back into Germany. With the laming of the *Himmelbett* close-control system, the jamming of *Lichtenstein* airborne intercept radar and the introduction of the two commentary-based freelance night-fighter operations, *Wilde Sau* and *Zahme Sau* respectively, the advantages of Leeuwarden's location near the western coast of Northern Europe had to a large extent been lost. There was little point in sending fighters out to meet a bomber stream when they could not be close-controlled into attacking position and

Another shot of the jovial Reichsmarschall. (Fengler)

Below: *IV./NJG 1 on parade during the visit of Hermann Göring to NJG 1 in Autumn 1943. Schnaufer may be seen in the front row between Jabs and Drewes.*

when they could not with confidence pick up their targets on their radar. It was better, particularly when the target was likely to be a long-range one, to wait until the position, heading and altitude of main bomber stream were established and then feed some fighters in by Tame Boar while also scrambling others to freelance in the target area as Wild Boar. And there was yet another complication for the defenders, which added to the desirability of being confident of the bombers' route and target before committing fighters: Harris was now sending smaller forces out simultaneously with the main force but to different targets in order to divert the fighters from the principal objective.

Erich Handke was back with Schnaufer for his next operational sortie when the target was Mannheim. They were flying Wild Boar, and there was a third man on board: as Handke wrote in *Jägerblatt*:

On 23 September we took off for *Wilde Sau* again. I went over the Wild Boar frequency straight away, where the current position of the enemy was continuously being broadcast in a sort of running commentary. I heard, 'Leading bombers over Brussels, heading 090 degrees, 4 to 6,000 metres. Bombs dropping over Aachen. All Wild Boars gather at Pundit Ida. Further incoming enemy aircraft over Dunkirk, heading 130 degrees, bombs being dropped over Frankfurt, enemy activity over Darmstadt, new target Mannheim,' and so on. The main targets were Aachen and Mannheim. [In fact, Mannheim was the main target, with a diversionary attack on Darmstadt. There was a minor Mosquito attack on Aachen]. We flew past the Ruhr area on an easterly heading so that we wouldn't run into the Flak and entered the stream to the south-west of Bonn. We knew we were in the stream by the many flares and cascades and by the heavy 'Window' jamming I had on my set and against which I could do nothing. We arrived in the Mannheim area, where fires were already burning. Now and then we were caught by a slipstream, and we expected to see a bomber at any time. To the north-west of Mannheim we were in luck. Since we had been flying *Wilde Sau* we had had a third man as look-out, who kept an eye open to the rear, particularly for enemy intruders. *Unteroffizier* Gänsler, nicknamed 'Willem', who had already participated in 17 kills as *Bordmechaniker* with *Hauptmann* Ludwig Becker, was flying with us. We sat back to back, and it was of course very cramped in the aircraft now.

Schnaufer had very good eyesight, but Willem's was possibly even better. Suddenly he shouted out, 'Hold it, hold it, – I can see one!' High above us there was a Stirling, flying very slowly. Our overtaking speed was too great, and we went so far ahead that Willem could hardly see him any more. Then Schnaufer saw another one ahead and above. By throttling back and pulling off and down to one side rapidly in an attempt to get beneath it he lost it momentarily, but I gave him a rapid correction from my *Lichtenstein* radar, and we quickly picked it up again. We adjusted our speed to the bomber's but then we pulled up too steeply and fired from too great a range – almost 200 metres. It wasn't until his fourth burst of fire that Schnaufer hit the outer engine that he had been aiming at from the beginning. For some strange reason the rear-gunner hadn't opened fire. We flew in close to the burning aircraft. It was losing height, and it went into a dive at 4,600 metres.

That same night *Leutnant* Kröner and *Unteroffizier* Damman were shot down while landing at Mainz-Finthen, carelessly having switched on their navigation lights. Kröner was a new man, but he already had two kills to his credit.

As illustrated by Kröner's demise, RAF intruders were rapidly becoming a grave threat to German night-fighter operations. Mosquitoes had to a great extent replaced the Beaufighters, so making the threat even greater. There was a device that some of the intruders carried that enabled them to home on transmissions from German *SN-2*[1] radar, and it was called *Serrate*. *Serrate*-equipped aircraft would patrol areas where they were likely to come across night fighters – as evidenced by Braham's activities on the night of the Peenemünde raid – and non-*Serrate* intruders headed for airfields known to house night fighters and attacked their prey when they were taking off or landing. In an effort to defend, in part at least, against this menace a third man was being introduced into the Bf 110 crews. Sometimes he was called the '*Bordmechaniker*' (Air Mechanic), sometimes the '*Bordschützer*' (Air Gunner), sometimes the '*Beobachter*' (Observer) and most frequently simply the '*Dritter Mann*', or Third Man. He was, in fact, intended as a third pair of eyes, primarily to watch for hostile aircraft that might attack. He was also of considerable use in looking for targets within the bomber stream, particularly when the *Funker* was occupied with his radar set. And in emergency he could use the rearward-facing machine-gun. Some pilots, including Schnaufer, however, had had the rear gun removed from the Messerschmitt in order to cut down wind resistance and increase the aircraft's speed, in which case the task of the '*Dritter Mann*' was confined to keeping a look-out. Schnaufer's Third Man was, as Handke relates, Wilhelm Gänsler.

Wilhelm Gänsler originated from Arnstadt, south of Erfurt in Thuringia, in what was later to become the German Democratic Republic. He brought with him a great deal of experience from his time as *Bordmechaniker* to the legendary Ludwig Becker, the 'Professor of Night Fighting', and, together with Fritz Rumpelhardt, he too was destined to become a legendary figure, in his case as part of the three-man Schnaufer team. As Erich Handke says, his eyesight was good: part of the Gänsler legend is that he had almost miraculous night vision, but Fritz Rumpelhardt disputes that:

We all had above-average night-vision capabilities. Even before Gänsler arrived on the scene we had a night-vision test, while we were still at II./NJG 1. And Schnaufer and I came out at the top of the whole *Gruppe*. There has been a great deal of nonsense talked about our crew, and an example of it is that Gänsler's night-vision was super-human. If there is any reason for our success, apart of course from Schnaufer's ability, it is because we were an excellent team.

---

[1] SN-2 was a development of *Lichtenstein* AI radar. It is described below.

But Rumpelhardt concedes that Wilhelm Gänsler's experience as a trained flight mechanic was a great advantage. Wilhelm had, he said, a fine feel for engines and would often express useful opinions or give useful tips concerning the motors. Rumpelhardt describes how, on one occasion after he had rejoined the crew, Schnaufer went on a 'Mosquito hunt' – unsuccessfully, because Schnaufer never shot down a Mosquito. The Mosquitoes flew at such a high altitude that weight was at a premium, so on the night in question Schnaufer left Gänsler behind. They took off, but the aircraft would not climb properly, and Schnaufer decided that the altitude compressor pump, which feeds the engine with extra oxygen for high-altitude flying, was unserviceable, and they returned to base. After they landed Schnaufer said to Rumpelhardt that it was a pity they hadn't taken 'Willem' with them. Schnaufer, who according to Rumpelhardt was a surprisingly superstitious man, attributed his comment to superstition, but it was Rumpelhardt's belief that Schnaufer had failed to switch the compressor pump on. Gänsler would have noticed the mistake. Nevertheless Rumpelhardt, in his 'early-return' report, agreed with Schnaufer that the pump was not working.

But that was still in the future. From Quakenbrück Handke flew two more missions with Heinz Schnaufer and Wilhelm Gänsler. The main target of the first raid was Hanover, but Harris sent 21 Lancasters and six Mosquitoes of the Pathfinder Force further east to Brunswick, succeeding in drawing off some of the fighters from the main force:

> We were on again against the raid on Hanover and Brunswick on 27 September. There were already big fires in both cities. We were losing height over the burning town when Schnaufer saw a Halifax going in the opposite direction. He turned in as quickly as lightning, behind and below. Then Willem and I saw another Me 110 two hundred metres behind it. 'He'll shoot the bomber down under our noses,' we thought. But not at all; he flew past the bomber, quite slowly, not a hundred metres away, without seeing him. We were holding our breath, but we breathed again when the other 110 had gone. Now it was our turn. But Schnaufer pulled up too steeply, so that when he went into a dive the ammunition-belts for the cannon jammed and it would only fire intermittently. At last the Tommy caught fire in his left wing and crashed to the south-west of the Steinhuder Meer. The rear gunner didn't fire.
>
> On the two following days our *Geschwader* suffered two great losses. *Hauptmann* Frank collided with *Hauptmann* Friedrich when coming in to land, and *Hauptmann* Geiger was shot down by an intruder. [Frank and Geiger died, Frank with 55 victories to his credit, Geiger with 53. Both were holders of the Oak Leaves to the Knight's Cross of the Iron Cross].
>
> On 3 October there was a light attack on Hanover and Brunswick (only spoof TIs) in order to disperse our night-fighter force, while the main attack was on Kassel. Schnaufer saw a bomber flying past. He lost him momentarily when turning in, but he picked him up again at 800 metres. There were stars, but no moon. This time he carried out a very good attack from astern and below at a range of 50 metres. The port wing caught fire. Schnaufer preferred firing into the wings, because they burnt quicker. That is very dangerous, however, because the rear gun-

ner could fire without hindrance. Although we had reminded him immediately before, he forgot to press the cannon firing-button and shot with
machine guns alone. He fired again, from a greater distance, this time
with his cannon, and the Halifax went down. The rear gunner fired but
missed. There was a huge explosion when the bomber hit the ground,
because he had been on the way to the target and still had all his bombs
on board.

The night fighters, in their unremitting battle against Bomber
Command, were suffering steady casualties, as Handke illustrates:

> That night we had further losses. *Hauptmann* Sigmund, with *Feldwebel*
> Bayer, was shot down by flak over Kassel. [Sigmund was killed. A hold-
> er of the Knight's Cross to the Iron Cross, his score at the time of his
> death was 28]. *Major* Lent, after shooting down a Stirling, was wounded
> and lost a finger. *Oberleutnant* Drewes exchanged fire with a Stirling,
> which shot him down in flames. The *Funker*, *Feldwebel* Hradchowina, and
> the *Beobachter*,[1] *Feldwebel* Petz, baled out. Drewes, however, could not get
> out because the roof jammed. He was still at an altitude of 800 metres
> (over Sauerland) when he suddenly saw a village 50 metres below. He
> switched on the searchlight, and he saw a tree ahead of him. He pulled
> the machine up and then, at a speed of 380 kmph., ploughed through
> an orchard situated on an upward slope. Wanting to get out, he swiftly
> unstrapped himself, holding his arm in front of his face. The starboard
> wing broke off, the starboard motor lay on the port side, and the fuse-
> lage was broken in five places. At last he was able to struggle out of the
> side window, but one of his fur boots was jammed and he had to leave
> it behind. He was scarcely 20 metres away when the wreckage of the air-
> craft exploded. His only injuries were bruises to the arm he had held in
> front of his face and a slight scratch on his forehead!

This was Handke's final operational flight with Schnaufer. Since
Schnaufer had been appointed *Staffelkapitän* of 12./NJG 1 in mid-
August, Handke had acted as radar operator for five of the seven kills
he had scored. Now Fritz Rumpelhardt, not yet commissioned but with
the improved rank of *Feldwebel*, rejoined the crew at Quakenbrück.

Since Rumpelhardt had been detached from Schnaufer's crew there
had been great changes. *Himmelbett* was, to all intents and purposes, no
more. There was a third man in the crew. And there were two further
changes at about this time, both much to the disadvantage of the
bomber crews. One was a new radar, the other a revolutionary and
lethal form of armament. It is not clear exactly when these two devices
were fitted into Schnaufer's Messerschmitt, but it is convenient to deal
with them here. They were SN-2 and *Schräge Musik* – 'Jazz Music'.

SN-2 – full name 'Lichtenstein SN-2' or FuG 220 – was, as its name
suggests, a version of *Lichtenstein* air-interception radar. The operator's
display was a little more sophisticated than that of the original equip-

---

[1] '*Beobachter*' – observer. There was no such crew-position in a night fighter. The word is used
here in the sense of 'look-out'.

ment, but the main difference was in its frequency, hence its wavelength. For maximum efficiency an aerial must measure half the wavelength of the equipment it feeds with signals. The same consideration applies to jamming devices such a 'Window' – optimum interference occurs if the jamming substance is half the wavelength of the receiver it is designed to jam. The wavelength of SN-2 was much longer than that of *Lichtenstein*, and hence 'Window' cut to the proper size to jam *Lichtenstein* was not as effective against SN-2.

There was a disadvantage. The longer wavelength of SN-2 meant that it was necessary to mount much bigger aerials on the nose of the night-fighter machines, and that reduced the speed of the aircraft quite noticeably. But the ability to pick up targets again outweighed the inconvenience of the loss of speed – particularly when it was used in conjunction with a devastating new form of armament, 'Jazz Music'.

CHAPTER SIX

Jazz Music – an Interlude

Comrades disagree. Myths abound. Georg Fengler.

The standard attack technique used by German night fighters until the arrival of 'Jazz Music' has been mentioned earlier in this book, *von hinten unten*. The method, which, it is believed, was developed by Ludwig Becker, with whom Wilhelm Gänsler gained the early experience that was to stand him in such good stead as a member of Schnaufer's crew, involved approaching the bomber from astern (*hinten*) and below (*unten*) and then pulling up and firing so that the burst of bullets and shells from the fighter's forward-firing machine-guns and cannon swept through the bomber (some pilots could fire much more accurately than this suggests) and then diving away. The fighter came in from below because in so doing he would be hidden against the darker background of the earth while he himself could see his prey silhouetted against the lighter sky. The fighter's main enemy in this manoeuvre was the rear gunner of the bomber, and the fighter's most vulnerable moment came as he fired, because his tracer ammunition gave away his position, and if he peeled off to one side rather than attempting simply to go into a dive when he had completed his attack he risked presenting his underbelly to the rear gunner. It was a manoeuvre that required considerable skill on the part of the pilot, not only in controlling his aircraft precisely but also in judging the deflection angle necessary to ensure accurate fire, and the natural abilities of pilots varied. Some – and Schnaufer was among them – had an built-in ability to 'aim off' to allow for the difference in speed, rather as some men have an instinctive ability to hit clay pigeons with a shotgun. Pilots so gifted would usually give very short bursts of fire and aim to hit the petrol tanks in the wing, while others would need to give long bursts and hope that some of the spray of projectiles would hit a vulnerable part of their target. Then came 'Jazz Music', and with it the night-fighter pilot could, in addition to firing directly ahead of his aircraft, fire upwards while still flying level.

The idea of having cannon fitted into the fuselage of a fighter and pointing upward was not new: a similar scheme had been tried as early as the First World War. Now, however, the idea was more soundly based. Who was the originator of the concept is open to debate and, to

Hauptmann *Heinrich,*
Prinz *zu Sayn-*
Wittgenstein, killed in
January 1944 with a
score of 83. (Hinchliffe)

some extent, to dispute. Several leading night-fighter aces experimented with the idea before it was officially adopted: for example, the
famous Heinrich *Prinz* zu Sayn-Wittgenstein, killed in January 1944
after having shot down 83 enemy – British and Russian – aircraft by
night, had upward-firing cannon unofficially fitted into the fuselage of
the Ju 88 he used on the eastern front in 1943. It is generally accepted, however, that the man who brought the attention of such weapons
to official notice was *Hauptmann* Rudolf Schoenert of II./NJG 5, who
had first experimented with an installation in his Do 217 in 1942.

The concept was one of beautiful simplicity and great practicality.
The night-fighter pilot would position his aircraft some distance below
the enemy bomber, which could usually be seen from there as a silhouette against the sky: and if the sky were very dark, the tell-tale
exhaust flames from the bomber's four engines would mark its position
clearly. Then he would climb gradually and bring his fighter closer,

confident in the knowledge that he was unlikely to be seen by the crew of the bomber, because very few RAF heavies had gun-turrets beneath the fuselage. He was, therefore, in the bomber's 'blind spot'. Two 20 mm. Oerlikon cannon fitted in the top of the fuselage, pointing upwards at a predetermined optimum angle of about 70 degrees to the fuselage and synchronised according to the pilot's preference for range, sometimes as close as 100 feet, were aimed by means of a reflector-sight in the cabin roof. Because the pilot would by now have adjusted his speed to that of his target, there was no need for to aim off for speed difference. As he was unlikely to be seen by the enemy, he had time to make sure his aim was accurate, and he would not be carrying tracer ammunition, and therefore his position below the bomber was unlikely to be betrayed even if he fired and missed. He would usually aim between the fuselage and one inboard engine, where the petrol tanks were located. So accurate was the method in the hands of a competent pilot, and so heavy was the hitting power of the twin cannon, that a burst of less than ten rounds – a brief touch on the firing button – was usually sufficient to set the wing of the bomber aflame and thus ensure its fate. Firing at the wing had the extra advantage that, should there be any bombs on board, the bomber was less likely to explode if explosive cannon shells hit the fuselage. Many German night fighters had themselves been destroyed when their prey exploded close to them. With 'Jazz Music' the main danger was that the bomber would go down so quickly that it would collide with the fighter, but in practice that seldom happened. Some pilots would dive swiftly to one side or the other immediately on firing, but others would calmly move over to one side and observe their victim's final moments.

Why 'Jazz Music'? In the Third Reich jazz music – 'the music of Negroes and Jews' – was labelled 'decadent' and was banned. In the vernacular it was called '*Schräge Musik*': '*schräg*' means slanting, oblique or, as a slang expression, unorthodox or deviant. The cannon were slanting – *schräg* – so someone called it '*Schräge Musik*', and the name stuck.

The official *Schräge Musik* took the form of a conversion set, factory-fitted, and the programme to equip night fighters began in Spring 1943. Reportedly the first British bomber shot down using the upward-pointing guns (twin 30 mm. MK 108 cannon, in this case) was destroyed over Berlin in May 1943 by *Hauptmann* Schoenert, and several kills were obtained by this new method during the attack on Peenemünde in August. Fritz Rumpelhardt cannot remember exactly when the new device was fitted to Heinz Schnaufer's aircraft, but places it in the latter part of 1943, possibly before he, Rumpelhardt, rejoined Schnaufer's crew in October.

Since the end of the war there has been a lot of debate about the effectiveness or otherwise of *Schräge Musik*, just as during the war there were those German nightfighters who swore by it and those who disliked it. Two factors, seen from the Bomber Command side, are worth mentioning. Firstly, the 'scarecrow' debate: from mid-1943 onwards

Twin Schräge Musik *cannon are clearly visible on this crashed Ju 88. Photos of* Schräge Musik *on the Bf 110 are rare.* (Hinchliffe)

there were increasingly frequent reports from Bomber Crews of what looked like aircraft exploding in the bomber stream. It was eventually accepted that these were devices fired by the German Flak services, specially designed shells that exploded in such a way as to simulate a bomber blowing up, the belief being that they were intended to have an adverse effect on the morale of the bomber crews. They were dubbed 'scarecrows'. In fact no such device existed. What many of the crews were seeing were in fact bombers exploding without seeing the tracer that usually marked a fighter attack, probably the result of *Schräge Musik* slightly misaimed. Secondly, it was not until late in 1944 that the existence of such weapons was confirmed by RAF Intelligence, and even then no warning was given to the crews that they might be attacked from directly below. Frequently, crews – or at least those who survived – thought they had been hit by flak, which was quite natural. With flak, as with *Schräge Musik*, there was no warning, just sudden, violent noise and the awareness that your aircraft was on fire and mortally damaged: possibly, for the fortunate, there would be just time to escape by parachute before the bomber went into a near-vertical dive from which there was no escape.

As already said, *Nachtjagd* pilots varied in their attitude to *Schräge Musik*. Some found it uncomfortable to bend their head backwards to look through the roof-mounted sight while attempting to control the aircraft and fire the guns, which they had to do by sense of feel. Some, like Hans-Joachim (Achim to those close to him) Jabs, *Kommodore* of NJG 1 and with a score of fifty victories, found that it went against their natural instincts of fighter pilots: Jabs even had *Schräge Musik* taken out of his aircraft. Many, on the other hand, found the method so safe, so simple to use and so effective, that they virtually abandoned the more dangerous, more difficult '*von hinten unten*'.

According the Fritz Rumpelhardt, who shared 100 kills with Schnaufer, Schnaufer favoured *Schräge Musik* and used it whenever he could in preference to the more traditional form of attack. Yet Fritz Engau, on the basis of remembered conversations, maintains that Schnaufer opposed the idea and preferred to approach his target from astern and below. In support of his contention Engau quotes a British Air Ministry Intelligence report based on a debrief of Schnaufer at the end of the war, in which, Engau says, Schnaufer told his interrogators that he had shot down 'twenty to thirty' using his upward-firing guns. It is of interest to look at this controversy, which is a good example of the many myths and bones of contention that still attach to Schnaufer.

Engau writes positively:

> When *Schräge Musik* was being installed here and there, Schnaufer was in no way enthusiastic about it. He would not think about giving up his fixed guns [sic – Engau means his nose-mounted guns. *Schräge Musik*, too, was fixed]. He called it an unnecessary 'crutch'. He expressed himself along these lines: 'It's no more than a crutch! You fly underneath as if you going into a parking place, stay nice and horizontal and press on the button. A few times doing that and I'll have forgotten how to fly!'
>
> That was pure Schnaufer! He didn't want to divorce himself from his steep attacks, his inimitable 'peel-offs', the freedom and mobility he had as a pilot. For him flying was something more than sitting like a dummy behind the joystick.

Engau goes on to say that Schnaufer would not have been Schnaufer, however, if he had not considered the pros and cons of the matter, and he concludes: 'His airman's temperament, however, meant that he didn't worry himself about the subject too long. In order to justify sticking with his old method of attack he took refuge in the statement, which is certainly correct, that one simply couldn't attack a bomber from below every time.' Engau then makes the somewhat surprising statement that Schnaufer did not have *Schräge Musik* fitted in to his machine until shortly before the end of the war, possibly in October 1944. Against this we have Rumpelhardt's comment, which could scarcely be more diametrically opposed. When asked, 'According to some people, Schnaufer didn't like *Schräge Musik*. Can you comment?' Rumpelhardt answered:

> That is quite wrong. Schnaufer was, in fact, one of the initiators of the weapon. We had been discussing it for a long time. And in 1942 he went to Messerschmitt in Augsburg for a week for talks on the subject. I wasn't personally present at the talks, but we spoke about it afterwards. Schnaufer used to say, '*Wir brauchen eine andere Bewaffnung*,' – 'We need some other kind of armament.' And after we had *Schräge Musik* installed, in late 1943, we used it most of the time. He always used it, unless it was

unserviceable. I can't remember exactly when we had it put in, but I know it was before the end of 1943, probably while I was away at *Kreigsschule*.

And then he went on to describe how Schnaufer would attack using the upward-firing cannon. Again this compares markedly with Fritz Engau's description of the way in which Schnaufer preferred to attack a bomber:

> I would pick up a target on my radar and give continuous corrections, height and azimuth, until I was very close and Schnaufer could see the bomber. Then he would be underneath the bomber. We could see it, because no matter how dark it was the sky was always just a little bit brighter. Then there was nothing more for me to do, and Schnaufer would take over. Then, flying horizontally, he would ease up gradually and fire into the wing of the bomber, usually the starboard wing. We usually went in very close, sometimes as close as thirty metres.
>
> And we had been told that the crew couldn't see downwards. The beauty of *Schräge Musik* was that we could take advantage of the dead angle. Because they didn't have a belly turret, and they couldn't see anything below. Schnaufer seldom needed to make a second attack. In early days, before *Schräge Musik* came along, he sometimes had to do so, sometimes three attacks. And we needed very few shells – I remember one night we shot down a bomber with less than twenty rounds.
>
> And then he was very concerned to get away as quickly as possible, not only because of the bomber's guns. Sometimes there were pieces of the bomber coming off! And I would be pressed against the roof with the G-force. And the wing began to burn fiercely, but the crew had more time to bale out.

These two points of view, those of Engau and Rumpelhardt respectively, are difficult to reconcile, and possible it would be churlish to sit in dogmatic judgement: that is better, in this instance, left to the reader. In the interests of historical correctness, however, comment would seem appropriate. Fritz Engau's acquaintance with Schnaufer, as recorded in his book, lasted from December 1942 to the time that Schnaufer left Saint-Trond for Leeuwarden, August 1943, which was before *Schräge Musik* came into general usage and certainly before Schnaufer himself had it in his aircraft. It would be interesting to know the source of Engau's contention that that happened 'towards the end of the war': and, in all conscience, it would be difficult to envisage a source more reliable than Fritz Rumpelhardt, who was in the same aircraft when Schnaufer was attacking the bombers, even though we must allow for the possibility that even he, being human, might be subject to fallibility of memory after more than half a century.

Leaving to one side the conflicting evidence for a moment, it would seem a good idea to look at the nature of *Schräge Musik* as an item of armament and the different approaches of the night-fighter pilots who used it. As already said, some, like Achim Jabs, didn't like it and wanted nothing to do with it. Others, for their own reasons, used it almost exclusively: it

Major *Paul Zorner,*
Kommandeur
III./NJG 5.

was a very effective weapon and had the attractive advantage of being less hazardous in use. But, for the dedicated fighter pilot, motivated to shoot down as many bombers as possible, it had one great disadvantage: you could not use it spontaneously, as you might do with the cannon in the nose of your aircraft. It was essentially a weapon of stealth, not of reaction. You had to position yourself carefully, come in behind and below your target, creep up, climb slowly, and then press the firing button, a deliberate sequence that took some time. If you found yourself in a stream of bombers, perhaps crossing the stream at an angle, and you glimpsed a Lancaster or a Halifax sliding away below, you could not hope to attack it with your upper guns, but the pilot who reacted rapidly to combat situations and was at home with his nose guns could flick, almost automatically, into an attacking position. The best pilots were the all-rounders, those whose attack was chosen according to the tactical situation he found himself in. Like *Oberleutnant* Erich Jung of II./NJG 2, who, flying a Ju 88, shot down eight in a night in March 1945: 'There were Lancasters here, Lancasters there, Lancasters everywhere. We fired with front guns, upward guns, even with the rear gun, until we had no ammunition left.' And like Heinz Schnaufer who, according to all who knew him or of him, was a most gifted, 'natural' fighter pilot.

Another versatile nightfighter was *Major* Paul Zorner of NJG 5, who scored 59 kills. To try to produce a perspective, we might look how he obtained his kills: fortunately he kept a meticulous list of them and how he made them. His first victory using *Schräge Musik* was his 23rd, in January 1944. Including that one, we are able to look at a sample of 36 of his victories: sixteen were made with his upward-firing guns, twenty with his forward guns. This fits in nicely with what Schnaufer told his British interrogators at Schleswig on 21 May 1945, as recorded in an Air Defence Intelligence report: 'Schnaufer considered that in the later stages of the war 50% of the attacks were carried out with upward firing guns. With the less experienced pilots the tendency was towards upward firing guns.'

This is in fact the very report that Fritz Engau refers to when claiming that Schnaufer shot down only 'twenty to thirty' bombers with *Schräge Musik*[1], and it was summarised in *Luftschlacht über Deutschland*, the German translation of Alfred Price's *Battle over the Reich*. It would not be amiss to look at the report itself. The relevant passage, which occurs in a discussion of the bombers' 'corkscrew' evasive tactic, is badly drafted and confusing, and on close inspection it poses more questions than it answers:

> Schnaufer had attacked 20 to 30 bombers with his upward firing guns at about 80 yards range and of those only 10% saw him, at a range of approximately 150 to 200 metres, and corkscrewed before he could open fire. This pilot claimed to have shot three bombers down with his upward firing guns while they were actually corkscrewing...

The first noteworthy thing is that the report does not say that Schnaufer had 'shot down' these bombers, only that he had 'attacked' them. And there is a confusion in the distances the writer gives, as there is in Schnaufer's reported claim to have shot down three bombers while they were already corkscrewing: three would represent the entire 10% of the 20 to 30 he is reported as saying had attacked and had seen him. The report was simply badly written, and further reading of it shows that it was also grossly inaccurate on at least one point: it claims that Schnaufer said he had been shot down by a Fortress during a Frankfurt raid in 1943. In fact Schnaufer was never shot down. In all, it is unwise to quote this report selectively in support of any contention.

One of the difficulties one meets when trying to write about someone like Schnaufer is that over the years there has been a proliferation of irresponsible articles, booklets and other material written about him, and much of what has appeared in such publications has found it way into the collective but indiscriminate memory, so that myths have been established and legends created. An example relevant to *Schräge Musik* may be found in a long article about Schnaufer in a popular German-language magazine that deals with military subjects, '*Der Landser*'. (A '*Landser*' is an ordinary Germany soldier, the equivalent of a 'Tommy'). The following extract is typical of the whole article – demonstrably wrong on almost every

---

[1] A.D.I.. (K) Report No. 337/1945, in PRO (Kew) file Air 40/1397.

point. The period under discussion is 1944:

> During this phase of the war Schnaufer conceived the idea of not attacking the enemy in the old way, from behind, but doing it in a completely different manner. As he himself had very often attacked bombers from below, aiming at the petrol tanks or the fuselage, always successfully, he foresaw that such a tactic would produce good results in the future. But it was not solely a matter of attacking from below. First of all it was necessary to create the necessary prerequisites: four fixed two-centimetre cannon that could fire obliquely upwards.
>
> Schnaufer passed this proposal up to the *Geschwader* and convinced his superiors of the effects it would have on the enemy. He demanded that this new armament should be fitted in all night fighters.

It might perhaps be though that too much time, too many words, have been devoted to the discrepancy. But in the context of this book the discussion serves to illustrate the fallibility of human memory, the dangers of dogmatism, and the difficulty of producing a historically accurate record after the passage of so many years.

*   *   *

Before we return to Heinz Schnaufer's operational progress, it might be well to introduce another principal character into the chronicle, the then *Leutnant* Georg Fengler. Firstly, something about his background.

Georg Fengler was born in 1921 in Peterswaldau, near to Breslau in East Silesia, of farming stock. He passed his *Abitur* in 1940 and, having volunteered to fly, was called up in October the same year. Why did he volunteer as aircrew?

> That's quite easy to explain. We were going to be called up any way. If you volunteered you could pick what you wanted to do. That's why we volunteered. We wanted to be officers, and volunteering for flying was one way. I was interested in technical things, and the idea of flying attracted me. I hadn't flown before, not even gliders, but flying was the thing to do in those days. As early as 1939 I went with three others from my class to Vienna for aptitude tests. After a few months we got the results, and mine were positive. Then when the results of the *Abitur* were announced I was called up.

Fengler's training as a pilot followed the normal pattern, and he was selected to fly multi-engined aircraft. Then:

> Let me tell you briefly how I came to be a night fighter. I was at Blind-Flying School in Stargard in Pomerania. After blind-flying training we were supposed to go on to bombers. At this time England was being bombed, and the bombers were having a rough time. That was the time of Hitler's craziness – 'We will eradicate London!' – and Göring was part of it as well, they ganged up with each other. I had no intention of being a bomber pilot. I was told that I could stay on at Stargard as an instructor or, if I wanted to see action, there was only one possibility, the *Nachtjagd*.

Fengler was posted to IV./NJG 1 on 1 August 1943:

> So I went to Leeuwarden. Heinz was already with the Second *Gruppe* at
> Saint-Trond. I didn't know him at that time. That was about the time when
> *Major* Lent became *Geschwader Kommodore* and *Hauptmann* Jabs took over as
> *Gruppenkommandeur*. But I didn't start my operational flying at once. I was ill,
> I had diphtheria. But I had enough to keep me busy. I was made Adjutant
> to *Hauptmann* Jabs. We had an excellent Senior Clerk, *Oberfeldwebel* Horst
> Diener.

Achim Jabs was a splendid commanding officer, personally supervising the
on-the-job training of new pilots, including Georg Fengler. 'I owe my life
to *Oberstleutnant* Jabs, as he later became. I flew with him as his Number
Two – formation flying, air tests, all sorts of things, and he made me stick
to his wing-tip, whether left, right, climb, dive, and I had to do it right!
It's the kind of thing they don't teach you when you're being trained. The
most important thing for a night fighter is to know his aeroplane thor-
oughly, and that is what he taught me.' Fengler also gives a vivid picture
of night fighting at that period. He is also interesting on the subject of
Heinz Schnaufer and *Schräge Musik*:

> The radio traffic in England was monitored, and according to the weather
> situation there we knew 99% where the bombers were likely to strike. The
> question was, what direction will they come from? Will they come in from
> the north, over the Scheldt, or will they come in over France? And the most
> important thing was the target – was it North Germany, or the Ruhr, or
> Berlin? When that was clarified, and it was quite obvious that only such-
> and-such a town was likely, we frequently transferred the very same day to
> another airfield, and when things started we took off. And when it was all
> over, and the bombers had gone back, we often had to land away because
> of shortage of fuel, perhaps in Munich, for example, or Nuremberg or
> Stuttgart, or perhaps in the Berlin area. And we would refuel and fly back
> to our own base.
>
> That was what was good about being in the *Luftwaffe* as a flyer. The
> weather was sometimes very bad. And we, the senior crews, the *alte Hasen*,
> we could take our own responsibility for the flight back, and we did so, often
> the same night, even when the airfield was to all intents and purposes closed
> and there were officially no take-offs. It was very pleasant. There was a
> great freedom about flying. In the infantry, or if you're a tank-driver, you
> can't do that!
>
> We were so small, compared with a Lancaster and so on, and we would
> position ourselves under one wing, and then we would aim at the port
> engines, or the starboard engines. We always had the advantage of surprise.
> And it was very difficult for the British gunners to be 100% alert, particu-
> larly when we got *Schräge Musik*. With my crew I would go very close under-
> neath a Lancaster, perhaps thirty metres, and we would talk about it –
> 'Shall we fire at the right engine or the left one?' We always fired blind,
> without tracer, that is. That went for the whole *Nachtjagd*. And I just had to
> touch the button, and we shot off perhaps three or four cannon shells, and
> the bomber was on fire... Of course, before we had upward-firing cannon
> it was different. Then the rear gunner was the *Todeskandidat* – the candidate

for death … Either you had to kill him or he would kill you. Of course, the cannon and machine guns in the nose were more powerful, but in terms of accuracy and potential for causing damage to the bomber *Schräge Musik* was much more effective. And I know, one hundred percent, that Heinz shared that opinion. He was one of the people who developed and tested it. The accuracy was astounding. Heinz shot down a lot of *Viermots* with just a few shells. Just a very short burst, and it was all over. When it was properly synchronized the shells went just where you wanted them to go. And you might say it was a more humane weapon, because there was little direct danger to the crew. With the normal type of fighter attack, firing ahead, then it was very bad for the men in the bomber.

Heinz was a *Staffelkapitän*. Those operational days were in fact a very enjoyable period. We became very close to each other as comrades, and we spent many pleasant hours with each other. We aircrew were all of one age – twenty or twenty-one years old – and as officers we bore a great deal of responsibility on our young shoulders. A *Gruppe* had a strength of about 1,000 men, and there were thirty aircraft that had to be kept operationally serviceable.

For reasons that will eventually become apparent, it might be suspected that Georg Fengler is possibly a biased witness when it come to speaking of Heinz Schnaufer. Nevertheless, his comments are typical of others who knew him:

I know of no one so exemplary, so near to being a genius. He was of highest intelligence, and he set a very fine example. He was very strong-willed and determined in action, so we were always very surprised when we had seen nothing whereas he had shot one or two down. He was an outstanding leader, and he would go through fire for his men. Everybody, without exception, admired him. I never heard any criticism. Yet at the same time he was very unselfish, very modest.

Possibly less likely to be a biased commentator on Schnaufer's personality is Georg Hermann Greiner. Greiner himself was a very successful night-fighter pilot who notched up 51 victories during the war. He had first met Schnaufer on II./NJG 1 at the end of 1941, but the two did not get to know each other well before Greiner went to a different *Gruppe*, II./NJG 2, and their ways parted. In October 1942, when Hitler abruptly called off the intruder offensive against Britain, Greiner's unit moved to Leeuwarden, where it was subsumed into IV./NJG 1, and when Schnaufer joined that *Gruppe* in August 1943 the two met again. Greiner recalls:

When I knew Heinz Schnaufer at II./NJG 1 there was neither time nor opportunity for a close friendship to develop. When we met again at Leeuwarden we were on the threshold of a comradeship that would be tested and proven during war, a solid relationship that developed into a very close friendship and which was destined to last until his tragic death took him from our midst. At the time the thought of such a frightful end would have seemed impossible to us. Despite the dangers and risks of operational flying we never thought of death – probably that was a phenomenon of youth. Such thoughts would probably have had an adverse effect on our readiness to fly. Despite all the tensions of those days we had some very pleasant times together, and the comparatively few losses we were having on the unit then didn't have a great effect on us.

Arising from the friendship that began when we met again, visits to the Schnaufer family home in Calw became a firm component of our relationship. I remember all too well a hospitable, welcoming family house in the *Ledergasse* with its endearing occupants. Firstly there was the dynamic mother, and then the charming brothers and sister. There were also two hard-working servants, always ready to help. Here I met a family without a father, but close and integrated to a degree that one seldom comes across. Each member treasured and cultivated the principle that each of them would support the others, and in return it was taken for granted that all would stand up for any one of them if necessary. After the death of their father the energetic, prudent Martha took the reins of the wine business firmly into her hands together with the responsibilities of the large household. But when it came to important matters she never acted without first getting the opinion of the eldest son, Heinz, to whom his younger brothers and sister willingly deferred when it came to making decisions, realising that their mother had a special affection for him. This is always a difficult situation, but they were probably so unselfish in their attitude because Heinz never used his privileged position to his own advantage.

Hermann Greiner

Hermann Greiner describes Heinz Schnaufer's character as a complex one made up of contrasts, and Heinz himself as a man of great natural talents who, while realising that he was gifted, did not see that as any reason to dominate his less gifted fellows:

> Heinz was a completely social being, yet at the same time he was the typical individualist. He was certainly not a loner, yet at the same time he was not the direct opposite, the pathetic type who tries to be friendly with everyone. He possessed the instinctive, healthy and basically decent self-confidence that is frequently found in those who are born gifted. He was by nature modest and reserved, yet he had a charismatic charm that was hard to resist. It was a combination of personal characteristics typical of the multi-talented. He would have succeeded in any walk of life. Fate had made him a *Luftwaffe* officer and night-fighter pilot, but he could equally have been a captain of industry, in which case whatever he was producing would have sold not because of its intrinsic quality but because of his leadership strategy. He was a born leader of very high quality, and he understood quite clearly, and used to his advantage, the 'long-rein' style of leadership. Despite having high command responsibility at a very early age he never showed signs of stress, but always seemed calm and relaxed. Natural genius and a sense of humour do not always go together, but Heinz was the exception that proved the rule. He would often burst into boyish laughter, hearty or kindly, but never disproportionately. When he had reason to complain or to admonish someone, which happened occasionally, he never raised his voice to give emphasis to what he had to say. Just the opposite: we all knew that the more he toned down his voice the more seriously he meant it.
>
> To try to describe Heinz Schnaufer as a human being, as I am doing now, must inevitably end up in repetition, and that is because his humanity emerges as the central component of every chapter of a description of his life.

There was unanimity among those sources who knew Schnaufer personally interviewed in preparation for this book when they spoke of his character. None of them had a bad word to say about him. Their views are summed up succinctly by Ludwig Meister:

> Heinz Schnaufer was a true comrade, also ready to help. His achievements were the result of a remarkable calmness and balanced character, as well as a very acute intelligence. In contrast to many highly-decorated officers he was the personification of modesty. It was no wonder that he was extraordinarily popular among his subordinates.

Others, Martin Drewes, Kurt Meyer and Georg Fengler among them, have already asserted that Schnaufer was politically neutral despite having been educated at a Nazi school for the élite of the Third Reich, and their views will be looked at more closely later in the book. When approached for his views, Hermann Greiner was at first reluctant to comment. He pointed out that anything he might say would almost inevitably generate speculation, possibly of an adverse kind; and equally, he said, there might be similar speculation if he didn't comment. 'Therefore,' he wrote after some consideration, 'it is my opinion that this decision should be left to

Kurt Meyer, who was at Napola with Schnaufer, later became a bomber pilot. He was shot down and severely wounded on the Eastern Front. This photograph was taken in 1941 during his bomber training. (Meyer)

the author. He can best decide what is appropriate to the biography as he conceives it.'

Hermann Greiner's concern is easy to understand. Nazism was an evil thing, and many unspeakable crimes were committed in its name, and today's Germans, particularly those who survived the war, have to bear the legacy of those tragic days. To say that the *Napola*-educated Schnaufer was not a died-in-the-wool Nazi, as the term is generally understood, is to risk being accused of whitewash, if nothing worse. But Greiner did contribute, and his views remain relevant:

> I will confine myself to a small number of comments. The fact that Heinz Schnaufer attended a *Napola*, and the type of education dispensed there, should not be taken as indicators of the political attitudes of my friend. I do not know what was behind his choice of such a school, but presume that he was attracted to it by reason of his exceptional natural talents. *Napolas* were known by the high standards of the education that they provided, and were reserved for young men of high intelligence. From this comment on the high standard of education one must exclude the dis-

semination of political ideology: and after all one could let that in through one ear and out through the other. You must take it from me that Heinz could not have been in the least brainwashed, and that he kept his fundamental principles, which stemmed from a liberal family, undiminished. After all, I knew him for more than nine years, including four years of close friendship during the war, and for him those were the decisive years during which his character was moulded. Despite the type of school he went to he was, when I knew him, quite positively on an opposite course to the ruling caste. To young men of our year, mostly brought up in a solid, humanistic environment, Nazi propaganda seemed pathetic, strident, unbelievable and tasteless. We in the *Nachtjagd* reacted against it, and we did so with immunity. And the organised informing that was carried out by supporters of the system was so blatant and insulting that good citizens could not help but be repelled by it.

Shortly after the invasion, when Schnaufer was *Kommandeur* IV./NJG 1, there was a *Führerbefehl* attaching so-called *NS-Führungsoffiziere* – 'National Socialist Leadership Officers'[1] – to military units of company level and above. These people had personal powers greater than those of the commanding officer. They reported on the morale of the units, but from the point of view of Party attitudes. Heinz quickly came to a judgement of Solomon. He resolved the difficult situation to the satisfaction of all members of the *Gruppe* in a simple yet ingenious manner, although in doing so he risked being called to account despite his reputation, his rank, his position or his achievements. He appointed an elderly *Oberleutnant*, experienced and worldly wise, to do the job. The appointment was not without danger for the officer himself. Heinz Schnaufer made it a condition of the appointment that he, the *Kommandeur*, would see and approve the officer's monthly report on the morale and political attitudes of the men before it was sent off to headquarters. But they had to produce a moderate report in such a way that it spoke of political attitudes that the Party expected but which the men in no way practised.

Georg Fengler, who was to become Schnaufer's adjutant when Schnaufer took over command of IV./NJG 1 from Jabs, recalls a different aspect of this subject; possibly he is speaking about another incident. According to him, the officer who was officially appointed as *NS-Führungsoffizier*, *Oberleutnant* Kühnel was an unpopular man and was never accepted by the other officers as one of them. At some subsequent point there was a call from the military authorities for personnel who were considered dispensable to be nominated for service on the Eastern front, a requirement that was known in the vernacular as '*Soldatenklau*'– 'soldier-stealing'. Schnaufer, according to Fengler, nominated Kühnel. It seems likely that the officer that Greiner speaks about was appointed in his place.

---

[1] These were officers appointed to monitor the political attitudes of personnel on the unit and to report to the Party on their morale.

CHAPTER SEVEN

October to December 1943

Berlin. Detachment to Quakenbrück.
The Knight's Cross, belatedly.

On the night of 8/9 October 1943 there were 26 Wellingtons among the 504 aircraft that went forth to attack Hanover, and one was lost. This was the last Bomber Command in which Wellingtons participated, and from now on all the heavy bombers used by Harris were four-engined. There was also a diversionary attack on Bremen comprising 119 aircraft, while small numbers of Mosquitoes flew nuisance raids against German cities. These Mosquitoes were part of the Light Night Striking Force[1], initiated in mid-1943 by Air Vice-Marshal Donald Bennett, commanding the Pathfinder Force, when he used No. 139 Squadron:

> …as a 'supporting squadron' to carry out diversion raids to attract fighters away from the main stream at appropriate moments during the attack. This tactic proved very successful, and often diverted the fighters away from the main target. I also used the squadron for nuisance raiding – an idea entirely of my own, which I quietly insinuated into the operations of the Group, without its being particularly noticed for some time. When the C-in-C did notice it, he thoroughly approved of it, and the idea grew.[2]

Mosquitoes acting in this rôle undoubtedly had a great effect on the night-fighter reaction to Bomber Command: it was impossible to differentiate on a radar picture between a small machine like a Mosquito and a large one like a Lancaster, and many a German night fighter was scrambled to try to catch aircraft – Mosquitoes – that it had no change of intercepting, in the mistaken belief that they were heavy bombers. The use of the Light Night Striking Force also had the added bonus that the 'Mossies' triggered off air-raid alarms in the cities they passed near to, thus interrupting the sleep of the civilian population, including

---

[1] A confusing name but it does not imply that the force only flew on light nights, but that the aircraft were light.

[2] Quoted from Bennett's book *Pathfinder*, first published 1958 by Frederick Muller Ltd. The 'Light Night Striking Force' does not imply that it operated on light nights, but with light aircraft.

Heinz Schnaufer in his Bf 110.

workers. Nor must it be forgotten that the Mosquito carried a power-ful weight of bombs, so that its attacks were in effect rather more than a 'nuisance'.

On the October night in question, however, the LNSF failed in its ideal of drawing off the fighters. Hanover was quickly recognised as the main target and night fighters scrambled. Of the 27 bombers that were lost, Schnaufer, Rumpelhardt and Gänsler claimed two Halifaxes, Schnaufer's 29th and 30th kills. It is likely that Schnaufer's first victim was a Halifax II from 158 Squadron, Lissett. Captained by Sgt D C R Cater, the bomber had taken off at 2258 hours and was damaged by flak before being attacked by a night fighter, almost certainly that of Schnaufer, and coming down at Schwaförden. Most unusually the entire all-sergeant crew escaped, presumably by parachute, and were taken prisoner.

The hard-pressed city of Hanover – more than 1,200 people had died there on the 8th/9th – was the target once again on the night of the 18th October, but this time cloud over the city meant that the attack was scattered, and the city itself suffered comparatively little damage. Light casualties on the ground do not imply light casualties in the air. The *Nachtjagd* was again active, and eighteen, or five percent of the all-Lancaster force, were missing. This night saw the loss from all causes of the 5,000th Bomber Command machine since the beginning of the war. The night fighters were generating an impressive reputation. From the beginning of 1940 to the beginning of October 1943 they had claimed 2,520 kills. In August 43 alone they had flown 7,807 sorties and

registered 290 victories – but Bomber Command, according to official figures, only lost 275 from 7,807 sorties, an average loss rate of 3.5 per-cent. There was clearly some degree of over-claiming – not really sur-prising in the conditions in which the antagonists were grappling with each other – but nevertheless the figures do give a sobering idea of the strength of both Bomber Command and the *Nachtjagd*, and, on closer reflection, of the frightening nature of the task that the men crewing the bombers were expected to carry out. Loss-rates were averaging 3.5 per-cent per night, and a tour of operations was set at 30. The mathemat-ics were inescapable: 30 multiplied by 3.5 comes to 105, which means that if you completed a tour you were living a charmed life. And indeed the mathematics were supported by the facts: for a Bomber Command crewman to survive a tour at this period of the war was a rare event.

Schnaufer's score increased by one that night, and the entry in his *Leistungsbuch* reads, 'Halifax, 18.10.43, 2025 hours, near Negenborn (NNW Hanover), 5,300 metres', a further example of the difficulty of correct identification in the darkness of the night and the stress of aer-ial combat. Chorley in his *Bomber Command Losses* records that a Lancaster III of 101 Squadron, DV 230 SR-T:

> Took off 1715 from Ludford Magna. Believed shot down by a night fighter and crashed between Brelingen and Negenborn, 20 kilometres NNW of Hanover. Funerals were initially held at Brelingen, since when their bodies have been buried in Hanover War Cemetery.

In late 1943 and early 1944 the new version of Lichtenstein, SN-2, was being introduced. This meant the aircraft carrying larger aerials on their nose, which adversely affected their performance. (Hinchliffe)

All on board perished. Unusually, there were nine. Chorley says that one member of the crew, although recorded as a Bomb Aimer, was probably flying as a special equipment operator. The 'special equipment' was Airborne Cigar, more commonly referred to as ABC, which was operated exclusively by No. 101 Squadron, and this was the first ABC aircraft to be lost in action. The Lancasters of this squadron operated in the main bomber stream exactly as other main-force aircraft, but in addition to a normal bomb-load they carried an extra crew-member, who could speak German. He had at his disposal electronic facilities that enabled him to tune in on German fighter-control frequencies and broadcast a warbling jamming tone to interfere with the night-fighter radio traffic. It did so to some considerable effect, earning among the German crews the nickname '*Dudelsack*', or 'Bagpipes'. ABC could also be used to jam the Germans' VHF system '*Ypsilon*', employed by the ground controllers to track their fighters and by the fighter crews to fix their position. ABC had first been used operationally just ten days previously, when Bomber Command had attacked Stuttgart. Of the 343 Lancasters committed only four, or 1.2 percent, had failed to return, and this at a period when the average loss per night was hovering at around five percent. It is not known whether the low casualties were the result of disruption caused by ABC or because the controllers were fooled by a Mosquito diversionary attack on Munich.

Even though this period is generally called the Battle of Berlin, the longer nights of autumn meant that Harris could also send his force to other long-range targets. Leipzig lies to the south-west of Berlin, and when 358 Lancasters set out to attack the city on the evening of 20 October they met appalling weather conditions. One Bomber Command navigator[1] recalls the raid to this day as 'shambolic', and in the diary he kept during the war he wrote, 'Cloud up to 20,000 feet all the way. Severe icing. Ten-minute orbit and a dummy run. Landed with no petrol at Wickenby. Shaky do.'

The bad weather meant that Leipzig suffered only comparatively insignificant damage, but it did not deter the night fighters, who shot down most of the sixteen Lancasters lost that night. Schnaufer took off from Quakenbrück at 1838 hours and headed west into the approaching bomber stream. Once there he destroyed two Lancasters in quick succession. Both his victims were Pathfinders, and as such were flying towards the head of the bomber stream. The first, from No. 7 Squadron, crashed in flames at Gieten in Holland, to the south-east of Groningen: the second was from No. 405 (Vancouver) Squadron, the only Canadian Pathfinder squadron, and it came down twelve minutes later and about forty miles further east near the small German township of Harrenstätte. Of the fourteen men on board the two machines there was only one survivor, a Canadian gunner from the 405 Squadron aircraft. The navigator of the first Lancaster, Sgt Frank White, was a 'spare bod' flying in place of the crew's regular navigator,

[1] Flight Lieutenant John Chaloner, DFM, No. 49 Squadron.

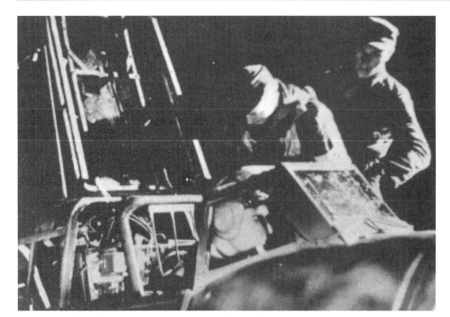

who was sick.

Two night's operations by Schnaufer – low-scoring by his standards – had cost the RAF three Lancasters and twenty-two trained aircrew. And none of them was an 'ordinary' main-force machine. The two Pathfinder aircraft carried highly trained personnel, special radar equipment, and marker flares that would, it was hoped, guide other bombers to their precise target in Leipzig, while the No. 101 Squadron Lancaster Schnaufer had shot down two nights previously had been carrying at least one specialist crewman and specialised jamming equipment. It is, of course, impossible to calculate the indirect negative effects that these kills might have had on Harris's bomber offensive or the positive ones, from the German point of view, on German cities and population, but there can be little doubt about the cost-effectiveness of the 21-year-old Heinz Schnaufer.

Heinz Schnaufer scored just two more kills from Quakenbrück before IV./NJG 1 returned to Leeuwarden on 1 December 1943. They were Schnaufer's 35th and 36th, and they took place in the early evening of the 23rd of November. Harris' Battle of Berlin was entering its most intensive and bloody phase and, encouraged by a comparatively successful attack on the 'Big City' the previous night, the Commander-in-Chief despatched a force of 383 bombers, of which 365 were Lancasters. The Pathfinder marking was to begin at 1958 hrs, which meant an early take-off for the Bomber Command crews, and the force's route took them over the southern tip of the island of Texel and then slightly south of east, passing north of Hanover and then continuing on due east for Berlin. Schnaufer took off from Quakenbrück and headed west. His first victim was another Pathfinder machine, Lancaster III LQ-C of No. 405 (PFF) Squadron, which had lifted off at

Die Me 110 Mit SN 2 Suchgerät und Bordkanonen.

The 'business end' of a Bf 110 with SN-2 radar. By this time some aircraft were also carrying Schräge Musik *upward-firing cannon in addition to the formidable weapons in their nose.* (Buschmann)

1712 from Gransden Lodge and which fell to Schnaufer's guns at 1850 hrs, coming to earth near Meppen. Ten minutes later Schnaufer claimed his second bomber, a main-force Lancaster I from No. 44 (Rhodesia) Squadron. There was one survivor from each crew.

Their detachment to Quakenbrück finished, IV./NJG 1 returned to their Dutch base. Harris was persisting with the Battle of Berlin, and on the evening of the 16th of December he sent 483 Lancasters and 10 Mosquitoes to the 'Big City'. One of the problems that faced Harris when it came to mounting his campaign against the capital city of Germany and the seat of the National Socialist government of the Third Reich was that of routing. The location of the target he was sending his bombers to and its distance from their bases in England left him very little scope for varying the course that they should follow: planning the routes involved a complicated balance of aircraft endurance, bomb- and fuel-loads and the need to minimise losses from flak and fighters. Diversion raids were of course now being flown by forces of heavy bombers of varying strength and by the versatile Mosquito, electronic and radio counter-measures (ECM and RCM) were used and *Serrate*-equipped intruders patrolled the vicinity of enemy radio beacons and fighter airfields in ever-increasing numbers, but the inescapable fact remained that there was no alternative for the Pathfinders and Main Force crews but to run the gauntlet of a night-fighter force hungry for kills and operating at an increased level of efficiency, thanks largely to von Lossberg's *Zahme Sau* strategy. In the course of the nineteen major attacks on Berlin mounted between August 1943 and March 1945, when the Battle of Berlin was discontinued, the bomber stream had to overfly the Zuider Zee area of Holland thirteen times on its way to the target and eleven times on its way back to England, so that the front-line night-fighter crews of NJG 1, including IV./NJG 1 at Leeuwarden, formed the spearhead of the defence of the *Reich*.

The attack on Berlin on the night of 16/17 December 1943 is extremely well – if not always accurately – documented. After the war had ended Air Ministry Intelligence issued a report[1] on the History of German Night Fighting. Extracts from the War Journal of the General Command of the First Fighter Corps, which had come into the posses-sion of the Allies, were appended. One extract, entitled, in translation, 'Example of Combined Operation of Pursuit, Target-Area and *Himmelbett* Night Fighting', dealt with this raid. 'Pursuit' and 'Target-Area' night fighting were '*Zahme Sau*' and '*Wilde Sau*' respectively.

First indications that a raid was impending came, according to the diary, at 1800 hours, when the radio monitoring service, the *Horchdienst*, detected 'Jay Beams'[2] being switched on in England. There appears to be an error in the time given, because the order to scramble had been given to some of the German night fighters at least half an hour before six o'clock. Be that as it may, the assembly and course of the bomber stream were 'plotted correctly by H2S bearings. Mosquito diversion attacks on Kassel and Hanover were clearly recognised'. The diary summarises British jamming as follows:

> *Korps* VHF jammed by bell sounds, R/T traffic hardly possible, jamming of *Korps* H/F by quotations from Hitler's speeches, *Korps* alternative fre-quency and *Division* frequencies strongly jammed, very sudden jamming of the *Soldatenrundfunksender* [forces' broadcasting station] 'Anne Marie' by continuous sound from a strong enemy jamming station.[3]

The weather was 'widespread mist and fog at 150 to 300 feet in the North German plain, and good in South Germany', and the diary records that because of the bad weather only crack night-fighter crews were scrambled. A total of 92 night fighters, not counting single-engined *Wilde Sau* machines, which operated independently, were sent aloft. Fighters from the First Fighter Division (*1. Jagddivision*, Holland and Belgium) were ordered to fly towards the radio beacon at Hanover and listen out for the running commentaries that would help them to pen-etrate the bomber stream (*Zahme Sau*) while others from the same *Division* headed directly for Berlin to do battle freelance (*Wilde Sau*).

---

[1] A.D.I.(K) Report No. 416/45, held at the Public Record Office, Kew.

[2] 'Jay Beams' (or J-Beams) were Lorenz-type homing beams sometimes used by Bomber Command crews on their way back from operations. They were in reality part of a British decep-tion operation mounted against the Germans.

[3] A commentary for use by night fighters was broadcast on public broadcast stations, to which category the *Soldatenrundfunksender* (there were several) belonged.

Machines from the *3. Jagddivision* (France), also flying *Zahme Sau*, headed in the direction of the radio beacon at Osnabrück, while some aircraft from the *2. Jagddivision* (North Germany, Schleswig Holstein, Denmark) flew towards the radio beacon at Bremen. Bomber Command took a northerly return route that night, and in an attempt to intercept the heavy bombers on their way back further fighters from *1. Jagddivision* were scrambled after the attack itself to *Himmelbett* areas over Schleswig Holstein and Jutland, but in the event they had little success. The *Nachtjagd* claimed eighteen kills, while the RAF figure for aircraft that did not return was twenty-five.

Martin Middlebrook[1] comments on this raid, as indeed he does on the majority of Bomber Command raids during the war. To give a glimpse of another dimension of the battle in which Schnaufer and other German night-fighter crewmen and their Bomber Command opposite numbers were engaged, and possibly to give pause for thought about the wider implications of a bombing war, Middlebrook is quoted here:

> Berlin was cloud-covered but the Pathfinder sky-marking was reasonably accurate and much of the bombing fell in the city. The local report says that the raid had no identifiable aiming point but the central and eastern districts were hit more than other areas. Little industrial damage was caused; most of the bombing hit housing and railways. Conflicting figures of the number of dead are given; the overall total may be 720, of which 279 were foreign workers – 186 women, 65 men and 28 youths. 70 of these foreigners – all from the East – were killed when the train in which they were travelling was bombed at the Halensee station. In the city centre, the National Theatre and the building housing Germany's military and political archives were both destroyed. The damage to the Berlin railway system and to rolling stock, and the large numbers of people leaving the city, were having a cumulative effect upon the transportation of supplies to the Russian Front; 1,000 wagon-loads of war material were held up for six days. The sustained bombing had now made more than a quarter of Berlin's total living accommodation unusable.

Flying in Bf 110 G9+DZ, Schnaufer, Rumpelhardt and Gänsler took off from Leeuwarden at 1737 hours. The heavy cloud over North Europe, with poor visibility and a cloud base of 100 feet, meant that Schnaufer's was the only machine to take off meet the advancing bombers: despite Leeuwarden being officially closed he had asked for, and been granted, special permission to scramble. The account that follows of his work that night indicates that he was freelancing, and was not one of those sent to the beacon at Hanover but went instead to the beacon code-named '*Eisbär*', which was located on the Zuider Zee, thus heading out towards the advancing bomber stream. According to Fritz Rumpelhardt:

---

1 *Bomber Command War Diaries*, by Martin Middlebrook and Chris Everitt, first published in 1985 by Viking Books.

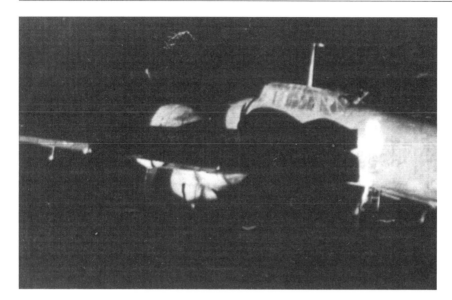

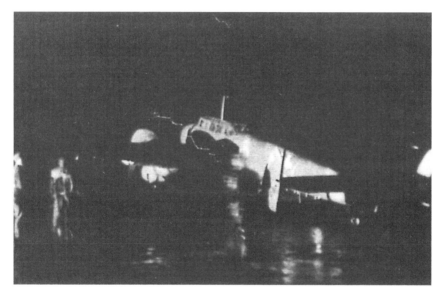

'A creature of the dark'. The Bf 110 in its allotted element. (Greiner).

We took off at 1737 hrs, one single night fighter against the enemy bomber stream. The crew didn't even ask themselves whether the risk was worth taking, but we were a little angry with him for volunteering. The cloud-base was 100 feet, and in the mist the obstruction lights could only just be made out. Within seconds the Me 110 was surrounded by thick cloud. The engines were turning at full throttle. It was very clear to Schnaufer that a dangerous period lay ahead of him, with a high risk of icing that could spoil the aerodynamic profile of the wings while adding considerably to the weight of the aircraft. But despite the aircraft becoming progressively less responsive to the controls Schnaufer suc-ceeded in coming through the danger zone, and after what seemed an age of climbing and hoping against hope we broke cloud at an altitude of 16,000 feet. There was a bright, starlit heaven, and we rapidly forgot the fears we had just come through.

R/T communication with the ground station in the *Eisbär* area was first class, and we were soon ordered to head due north. It was not before time, because the approaching bomber stream had already reached the north-west extremity of the area. Schnaufer and Gänsler stared into the night, while I concentrated on my radar screen. Soon I picked up an echo at a range of about 4,000 metres. Over the intercom I gave Schnaufer several alterations of course, and then Gänsler picked out a faint shadow – the bomber. With skill born of practice the pilot manoeuvred his aircraft below the Lancaster, which was heading east, unsuspecting. A slight adjustment of position, and Schnaufer opened up with *Schräge Musik*, two MK 108 cannon firing almost vertically and built into the rear half of the fuselage. Whenever he could Schnaufer liked to aim at the fuel tanks, which were located in the wing between the two engines. On the one hand, this was the most effective way to attack, because the petrol tank would explode, while on the other hand the crew had a better chance of getting out with their parachutes. Immediately after the first burst of fire a huge sheet of flame erupted from the wing. The night almost turned into day. Schnaufer flung the Me 110 into a dive so that we would not come into the field of fire of the bomber's guns, and also to avoid any falling wreckage.

With enormous speed, and trailing a long banner of flame behind it, the mortally wounded bird sped downwards, wheeling over one wing before disappearing into the bank of cloud. As we later found out, it crashed into the Friesian Canal near Follega at 1801 hours.

Schnaufer's victim was the No. 7 (Pathfinder) Squadron Lancaster MG-L captained by Warrant Officer W A Watson of the Royal Australian Air Force. There were no survivors.

Five of the crew of Lancaster III MG-L of No. 7 Squadron, PFF, shot down by Schnaufer over Holland on 16 December 1943. From left to right, back row: *Flight Sergeant W. M. Waterman, navigator; Sergeant (later Warrant Officer) W. A. Watson, RAAF, pilot; Flight Sergeant Lloyd Robinson, RAAF, Bomb Aimer:.* Front row: *Flight Sergeant John Butterworth. RAAF, Wireless Operator; Sergeant Doug McWha, RearGunner. All were killed.* (Cheetham)

In March 1944 an article in a German newspaper headlined 'Four British Bombers destroyed in an Hour' presented a rather different picture:

> The first enemy machine that they met was a so-called 'Pathfinder' aircraft. No sooner had the night fighter positioned itself behind the black giant[1], no sooner had the first shells left the cannon, than fire broke out in the huge fuselage. The Lancaster had been overwhelmed virtually without defending itself. The cargo of bombs that it was carrying had exploded and sealed its fate. 'The fragments of the bomber fell to earth beneath me like gold and silver rain,' said the night fighter, describing his success.

There is a graphic eye-witness account of the event from the farmer on whose land the Lancaster came down, *M'heer* Bangma:

> I was in the kitchen when an enormous explosion lit up the field facing the kitchen window. The window was smashed and a ball of flame flew straight over the farmhouse roof. Later this was found to be one of the engines, which landed in a ditch behind the farm.

Accompanied by his mother, *M'heer* Bangma went into the yard and saw four bodies quite close by, all looking as if they were just asleep. Pathetically, one was wearing a parachute that was partially open. The Germans came later and took the bodies away. Next day the cockpit canopy of the Lancaster was discovered resting against a hedge in the field.

Rumpelhardt goes on:

> By 1812 hours the second British Lancaster went down. It came to earth at Esterga, a few kilometres to the north of Lemmer.

The version in the newspaper article reads as follows:

> Shortly afterwards he came across his second victim, an aircraft of the same type. With lightning reflexes *Oberleutnant* Schnaufer flung his aircraft round. But the enemy had already seen him, and bullets from the English rear gunner were spraying towards him. He was a determined adversary, this man in the rear turret of the British bomber. With desperate tenacity he went on firing his well-aimed bursts, even as his aircraft became a flaming torch in the sky and then dived into the depths.

Schnaufer's second victim was once more a Lancaster from No. 101 Squadron – it will be recalled that he had shot one from that unit down on 18 October 1943 – carrying, in addition to the normal crew of seven, a specialist 'ABC' operator. All eight on board died. It was Schnaufer's practice to make a note in his *Leistungsbuch* when he came

---

[1] Schnaufer's kill was not made from astern, but from below by means of *Schräge Musik*. The device was on the secret list at that time, however, and could not be mentioned in the press.

under enemy fire, and it is of interest, despite what appeared in the press, that there is no such mention in his record of this kill.

The third aircraft that Schnaufer destroyed that night was Lancaster III EA-O of No. 49 Squadron, which had taken off from Fiskerton at 1627 hours. Again all the crew perished. Rumpelhardt:

> Because of the excellent visibility the bombers were able to see the tragic fate of their comrades, and they were warned. They tried to avoid the night fighters' attacks by means of the so-called 'corkscrew' defensive manoeuvre. But Schnaufer, who had a lot of operational experience, would not let himself be shaken off, and at 1823 the next enemy fell near Oudentrijn. After the attack this machine continued to fly on ahead before it went into its death-dive. We could not understand why the crew didn't bale out instead of going to their death with their aircraft, as we later found out that they did.

Anyone reading the 1944 newspaper article might be forgiven for thinking the writer was describing a different combat:

> Profiting from experience, the next victim was approached in such a way that the rear gunner had no opportunity for successful defence. But the plan failed. [Quoting Schnaufer]: 'We had ventured too close to the

Schnaufer boarding his Bf 110.

black giant. When he suddenly went downward in a defensive manoeuvre we nearly collided with him. To make matters worse, he was already blazing fiercely, so that I imagined that I could feel the heat on my skin. The glowing pieces that my shells had torn off him were spraying around us. In previous aerial combats I had almost had my own wings set on fire by flames from enemy aircraft. It could have meant the end for us. I don't know how we managed to avoid that fate now. The enormous air pressure from the exploding Lancaster made me lose control over my own aircraft for a matter of seconds, and I found myself diving earthwards, out of control. Only after we had gone down several hundred metres did I manage to pull out of the dive. But our nerves were still vibrating, and we were happy to see our dangerous opponent destroyed in the detonation of its own bombs as it hit the ground.'

Rumpelhardt records Schnaufer's fourth successful encounter that night somewhat laconically:

> Before the bomber stream had left *Raum Eisbär* behind I was able to carry out another successful radar interception. The enemy crew had seen us, and the pilot tried to evade by means of violent manoeuvres. After several attacks, however, his fate was sealed. His Lancaster crashed at 1841 hours only five kilometres from the airfield at Leeuwarden.

The fourth kill was a Lancaster Mark II, QO-N of No. 432 Squadron, which had taken off from East Moor at 1629 hours. The aircraft was captained by an American, Flying Officer W C Fisher, while two

Canadians, two Australians and two RAF men made up the crew of seven. This time two men survived to become prisoners of war, Sergeant O D Lewis of the RCAF and Flight Sergeant M A T Brudell of the RAAF. The newspaper version was once more rather more dramatic:

> It was the flight mechanic [i.e. Willem Gänsler], a comrade proven in many a combat who had so far participated in thirty-four victories, who was the first to make out the fourth victim that night. The enemy could not have failed to notice the fate of those who had gone before him, because on nights like that one can see from a long distance the burning torches that are crippled aircraft on their dive to the ground. And the British were on the alert. That was proved by the way that they were flying defensive manoeuvres in an attempt to avoid their unseen enemy. It was also proved by the way that tracer bullets sprayed from the bomber as the Me 110 was finally detected as it made its fourth stalking approach that night. Now the fight was on. A violent dog-fight developed beneath the stars, and when it finally ended, with victory going to the night fighter, *Oberleutnant* Schnaufer summed it up with the words, 'Soldiers' luck was on our side. I was lucky to hit the Lancaster in good time, otherwise it could easily have been us who were shot down.'

Within the space of forty minutes Schnaufer had destroyed four Lancasters and sent twenty-seven young men to their death. Now Schnaufer had to get back down to the ground, and the weather was still far from favourable. Fritz Rumpelhardt:

> Four kills in forty minutes – that was quite an achievement. But our greatest test was still to come. How were we to land our Me 110 in such impossible weather conditions? There seemed to be little chance of finding another airfield to divert to, because all of Western Europe lay under thick fog. We considered baling out, but decided against it. There was only one thing to do – to head back for our base, Leeuwarden. Using radio bearings we soon arrived there, and then it was a matter of descending though the thick layer of cloud with all its hazards. Our nerves were near to breaking-point, because even after four approaches we were still unable to see the airfield. Then, as if by a miracle, we found a gap in the clouds and we could see the perimeter and runway lights through a light mist. The quickest way of losing height is by side-slipping, and by doing that Schnaufer succeeded in landing his night-fighter aircraft safely. Believe me, until then I had never believed in a Higher Power!

Overleaf: Two post-war German magazines sensationalise Schnaufer's deeds. The contents are virtually identical, even though two individual authors are named.

It is interesting to compare these two accounts of the same events, the recollections of someone who was there and the version published in the press. Yet one can readily accept journalistic licence and the wartime necessity to maintain civilian morale by glamorising the fighting forces and retailing heroic deeds – the Germans were not alone in that – as reasons for the tone of the 1944 article. It is less easy to condone the distortion of history by irresponsible reporting long after the fighting was over: again '*Landser*' is the offending publication:

Alarm! A formation of bombers is flying in towards Holland, its target the Ruhr area. The *Gruppe* prepares to take off, the aircraft climb aloft and disappear into the night.

'*Achtung!* Enemy aircraft in the Follega area!'

Schnaufer has understood. At maximum speed he races into the designated area, peering into the sky. He is lucky – the visibility is good. There – a shadow. Dark and big. It can only be an Englishmen. Schnaufer speeds in behind it, loses it from sight, suddenly discovers it again beneath him. 'Lancaster,' he says to his radar man, and by now he is on its heels. Then everything occurs so quickly that the rear gunner never knows what has happened. After the very first burst of fire the bomber explodes and falls to earth like a rain of fire. The clock shows 1801 hours.

Eleven minutes later, north-west of Esterga [*sic*], he sees another two machines. One is already under attack by another German night fighter, so he takes the second one and shoots it down in his first attack.

A further eleven minutes afterwards the third Lancaster learns his lesson. That was near Obetrijsne [*sic*] at 6,000 metres altitude. At 1841 hours Schnaufer destroys another Lancaster near Wirdum.

This represents the greatest success so far for the young *Oberleutnant*. Four bombers in forty minutes! Indeed, the whole *Gruppe* enjoys good fortune this night. The British bomber force is completely scattered, and more than two-thirds of the attacking machines are shot down.

For this action Schnaufer is decorated with the Knight's Cross on 31.12.1943.

The writer is correct – for once – when he says that Schnaufer received the Knight's Cross to the Iron Cross on the last day of 1943, but not in saying that he was awarded it for this one action alone. The prestigious decoration was not given for any one single achievement, but came after an officer – or occasionally an NCO – had proved himself by a consistent run of achievement. There seemed, at that period of the war, to be no set number of kills after which a member of the *Nachtjagd* was honoured with the *Ritterkreuz*, although later in the war it was customary to receive it after making twenty-five kills. When he got his Schnaufer had exceeded that number by seventeen. Paul Gildner, for example, – an *Oberfeldwebel* at the time – had been decorated with the Knight's Cross after only 14 night victories and four by day; *Oberleutnant* Egmont *Prinz* zur Lippe-Weissenfeld after 21 night kills; *Oberleutnant* Helmut Lent after a total of 22, including eight by day; *Oberleutnant* Manfred Meurer after 23; and the 'Professor of night fighting', *Oberleutnant* Ludwig Becker, when his score had reached 25. Admittedly these night-fighter pilots were honoured in the earlier part of the war, and it might be that victories were coming so quickly in 1943 that the awarding of Knight's Crosses just could not keep up with the demand. But when one takes into account the fact that Schnaufer's promotion to *Oberleutnant* had also been delayed, one cannot help but wonder whether, perhaps, he was looked upon with disfavour somewhere at a higher level in the *Luftwaffe*. Perhaps he had 'put up a black' – blot-

ted his copybook in some way. But that is idle speculation, and we must revert to the task of detailing the successes of his career.

In addition to those destroyed by Schnaufer, another Lancaster went down in the same general locality, on the banks of the Zuider Zee, that night, and it too, like Schnaufer's first victim, was from No. 7 (Pathfinder) Squadron. The satellite airfield at Bergen, situated near Alkmaar on the west coast of Holland, was less affected by the mist that had to all intents and purposes closed Leeuwarden down, and *Leutnant* Heinz Rolland took off from there and shot down Lancaster II MG-D, which crashed with the loss of all on board just a few kilometres east of Alkmaar. No. 7 Squadron was destined to lose four aircraft that night, with only three crewmen out of the total of twenty-eight surviving.

The twenty-five bombers lost represented 5.2 percent of the Lancaster force, but there were other hazards besides fighters and flak that had to be faced by Bomber Command crews whenever they took to the air, and this night the bad weather, which was not confined to the Continent, took an even heavier toll than did the German defences. Thirty Lancasters crashed in England on return because of low cloud at their bases and a shortage of petrol: the long route back from Berlin that had taken them over Denmark and the North Sea had left little room for error in the calculation of fuel consumption. No. 97 (Pathfinder) Squadron alone lost seven machines in this way, but only one to enemy action. In addition to the Lancasters that came to grief when they arrived back from the Berlin raid, two others had crashed in mid air soon after take-off and a further six aircraft from other opera-

tions – two Stirlings, two Halifaxes and two Lysanders – also succumbed to the bad weather conditions. The human cost was high:
despite being over home territory, over 150 men died in their crashing
machines.

Heinz Schnaufer marked the end of the year 1943 by adding two
more RAF bombers to his score on the night of the 29th/30th. As Fritz
Rumpelhardt continues:

> On 29.12.43 the crew of Heinz Wolfgang Schnaufer took off again in
> similar weather conditions. Once more the RAF's aim was the destruc-
> tion of Berlin. At 1848 hours we succeeded in destroying a Halifax near
> Dijkhuizen and at 1903 hours a Lancaster near Lingen.

The Halifax was from No. 10 Squadron, No. 4 Group, based at
Melbourne, Yorkshire, while the Lancaster was a No. 408 Squadron
aircraft. 408 Squadron belonged to No. 6 (Canadian) Group, and its
pilot, Flight Lieutenant W T Wilton, and three other members of the
crew belonged to the RCAF. Again all on board went to their death:
there seemed little to substantiate the belief, professed by many German
night fighters, including Fritz Rumpelhardt and Georg Fengler, that
'*Schräge Musik*' was a more humanitarian weapon than forward-firing
cannon.

In the course of the year Schnaufer had destroyed 35 bombers, and

*Probably February 1944.
Oberleutnant
Schnaufer,
Kommandeur
IV./NJG 1, is now
wearing the
Ritterkreuz, awarded to
him on 31 December
1943, by which time he
had scored 42 kills.
Jabs, Kommodore
NJG 1, is in the centre
and to the right is
Weissflog, Jabs' radio
operator. (Jabs)*

his score now stood at 42. He was at fourteenth place on the 'league table' of successful night fighters, which was headed by Lent with 76 kills and *Prinz* zu Sayn-Wittgenstein with 68.

The combination of freelance interception, as exemplified by *Zahme Sau*, *SN-2* radar and *Schräge Musik*, plus the great bravery and skill of such as Heinz Schnaufer, made the *Nachtjagd* a formidable adversary for Bomber Command. Once having infiltrated the bomber stream a good team – because the radar operator was indispensable in the matter of bringing his pilot into visual range of a target, while the eyes of the 'Third Man' were an extra aid to picking out the shadows that repre-

Schnaufer wearing the Knight's Cross (Ritterkreuz). This was a prestigious decoration, much sought after by Nachtjagd *pilots. It was usually awarded after about 25 kills, but Schnaufer did not receive his until he had shot down 42 bombers.* (Diener)

sented enemy bombers – could frequently, as Schnaufer had demonstrated on the 16th December, move on rapidly from one victory to
another. Yet Schnaufer's four in a night was not, by standards prevail-
ing among the night-fighter men at that time, outstanding. There had
already been thirteen cases of individual night-fighter pilots having shot
down five or more in a night, and on 20/21 December 1943, when
Bomber Command had hit at Frankfurt, *Hauptmann* Wilhelm Herget,
Kommodore of I./NJG 4, with whom, it will be recalled, Schnaufer had
disputed a kill exactly a year previously, had himself destroyed eight
bombers.

Membership of a Bomber Command crew, it might safely be said,
was by no means a sinecure.

CHAPTER EIGHT

January to March 1944

Back to Saint-Trond as Kommandeur IV./NJG 1.
Harris persists with Berlin. Past the half-century.

The concentrated series of attacks on Berlin had begun on the night of 23/24 August 1943, and the city had been attacked by Bomber Command eleven times by the end of the year. Losses of bombers in the course of these raids had been daunting, only falling below five percent on four occasions, while on four nights they had exceeded seven percent of the force despatched. In terms of percentage losses the worst night had been that of 2/3 December, which had cost the RAF forty machines, 8.7 percent of the 458 involved. Berlin, although grievously hit, showed no sign of the collapse that Sir Arthur Harris had predicted when embarking on the battle – but then Harris, in his now notorious 'We can wreck Berlin from end to end' minute to the Prime Minister dated 3 November 1943 had added, 'if the USAAF will come in on it,' and the USAAF hadn't: nor, it is only fair to add, could Harris have had any real belief that they would do so. Nevertheless, despite having lost over three hundred machines, Harris persisted with his attacks on the capital.

Berlin was, of course, not the only city against which major forces of bombers were sent during this period, nor was it the only target that cost Bomber Command dear in terms of losses. 569 heavies went to Kassel, for example, on the night of 22/23 October, and 43 did not come back. And the night fighters caused the majority of the losses. Against raids on Berlin alone up to the end of 1943, Schnaufer had shot down 22 bombers.

There would only be eight more operations against Berlin before Harris called it a day in March 1944. Some historians maintain that the losses during this phase of the air battle against Germany were simply too heavy to sustain, and that the Battle of Berlin was a defeat for Bomber Command. Others take an opposite view, pointing to the immense damage in the metropolitan area to both civilian and industrial premises, the heavy loss of life and, above all, the psychological effect of the repeated bombardment.

Be all that as it might, one thing may be stated without fear of contradiction. This was the most successful period for the *Nachtjagd,* which

Leeuwarden, early 1944.
Heinz Schnaufer speaks
with a mechanic working
on his Bf 110.
(Fengler)

claimed 1,674 bombers destroyed from the beginning of August 1943 to the end of March 1944. In the month of January, the most success-ful month for the German night fighters of the whole war, 308 were claimed out of a total of 314 listed by Bomber Command as lost. The Bomber Command aircrew losses for the whole period under consider-ation were in the region of 11,000. Civilian casualties in both Berlin and other cities had been enormous.

Schnaufer's first kill in 1944 did not come until the evening of the 27th of January. The target that night was once again Berlin and Harris had mounted a raid against Heligoland and despatched a mine-laying

Leeuwarden, early 1944, Schnaufer, Kapitän *of 12./NJG 1, at the burial of a comrade,* Leutnant *Rühle, killed in action.*

force to the North Sea, which went ahead of the main force in order to divert fighter attention from the stream. Night fighters were scrambled against these diversionary forces, which is possibly why Schnaufer, flying from Leeuwarden, did not achieve his victory until the leading bombers had passed over Dutch territory and penetrated into Germany. His Lancaster, which came down near a small town called Essen, just to the north of Quakenbrück, was one of four claimed by IV./NJG 1 that night. Despite the early diversion of the fighter force from the main bomber stream, fighters further east were able to get to grips with the bombers, and Bomber Command again suffered heavy losses, 6.4 percent of the force failing to return.

The force of 673 heavy bombers that was routed back to Berlin the following night was sent well to the north, crossing Denmark on both the inward and outward tracks, and so the fighters based in Holland and Belgium did not come into contact with them. There was, however, a strong concentration of German night fighters in the target area, and once again nearly seven percent of the force was lost. The next night, with Berlin the target for the third night out of four, the bombers went in from the north, over Schleswig Holstein, and returned over Holland, so they had to run the gauntlet of the night fighters both in the target area, where more than twenty of the attackers were shot down, and on the way back home as well. The total number of RAF heavy bombers lost, 33, represented 6.2 percent of those that went out, and of them Schnaufer claimed one. The unfortunate Lancaster crew had just crossed the Dutch coast on the way home, possibly congratu-

Heinz Schnaufer by the tail of his aircraft in February 1944. Left to right, *Matzak, Rolland, Schnaufer, Potthast.*

lating themselves on having left the worst of the danger behind, when their machine succumbed to Schnaufer's guns and came down in the sea to the west of Amsterdam at 2215 hours, Schnaufer's 44th kill.

The 45th victory came on the 15th February 1944 – and so did the 46th and the 47th. Once more Berlin was object of Bomber Command's attentions, and this time Harris sent out the largest force, with the exception of those used on the three nominally thousand-bomber raids in 1942, that he had used so far in the war. But whereas the forces used in 1942 had included a large number of twin-engined Wellingtons, now the heavy bombers were all four-engined load-carriers. There were 561 Lancasters and 314 Halifaxes, and they carried a total of 2,642 tons of bombs. Mosquitoes, too, were active, and in addition to the 16 that went with the main force, a further 23 attacked airfields in Holland using *Oboe*, while 14 carried out *Serrate* patrols against the night fighters of the *Luftwaffe*. The route used by the bombers was similar to that which they had used on the previous visit to the 'Big City' – in over southern Denmark, south-east to the target, and back more or less directly, which took them over Holland and exposed them to NJG 1 fighters.

Despite the northern route used by the bombers on the way out, however, night fighters based in Holland and Belgium, listening in to the broadcast *Zahme Sau* commentary, flew north and succeeded in catching the tail-enders of the stream as it crossed the east coast of

Heinz Schnaufer after his 47th kill, February 1944. The fin of his Bf 110 carries the officially authorised 'kill' icons. Later he changed these for small symbols, unique to himself, comprising a silhouette of his victim (twin-engined or four-engined), an RAF roundel and the date of each kill. See Appendix A. (Fengler)

Denmark prior to turning on to its south-easterly heading for Berlin. There the aircraft from Dutch and Belgian bases joined fighters from bases in Germany and pursued the bombers to the outskirts of the city, many of them running so short of fuel that they had to land at bases in Germany. About twenty bombers were shot down during this phase of the attack, and then those who had come through had the long run back home, a distance of some 800 miles, nearly all of it over hostile territory. Among the night fighters held in reserve and waiting to welcome them was that of Heinz Schnaufer. He scored at 2258 hours, 2319 hours and 2333 hours. His first victim came down in the sea off the Dutch coast, his second, No. 115 Squadron Lancaster LL689, near Hoorn and his last in the Zuider Zee. Twenty-seven minutes after the third kill that night – and his 47th overall – Fritz Rumpelhardt congratulated him over the intercom on his 22nd birthday.

When Schnaufer and his crew landed at Leeuwarden at 0014 hours their fellow-aircrew were awaiting them: a celebration was planned. What had originally been conceived as a just a birthday party now had an extra *raison d'être*, Schnaufer's three victories that night. Bottles of champagne were on ice, yet although some of the wine was drunk there was little atmosphere of celebration. Schnaufer had been suffering from stomach pains most of the day but had been unwilling to report sick and so miss an operational flight – with good reason, as it had turned

out. Now the pain was worse. A birthday party at a local Dutch inn had been planned for that afternoon, and on his way there Rumpelhardt learned that Schnaufer had been rushed into hospital with appendicitis. At once Rumpelhardt went straight to the hospital, where he just had time to shake his pilot's hand and wish him well before he went into the operating theatre. Schnaufer was in hospital for about two weeks. He then flew to Stuttgart on leave in a twin-seater aircraft with Wilhelm Gänsler and, in trying to lift his suitcase, burst his stitches and had to go back for further hospitalisation. The next time he flew the Bf 110 was on the 19th March, and the crew's next kill was not until the 23rd.

In the seven months that had past since he had joined IV./NJG 1 at Leeuwarden and assumed command of the 12th *Staffel* Schnaufer had shot down 26 British bombers to add to the score of 21 he had brought with him from Saint-Trond. Now there was a reorganisation within NJG 1. On 1 March Schnaufer, still with the lowly rank of *Oberleutnant* and only just 22 years of age, was appointed *Kommandeur* of IV./NJG 1 to replace Hans-Joachim Jabs, who himself went up in the hierarchy to become *Kommodore* NJG 1. Schnaufer now had charge of three *Staffeln* with a total, including the Staff Flight, of thirty aircraft. Just four days later the *Gruppe* was relocated from Holland to Belgium, and Schnaufer found himself back at Saint-Trond, where he had cut his teeth in the deadly business of night fighting.

Lunching al fresco. *Schnaufer is at the head of the table.* (Greiner)

With the advancement of Achim Jabs to *Kommodore* of the *Geschwader* and of Heinz Schnaufer to *Kommandeur* of the *Gruppe*, Georg Fengler now became Schnaufer's adjutant. The two were already friends as members of the same mess, but now the official relationship strengthened the friendship. Fengler was, one might say, an average night-fighter pilot whereas Schnaufer was clearly a rising star, a holder of the Knight's Cross and destined, should he survive, for even higher things. But Georg Fengler stresses Schnaufer's unassuming nature: it would have been easy, he says, for a man of Heinz Schnaufer's tender years to let his comparatively high appointment go to his head, but that did not happen in the case of Schnaufer. With the officers he was friendly, very popular, but never over-familiar. Nor did the other officers take advantage of his friendliness and his somewhat retiring nature. He was a born leader and both he and his subordinates accepted the relationship unquestioningly.

Hermann Greiner, too, is interesting on the subject of Heinz Schnaufer as commanding officer. Speaking of his qualities as a host, both on duty and in the Officers' Mess – the *Kommandeur* of a *Gruppe* had social responsibilities as well as administrative and operational duties – Greiner writes:

Hans-Joachim Jabs is still wearing the insignia of a Hauptmann. *He was promoted to* Major *on 1 January 1944 and finished the war as* Oberstleutnant. (Greiner)

We had plenty of visitors and guests, for example leaders of other flying units, Commodores and Commanders, to exchange experiences of new weapons, new electronics and new concepts and procedures within the framework of air defence by night. On such occasions Schnaufer demonstrated both his wide knowledge of his subject and his skill and sureness of touch when dealing with high-ranking officers. He also showed his winning ways with his equals in rank and subordinates, who held his experience and his precisely expressed expertise in high regard.

In addition to senior *Luftwaffe* personnel, frequently holding the rank of *General*, we often had local civilian officials and Party functionaries as our guests. Schnaufer was a good host, the son of a generous, hospitable family, and he had breathed hospitality from his early youth. He liked having visitors, inviting guests and giving parties. His wine business enabled him to produce select wines for any occasion, and he offered them to guests and friends in generous measure.

His hospitality to members of the *Gruppe* also arose from his inherent social awareness. As an example, he suggested that the extra flying rations that aircrew received should be drawn weekly in bulk so that a formal, festive dinner could be held, to which the technical personnel, who did not get extra rations, were invited. The suggestion was very popular to all concerned, and it became a firm tradition of the *Gruppe*. Heinz took the opportunities of these dinners to make a short speech thanking all his men for their loyalty and their readiness for operations, which was a great encouragement to them.

Officers of IV./NJG 1, early 1944, left to right: Oberleutnant *Greiner;* Leutnant *Matzak;* Leutnant *Rolland;* Major *Sutor;* Oberleutnant *Schnaufer,* Kommandeur; *unknown;* Leutnant *Potthast;* Leutnant *Fengler. After the war Sutor was able to help Fengler with his resettlement.* (Fengler)

Greiner also comments on Schnaufer's officer qualities, innate powers of leadership and charisma:

> His striking appearance and personality attracted the attention of all those who came into contact with him. His everyday speech was clear, to the point and precise, so much so that it was almost suitable to go directly into print. In this exceptional person the combination of his impeccable appearance, his sympathetic nature and his first-class general education made for a very fine human being.
>
> Schnaufer rapidly formed the reputation, despite his youth, of being a highly gifted leader of men who felt himself duty-bound to look after the interests of his subordinates. He had an uncanny ability to assess a situation and form a judgement – when, for example, to rely on common sense or when reality and reason had to be applied. This is a trait that cannot be learned – it has to be inborn. He was a gifted military leader to whom a generous Nature had given the unusual advantage of being able to attract his subordinates to him by reason of his exceptional personality and the charisma he exuded. He was able to lead his men on a long rein, but he knew instinctively when something was troubling them.

Hauptmann *Breves and* Oberleutnant *Georg Fengler.* (Greiner)

Schnaufer's *Napola* training was a great asset, both in terms of the way it had prepared him for leadership and, no doubt, in the eyes of his superior officers when it came to his selection for appointment to positions of command. But all those who knew him – Achim Jabs, Georg Fengler, Kurt Meyer, Martin Drewes, Fritz Rumpelhardt and others – stress that there was no sign of his having been affected by extreme National Socialist indoctrination. They add, however, that politics were seldom a subject of discussion among the aircrew. There were more important things, such as defending their homeland.

Martin Drewes was *Kapitän* of the 11th *Staffel* at Leeuwarden when Schnaufer had the 12th *Staffel*. A holder of the Oak Leaves to the

12 March 1944: Schnaufer sends a telegram to Martin Drewes congratulating him on the award of the German Cross in Gold. (Drewes)

Knight's Cross with 49 kills to his credit, Drewes is now resident in Brasilia, and he holds Schnaufer's memory in great affection:

I joined the 4th *Gruppe* of *Nachtjagdgeschwader* 1 on 15 August 1943 and took over the 11th *Staffel* from Jabs, who had just been made *Gruppenkommandeur* of IV./NJG 1. Heinz Schnaufer must have arrived at Leeuwarden shortly before me, and he had the 12th *Staffel*. We remained together under Jabs' command until February 1944, when I was given the III./NJG 1 when *Prinz* zur Lippe-Weissenfeld took over NJG 5. A few days later Jabs took over NJG 1 from Streib, and Heinz became *Kommandeur* of IV./NJG 1. We kept in touch. Part of the keeping-in-touch was the frequent Command Conferences that Jabs called at Deelen for inter-unit discussion. During his time as *Kommandeur* Heinz sent me two messages – a teleprinter message and a telegram – which I still have in my possession.

The two messages that Martin Drewes speaks of came in March and May 1944 respectively. At the risk of running ahead of the story, they are translated here. The first, a teleprinter message dated 12 March 1944, is self-explanatory:

To *Oberleutnant* Martin Drewes, III./NJG 1, Athies-Laon.

Dear Martin,

Most sincere congratulations on the award of the long overdue and bitterly earned German Cross in Gold.

Your comrades of IV./NJG 1.

The second message came after Drewes – meanwhile promoted to *Hauptmann* – shot down five bombers on the night of the 3rd/4th May 1944: on the 8th he received this telegram:

To the new star in the night-fighting sky the *Gruppe* congratulates you most sincerely on the latest successes you have achieved and wishes you further fat pickings.

Signed, Schnaufer.

The telegram seems possibly to have inspired Drewes, because before the month of May was out, on the night of the 21st/22nd, he had repeated his feat, destroying a further five bombers. As if not to be outdone, Schnaufer himself, promoted *Hauptmann* on 1 May, claimed five bombers just three nights after Drewes had done it for the second time.

But there were other sides to life in the front line, and another side to the character of Heinz Schnaufer: Martin Drewes writes:

As a form of relaxation we would occasionally go out and do a bit of hunting. The area around Leeuwarden is ideal for hunting duck. Heinz and I once got a shotgun, slung it over our shoulder and trailed along behind a group of enthusiastic 'huntsmen'. Because we had a lot to talk about, and because we didn't come across any 'enemy' ducks, we didn't shoot anything. In itself, that's not a very interesting story, but I tell it simply to show that Heinz was in no way a person who had to be the best at everything he did, including duck-shooting. Had he been that way inclined he would have gone out of his way to shoot as many ducks as he could. His dedication was to his job, and that was night fighting. His motivation never rose from ambition or a desire to be someone special, but rather from a decision of conscience, which was itself a facet of an outstanding character.

Following on from this little story about hunting, I would like to add a sequel. About a kilometre ahead of us the hunters gathered for the '*Streckenlegen*' – that's what German hunters call the laying out of the kill. And Heinz and I had – nothing! And then, to our right and near the river, I saw a wildcat. There was a bang – Heinz had shot it. We walked slowly to where they were laying out the kill, and Heinz laid the wildcat out alongside the ducks on display. Protests and laughter! Smiling, Heinz said it had been a right and proper thing for a fighter pilot to do. He had seen the cat, so he had fired on it. Wildcats destroy young cattle, birds' nests and so, and they have to be shot as long as they are away from built-up areas.

I have told this hunting story to show that Heinz was never the sort of man who had to be the best in anything and everything. There are some unpleasant people who make a point of doing just that. For us Heinz was always the same, no matter how high he climbed. Jabs will certainly confirm that: Heinz and I were members of his *Gruppe* when we first met. Jabs had a felicitous way of leading his unit commanders, his officers and his men. For us he was always a clear-sighted man who never had a great deal to say, but he was a personal example in every situation, and to this day he remains a shining personality.

Unknown occasion at Saint-Trond. Left to right: Weissflog; Schnaufer; Drewes; Sutor; Jabs; Dormann; Förster; von Bonin; Knickmeyer (Fighter Control Officer). Hermann Greiner is lying on the ground. (Greiner)

'Playing the fool'.
Schnaufer is second from
the left, Greiner on his
left. (Greiner)

Independently, Achim Jabs confirms what Drewes says about Heinz Schnaufer's lack of personal ambition for the sake of ambition: 'He was ambitious, but not for himself, only to do his best to protect his homeland. He was no Wittgenstein.' Heinrich *Prinz* zu Sayn-Wittgenstein, the leading night-fighter pilot when he was shot down and killed in February 1944, was ruthlessly ambitious, determined to be the best, which he felt was his vocation and his duty as an aristocrat. Wittgenstein would use his rank to remain on the ground in the operations room until he saw from the general situation map where the bombers were coming, and only then would he take off, often dismissing junior pilots who had been waiting overhead at a beacon for a long time with an R/T message: '*Hier Wittgenstein, geh' weg!*'[1], so that could have the pick of the bombers to boost his own score. Jabs again: 'Schnaufer would never do that – never. On the contrary, he would help his pilots and be happy for them when they were successful.'

There was, in general, far greater rank-consciousness in the *Luftwaffe* than in, for example, the Royal Air Force – far more smart saluting and coming to attention (in the German armed forces accompanied by heel-clicking) in the presence of one's seniors, far more use of formal modes of address: there is no equivalent in German of the generally used 'Sir', and a subordinate usually addressed his superior NCO or officer by his rank: '*Herr Oberfeldwebel*', '*Herr Hauptmann*' and so on. Strict observance

[1] 'Wittgenstein here. Clear off!'

of rank was far more general within the crew of a German aircraft than in a British machine. Whereas the captain of a British bomber was normally 'Skipper', no matter what his rank, and all members of a crew usually addressed each other by their Christian name (there were, of course, exceptions), many German pilots insisted on formality both on the ground and in the air, although others were more relaxed. Similarly, some pilots never allowed those crew-members who were junior in rank to them to use the familiar pronoun, '*Du*', but insisted on being addressed by the formal '*Sie*' at all times. Schnaufer, Rumpelhardt and Gänsler were on '*Du*' terms both in the air and, when there was not a third party present, on the ground, even before Rumpelhardt was commissioned. But, as he makes clear, there was no easy slipping into informality such as more often than not happened within RAF crews:

Fritz Rumpelhardt (centre). (Greiner)

> I was only a *Gefreiter* when I joined Schnaufer, and he was a *Leutnant*. You ask about the degree of familiarity within the crew. In addition to normal home leave, by which Schnaufer set high store, we used to go on ski-leave once a year. We went on four such leaves, as a crew, at the beginning of 1942, 1943, 1944 and 1945. And during the second of these leaves he suggested that we should use '*Du*' to each other. This was exceptional. There was an infantry *Hauptmann* at the lunch table, and he heard us calling each other '*Du*', and he was very angry. He said it was a disgrace, a scandal, that an officer and an *Unteroffizier* should speak to

each other so familiarly. He objected violently. Schnaufer explained that we were both members of the same crew, and that it was like a secret society, where '*Du*' was the accepted way of addressing each other. But after that we never used it when third parties were present – on the ski-leave it was an oversight. Never on the unit. Willem Gänsler was not there at the time – he didn't join the crew until August 1943 – but he quickly became '*Du*' as well.

Let us, however, return to the mainstream of the chronicle. When Schnaufer went back to Saint-Trond in early March 1944, already one of the most successful *Nachtjagd* pilots – even though still well behind such prolific scorers as Lent, Streib and the recently deceased zu Sayn-Wittgenstein – the so-called Battle of Berlin had all but run its course. Schnaufer added to his score on 22 March when Harris attacked Frankfurt, shooting down a Lancaster near Münster, his first victory flying from Saint-Trond as *Kommandeur*. Then three nights later there came the final attack against Berlin during the so-called 'Battle'; it was also Harris' last heavy-bomber attack on the city in the war, and it was a disappointing, high-cost raid. Nearly nine percent of the attackers did not come back, and Schnaufer claimed three out of the total of seventy-two, making his kills within the space of only twenty minutes. His tally had now passed the half-century mark.

This final raid on Berlin had been a costly failure. The calculated 'break-even' figure for losses in the bomber offensive was five percent; above that figure it was considered doubtful whether the effort could be

In mid-March 1944 IV./NJG 1 moved from Leeuwarden to Saint-Trond. This is the Kasteel Nonnen-Mielen in which the aircrew officers were accommodated. (Greiner)

sustained. At 8.9% of the heavy bombers involved the losses on the Berlin raid far exceeded this yardstick. But there was even worse to come.

On the evening of the 30th of March 1944, at about nine o'clock, the first of 786 heavy bombers took off, their target Nuremberg. The route that had been chosen was tactically bad, the weather forecast was grossly inaccurate. The German night fighters found their way into the bomber stream at an early stage, and they enjoyed a field day. Ninety-five heavy bombers were shot down, and many more crashed back in England. The target city was little damaged. It was Bomber Command's worst night of the war and the most successful for the *Nachtjagd*. Yet despite being scrambled against the bomber stream, Schnaufer did not enjoy a single victory. Fritz Rumpelhardt:

> Our intercept service had been monitoring the radio traffic in England, and we knew that there was going to be a heavy attack. Schnaufer was sent out against the stream in the direction of the Channel, taking off from Saint-Trond, to find out where the bombers were coming in and to broadcast the information back. But we missed them – we were going

This photograph was taken in March or April 1944 at Saint-Trond and shows Major Hans-Joachim Jabs *(right)*, Kommodore *NJG 1, with* Oberleutnant *Heinz Schnaufer, recently appointed* Kommandeur IV./NJG 1. Jabs is *wearing the* Eichenlaub, *awarded to him on 25 March.* (Jabs)

in the opposite direction. When we got to the coast they had all gone. On the way back we saw combats and crashes all over the place, but we were too late. And then our SN-2 went unserviceable, and we landed at Hanau/Langendiebach. And the young pilots, some of whom had had their first kills, some of them shooting down two or three, came up to us and said, 'May we congratulate the *Herr Oberleutnant* on his victories?' Schnaufer took it in good part.

In what is now common usage, the disastrous Nuremberg raid marked the end of period known as the Battle of Berlin. During the latter part of this period, however, the general nature of the bomber offensive had been changing. Firstly, planning was already well under way for the invasion of the Continent, in which a major rôle was foreseen for Bomber Command, and a number of raids had already been mounted against targets within that context, mostly transport-related objectives in France. In March, for example, there were seven major attacks against German cities, eleven attacks in moderate strength on targets in France. Secondly, a new threat had been perceived that was destined to divert Bomber Command strength from the main offensive: concrete constructions, dubbed 'Ski Sites' from their elongated, upswept shape, were being erected in France, intended as launchers for the pilotless flying bomb, the V1.

From April 1944 onward the main effort of Bomber Command was transferred from Germany cities to invasion-related targets. Communications targets predominated – roads, railways, traffic centres

The officers of IV./NJG 1 on the occasion of the marriage of Hermann Greiner. Schnaufer is on Frau Greiner's right, Greiner on her left. (Fengler)

and so on. Shallower penetration by the bombers streams – for now several attacks against different targets the same night were being mounted in increasing numbers – meant that the night fighters had less opportunity to get in among the bombers before they turned back for England, but the *Nachtjagd* remained a potent force. Saint-Trond was well located for IV./NJG 1 to oppose raids against targets in Belgium, of course, and in Northern France, but it also remained a strong-point against penetration into Germany.

Now was to begin Schnaufer's most prolific period. In twenty-nine months as a front-line night fighter he had by this time downed fifty-one enemy bombers. History records that he would more than double that score within the next seven months. During that seven months he was successful on twenty nights, destroying in all a further fifty-two bombers: remarkably, there were only three nights in the period when his score was confined to a single *Viermot*.

CHAPTER NINE

April to June 1944

The peak months. Promotion and the Eichenlaub.
The invasion of France.

The first main-force attack on a German city in April, sandwiched in between a series of attacks on targets in France, was against Aachen on the night of the 11th/12th. Possibly the German defence commanders were expecting another raid against France, possibly it was due to the comparatively shallow penetration, possibly British deception measures, perhaps a combination of all, but only nine Lancasters were lost, and Schnaufer claimed two of them, shooting one down near Turnhout at 2315 hours and another near Sint-Lenaarts ten minutes later. The first aircraft to go down to Schnaufer was from No. 83 (PFF) Squadron, the second from No. 49 Squadron. Additionally, one single night-fighter pilot, *Hauptmann* Bergmann of III./NJG 4, was credited with having shot down seven, so that he and Schnaufer alone were responsible for all the Bomber Command aircraft lost that night.

The crew of Lancaster LL899. (Coward)

The No. 49 Squadron Lancaster that Schnaufer shot down was piloted by Flight Lieutenant Donovan J Bacon, DFC, a Deputy Flight
Commander known on the Squadron as 'Max' after a well-known radio
comedian of his surname. Bacon's Lancaster's serial number was LL899
and its Squadron letters were EA-P. This, Schnaufer's 53rd kill is well
documented. There were similar stories, almost always untold, each
time Schnaufer – or any other *Nachtjagd* pilot, for that matter – sent an
RAF bomber to its doom.

No. 49 Squadron, which was stationed at Fiskerton in Lincolnshire
and belonged to No. 5 Group, only sent four aircraft to that night's
main target, Aachen. One of the four, Bacon's aircraft, took off at 2031
hours local time in conditions of poor visibility, an overcast sky and light
drizzle. The navigator was Pilot Officer Clifford W Coward, the Bomb
Aimer Flying Officer Nicholas Melnick, RCAF, the Wireless Operator
Sergeant Peter Monck, the Flight Engineer Sergeant John Hennessey,
the Mid-upper Gunner Sgt Stanley W Weedon and the Rear Gunner
Flight Sergeant Alvin Richards, RCAF. All were killed when their aircraft crashed in flames. At that time of the war, despite the complexi-
ties of Double British Summer Time and its German equivalent, local
time in England and in German-occupied Belgium was the same.
Schnaufer took off in his Bf 110, identification letters G9+DF, at 2008
hours, twenty-three minutes before the Lancaster did. Presumably the
Germans' early warning system had alerted the *Nachtjagd* in good time,
and Schnaufer, as usual, had been one of the early ones off. Despite his
prompt start, however, it was not until 2315 hours, when he had been
airborne for over three hours, that he made his first kill. His second,
Bacon's Lancaster, came just ten minutes later. The No. 49 Squadron
aircraft had been scheduled to attack the target at about 2245 hours, so
that it was well on its way back home when Schnaufer intercepted it.

Bacon and his crew were experienced flyers. They had flown their
first operation, against Berlin, on the 18th of November 1943, and this
one was their twenty-third. Their introduction to operational flying had
coincided with Harris's intensification of his Berlin campaign, and their
first four operations had been against the 'Big City'. This was really
'deep end' indoctrination. Before fate overtook them they had been to
the Reich capital eight times in all. After the crew's fifteenth operation,
to Stuttgart on 1 March 1944, the skipper had been awarded the DFC.
The citation had included this passage:

> This officer joined 49 Squadron in time to take part on 18th November
> in the first of the series of assaults on Berlin that are leading to the elim-
> ination of that enemy centre. It was his first operational sortie as a
> Captain of a Lancaster night bomber.
>   On the night of 30 January he was over Berlin for the eighth time. He
> has gone into these great air battles with a fearless enthusiasm that has
> infected the very heart of the squadron.

The twenty-second mission that Bacon and his crew had flown on, the
one before that on which they destined to die, had been the infamous

attack on Nuremberg on the 30th March 1944. The Flight Engineer, John Hennessey, had maintained a diary of the crew's operational trips, and after that night he had written in it: 'The greatest mistake the RAF have made, for we went to do the attack in moonlight. Fighters intercepted us as soon as we crossed the enemy coast and kites were being shot down all around us. 96 aircraft were missing from this operation – the greatest number yet lost on a single operation.'

The odds against Donovan Bacon and his crew surviving were very great. At this period, the worst comparable one that Bomber Command experienced during the war, losses were such that it was becoming doubtful whether Harris could continue his long-range attacks. On the twenty-two raids that Bacon had flown the average loss rate had been almost six percent. In simple statistical terms, that meant that the number of operations that one might expect a crew to survive was seventeen. The 49 Squadron crew had passed that point and now the odds were to catch up with them.

Hennessey's laconic entries in his diary give a glimpse – no more, because no one who has not flown operationally can ever remotely imagine it – of what these men, and tens of thousands like them, experienced:

Berlin, 18 November 1943 [440 Lancasters dispatched, nine failed to return]: On our way to the target we went over a defended area and we received a real hammering from flak. Our kite was holed in ten places, the worst two places being in the windscreen. Our petrol supply ran short and we had to land away from Base with only twenty-five gallons of petrol left in our tanks.

Berlin, 23 November 1943 [375 heavies dispatched, twenty Lancasters lost. Schnaufer claimed two]:
   As we left the target we had to make our way back through flak from the Big City to Hanover. We saw two planes brought down by flak after they had been coned over the target.

Berlin, 2 December 1943 [440 heavy bombers despatched, thirty-nine lost]: The first time we had the opportunity of seeing Berlin's searchlights at work in their full capacity. It was an experience which we have no desire to repeat. The master beams made several attempts to catch us but by excellent work on the part of the crew we evaded them. On one occasion we had to drop two thousand feet in as many seconds to avoid being caught.

Berlin, 27 January 1944 [515 Lancasters, of which thirty-three failed to return. Schnaufer claimed one]:
   An Me 109 attacked us just as we were coming out of the target area, and Al (Richards) gave directions to the skip for the necessary evasive action, which succeeded in getting us away safely.

Stuttgart, 1 March 1944 [544 heavy bombers, of which only four were lost]: There was a heavy snowfall this morning. We were told there

Date	Aircraft Type & Number	Crew	Duty	Time Up	Time Down	Details of Sortie or Flight
1/12.4.44	LANCASTER ND.512	F/Lt. Adams J.P. / Sgt. Seymour F.S. / S/Ldr. Evans J.H. / Sgt. Daines R.A. / P/O. Hamilton W.J. / P/O. Lowans E.J. J.18661 / F/Sgt. Weller G.M.	BOMBING AACHEN	2035	0026	AACHEN 2248 hrs. 17,000 ft. Second wave. Thin layer of clo[ud] Bombed remnants of Red TI. Attack reasonably concentrate[d] with a number of incendiaries dropped on wrong heading. O[ne] or two fighter flares seen on way out.
"	LANCASTER ND.647	P/O. Shinn A.W. / Sgt. Eyles D.G. / Sgt. Andrews B.A. / Sgt. Hawes S. / Sgt. Dicken A.E. / Sgt. Cully V.G. R.153885 / Sgt. Payne L.P.	BOMBING AACHEN	2033	0029	AACHEN Second wave. 2237 hrs. 17,000 ft. Bombed on H2S (as early and TI's not seen) No difficulties or congestio[n] No combats or interceptions. Route good.
"	LANCASTER LL.899	F/Lt. Bacon D.J. / Sgt. Hennessey J.P. / P/O. Coward C.W. / Sgt. Monck P. / Sgt. Weedon S.W. / F/O. Melnick N. J.21183 / Sgt. Richard C.E. R.154916	BOMBING AACHEN	2031		Missing without trace.
"	LANCASTER ME.675	S/Ldr. Miller D. NZ.402207 / Sgt. Poulter R.G. / F/Sgt. Benson L.B. / F/Sgt. Wilson W.S. / F/Sgt. Henderson D. / F/Sgt. Williams S.N. / D/Sgt. Hubbard F.W.	BOMBING AACHEN	2019	0018	AACHEN First wave. 2245 hrs. 17,000 ft. Bombed cluster of Red TI's cascading 2242. (H2S of no use at time, screen blurred). Target could be identified apart from Marshalli[ng] Yards. No explosions observed. PFF concentrated. At the height from which we bombed (17,000) photo flashes more dangerous than the flak.
18/19.4.44	LANCASTER LL.900	W/Cr. Adams A.A. / P/O. Reddish J.A. / P/O. Sergeev C.V. / F/Sgt. Murray G. / P/O. McKay H.G. A.415542 / F/O. Abbott S.J. / Sgt. Kennedy H.H.	MINING POMERANIAN BAY	2119	0416	POMERANIAN BAY Geranium I 0039 hrs. 14,800 ft. Liepe identified visually and by H2S at 0030 hrs. Vis. hazy. No cloud. Route excellent. Considerable flak from Peenemunde and flak ships in neighbourhood. First class conditions f[or] very accurate mine-laying.

were Ops. on and everybody cleared the runway so that we could get off. This was an extremely quiet trip, and we carried a second 'Dickey'[1] who, incidentally, is now missing from his first op with his own crew. I passed out through lack of oxygen and 'Funf'[2] came to the rescue. Afterwards I was violently sick.

Stuttgart, 15 March 1944 [847 heavies, of which thirty-seven did not come back]:

The flak was really heavy, and the fighters were up in strength. We saw three shot down in flames. Stan (Weedon) had his hand frost-bitten. When we returned to our base and were circling we saw two kites collide and hit the ground. None of the crews were saved.

Frankfurt, 22 March 1944 [804 heavies despatched, thirty-three missing. Schnaufer claimed one]:

There were hundreds of combats and plenty of kites being shot down. We had to fly the whole belt of searchlights and once we nearly got coned, but the one searchlight that was on us got hit by incendiaries. We lost two kites from the Squadron.

11 April 1944. This extract from the Operational Record Book of No. 49 Squadron RAF lists Lancaster LL899, Pilot Flight Lieutenant Bacon, as taking off at 2031 hours. The machine was shot down by Heinz Schnaufer: all on board perished. (Public Record Office)

[1] 'Second Dickey' — Second Pilot. A Second Dickey was usually an inexperienced pilot flying with an experienced crew as an introduction to operational conditions.

[2] 'Funf' was the bomb-aimer in the crew at that time, Flt Lt William Fitch, GM, DFC. He was subsequently killed in action when flying with a Pathfinder squadron.

Berlin, 24 March 1944 [793 heavy bombers sent out, seventy-two lost. Schnaufer claimed three]:

It was a deadly route, for as soon as we crossed the coast of Denmark we ran into a belt of searchlights and saw four kites coned, and two were shot down immediately.

The seven who died when Schnaufer destroyed LL899 were not untypical of the thousands who flew with Bomber Command during the Second World War – ordinary young men doing extraordinary things, and risking their life every time they flew. In the course of the war, over fifty percent of those who flew in the bombers were killed. The pilot, Flight Lieutenant Bacon, whose home was in Beeston, Nottinghamshire, was born in 1915, and was therefore somewhat older than the average Bomber Command man: he was also better qualified academically than most, having studied at Nottingham University College and obtained a Bachelor of Arts degree. He had joined the Army Education Corps shortly before the war and volunteered to transfer to the RAF for flying duties in 1941, when he was a Sergeant Instructor. He had done his pilot's training in Canada, and had been commissioned when he qualified. He was a married man and had a daughter three years old; a son was born after his death.

The navigator of EA-P was a Londoner, Pilot Officer Clifford William Coward, who was twenty-three years of age. Cliff Coward had left school at the age of sixteen and had become a trainee accountant. He too had volunteered for flying duties in 1941 and done his training in Canada, and he had passed out as a Sergeant. He had later been promoted to Flight Sergeant, and had been commissioned as a Pilot Officer in January 1944. Like his skipper, he was married. He was the eldest of four sons. His youngest brother Eddy, seven years his junior, writes:

I had a strong schoolboy hero-worship for Cliff, which has always stayed with me. He and I shared many interests. We both attended the same school, sang in the same church choir and learnt to play the piano; we both became accountants, we both had a passion for flying and we both subsequently joined the RAF.

My parents were absolutely shattered when they had the telegram to say that Cliff was missing. My mother was very tearful, while my father was quiet and sad. He had been a sergeant in the Army in the 1914-18, and he knew the toll of war. As for myself, I just could not believe it. Every RAF officer I saw, I thought it was Cliff coming home. Eighteen months later I joined the RAF and still expected to find Cliff. When I came home on leave my RAF uniform upset my mother so much that I kept it in the wardrobe and wore civilian clothes. My parents were very upset after the war when Cliff's remains were taken from his temporary grave and re-interred in a Commonwealth War Graves cemetery.'

The Lancaster in which Bacon, Coward and the other five members of the crew died crashed in flames on agricultural land at Henzbroek, a small hamlet just north of Sint-Lenaarts. On the 15th of April their remains were buried at the '*Feindfriedhof*' — 'enemy cemetery' — at a site known as 'Fort 3' in the Deurne district of Antwerp, where they rested until, as Eddy Coward writes, they were moved to the War Graves Cemetery at Schoonselhof in 1946. In 1980 Eddy Coward began to research the circumstances of his brother's death, and in 1987 he erected a brass plaque to the memory of his brother's crew in the Parish Church at Sint-Lenaarts. Then, in June 1994, a memorial was unveiled in Borsbeek, Antwerp, to all the 240 aircrew who had been buried at the Fort 3 'enemy cemetery'. The idea that there should be such a memorial was Eddy Coward's.

A third member of the crew is recorded in less detail, but no less poignantly. In the course of his researches into the death of his brother Cliff, Eddy Coward met Joe Melnick, the brother of Flying Officer Nick Melnick, the Canadian bomb-aimer of LL899, and they visited Sint-Lenaarts together and laid wreaths on the graves of their respective brothers. Joe's wife spoke of Nick to a local newspaper in Canada:

> She knew Nick well because they all grew up in tiny Plunkett, Saskatchewan. Nick, the dark, handsome star goalie of the Plunkett hockey team, was twenty-eight when he died. He'd left for the war six weeks after his wedding day.

In terms of kills April 1944 was Heinz Schnaufer's most successful month to date. So far his highest score in a month, October 1943, had been seven. In April he shot down ten. April was a good month, too, for Fritz Rumpelhardt: apart from the satisfaction in having contributed to the successes attributed to Schnaufer, which were in reality largely a team effort, he had another reason for self-congratulation. On the first of the month he was promoted *Leutnant*.

This photo was taken during a visit to Saint-Trond by Generalmajor Grabmann. *Left to right:* Weissflog *(*background*), Grabmann, Schnaufer, Jabs.*

Harris was now splitting his main force into lesser, but still very strong, attacks over a wide geographical area, thus setting difficult problems for the defenders when it came to deciding which fighters were to be sent where, problems which were exacerbated by the many small, but nevertheless highly effective and low-cost, raids by Mosquitoes of Donald Bennett's Light Night Striking Force. The night on which Schnaufer achieved his next successes, the 24/25 April, was typical of the pattern. The main target, visited by 639 aircraft, was Karlsruhe, but a further 244 Lancasters and sixteen Mosquitoes went to Munich. In addition 165 aircraft from Operational Training Units carried out a diversionary sweep over the North Sea, producing returns on the Germans' coastal radars and so tempting them to put fighters into the air before the OTU machines turned back for the safety of England. Twenty-three Mosquito bombers went to Düsseldorf, adding to the German controllers' problems and at the same time ensuring that the air-raid warnings would sound and the population, including workers, would be deprived on sleep – and, of course, causing further not insignificant damage to the badly battered city on the Rhine. As a diversion in support of the Munich raid six Lancasters from No. 617 'Dambuster' Squadron dropped marker flares on Milan.

No. 100 (Bomber Support) Group was in action, too: formed in November 1943, the Group exercised various functions. Its Mosquito squadrons would set out to attack *Luftwaffe* night fighters in the air, using *Serrate* to home on the transmissions from their intercept radars, and to strike at *Nachtjagd* airfields and destroy the machines on the ground or, preferably, as they were taking off or landing. The word '*Moskito*' swiftly became a much-dreaded addition to the vocabulary of the German night-fighter pilots, and few of them did not at one time or the other experience an attack from the 'wooden wonder' either when airborne or on the ground. Countless crews were shot down, many on two, three or more occasions, either having to take to their parachutes or to crash-land in their aircraft. Very many gallant men, ranging from newly arrived, inexperienced crews to leading aces – for the Mosquito was no respecter of rank – perished in the process. Schnaufer and his crew, miraculously, it might seem, never came under Mosquito attack.

Doubtless sheer good luck played its part in Schnaufer's apparent immunity to Mosquitoes, but there were other contributory factors. Take-off was one of the most dangerous times, and as the night-fighter airfield illumination attracted the British intruders as a candle attracts moths, the Germans did not switch on the lights until an aircraft was at the end of the runway awaiting take-off clearance, and once that machine was airborne they were switched off again until the next machine was ready to go, and so on. By the period of the war when the threat from the intruders, firstly Beaufighters and then Mosquitoes, was becoming more and more serious, Heinz Schnaufer was usually in a position, to some extent, to decide his own place in the take-off sequence, firstly as *Staffelkapitän* – if his *Staffel* alone from the *Gruppe* was

flying he had absolute choice, but if other *Staffeln* were also operating the decision was that of the *Gruppenkommandeur* – and later as *Gruppenkommandeur* himself and, ultimately, as *Geschwaderkommodore*. Schnaufer always led from the front, and was, as far as he could possibly manage it, first into the air, which meant that he was usually aloft before the intruders had, by seeing the airfield lighting, positively established the precise position of the airfield. Once in the air, Schnaufer seldom flew straight and level, preferring a gentle weaving motion, and coupled with this Rumpelhardt did not leave his AI radar transmitting all the time, as some radar operators did, but only switched it on when in the stream and looking for targets. In this way he limited the periods during which Schnaufer's aircraft could be picked up by *Serrate*. Then there was the landing period, which was even more dangerous for the German fighters than take-off.

A fighter approaching his base, possibly having been in the air for up to three hours and possibly having been engaged in combat with one or more bombers, possibly even damaged and with one or more members of the crew injured, would call up the airfield control, report he was coming in for landing and ask for the airfield and runway lighting to be switched on, using the codeword '*Christbaum*' (Christmas Tree): incidentally, the German civilians, with a macabre sense of humour, used the same nickname for PFF flares. On the approach the pilot would usually come in at low altitude, gradually losing further height as necessary, and switch on his own navigation lights, which made him an

Leisure time at the Château Nonnen-Mielen, Saint-Trond, Spring 1944. Fritz Rumpelhardt has his back to the camera, bottom left, while Heinz Schnaufer is in the back row. (Greiner)

easy target for a predatory Mosquito. Schnaufer, according to Fritz Rumpelhardt, preferred another method of approach. He was, says Fritz, a consummate pilot and 'the master of the side-slip': he would come in comparatively high and then, at the last moment, lose height by side-slipping, lower his undercarriage and touch down, in one rapid sequence, switching off his navigation lights as soon as he was taxying,

Hermann Greiner (right) and Oberleutnant Koltermann *relaxing with a* Luftwaffen-Helferin, *the equivalent of a WAAF. Strictly social contact between other-rank females and officers was forbidden, but the girls were allowed to wear civilian clothes (unlike members of the WAAF), and discreet off-duty and off-camp friendships were generally overlooked.* (Greiner)

by which time the airfield lights would also be extinguished.

Another function of No. 100 Group, equally important, was the jamming of German radio, radar and navigational systems, and this task too they carried out to great effect. The *Nachtjagd* crews coined appropriately descriptive names for the various methods of jamming, for instance '*Seelenbohrer*' (Soul-drill) for 'Tinsel', the jamming of R/T traffic by means of microphones in the bombers' engine-nacelles; '*Dudelsack*' (Bagpipes) for 'Airborne Cigar', a jammer that transmitted a warbling interference on speech channels; and '*Sauerkraut*' for the mushy signals that appeared on an AI radar screen jammed by such devices as 'Window', 'Ground Grocer' and 'Piperack'. To add to the confusion experienced by the German *Funker*, false and misleading fighter-control instructions and commentaries were broadcast on German frequencies by German-speaking personnel: the British code-name was 'Corona'. At one time, according to Rumpelhardt, it was suggested that controllers and aircrew should learn English so that the British in their turn could be deceived, but nothing came of the idea. And as one German night-fighter pilot[1] wrote, deception went further than simple interference with fighters already in the air:

> The British were very cunning gentlemen: it apparently amused them to lead the German night fighters astray when the opportunity presented itself. It would all start in the later afternoon. Radio transmitters in large numbers would be tuned in, coded messages broadcast, and everything done to give the impression that there was going to be a major attack that night. The result of these activities was that at the evening briefing the words 'immediate readiness' were appended to the code-word *Fasan* (enemy attack expected). And then during the night only a few

---

[1] *Leutnant* Otto Fries, II./NJG 1.

Off duty and at ease.
Left to right
Rumpelhardt, Schnaufer,
unknown.
(Rumpelhardt)

Mosquitoes would come, simulating a bomber stream by means of both radio measures and dropping 'Window', and so throwing the whole of the German night-fighter organisation into confusion.'

On one occasion Fritz Rumpelhardt, at home on leave, was listening in to a music broadcast on the radio: he turned to his father and said, 'The English are bombing Munich tonight'. His father asked him how he knew, and Rumpelhardt explained. In an attempt to counter R/T jamming and identify the target to the fighters, the Germans had introduced a system of area-related music broadcast on the public radio frequencies – nautical music, for example, indicated the Hamburg area; military marches meant Berlin, waltzes Vienna, and so on. Striving to make out snatches of information that would tell him where the bomber stream was heading, a night-fighter *Funker* had a wide choice of frequencies he could listen in to, all of which were more likely than not to be jammed to a greater or lesser degree. One practice employed by some fighter radio operators, in an attempt to filter scraps of operational information from the saturated frequencies, was to broadcast on one frequency until a British jammer switched in and then rapidly change wavelength, hoping that the attention of the jamming RAF operators would be momentarily diverted.

The British initiatives – the tactical and diversionary use of his forces by Harris, the offensive patrols by No. 100 Group and other formations, and the plethora of technical offensive and defensive measures deployed – made the life of the night-fighter crews difficult and hazardous in the extreme. New crews arrived on units, were noticed a few times in the messes, then were not seen again: they had fallen victim either to British intruders or to their own lack of experience. Losses due to pilot error were very high. Many crews never developed the ability to find the bomber stream and then to infiltrate it and fulfil their primary function, that of shooting down bombers. Understandable caution and hesitancy – one hesitates to use the word cowardice in this context – doubtless played its part: just as similar feelings among RAF aircrew contributed to the high 'early-return' rate on some dangerous operations. Some crews, notable among them Schnaufer's, on the other hand, seemed to develop an almost uncanny ability to get in among the bombers and exact retribution. The first requirement was dedication to the task in hand, particularly on the part of the man at the flying controls, and an implacable determination to destroy the enemy. Then came the ability to interpret the jumble of information from the ground and decide where the bombers were, in which direction they were flying and what their target was, and for this a high degree of navigational ability on the part of both *Funker* and pilot was necessary: this was not dead-reckoning navigation such as was practised by the Bomber Command navigators, but instinctive, rule-of-thumb, 'seat of the pants' flying coupled to an intimate knowledge of the territory above which they were operating, and both Schnaufer and Rumpelhardt possessed this ability in

20 April 1944 - Adolf Hitler's birthday. A Parade in his honour, with Heinz Schnaufer taking the salute at Saint-Trond. (Rumpelhardt)

*Officers of IV./NJG 1
assemble at the parade to
mark Adolf Hitler's
birthday, April 1944.*
(Fengler)

abundance.

When Schnaufer took off from Saint-Trond in the early hours of the morning on the 25th April 1944 he had fifty-three confirmed kills to his name: when he landed his score had increased by four. He had shot down three four-engined bombers – they are entered in his *Leistungsbuch* as 'Lancaster or Halifax' – over Belgium itself, and one just off the coast where Holland meets Belgium. Victim number one went down at 0203 hours at Alken, only seven miles or so north-east of the airfield at Saint-Trond; Schnaufer headed west, and the second kill followed twenty-five minutes later near Mechelen, south of Antwerp; still heading into the approaching bomber stream, and at an altitude of about 18,000 feet, Schnaufer found and destroyed his third *Viermot* that night a mere two minutes later, at Haasdonk; it took him a further ten minutes to locate and shoot down his fourth. The target of the four bombers he destroyed was Karlsruhe, and nineteen in all were lost from the 628 heavies that took part in the raid. It was a sign of the times that the total number of Bomber Command aircraft attacking their various targets in Germany, together with those flying in support, totalled 1,160.

Schnaufer's tally of kills for April was now six, and there were more to come before the month was out. Two nights after the four successes just described, during the night of 26/27 April, he claimed another two from the force that went to Essen. Heavy-bomber casualties on this raid, at seven out of 475, were light, and Schnaufer accounted for two of the six Lancasters destroyed. But if losses against comparatively short-

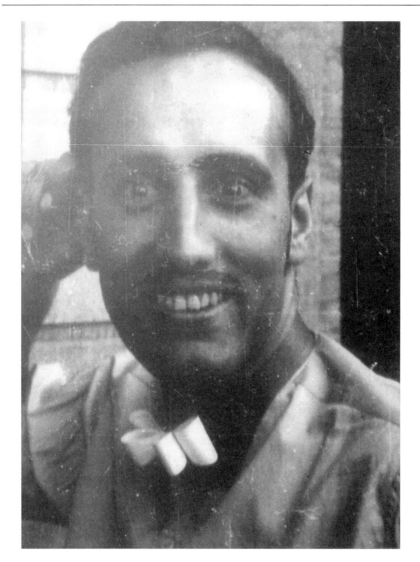

range targets such as those in the Ruhr Valley were, for the time being, showing a downward trend, no doubt as a result of Harris' multiple-target, diversionary and spoof tactics, there was a chilling reminder that same night that a bomber stream detected and penetrated by the *Nachtjagd* was still a very vulnerable entity. A force of 206 Lancasters and eleven Mosquitoes from No. 5 Group, which was operating in a quasi-independent and largely experimental rôle at that period, had set out to attack Schweinfurt, home of the strategically important ball-bearing works. The attack was inaccurate in the extreme and very costly, with twenty-one Lancasters, over ten percent of those taking part, being lost, almost all to night fighters.

The following night the principal target was another long-range one, Friedrichshafen on Lake Constance, and that, with 5.6 percent of the all-Lancaster force failing to return, was also expensive in terms of casualties. There were two short-range targets, too, Aulnoye railway yards, south of Mons and just on the border between Belgium and France, and Montzen, also near the Belgian border, but this time the border with Germany, another railway communications target that was bombed in preparation for the invasion of France. While only one bomber out of 207 was lost on the Aulnoye raid, night fighters penetrated the force of 136 heavies aiming for Montzen and shot down fifteen of them, again more than ten percent. Montzen lies close to Aachen, and to get there the force had to pass perilously near to Saint-Trond. Schnaufer claimed to have destroyed a Halifax and a Lancaster within ten minutes of each other, but the only Lancaster lost on the Montzen raid that night crashed near Diest, about forty miles from where Schnaufer scored his successes. It seems certain that Schnaufer's two victims were in fact both Halifaxes, LL 258 of 434 Squadron, which crashed five miles north of Aubel, and MZ 588 of No. 432 Squadron, which came down at Verviers. Both 432 and 434 Squadrons belonged to No. 6 (Canadian) Group. For the Canadians, this was a bad night: No. 419 Squadron lost one Halifax, No. 431 Squadron four, No. 432 Squadron three and No. 434 Squadron two, eleven of the total

Heinz Schnaufer. This photograph, exact date unknown, was taken after he was promoted to Hauptmann *(1 May 1944) but before he was awarded the* Eichenlaub. (Diener)

of fifteen bombers that were shot down on the operation.

These were Schnaufer's 60th and 61st victims respectively. It is an interesting comparative statistic, and a useful one as a pointer to the unique genius of Schnaufer, that when the war ended only another twenty night-fighter pilots could claim fifty or more night-time victories, and of them only five – Helmut Lent (102), Heinrich zu Sayn-Wittgenstein (83), Manfred Meurer (65), Werner Streib (65) and Rudolf Schoenert (64) – scored more than Schnaufer had done by this time, and there was more than a full year of war yet to come.

On the first day of May 1944, Schnaufer was promoted *Hauptmann* – the direct equivalent of Flight Lieutenant in the Royal Air Force and still a junior rank. It is impossible to imagine that a fighter pilot of his abilities and attainments would not have already been promoted to a much higher rank had he been in the British, Commonwealth or American Air Force. Fritz Rumpelhardt was a *Leutnant*, and Wilhelm Gänsler was by now an *Oberfeldwebel*, the equivalent of a Flight Sergeant in the RAF.

Schnaufer's outstanding run of successes continued in May 1944, the month in which he scored the highest number of kills of his entire career, thirteen. The sequence began on the night of the 8th/9th of the month, when he destroyed a Halifax III from No. 432 (Leaside) Squadron, flying out of East Moor, Yorkshire. The pilot, Pilot Officer

8 May 1944. Schnaufer congratulates the Kommandeur *of III./NJG 1, Martin Drewes, by telegram after he had shot down five bombers in a night.* (Drewes)

S A Hawkins, and three of the other members of the crew belonged to the RCAF. Three, including Hawkins, died, two were taken prisoner of war, and the remaining two evaded capture and, presumably, eventually returned to England.

Further successes followed, all achieved against comparatively small forces of bombers engaged on communications targets in France and Belgium. On the 13th of the month, when the target was Hasselt, just to the north-east of Saint-Trond, Schnaufer claimed two Lancasters and a Halifax: official RAF records, however, only show one Lancaster as missing that night, so it is fair to assume that Schnaufer's identification of one of his victims was again faulty. The nights of the 21st/22nd and the 22nd/23rd of May saw attacks against Germany, to Duisburg and Dortmund respectively, and on each night Schnaufer shot down two Lancasters. Then, on the night of the 24th/25th May, 426 heavies and sixteen Mosquitoes headed for Aachen. Eighteen Halifaxes and seven Lancasters were destined not to come back.

As mentioned earlier, Heinz Schnaufer's colleague and friend Martin Drewes, *Kommandeur* of III./NJG 1, had shot down five bombers on the night of the 22nd/23rd, repeating a feat he had accomplished for the first time eighteen days previously. Now it was Schnaufer's turn to join the 'Five in a Night' club. His first kill, a Halifax from No. 51 Squadron, came down in Eindhoven at 0115 hours, his fifth at 0129 hours. Numbers two, three, four and five were all shot down in the space of eleven minutes in the vicinity of Tilburg, a short distance further west. This was yet another demonstration of the vulnerability of a closely concentrated bomber stream when penetrated by a determined and skilled night fighter. On the other side of the coin, it also evidenced – in an ominous fashion – the skill of the navigators of Bomber Command. For obvious reasons, the bombers could not fly in visual formation, close or even loose, by night. Each aircraft was individually navigated, yet the concentration achieved provided the German night-fighter crews with the opportunity to create mayhem once in the stream.

For such as Schnaufer, Rumpelhardt and Gänsler episodes of this nature represented the fulfilment of their *raison d'être*. As young adults they had entered the *Luftwaffe* on the wave of patriotic enthusiasm that characterised Germany in the second half of the nineteen-thirties, caring little for – and probably not even giving other than superficial thought to – the complex ramifications of the internal and international politics of the age. They had begun their aircrew training at a time when their country, their kinsfolk, were being threatened by the ever-increasing brutality of high explosives and fire-bombs, and by the time they became operational that threat had multiplied many times over. It was an easily understandable, elemental situation: the bombers were coming by night and it was their job to do their utmost to stop them. It was what they had been trained for, and, despite the fear that was a constant companion, there was an enormous sense of achievement, of professional pride, of self-justification, in demonstrating their excellence in their particular field of expertise.

And what of their immediate enemies, the young men of Bomber Command who risked violent, indescribable death at their hands night after night? They too had been spurred on by patriotism to volunteer to fly in the defence of their country, as they saw it. In the same way that their enemies in the *Nachtjagd* perceived the situation in black-and-white terms, so did they: Germany, territorially ambitious and ruled by an unscrupulous clique of wicked men, had spread her evil domination over Europe, had attempted to invade England but had been prevented from doing so by the heroism of the Royal Air Force, had bombed British cities and killed thousands of British civilians: 'They started it, and we're going to finish it!' was their cry. And on the night of the 24th/25th of May, when what might correctly be described as a minor force of bombers went to hit at railway targets in Aachen, 175 Bomber Command aircrew were lost, of which *Hauptmann* Heinz Schnaufer and his crew accounted for thirty-five. History does not record how many night-fighter men perished that night, but in and around Aachen something in the region of 300 civilians died: in Aachen alone nearly 15,000 people were bombed out – and bombs also fell in a number of other townships and villages – and that the number of fatalities was so low was a tribute to the excellent air-raid shelters that were typical of major towns in Germany.

It was a world once again inflicted with the recurrent madness of war, and as always it was largely the young men who were paying the price in their blood. But aerial bombing, which reached a dreadful climax in World War Two – but who would dare to say that the future does not hold worse? – meant that now not only young fighting men, but also civilians of all ages, from babies to old men and women, had to bear the brunt of the slaughter. There was no true front line. Impotently, one can but blame the apparently inherent stupidity of what we choose to call, rather quaintly, *homo sapiens*: 'Lord, what fools these mortals be!'

It is unlikely in the extreme that the name Schnaufer would have meant anything to the Bomber Command crewmen against whom he was pitted, despite the fact that by May 1944 he had already accounted for well over four hundred of their colleagues. Unlike the air battles on the Western Front from 1914 to 1918, when aces on both sides – Ball, von Richthofen, McCudden, Guynemer and others – were known to and respected by their enemies, this was not an intimate, frequently chivalrous aerial war but a bitter, anonymous, high-risk confrontation in which chivalry played little part and quarter was neither given nor expected. Yet the myth has grown, and is firmly believed in some quarters – but certainly not by former Bomber Command men – that the name Schnaufer was known to and feared by the aircrew in the bombers, and that they called him 'The Night Ghost of Saint-Trond'. Agreed, it is probable that his name and position in the hierarchy were known to RAF intelligence as a result of their monitoring of fighter-control frequencies and from *Enigma* and

Saint-Trond, 1944. Hans-Joachim Jabs, Kommodore *NJG 1, with his* Gruppen-kommandeure. Left to right: *Schnaufer (IV.* Gruppe*); Drewes (III.* Gruppe*); Jabs; Förster (I.* Gruppe*); and von Bonin (II.* Gruppe*). The officer in the background is* Major Sutor. (Jabs)

other intelligence material, but, to the men flying the bombers, in the dark all night fighters, like all cats, were black. There were other myths that circulated – and still do to this day – about the 'Night Ghost of Saint-Trond', one of which endows a Belgian pilot in the RAF with the sobriquet, claiming that it was he who carried out regular intruder attacks by night against the airfield. As is frequently the case with myths, none can be substantiated, although they are presumably believed by those who retail them. The 'Night Ghost' legend must, however, take second place to another palpable nonsense – that the RAF considered Schnaufer to be so dangerous that they mounted special operations to eliminate him. The self-styled 'history' magazine *Landser*, mentioned previously, perpetuated this myth in its issue No. 426, as follows:

> It is characteristic of the British that they pay very particular attention to a dangerous enemy. In this way the British commanders in Africa focused their attention on the person of *Feldmarschall* Rommel; or, again, the British fighter pilots, who not only knew the names of their enemies, but also details of their careers.
>
> For Schnaufer, the terror of the bombers, the British had thought out a particularly shocking programme. Together with their American allies, in England getting ready for the invasion, they laid on whole swarms of Mosquitoes (night fighters) against Schnaufer and his *Staffel*, then his *Gruppe* and his *Geschwader*. They hoped to be able to eliminate him before take off and to destroy the runway with bombs.
>
> This plan failed. Despite the fact that the British sent agents to find out where Schnaufer was, the Mosquitoes always arrived too late. Either Schnaufer was already in the air or he had moved to another airfield.

Finally the Allies sent out a special force before every bombing raid on
the Reich to deal exclusively with Schnaufer. The airfield they thought
he was at was bespattered with thousands of high-explosive and incendiary bombs.

   These precautions were unsuccessful. Schnaufer continued to fly without being defeated by the enemy.

Two other persistent myths about Schnaufer might conveniently be dismissed at this point. Firstly, that he and his crew took drugs to enhance
their night-vision: 'Nonsense,' says Rumpelhardt. 'We sometimes wore
dark spectacles in the crew room before flying at night, but that was the
extent of it. As I said before, we all had good night-vision, and we
didn't do anything extra to improve it.' The other story concerns the
unconventional and extremely potent fighter-bomber aircraft, the Do
335, which had two engines, one driving an airscrew in the nose of the
fuselage and the other an airscrew in the tail. The Do 335 came late in
the war and did not see action. The story is that Schnaufer flew one of
the machines and crashed it. That, says Fritz Rumpelhardt, is also
untrue. Schnaufer did indeed fly one unofficially, probably while they
were at Dortmund, and he was very enthusiastic about it. He landed
without any trouble despite the unfamiliar nose-wheel undercarriage,
but higher authority was peeved that he had taken it into the air without permission and decreed that he was not to fly it again. A lesser mortal, says Fritz, would have been severely reprimanded.

*Berlin 1944. Three
Geschwader-
kommodore at a
conference at the Air
Ministry. Centre Jabs
(NJG1), left Radusch
(NJG 3) and right
Griese (NJG 6). (Jabs)*

On the 6th of June the Allied invasion armies landed on the Normandy beaches, and the weight of Bomber Command was deployed in support. For some weeks following the invasion the bombers' priority, under the overall direction of General Eisenhower, was to give continued support to the ground forces, and communications targets predominated. Schnaufer's first successes following the Allied landings were achieved a week later, during the night of 12/13 June, when railways at a number of points in France were attacked by a total of 671 bombers. Cambrai was among the target towns, and Schnaufer shot down three of the attacking aircraft, logging one as a Lancaster and the remaining two as 'Lancaster or Halifax', between 0027 and 0034 hours.

The force of ninety-two Halifaxes and Lancasters that attacked Cambrai came from No. 6 (Canadian) Group, stationed in the north of England, the only non-British Group to serve in Bomber Command. In the run-up to the invasion, when there were a high proportion of short-range targets, operations to France had, in general, been less costly in terms of casualties than the longer trips to Germany. In the weeks immediately following the invasion, however, when the majority of the German night-fighter force was brought forward to support the ground forces of the *Wehrmacht* against the RAF bombers – and some of them, incidentally, to act in a ground-attack rôle – losses on French targets increased considerably. So it was that when the Canadians attacked Cambrai they lost nine of their aircraft, one out of every ten of the force.

One of the Lancasters that were destroyed came from No. 419 Squadron. It is unlikely that it fell to Schnaufer, because a survivor from the crew later reported that it had been attacked by a Ju 88. A vivid account of the meeting between bomber and fighter appears in a history of the Canadian 6 Group [1] and it is worth reproducing it in its entirety, whether or not Schnaufer was the night-fighter pilot involved, to give an idea of what it was like to be in a stricken bomber. On this occasion heroism was officially recognised – eventually – but countless Bomber Command men died without their bravery becoming known, because, as so frequently happened, there were no survivors to bear witness:

Another of the casualties on that eventful night was A-Able, a Lancaster of 419 Squadron skippered by Flying Officer Art deBreyne. He and his crew were on their thirteenth sortie. Before they reached the target, a Ju 88 night fighter attacked from below, pouring an accurate stream of cannon fire into the port wing and rear fuselage. Three explosions staggered the Lancaster. 'I noticed a strong smell of burning', recalls Jim Kelly, the wireless operator. 'Smoke started to fill the cabin and the navigator, Bob Bodie, got up and reached for his parachute.' A moment later Kelly saw that the port wing was in flames. Both engines on that side had stopped; fire streamed from the No. 2 fuel tank between them. In the pilot's seat,

[1] *Reap the Whirlwind*, by Spencer Dunmore & William Carter and published in the UK by Crécy Books, 1992

deBreyne glanced in vain at his instrument panel. There wasn't much to see; the lights had gone out. Realizing that the situation was hopeless, deBreyne ordered the crew to bale out. But the intercom was no longer working. He told the flight Engineer, Roy Vigars, to pass the word to the others. Abandon aircraft! Immediately! He used the emergency warning-light system to convey the message to the gunners. Then, unable to do more than hope the faltering aircraft wouldn't blow up before everyone jumped, he held it as steady as he could. And waited. One by one the crew escaped. Now the Lanc. was down to little more than a thousand feet. It was now or never. Art deBreyne heaved himself out of his seat and hurriedly made his way to the emergency exit in the nose while the aircraft was still on an even keel. He jumped, believing that all his crew had jumped.

He was wrong. The rear gunner was still aboard, trapped in his tur-ret when the port outer stopped, since that engine powered the hydraulic system that operated his turret. The turret jammed at an angle to the fuselage. The gunner, Pat Brophy, managed to pry the sliding doors open wide enough to reach into the rear fuselage and grab his parachute pack. Now he tried to hand-crank the turret around to a ninety-degree posi-tion which would enable him to roll out backwards. But the mechanism broke. He would go down with the kite like countless gunners before him. The only hope was that the bombs might go off and blow him to bits. It was preferable to being burned to death. Meanwhile, the mid-upper gunner, Andy Mynarski ('A quiet, cheery guy,' remembers Jim Kelly), had extricated himself from his turret and had made his way aft along the fuselage, by now a nightmare of smoke and flames. He opened the main door on the starboard side near the tail unit to make good his escape. An instant before jumping, he happened to glance back – and glimpsed Brophy in the rear turret. Did Mynarski fight a fierce little bat-tle within himself, a tug-of-war between self-preservation and the desire to help a crew-mate in trouble? When a fully loaded Lancaster is on fire, time is in desperately short supply. Mynarski could have jumped. But he didn't. He left the open doorway and struggled back along the narrow aft-fuselage. Fingers of flame clutched at him. Mynarski's flying suit start-ed to burn. He beat out the flames. They sprang up again. Ignoring them, he took the axe from its stowage and attacked the stubborn doors of Brophy's rear turret. In the shuddering, swaying, claustrophobic metal tube, there was hardly room to move let alone swing an axe. But Mynarski kept at it, smashing at the stubborn doors as smoke and fire swirled around him. The doors gave a little, but not enough. Furiously he wielded the axe again and again. It was hopeless. Brophy knew that Mynarski had done all he could. He gestured for him to jump while there was still time. Mynarski continued to attack the doors but finally he accepted defeat. Eyes glued on Brophy, he backed away, his flying suit and parachute pack burning. But even now he didn't jump. With mag-nificent contempt for the flames and smoke, he dragged himself to atten-tion and saluted Brophy. Then at last he leapt from the aircraft, vanishing into the hostile darkness. Trapped in the rear turret, Brophy could do little but await death. It wouldn't take long, he knew. The kite was low when it was hit, so it would dive in.

The din of bombs exploding woke him. He found himself lying in a French field. Somehow, by a shuffling of impossible odds, he had sur-

vived the crash of the burning Lancaster with its load of bombs; it had
hit the ground on a relatively even keel. The impact had torn the rear
turret free of the fuselage and had ripped the turret doors off so that he
had tumbled out onto the grass. Incredulous, he got to his feet. He
appeared to be uninjured — except for the loss of his hair, which fell out
as he tugged off his helmet. He had no right to be alive. But he was.
And so was the rest of the crew; except for the gallant mid-upper gunner, Andy Mynarski. Resistance workers had seen his descent, his parachute trailing fire. Mynarski fell into a swamp. Eager hands quickly
pulled him out, but the young man died of his terrible burns. When
Brophy met up with other members of his crew he was able to relate the
story of the gunner's self-sacrifice. In October 1946 Andrew Charles
Mynarski of Winnipeg, Manitoba, was posthumously awarded the
Victoria Cross, the only Victoria Cross ever won by a member of 6
Group.

Three nights later Schnaufer shot down a Lancaster, his 78th victim,
near Arras, while the leading night-fighter pilot, Helmut Lent, shot
down his 99th and 100th. The target that night was a synthetic-oil refin-
ery at Sterkrade, in the Ruhr. With the Normandy beachheads becoming more established, it was now possible for Harris to turn his

*Helmut Lent (*right*),
Kommodore NJG 3,
in conversation with
Heinz Schnaufer,.*
Kommandeur
IV./NJG 1.

attentions, in part at least, back to Germany. But he could not do so on his own terms. For some time, beginning shortly before the invasion, the United States Air Force had been attacking German fuel plants, believing that to be the most likely way to cripple the Germans' military and air potential. Now the Allied Supreme Commander, General Dwight D Eisenhower, under whose ultimate command Harris' force had been placed before the invasion, decreed that Bomber Command should also give priority to oil-related targets. To Harris, Commander-in-Chief of Bomber Command, this was yet another in what he saw as an endless succession of 'panacea targets' – ingenious-sounding but impracticable, sometimes simply crazy, schemes by earnest planners in which his bombers were to be used to shorten the war. To the unequivocal Harris there was only one way to do that – to use bombers to pound Germany into submission. Any diversion from that direct route he saw as ill advised:

> I had therefore learnt from bitter experience to regard their [i.e. economic experts'] predictions with the greatest suspicion and largely to discount their claims in advance.
>
> When Bomber Command was required to begin bombing the synthetic oil plants in conjunction with the Americans in June – at least we had the means to find and hit the targets in reasonable weather. My main objection was that we were swapping horses in mid-stream. Though the bomber offensive had only begun in 1943 and had ended within a year when we were put on invasion targets, the vast damage that had been done in that short space of time showed that if the available bomber forces – ourselves and the Americans – went on and developed the weight of the attack that was by then possible, Germany would then without a shadow of doubt be knocked right out in a few months. I therefore strongly objected to stopping the offensive for which we had worked for five years, and which was succeeding hand over fist at the very moment when we at long last disposed of such weight of attack as to put all question of failure out of court. On the one side I saw certainty of success, and on the other still many chances of failure.[1]

Despite Harris' forebodings, there can be no doubt that the oil offensive was in fact a great success, a major factor in bringing the war to a comparatively early close, as Harris himself subsequently conceded, while still maintaining that it had been a gamble, albeit it one that came off. Bomber Command achieved a degree of accuracy by night, thanks to new navigational and target-finding aids and to the decreasing efficiency of the German defences, that surprised even Harris, and he quotes the Reich Minister for Armament and War Production, Albert Speer as saying, 'Owing to their greater effectiveness night attacks caused considerably more damage than day raids.' Like the Good Book, Speer is very quotable in support of almost any point one wishes to make, but what is certain is that the efficiency of Bomber Command as

[1] From *Bomber Offensive*, by Marshal of the Royal Air Force Sir Arthur Harris, GCB, OBE, AFC, published by Collins, 1947.

an aggressive, and possibly war-winning, weapon increased enormously in the final eleven months of the war. But the *Nachtjagd* was still a potent force, and the German flak was always a threat, even if a lesser one. Of more than three hundred four-engined bombers that attacked the oil plant at Sterkrade, over twenty fell to night fighters, including Schnaufer's singleton, and ten to flak. The majority of bombers that failed to return were Halifaxes: No. 77 Squadron., flying from Full Sutton in Yorkshire, lost seven of the twenty-three that it despatched that night.

There was another type of target which, at this period, was perforce diverting Harris's bomber resources from German cities, which he believed should be his first priority. Since December 1943 Bomber Command and the USAAF had been sporadically attacking, on a very small scale, so-called 'ski sites' in France, the launching ramps for the V1 pilotless flying bomb mentioned earlier. The Germans fired their first flying bombs against London on 12 June, less than a week after the invasion, causing heavy casualties, and there was a sudden urgency to do something about the new threat to the civilian population in England. Starting on the night on which Sterkrade was attacked, large forces of Halifaxes and Lancasters would attack the launching sites in France by both day and night, usually, thanks to *Oboe* marking, with great accuracy. In general the sites were only weakly defended by anti-aircraft guns, and the short distance that the bombers penetrated the Continent meant that fighters seldom intercepted the attackers, so that casualties on such raids were usually – but not always – very low. The campaign against the flying-bomb sites was destined to last until the end of August, by which time the Germans had retreated so far inland that all the sites that threatened England had been overrun by the Allied armies.

On the night of 21/22 June fifteen Mosquitoes, mostly acting as pathfinders, and 156 Lancasters, the majority of which were from No. 5 Group, reverted to the synthetic-oil target after a period of five days during which bad weather had restricted operations to comparatively small-scale raids against V-weapon objectives. The targets were the Scholven refineries at Buer, near Duisburg in the Ruhr Valley, and Wesseling, to the south of Cologne, and the attacks took place simultaneously. The night fighters were scrambled in good time and found their way into the bomber stream, where their task was made much easier than usual by a blanket of low cloud against which the bombers were silhouetted, and they enjoyed considerable success. Of the force bombing Wesseling, 37 Lancasters were lost – more than a quarter of those who had set out – while against Buer the tally was 9 from 123. The German pilot with the highest score was *Hauptmann* Ernst-Wilhelm Modrow, who scored five, with Heinz Schnaufer coming second with four.

Modrow, from I./NJG 1, stationed at Venlo, was flying the He 219, a revolutionary, custom-built night fighter which, had it come into service earlier and in greater numbers than it did, might well have proved

to be a decisive factor in the battle against the British bombers. As it was, opposition to the machine in high places in the *Luftwaffe* – Göring himself and Kammhuber were numbered among those who opposed its introduction – meant that it was slow in coming on stream and only one *Gruppe*, I./NJG 1, was equipped with it. It was the only German night fighter that had a performance that came near to matching that of the Mosquito. Flown by *Major* Werner Streib, *Kommandeur* of I./NJG 1, on its first operational trial on 12 June 1943, it had destroyed five four-engined bombers, but had unfortunately crashed on the runway on its return to Venlo, so giving fuel to the arguments of those who opposed its introduction into the *Nachtjagd*.

The night of the attacks on Buer and Wesseling were successful ones for the first two *Gruppen* of NJG 1, who together destroyed twenty Lancasters. He 219 pilots from I./NJG 1 shot down thirteen: in addition to the five[1] claimed by *Hauptmann* Modrow, *Hauptmann* Strüning shot down four and *Feldwebel* Willi Morlock and *Oberleutnant* Josef Nabrich two each. Among the other successful pilots that night, also with two victories, was Schnaufer's friend Martin Drewes, who was flying a Bf 110.

Flying north from Saint-Trond towards the incoming bomber stream,

Oberleutnant *Augenstein returns to Saint-Trond from hospital after being wounded in action. Here he is seen with Schnaufer* (right) *and Georg Fengler.* (Fengler)

---

[1] Records are unclear on this, some saying that Modrow only shot down four.

Schnaufer (right) with Major *Greisig, Station Commander, Saint-Trond. Schnaufer is wearing the* Eichenlaub, *awarded on 24 June 1944.* (Fengler)

Schnaufer destroyed his first victim at 0125 hours. It came to earth at Valkenswaard, south of Eindhoven and just over the Dutch border. Following the stream south, and back over Belgian territory, he shot down his second at 0130 hours at Meeuwen-Gruitrode and this third at 0136 hours at Opoeteren, only about seven miles away. Then, after a break of twenty-eight minutes, he attacked and destroyed his fourth near Hamont. Against the entry in his *Leistungsbuch* referring to his final victory are the words, *'Starke Gegenwehr'* – strong defensive fire.

Two days after these four successes, which brought his total of kills

up to 84, Schnaufer was awarded the Oak Leaves (*Eichenlaub*) to the Knight's Cross of the Iron Cross. That the Oak Leaves were not awarded lightly may be judged by the fact that by the end of the war only twenty-eight night-fighter pilots had achieved the distinction. What is noteworthy – and puzzling – about Schnaufer's award, however, is that it came so late in his operational career. He had been awarded his Knight's Cross when his score was 42, at a time when 25 was the average score at which the decoration might be expected, and now he had had to wait until he had doubled that number before reaching the next higher stage, the Oak Leaves. The leading night-fighter pilot was still Helmut Lent, who had 100 victories to his name, but Schnaufer, with 84, was running him a close second. The rest were far behind. As has already been mentioned, Lent had been awarded his *Ritterkreuz* when he had scored fourteen night victories (he had already shot down eight by day as a Zerstörer pilot), and his Oak Leaves had followed after only 35 kills by night.

CHAPTER TEN

July and August 1944

Invasion-related targets. Awarded the Schwerter.

By the beginning of the month of July 1944 Allied troops, pushing forward on a broad front from their original beachheads, were well established in Normandy, and back-up units and vast quantities of supplies were pouring into France. In England the German V1 offensive, which had begun on the 17th of June, was taking its toll. The first ten days of the onslaught by the pilotless aircraft caused over 6,000 casualties, mostly among civilians, of which 1,600 were fatal. July saw, on the 20th, the unsuccessful attempt on Hitler's life at Rastenburg in East Prussia.

For the night fighters stationed in Holland and Belgium the month started slowly. Raids by heavy bombers on Germany at this juncture were few, because there were, in the view of the Allied Supreme Commander, more important tasks for Bomber Command. V-weapon sites and communications targets had priority, as did operations in direct support of the ground troops in France. Most of these attacks were carried out in daylight. In complete contrast to the early months of the war, when German day fighters had wreaked terrible attrition against unescorted RAF bombers, casualties among those attacking targets in France by day at this period were very low indeed. The *Luftwaffe* was numerically overwhelmed, both in the east and the west, and its day-fighter force had suffered huge losses of aircraft and pilots in its desperate defence of the homeland against the Fortresses and Liberators of the USAAF and their escorts, the P-51 Mustangs, the P-47 Thunderbolts, and the P-38 Lightnings. While the *Luftwaffe* aircraft could be replaced – albeit with increasing difficulty as the war progressed – experienced pilots could not. It was a situation that had been developing since well before the invasion, and which had had its roots in a joint American/British policy decision at the Washington Conference in May 1943 to attack the German aircraft industry in the air and on the ground: the brunt of the implementation of this policy had fallen to the Americans, who, because they operated by day, were uniquely placed – and equipped – to destroy German fighters in direct conflict. At the end of May 1944 *Luftflotte 3*, responsible for air operations on the western front, had only 115 serviceable single-engined fighters, while *Luftflotte Reich*, defending Germany itself, could muster only just over 500. The situation pertaining as early as in April 1944, two months before the invasion, had been summed up by the *General der Jagdflieger*, Adolf Galland[1]:

> The problem of fighter aviation, which the Americans have created, is simply one of air superiority. The ratio of numbers which we fight in the day time lies approximately between 1: 6 and 1: 8. The standard of the enemy is extraordinarily high. Daylight fighting in the last four months has caused a loss of more than 1,000 men of the flying personnel, among whom, of course, were many of the best squadron leaders, wing commanders and group commodores. We have trouble in closing these gaps, not with numbers, but with experienced pilots.

Now, following the invasion, and despite the deployment of further fighters from *Luftflotte Reich*, the Germans simply could not come near to matching the vast numbers of Allied fighters that filled the skies over France, escorting the bombers, shooting down any German aircraft that dared to show itself or strafing the fighter airfields and preventing the comparatively few available German fighters from getting into the air to do combat. A major change in Bomber Command tactics had come about, and it would persist until the end of war. Harris could now send large forces of bombers during the daylight hours with little fear of their being intercepted by hostile fighters. Gradually, as the Allied forces advanced and the German forward airfields were overrun, Bomber Command would be able to penetrate more and more deeply into the Fatherland without having to rely on darkness for a degree of protection.

Two raids in July, one by day and one by night, provide an interesting contrast, underlining as they do the dramatic change that Allied air superiority had brought about to the bomber war. During the daylight hours of 18 July, 667 Lancasters and 260 Halifaxes bombed fortified villages in Normandy in support of the British Second Army advance, and only six were shot down, all by flak. *Luftwaffe* fighters did not put in an appearance against what, had Allied fighters not been in action, would have been a very vulnerable force. That very night a further 253 heavy bombers attacked railway junctions at Aulnoye and Revigny, admittedly much deeper in France, and twenty-six were shot down by night fighters. Of those twenty-four were from the force of just over a hundred Lancasters attacking Revigny, which lay near the German night-fighter base of St-Dizier.

If July 1944 started slowly for the *Nachtjagd*, the tempo increased as the month progressed. By the 31st the month's claims amounted to 258. It is impossible to say how many of them were Bomber Command machines, because some of the Bf 110s and Ju 88s of the night-fighter force had been operating by day and had shot down a number of aircraft from Fighter Command, Coastal Command, the Second Tactical

---

[1] *The First and the Last*, by Adolf Galland, published 1955 by Methuen and Co. Ltd.

7 July 1944. A publicity photograph of Schnaufer. The official press release reads, 'The holder of the Eichenlaub, Hauptmann *Schnauffer [sic], one of our most successful night fighters, who has destroyed 80 enemy bombers, is the Commander of the most successful night-fighter* Gruppe. (Fengler)

Air Force and the United States Air Force. They had suffered severe casualties themselves. Bomber Command losses, at 229 aircraft from 11,500 sorties, represented rather less than two percent, an interesting contrast with the figure of from four to five percent average that prevailed at the time of the Battle of Berlin.

For Heinz Schnaufer, July 1994 was less successful, operationally speaking, than the preceding three months had been, but still impressive. He shot down two heavy bombers on the night of the 20th/21st of the month, and three on the 28th/29th. But there were other happenings of interest in the context of both the Schnaufer story and that of the night fighters in general.

As already described, the original *Lichtenstein* intercept radar carried by the German night fighters had been effectively rendered redundant by the introduction of *Window* in July 1943, so the Germans had introduced, as rapidly as production and installation difficulties would allow, the SN-2 radar, which operated on a longer wave-length. Since early 1944 the majority of the night fighters had been equipped with *SN-2*, and so far the British scientists had not discovered its wavelength and so been able to jam it. Bomber Command aircraft were still dropping the original short 'Window', which was effective against the now obsolete *Lichtenstein* but not against *SN-2*. Indeed, the value of 'Window' at this period is debatable: not only did it not jam the fighters' intercept radar, but on the new panorama radars such as *Mammut* and *Wassermann* that the Germans were introducing 'Window' gave a clear 'paint' of the track of the bomber stream and so was a useful aid to the controllers in their efforts to direct fighters into the concentration of bombers.

Then, at 0430 hours on 13 July 1944, at the airfield of Woodbridge in Suffolk, an aircraft that the runway controller took to be a Mosquito came in on the approach, got a 'green', and landed. In his book, *Instruments of Darkness* the aviation historian Dr Alfred Price describes what happened next:

> The plane touched down and taxied to the end of the runway, where it switched off its engines. Its crew were standing around on the apron, stretching their legs, when the crew bus arrived to pick them up; and it was in this way that an RAF fight-sergeant came to find himself confronted with three live German air crewmen. The surprise was mutual, but the British NCO produced a Very pistol and forced the Germans to surrender. The 'Mosquito', it now transpired, was a fully equipped Ju 88 night-fighter. Its inexperienced pilot had inadvertently steered a reciprocal course on his compass and arrived in England without knowing it. He had been lucky to reach Woodbridge; when RAF technicians attempted to take a sample of fuel from the aircraft they found that there was insufficient even for analysis.

There is another version of the event that gives further detail. In Ab A Jansen's book, *Wespennest Leeuwarden*, Part III, the author identifies the aircraft as a Junkers 88 G-B, identification number 4R+UR, of 7./NJG 2, which had taken off from the Dutch airfield of Volkel in the early hours of the 13th July on a night-fighter patrol over the North Sea. The pilot was *Obergefreiter* (roughly equivalent to Lance-Corporal) Hans Mackle. According to Jansen, Mackle's navigation instruments went unserviceable and, running short of fuel and completely disorientated, he saw an airfield, which he took to be Venlo, and landed there.

Mackle's incompetence proved costly for the *Nachtjagd*. The Ju 88 was equipped with *SN-2*, so that it was a very simple matter for the RAF technicians to discover its wavelength so that 'Window' of the correct size – half the wavelength – could be introduced. There was in fact some suitably sized 'Window' already available, and the bombers began dropping it within ten days of the unexpected arrival of the Junkers night fighter at Woodbridge. There were further benefits: firstly, the *Serrate* sets fitted to Mosquito intruders were still tuned to the *Lichtenstein* frequency, and now they could be retuned to pick up transmissions from SN-2. Secondly, the aircraft was fitted with a device the Germans called '*Flensburg*', which was used for homing on to signals transmitted by RAF aircraft equipped with 'Monica', a device that enabled them to detect night fighters in their vicinity. As a result, 'Monica' was removed from all Bomber Command aircraft, while restrictions were put on the use of other devices that transmitted radio signals.

Fritz Rumpelhardt recalls the night on which the longer 'Window' was first used:

> I talked Schnaufer into attack position on at least fifteen possible targets, and we never got a visual contact. We didn't see a thing. Schnaufer got very angry. He played hell, calling me all sorts of rude names. So I switched off my intercom, so I couldn't hear him and he couldn't hear me. He banged on the cabin roof to tell me to switch on again. And when we landed all the others had had exactly the same experience, and I was rehabilitated. Schnaufer apologized to me.

In addition to describing the effect of the new 'Window', this episode is a good illustration of the in-crew relationship that existed between Schnaufer and Rumpelhardt, both officers, albeit of different rank and seniority. Wilhelm Gänsler, however, remained an NCO, and in some crews that would have been a bar to anything approaching intimacy. But, as Rumpelhardt recalls today, that did not apply to them:

> We could, if necessary, be very critical with one another. I remember one particular occasion when had we had been in visual contact with more than one bomber, yet Schnaufer had aimed badly and we hadn't had any success. When we had landed, and Schnaufer was still in the cockpit, Gänsler stood on the wing and told him that he had shot *'unmöglich schlecht'* – impossibly badly – and that if he couldn't do better than that he wouldn't fly with him any more. Gänsler spoke very formally, not calling him 'you' but speaking in the third person and addressing him as *'Herr Hauptmann'*. That was the tone. We were all very critical of each other. Mistakes simply weren't allowed. Schnaufer encouraged it – we would talk every operational flight over after we landed, and everyone had to heed and accept the others' comments. But on this occasion they were almost at each other's throat, and I had to stand between them and try to calm Willem Gänsler down. I can't remember exactly when it happened. Yet Willem was normally a very quiet, reserved man.

Some of the night-fighter crews never fully mastered the new 'Window', but for Fritz Rumpelhardt, like many other experienced radar operators, it did not long remain an insuperable problem:

> When the new 'Window' came into operation we soon learned to cope with it. At that time we were already receiving broadcast information on the course and height of the bombers, and once we got into the stream we simply flew that heading. If we picked up a return on the SN-2 and it seemed to be flying very quickly, we knew it couldn't be a real bomber, so we ignored it. And then there was another piece of electronic equipment, which was introduced later and was fitted to the SN-2. I can't remember its name, and it was experimental when we first got it. I don't know if all the other crews had it, but it cut down the number of spurious echoes on the SN-2, and I found it very useful.

On the night of the 28th/29th July, Schnaufer scored his 87th, 88th and 89th kills. One came to earth at Malmsheim, thirteen miles to the west of Stuttgart, the other two in and near Pforzheim, twenty-five miles north-west of the same city. Stuttgart was the target of Bomber Command that night, and the night fighters had considerable success, intercepting the stream early and shooting down the lion's share of the thirty-nine Lancasters that were lost, 7.9 percent of the 494 that made up the attacking force. Another Schnaufer legend has grown up around the events of that night. In short it is that Schnaufer set out deliberately to shoot down the Master Bomber, and succeeded. There are two factors that seem to have contributed to this tale, firstly that Stuttgart was Schnaufer's birthplace, and secondly that it was unusual for Schnaufer to penetrate so far into Germany before claiming victims. One published account (which gives the date of the events as 25 July, when in fact Schnaufer did not score) promotes Schnaufer to *Major* prematurely, but that is a minor error when compared to the many other factual mistakes and flights of fancy it contains:

Oberstleutnant *Streib*, Kommodore *NJG 1*, *is in the centre. To his left are Schnaufer and Weissflog, to his right Greiner.*

> The 22-year-old *Major* Heinz Wolfgang Schnaufer from Calw, with 121 victories the most successful night fighter in the world, was stationed with his *Staffel* at Saint-Trond in Belgium. On the evening of the 24th July further incoming formations of heavy bombers were reported approaching

Germany. When it became known that a large formation that had come in over France was heading for Stuttgart, *Major* Schnaufer and his crew took off in their Me 110 and raced after the bomber stream, even though on that particular day he was standing by as reserve against unexpected developments. But he cannot allow 'his' Stuttgart to be bombed while he is sitting about idly in Saint-Trond.

He flies at a height of 5000 metres and soon reaches the end of the great enemy formation, which is made up of about 500 machines, mostly four-engined bombers. In order, as a single pilot, to be most effective against such a mass of aircraft, Schnaufer decides to shoot down the so-called 'Master of Ceremonies' aircraft, which carries the officer in command, in order to prevent a well-organized attack on the town: but he, the Master of Ceremonies, is flying at the head of a stream at least one hundred kilometres long. Schnaufer goes down some metres and flies below the enemy. He demands the last of his machine so that he can reach the Commander at the head of the stream before Stuttgart.

Schnaufer also knows that in order to protect himself against enemy fighter attacks the commander's machine will remain in the middle of the leading gaggle until shortly before the target, when he will pull away in order to reach a greater height in order to drop the first marker-bombs for the following illuminators, who will drop the 'Christmas trees'. The commander will circle in his aircraft above the town and direct the attack by R/T: but tonight that will not happen.

Schnaufer has already reached the head of the stream, when the expected happens. A bomber from the first wave draws away – that must be him! Schnaufer attacks at once. But the British rear-gunner is on the alert. He has seen Schnaufer's Me 110 and he lets fly with all barrels. The night-fighter's radar is hit and put out of action. The Me 110 wavers for a few seconds but then Schnaufer succeeds in picking up the Master of Ceremonies, who had been lost from sight for a few seconds, again. At 0150 hours he is shot down to the northeast of Horb. The British lead-aircraft strikes the ground with a mighty explosion.

All this happens at the very last moment, because within a very short time the Lancaster would have reached Stuttgart and dropped its marker as planned.

Major Schnaufer does a circuit of the crash site and then tears after the following bomber stream. The British must have realized that their commander had been shot down, because the bombers suddenly change course and split up into small groups. Without their chief they fly helplessly on at a height of 4,000 metres. A lot of them jettison their bombs, and woods and fields are ploughed up by high-explosive bombs and aerial mines. In Stuttgart this attack is far less heavy than following attacks.

One of the engines of Schnaufer's machine has been hit and is running lame. Despite this he shoots down another machine. But his Me 110 is becoming ever less manoeuvrable. All that Schnaufer can do is to reach the nearest airfield as quickly as possible and land there. He says to his comrades, 'I'm going to Echterdingen: we can make it there.' He holds his breath, flying on one engine until he reaches Echterdingen.

The airfield must be directly below him, but there is nothing but darkness, nothing can be seen. His radio is destroyed, and he has no contact with the flying control centre at Echterdingen base. And so Schnaufer must try to land 'blind'. But Schnaufer can still shoot off Very cartridges, and they are answered by flashing lights. They are understood. The air-field lighting is switched on. The crew breathe again; the approach fun-nel is ahead of them. A few moments later they are climbing out of their aircraft. Only when it has been repaired can the aircraft be flown back to its operational base at Saint-Trond.

A few comments might be appropriate, even although the nonsenses are largely self-evident. Firstly, *Hauptmann* Schnaufer was not with his *Staffel* at Saint-Trond, but with his *Gruppe*. As *Gruppenkommandeur* he belonged to the Staff, not to a *Staffel*. Secondly, there would be no pos-sible way in which the Germans could have known that the bomber stream was heading for Stuttgart. The thought of a Bf 110 taking off and pursuing and overtaking a bomber stream is ludicrous – the Bf 110 had precious speed advantage over the Lancaster – as is the idea of Schnaufer setting out to defend 'his' Stuttgart against the RAF bombers. The writer shows his detachment from reality when he describes the functions and operational methods of the Master Bomber, who was not the 'officer in command' or the 'commander' of the bomber force and who did not fly at the head of the stream, but usually arrived after the first markers had been dropped by the Pathfinders. He did not 'protect himself by remaining in the leading gaggle' and then pull away to drop the first markers – the Master Bomber was not primarily a marker, but a controller. Schnaufer's aircraft was not hit by enemy fire that night, and none of his three victims came down near Horb. And, finally, the loss of the Master Bomber would in no way have prevented the bombers from attacking Stuttgart – there were plenty of Pathfinder air-craft to mark the target, and there would certainly have been a Deputy Master Bomber.

It might be thought that it would be difficult to write a less truthful account of Schnaufer's activities that night, but our old friend '*Landser*', not to be outdone, has a very good try:

Other *Gruppen* are already airborne when the early-warning service reports a heavy formation of bombers from Italy with Stuttgart as their probable target. But simultaneously a second British formation is report-ed approaching from over the sea. There are not enough night fighters to attack the superior forces of bombers.

'I will fly to South Germany! The *Gruppe* can operate here,' Schnaufer tells his *Kommodore*.

'You're taking a great deal on! The British have got a head's start!'

'I'll cope.'

The course is worked out in the crew room. From Holland to Southern Germany – what a crazy idea! And the enemy is already head-ing for the target.

'We'll fly, even if the aircraft breaks into pieces,' says Schnaufer to his crew.

'We mustn't let them drop bombs on Stuttgart,' says Gänsler. 'Herr *Hauptmann*, you've got to get the most you can from the aircraft!'

They fly at a height of 5,000 Metres. There are stars everywhere.

The article goes on to describe how the bombers fly in great curves, hoping to deceive the Germans as to the identity of their target. Then Schnaufer reaches the end of the stream, and he promptly shoots down the last bomber. But that is not enough for our hero:

> Schnaufer knows that he cannot do anything by himself against the entire bomber stream. To oppose these 400 machines would mean certain death. If he is to thwart a successful attack on Stuttgart he must shoot down the Master of Ceremonies. But where is the Commander?

Schnaufer positions himself beneath the stream, alert for the escort fighters that are, the writer says, accompanying the bombers.

> Mile after mile Schnaufer flies beneath the formation, waiting for the moment that the Master of Ceremonies breaks away from the first wave and flies on alone to Stuttgart. The waiting tears at their nerves. Suddenly, when the stream is only a few miles from Stuttgart, an aircraft breaks away from the leading wave. 'There he is!' shout Rumpelhardt and Schnaufer with one voice.

Schnaufer attacks, but his machine is hit by enemy fire. Undeterred, Schnaufer presses home his attack:

> The airscrews of the Messerschmitt are less than twenty metres from the Lancaster's fuselage when Schnaufer presses the firing button of his cannon, which spew out death a thousand-fold, mercilessly tearing apart the belly of the bomber, exploding its tracer ammunition and creating an enormous explosion, blasting apart the aircraft, the men in it and everything solid, melting them, atomising them.
> A voice cries out – 'The formation!'
> Now hundreds of black shadows emerge from the background. The British will have seen their Master of Ceremonies shot down. Now they have no idea where to drop their bombs. Admittedly the pilots know what their target is, and they have maps with them. It would not be difficult for them to attack Stuttgart and unload their shocking cargoes. But what if night fighters and heavy flak are waiting there for them?

So Schnaufer has triumphed, and his hometown is spared. But Schnaufer's aircraft has been badly hit by the British rear gunner, and he has to get down. He heads for Echterdingen. On the way he encounters and shoots down another Lancaster. All in a night's work!

Fritz Rumpelhardt, however, is dismissive:

> I have looked in my flying log-book. We took off from Saint-Trond at 0045 hours on 29.7.44, and we landed back at Saint-Trond at 0306 hours with an intact machine and undamaged radar and radio equipment. We got three kills, all made by Schnaufer with his *Schräge Musik*. Heinz had long since had the rear machine gun, an MG 81Z intended to be used by the air gunner, taken out of the aircraft so that it would fly faster (weight and reduction of air resistance). And so there was no way in which Wilhelm Gänsler could shoot down a bomber himself. Both

these articles are based on rampant fantasy, presumably intended, by means of the romantic way in which they are written, to stimulate the interest of the readers. They have, however, very little in common with the hard facts. How, I wonder, could a 'Master of Ceremonies' be recognized as such, particularly in the dark? We did in fact once shoot one down, and there was a fantastic fireworks display[1]. Whether that was on the 29th of July I can no longer recall with any certainty. But in any case that was a matter of pure chance, in no way the result of any tactical consideration. And in fact our machine was only once damaged by enemy fire, and that was on the 2nd of June 1942, when we made an unsuccessful attack on a second bomber after our first kill. I have a vague recollection that on one other occasion we brought a very few bullet holes in our fuselage back home with us, but the aerodynamic qualities of our aircraft were not affected in the slightest.

The day after these happenings, the 30th July 1944, *Hauptmann* Heinz Schnaufer, *Kommandeur* IV./NJG 1, received a rather special letter. Carefully hand-printed in Gothic script, it read:

My dear Schnaufer,

With praiseworthy bravery and an exemplary operational spirit in the defence against the terror attacks, as both an individual fighter and unit commander, you have accomplished outstanding achievements and, with a unique series of successes, fought your way into the leading group of my best and most successful night-fighter pilots.

The *Führer* has now recognized your achievements in the defence of the homeland with the award of the Oak Leaves with Swords to the Knight's Cross of the Iron Cross.

I offer to you my most sincere congratulations on this high decoration for gallantry. Together with my acknowledgement I also send to you the thanks of the whole German people, who see in you one of their boldest and bravest soldiers.

May soldier's fortune remain with you and lead you to new, proud successes at the head of your unit.

Your,
Göring,
Reichsmarschall of the Greater German Reich
and Commander-in-Chief of the *Luftwaffe*.

'The Swords' *(Schwerter)*, as Schnaufer's latest decoration was generally known, was the second-highest of the six grades of the Iron Cross (*EK2, EK1, Ritterkreuz, Eichenlaub, Schwerter, Brillanten*)[2]. During the Second World War the Swords were awarded to 150 members of the armed forces, only five of whom were night-fighter pilots: Heinz Schnaufer,

---

[1] The machine Rumpelhardt refers to was probably a PFF marker, not a Master Bomber.

[2] Iron Cross (Second Class); Iron Cross (First Class); Knight's Cross; Oak Leaves; Swords; Diamonds. (These were the short forms in common usage of the names of the decorations. There were also two higher stages – the Knight's Cross with Golden Oak Leaves, Swords and Diamonds, and the Grand Cross – but they were each awarded to only one man, *Oberst* Hans-Ulrich Rudel and Hermann Göring respectively.

Mein lieber Schnaufer!

Mit bewunderungswürdiger Tapferkeit und mitreißendem Ein-
satzgeist haben Sie bei der Abwehr der feindlichen Terrorangriffe als Einzel-
kämpfer und Verbandsführer hervorragende Leistungen vollbracht und sich
in einzigartigem Siegeslauf in die Spitzengruppe meiner besten und
erfolgreichsten Nachtjäger herausgekämpft.

Der Führer hat nun Ihre Verdienste zum Schutze der
Heimat durch die Verleihung des

Eichenlaubes mit Schwertern

zum Ritterkreuz des Eisernen Kreuzes
gewürdigt.

Zu dieser hohen Tapferkeitsauszeichnung spreche ich Ihnen
meine herzlichsten Glückwünsche aus. Zusammen mit meiner Anerkennung übermittle ich Ihnen den Dank des ganzen Deutschen Volkes,
das in Ihnen einen seiner kühnsten und tapfersten Soldaten
erblickt.

Möge Ihnen das Soldatenglück auch weiterhin treu
bleiben und Sie an der Spitze Ihres Verbandes zu neuen stolzen Er-
folgen führen.

Ihr Göring
Reichsmarschall des Großdeutschen Reiches
und Oberbefehlshaber der Luftwaffe.

Hitler awarding decorations. Schnaufer, awarded the Schwerter *(second from the left) with Erich Hartmann to his right. This was shortly after the attempt on Hitler's life, and Hitler, wounded in his right hand in the explosion, is seen here shaking hands with his left hand.* (Fengler)

Awaiting Schnaufer's return from the award of the Schwerter. *Left to right:* Drewes; Breves; Jabs; Weissflog; Sutor. (Greiner)

Schnaufer returns to Saint-Trond after receiving the Schwerter. (Greiner)

Martin Drewes congratulates Schnaufer on the award of the Schwerter. (Diener)

Above: *Schnaufer is presented with a 'lucky pig' to mark the award of the* Schwerter. *The presentation was made by his official driver. To the driver's left are Fengler, Drewes, Schnaufer and Greiner.* (Diener)

Schnaufer is wearing the Schwerter *decoration. Fengler is in the background, left.*

Lfd. Nr.	Typ	Datum	Uhrzeit	Ort	Höhe	Zeugen	Bemerkungen
79	Lancaster oder Halifax	17.7.44	01.54	1 km N. Drenmel (12 km N Hertogenbosch)	4000 m	Lt. Rumpelhardt, Ofw. Gänsler	brennender Absturz nach 4 Angriffen starke Gegenwehr.
80	- " -	- " -	02.04	Berkel (5 km N Rotterdam)	3800 m	- " -	- " -	brennender Absturz nach 1 Angriff
81	- " -	22.6.44	01.25	Valkenswaard (9 km S. Eindhoven)	8000 m	- " -	- " -	(Einflug) anerkannt 498/44
82	- " -	- " -	01.30	2 km S Meeuwen (22 km NNO Hasselt)	5200 m	- " -	- " -	(Einflug) anerkannt Nr. 498/44
83	- " -	- " -	01.36	5 km S Opoteren (21 km NNW Maastricht)	5200 m	- " -	- " -	(Einflug) anerkannt Nr. 498/44
84	- " -	- " -	02.04	6 km S Hamont (27 km SSO Eindhoven)	2900 m	- " -	- " -	Starke Gegenwehr anerkannt Nr. 498/44
85	- " -	21.7.44	01.48	1,5 km N Boxtel	4500 m	- " -	- " -	Absturz nach 1 Angriff (explodiert) anerkannt Nr. 910/44
86	- " -	- " -	01.57	Zwischen Den Hout u. Made (8 km N. Breda)	2500 m	- " -	- " -	- " -
87	- " -	29.7.44	01.38	Friedhof Pforzheim	6000 m	- " -	- " -	- " - anerkannt Nr. 1138/44
88	- " -	- " -	1.50	bei Eutingen (3 km NO Pforzheim)	4800 m	- " -	- " -	- " - anerkannt Nr. 1138/44
89	- " -	- " -	01.57 / 02.44	bei Malmsheim (20 km W Stuttgart)	4900 m	- " -	- " -	- " - anerkannt Nr. 1138/44
90	- " -	13.8.44	00.48	Waxweilesen (14 km S. Trier)	4300 m	- " -	- " -	- " - anerkannt Nr. 1138/44
91	- " -	- " -	01.05	Coucy (28 km SSW Malmedy)	4300 m	- " -	- " -	- " - anerkannt Nr. 1138/44

A page from Schnaufer's Leistungsbuch *showing 13 kills between June and August 1944.* (Rumpelhardt)

Werner Streib, Hajo Herrmann, Heinrich zu Sayn-Wittgenstein and Helmut Lent. Heinz Schnaufer was now one of a very select band of Germans: not only that, he was also the second-highest scorer of the *Nachtjagd*. He had now passed the late Wittgenstein's total, and the only man ahead of him was Helmut Lent, who had scored his 100th kill on the night of the 15th/16th June 1944, when Schnaufer scored his 78th. The day after Schnaufer was awarded the *Schwerter*, Lent, *Kommodore* NJG 3, was awarded the *Brillanten*, the first night-fighter pilot to be so honoured. The *Führer* himself decorated Heinz Schnaufer with the *Schwerter*. It is said that when he came into the room in which the presentations were to take place his first words where, 'Where is the night fighter?' Hitler looked haggard, and he used his left hand to shake the hand of Schnaufer. His right hand was still in bandages, a result of the abortive attempt on his life the previous month.

CHAPTER ELEVEN

August 1944 to March 1945

**Ritterkreuz for Fritz and Willem. Retreat to
Germany. The death of Helmut Lent.
Schnaufer's 'century'. Awarded the Brillanten.
Becomes Kommodore NJG 4, promoted Major.
A brother's demise. Nine in a day. Further retreat.**

In the course of the few eventful weeks that had passed since the 6th of
June the Allied invasion forces in France had consolidated their hold on
the Normandy beachheads and begun their forward progress into
Hitler's '*Festung Europa*'. By the end of July the Germans had been driven out of the Cherbourg peninsula and the Americans had started the
breakout that was to develop into an incredibly rapid advance across
France. In the east, the Red Army was in the Baltic States, Lithuania
and Poland, and still rolling onward inexorably to the west. On the 15th

*The Schnaufer crew,
Gänsler, Schnaufer,
Rumpelhardt.* (Diener)

Vorläufiges Besitzzeugnis

Der Führer
und Oberste Befehlshaber
der Wehrmacht

hat

dem <u>Leutnant Friedrich Rumpelhardt</u>

das Ritterkreuz
des Eisernen Kreuzes

am <u>8. August 1944</u> verliehen

<u>Hauptquartier d.Ob.d.L.</u> ,den <u>10. August 1944</u>

Der Chef der Personellen Rüstung und
National-Sozialistischen Führung der Luftwaffe
I.A.

[signature]

Oberst

8 August 1944. Certificate of the award of the Ritterkreuz *to Leutnant Fritz Rumpelhardt. The same decoration was also awarded to* Oberfeldwebel *'Willem' Gänsler. Schnaufer's crew thus became the only one with all members wearing the Knight's Cross.* (Fengler)

of August American troops landed on the Mediterranean coast of France, presenting the hard-pressed *Wehrmacht* with yet another defensive problem, and ten days later Paris fell. By the 31st of the month the Allies' spearheads were approaching Metz and Nancy, and the German border was less that fifty miles away.

In the wake of Schnaufer's award of the *Schwerter* there were further distinctions for the Schnaufer crew. On the 8th of August both Fritz Rumpelhardt and Wilhelm Gänsler were awarded the Knight's Cross to the Iron Cross, and the crew so became the only one in the *Nachtjagd* of which all the crew members could wear the high decoration. Very few radio operators were so decorated during the war, and only one 'third man', and that was 'Willem' Gänsler.

The targets for Bomber Command on the night of the 12th/13th August – or at least the targets in Germany, because there were raids into France as well – were Brunswick and Rüsselsheim. Neither raid was successful, while casualties to both attacking forces were severe. Of

25 August 1944. Another photo-call. Caption: 'First...second ...third! There is a great deal to do if the organisation is to run at full revs., particularly when the Kommandeur *himself is short of time for office work because of an urgent air test. But, as* Hauptmann Schnaufer *knows, his faithful adjutant, himself a successful night-fighter pilot, will soon sort things out.* Oberleutnant F., *who recently came back to base after shooting down three bombers, has been the Commander's right hand for a long time.'* 'Oberleutnant F.' is Georg Fengler. (Fengler)

From the same photo-call: 'Hauptmann Schnaufer has not only earned fame as a night fighter. He has also attracted admiration as an exemplary leader of men. The Kommandeur *often engages in stimulating conversation with the ground staff on the operational airfield. The* Oberfeldwebel *goes away well pleased. Once again he has carried out his work well.'* (Fengler)

the 379 heavies that went to Brunswick, twenty-seven did not come back, and in the town the comparatively low number of ninety-nine people were killed: a morbid statistic is that it took approximately four bombers and about twenty tons of bombs to kill one German. A sad statistic is that twice as many RAF aircrew were lost. The other raid was against the Opel motor factory at Rüsselsheim, and 287 Lancasters and Halifaxes participated. The works were slightly damaged, but most of the bombs fell in open countryside. Human casualties on the ground were slight, totalling forty, of which a mere nine were killed and the remainder injured. Twenty of the bombers failed to return, and Heinz Schnaufer and his crew destroyed four of them with the space of twenty-one minutes. The total loss of Bomber Command men was 140, of which Schnaufer accounted for twenty-eight. These four heavies were Schnaufer's only successes in August.

At the beginning of September 1944 NJG 1 was forced to evacuate its airfields in Holland and Belgium in front of the advancing Allies following heavy daylight attacks by RAF and American heavy bombers and strafing by Allied ground-attack fighter-bombers. On 2 September IV./NJG 1 vacated Saint-Trond and moved back into the Reich, where they installed themselves at Dortmund-Brakel, sharing the airfield with a day-fighter unit. The degree of urgency with which this evacuation had to be carried out can be imagined by the fact that the following

Heinz Schnaufer with the Officer Commanding the Staff Company, Major Rotter. This photograph was almost certainly taken at the photo-call on 7 July 1944.

day the Germans were forced to withdraw from the city of Brussels, only about forty miles to the west of Saint-Trond.

There could have been little doubt in the mind of any German that the war was lost, nor that Allied troops would soon be in Germany itself. To encourage resistance to the Allies Hitler spoke of the wonder weapons that would turn the tide in Germany's favour – the V1 flying bomb, the V2 rocket, which first struck at London on the 8th of September, and other unspecified 'retaliation' weapons – and made great play of the Allies' demand for unconditional surrender, forecasting dire consequences for the German people if they were to yield. On the 25th of the month, in desperation, the *Führer* announced:

> After five years of struggle, and as a result of the failure of our European allies, the enemy stands at the borders of Germany. His ultimate aim is the eradication of the German people. Therefore, to strengthen the active forces of our *Wehrmacht*, I call up for front-line fighting duty all German men capable of carrying weapons. In all regions of the Greater German Reich all German men between the ages of sixteen and sixty capable of bearing arms will form the German *Volkssturm*.

Germany fought on, its leaders apparently unable, or unwilling, to see the impossibility of their position. 'Bomber' Harris had said – indeed, still maintained – that the morale of the German civilians could be broken by bombing their towns, and it arguable that, to a large extent, that aim had already been achieved. But what Harris never explained – per-

Schnaufer with other members of IV./NJG 1. (Diener)

haps never seriously considered – was how a breakdown in civilian, or even military, morale in a ruthless dictator state could be translated into a rising against the leadership that would bring an end to hostilities. The morale of the man in the German street was already broken, and he had little, if any, incentive to fight on. But the futility and the danger to oneself of coming out in opposition to the Nazi regime had been common knowledge in Germany from the early days of its existence, increasingly so as the war began and continued, and had been brutally demonstrated following the failure of the attempt on Hitler's life at Rastenburg in July 1944. There was simply nothing that the German people could do: it was too late for that. Fatalism, too, played its part. As Albert Speer, the Reich Minister for Armaments and War Production, commented succinctly: 'The powers of resistance of the German people were underestimated and no account was taken of the fatalistic frame of mind which a civil population finally acquires after numerous air raids.'[1]

September 1944 saw Heinz Schnaufer and his crew shoot down five more Bomber Command machines, a singleton – unusually for him – on the 12th and four in the space of thirty-two minutes on the 23rd. Dortmund is located on the eastern fringe of the Ruhr metropolitan

[1] From a report dated 18 July 1945 on the interrogation of Speer, quoted in the *Official History of Bomber Command*, Part IV, Page 378.

complex, and from this point in the Schnaufer story it becomes very much more difficult to pinpoint the location of his kills with any degree of precision. Until approximately this date his *Leistungsbuch* was carefully filled in with the name of the town or village near to which each victim had come down – for example, 'Three km. West of Mons' – but from now on kills were logged by means of a grid reference system – simply 'KO', for example, or 'MM-MN'. The grid map comprised rectangles measuring fifteen minutes of latitude by thirty minutes of longitude, so that the area of each rectangle was about 360 square miles. As a result, the identification of individual victims becomes almost impossible.

Heinz Schnaufer with his ground staff. August/September 1944. (Diener)

The reason for this change in the method of recording the location of kills is clear. Before the invasion the *Nachtjagd* was, one might say, fighting a static defensive war, and there was time to follow up and locate each kill so that it might be officially recognised. The *Funker* would note the time and the approximate location when the bomber was shot down and then that would be matched against reports of witnesses and, of course, the wreckage on the ground. It was a bureaucratic, painstaking process that sometimes lasted several weeks, and only when it was completed would the precise position of the crash be entered. Now the night fighters were involved in a different sort of war, a war of movement in which the enemy was advancing and they, along with all the other German forces, were retreating, and they no longer had the leisure to follow up each individual claim, so the radio operator's estimate of position had to suffice. Frequently, too, bombers came down behind enemy lines.

Another publicity photo, 25 August 1944. 'The night fighter without peer. The Divisional Commander (Grabmann) *pays a visit to the most successful* Gruppe *and listens to* Hauptmann *Schnaufer's experiences.' Georg Fengler is on the right.* (Fengler)

Schnaufer located his 94th kill, at 2307 hours on 12 September, as 'in RQ – RP', which would out put it some way to the south-west of Frankfurt am Main, that night's target, in the Hunsrück hills. It was unusual for Schnaufer to have to fly so far from his base before finding the bombers. On the 23rd, when Schnaufer claimed four, there were two Bomber Command attacks in the area of Münster, one against Handorf airfield, where I./NJG 1 was stationed, and one against the Dortmund-Ems canal, so that it not possible to say from which bomber force Schnaufer's victims came. All his claims were to the west of Münster and in the region of the border with Holland.

By the end of September 1944 virtually all of France and Belgium was in the hands of the Allies. United States troops, which had crossed the border between Luxembourg and Germany near Trier in the middle of the month, were also poised further north to advance on Aachen,

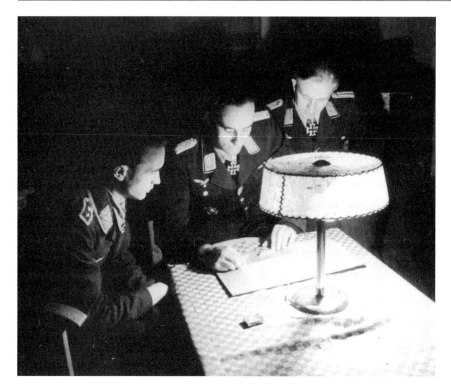

destined to be the first large German town that would fall to them. September had also seen the daring, but unsuccessful, airborne assault at Arnhem, which was intended to capture the two bridges over the Rhine and so open the way for a rapid advance across Holland and into Northern Germany. In the east the Red Army now occupied all of Romania and was well established in Poland, Hungary and Yugoslavia and moving inexorably forward. For the Germans there could be no escape from a crushing defeat; yet Hitler, the only man who could cry 'enough', fought on. Many more human beings on both sides, soldiers and civilians, would die before peace came to Europe again.

Hauptmann Heinz Schnaufer began the month of October with his tally of night-time victories standing at ninety-eight. Only one other pilot in the *Nachtjagd* could claim a higher score, *Oberstleutnant* Helmut Lent, who had by then made 102 kills as a night-fighter pilot to add to the eight he had achieved when flying the Bf 110 *Zerstörer* early in the war. He had already destroyed thirty-nine enemy aircraft before Schnaufer shot down his first.

Helmut Lent was born on 18 June 1918 at Pyrehne near Landsberg, later to be renamed Gorzow, then in Germany, now in Poland. He was the sixth child of the Protestant parish priest Johannes Lent, and was himself a deeply religious man. It is said that each time he shot down an enemy aircraft he would say a prayer for the crew. He was also a very modest and unassuming man: when he was already a senior and much-decorated officer, report has it, he was once asked by a friend in

Pyrehne why it was that when he was on leave he always wore civilian clothes rather than his uniform, and he replied, 'If I wear my uniform old friends have to stand to attention when they speak to me, which I don't like. This way I'm just the priest's Helmut, and they don't need to salute me.'

Lent, almost four years Heinz Schnaufer's senior, passed his *Abitur* examination in 1935 at the early age of seventeen, thus qualifying for entry to university. Instead of doing so, however, he chose to join the *Luftwaffe*, which had just emerged from clandestinity amidst a wave of popular enthusiasm and patriotism. He became an officer-cadet in April 1936 and was commissioned as *Leutnant* in March 1938, when Schnaufer, sixteen years old, was just moving from senior school in Calw to the *Napola* in Backnang. After completing his training he began his operational career as a *Zerstörer* pilot, scoring victories in the Polish campaign, against the RAF over the *Deutsche Bucht* in December 1939, and in the Norwegian campaign. In 111 operational sorties he shot down eight enemy aircraft – one Polish PZL 24/11C, two Wellingtons, one Blenheim, one Sunderland and three Gladiators. He was a member of Wolf Falck's *Staffel* of ZG 76 when Falck was called upon by Göring in May 1940 to form a night-fighter force, and Falck gave him the position of *Staffelkapitän* in the newly-formed NJG 1. Flying with 4./NJG 1, he made his first two night kills, both Wellingtons, during the night of 11/12 May 1940. Further operational successes, decorations and promotion followed. In August 1941 he was awarded the Knight's Cross, and in November the same year, with twenty-seven victories to his name, be became *Kommandeur* II./NJG 2 with the rank of *Oberleutnant*, although he was promoted to *Hauptmann*

Helmut Lent visits Saint-Trond. Coffee with Schnaufer and Jabs. (Fengler)

two months later. II./NJG 2 was renamed IV./NJG 1 in October 1942, by which time Helmut Lent had scored forty-six kills and was wearing the *Eichenlaub*, which had come to him in August after thirty-five victories. In January 1943 he was promoted to the rank of *Major* and in August, after shooting down sixty-five bombers at night — including the first Mosquito ever to be destroyed by a night fighter – he was made *Kommodore* NJG 3, almost simultaneously being awarded the *Schwerter*. Promotion to *Oberstleutnant* followed in January 1944 and his 100th victory came in July the same year. He was awarded the *Brillanten* on the 31st of the month, by which time his night-time score stood at 102.

At the beginning of October 1944 the *Geschwaderstab* of NJG 3 was temporarily located at Stade, west of Hamburg. At 1246 hours on the fifth day of the month Helmut Lent took off from Stade at the controls of a Ju 88. On board with him were three other men: his *Funker*, *Oberfeldwebel* Walter Kubisch, a holder of the Knight's Cross; a war reporter, *Leutnant* Werner Kark; and *Oberleutnant* Hermann Klöss, presumably flying as second radar operator, a customary crew-member in the Ju 88. Lent was heading south for the airfield at Nordborchen, near Paderborn, where he intended to visit his colleague and close friend *Major* Hans-Joachim Jabs[1], *Kommodore* of NJG 1. He arrived at Nordborchen at just after 1315 hours and began his landing approach. What happened then is told by an eye-witness, *Unteroffizier* Walter Kotecki:

> I was at the 'Ilsewerk' Flak site to the west of the airfield. I was watching the aircraft as it was coming in to land. The machine was coming in on the approach with the engines throttled back, and then it suddenly turned to the left. As it did I noticed that the port engine had stopped. The rear of the fuselage sagged downward, and the aircraft flew on for a short time in a stalled attitude. Then it seemed to me that the pilot had seen the high-tension lines and had pulled the aircraft to the left. As he did so the left wing-tip touched the ground and the right one cut through the high-tension line. There was a bright-blue tongue of flame. Then the aircraft hit the ground and began to burn immediately. I did not notice whether the undercarriage was lowered.

The crew of four were flung out of the Ju 88, all dreadfully burnt and injured. Today Achim Jabs he recalls the tragic loss of his comrade and colleague:

> Helmut and I were close friends. Our two young families lived together in the former law courts in Reinfeld in Holstein, and it was natural that we should become close to each other.
>
> In October 1944 he was coming to visit me at Paderborn to talk over a number of matters and requirements that we wanted to discuss with our senior authorities. He arrived in a Ju 88 flying on only one engine,

---

[1] Jabs was promoted to *Oberstleutnant* the following month.

Saint-Trond, Spring
1944. On the left
Helmut Lent,
Kommodore *NJG 3;*
on the right Hans-
Joachim Jabs,
Kommodore *NJG 1;*
in the centre, Heinz
Schnaufer,
Kommandeur
IV./NJG 1. (Jabs)

the other one having failed. On the approach he switched the unserviceable engine on, but he forgot to alter the trim and crashed the aircraft. Lent managed to tell me this in a fragmentary way on his death-bed.

After the aeroplane crashed all the four occupants were still alive. Lent was the least seriously injured. Both his legs were badly broken. His radio operator Kubisch died on the operating table of severe internal injuries, his radar operator Klöss died some hours after the crash of head injuries and the war reporter Kark died during the night of cerebral haemorrhage.

The Head Doctor of the Paderborn hospital told me that he had no alternative but to amputate because he believed that Lent had been infected with gangrene. I was ordered by Göring to tell the doctor that the Senior Medical Officer of the Second *Fliegerkorps*, a famous surgeon, would come and take over further treatment himself.

This involved a delay of some hours, which spelt the end for Lent. When the surgeon from the Second *Fliegerkorps* finally arrived he tried to amputate Lent's leg on the operating table, but the gangrene had already passed into his body and he died the following night.

Martin Drewes fills in the picture a little:

I was waiting outside the door to the ward that day. Jabs and I had to go quickly to Münster to attend the funeral of *Hauptmann* Förster,

Oberstleutnant *Helmut
Lent, killed in a flying
accident in October 1944
when his score stood at
110.* (Szardennings)

Kommandeur of the First *Gruppe*[1]. When Jabs came out of the sickroom he
said that he had told Lent he would be back soon: he hadn't said where
he was going or why. Lent had answered, 'Don't stay away long: I
haven't much time.' When we came back Lent was dead.

Helmut Lent, the survivor of uncounted night-time combats but a victim of his own human error, was given a full State Funeral Service in
Berlin on the 11th of October, at which the *Reichsmarschall*, Hermann
Göring, gave the commemorative address. Helmut Lent was buried in
the Stade town cemetery together with the other three who had died in
the accident. He was posthumously promoted to the rank of *Oberst*.

   With the death of Lent, Heinz Schnaufer now became the leading
surviving night-fighter pilot of all time, with ninety-eight victories to his
name, four less than Lent had scored with the *Nachtjagd*. He came clos-

---

[1] Paul Förster, *Kommandeur* I./NJG 1, was killed in action on 1 October 1944 with his score
standing at 10.

Generalkommando I.Jagdkorps   Korpsgefechtsstand, 18.10.1944
II

Korpstagesbefehl Nr. 41
==

Anerkennungen.

a)   Der Führer und Oberste Befehlshaber der Wehrmacht
hat

Hauptmann S c h n a u f e r , Kommandeur IV./N.J.G.1

als 21.Soldaten der deutschen Wehrmacht

das EICHENLAUB MIT SCHWERTERN UND BRILLANTEN
ZUM RITTERKREUZ DES EISERNEN KREUZES

verliehen.

In stürmischem, von höchster Kampfbegeisterung getragenem
Siegeslauf hat Hauptmann Schnaufer an Erfolg – häufig in hohen
Mehrfachluftsiegen während je eines einzigen Nachtjagdeinsatzes –
gereiht.

Die Erzielung von 100 NACHTJAGDABSCHUESSEN, unter denen
sich die Siege über z w e i u n d n e u n z i g feindliche Groß-
kampfflugzeuge befinden – hat nunmehr zur Verleihung dieser
höchsten deutschen Kriegsauszeichnung geführt.

Ich beglückwünsche Hauptmann Schnaufer hierzu in dankbarer
Würdigung seines immerwährenden heldenmütigen Einsatzes und spreche
i h m und seiner bewährten Besatzung, den Ritterkreuzträgern
Leutnant R u m p e l h a r d t und Oberfeldwebel G ä n s l e r,
meine vollste Anerkennung für ihre hervorragenden Leistungen aus.

Das gesamte I.Jagdkorps sieht heute mit stolzer Freude
auf

Hauptmann S c h n a u f e r !

gez. S c h m i d.

Order of the Day by General *'Beppo' Schmid congratulating Heinz Schnaufer on the award of the* Brillanten. (Rumpelhardt)

er to that score on the night of the 9th of October 1944 when Bomber Command hit at Bochum with 415 heavies, from which they lost four Halifaxes and a Lancaster, of which Heinz Schnaufer claimed two, so reaching his 'century'.

In recognition of this achievement, Schnaufer was awarded the *Brillanten* on 16 October 1944. After Helmut Lent, he was only the second night fighter to receive this prestigious and exclusive decoration, and only the twenty-first member of the German armed forces to be so honoured. On the 18th of October the Commanding General of the First Fighter Corps, Josef Schmid, issued an order of the day. It read:

<u>*Korps* Order of the Day No. 41.</u>

The *Führer* and Supreme Commander of the *Wehrmacht* has awarded to *Hauptmann* Schnaufer, *Kommandeur IV./NJG 1*, as the twenty-first soldier of the *Wehrmacht*,

The <u>OAK LEAVES WITH SWORDS AND DIAMONDS</u> <u>TO THE KNIGHT'S CROSS OF THE IRON CROSS</u>

In an eventful victory march carried out with the highest degree of combativeness *Hauptmann* Schnaufer has achieved great success, frequently in the form of multiple aerial victories in the course of a single night-fighting mission.

The attaining of <u>100 NIGHT-FIGHTER VICTORIES</u>, among them the destruction of <u>ninety-two enemy heavy bombers</u>, has now resulted in the award of this, the highest war decoration.

I congratulate *Hauptmann* Schnaufer on this award in grateful appreciation of his sustained heroism in action, and to him and his tried and trusted crew, the holders of the Knight's Cross *Leutnant* Rumpelhardt and *Oberfeldwebel* Gänsler, I express my most sincere appreciation of their outstanding achievements.

The entire First Fighter Corps today looks up with pleasure and pride to *Hauptmann* Schnaufer!'

Previously awards, just as promotions, had seemed to come to Schnaufer belatedly. Now the balance was redressed, and his achievements had been recognised promptly. On the 26th of October he was accorded further distinction, being nominated to take over command of an entire *Geschwader*, NJG 4., replacing *Oberstleutnant* Wolfgang Thimmig. With the lowly rank of *Hauptmann*, and with his twenty-third birthday still some four months in the future, he would now have under his operational and administrative command a unit that comprised four *Gruppen* plus headquarters staff. It was an awesome responsibility for so young a man. Schnaufer took up his appointment as *Kommodore* on the 14th November, and was replaced as *Kommandeur* IV./NJG 1 by his

Holders of the Ritterkreuz, IV./NJG 1. Left to right: Augenstein; Gänsler; Schnaufer; Greiner; Rumpelhardt. This was taken at Schloss Schwansleben at Lünen, near Dortmund. IV./NJG 1 retreated from Saint-Trond to Dortmund/Brakel at the beginning of September 1944. (Diener)

friend, colleague and subordinate of long standing, Hermann Greiner. Schnaufer wanted to take with him Georg Fengler, who had been his adjutant since he took over IV./NJG 1, but Jabs, *Kommodore* NJG 1, declined to give his permission. Schnaufer could not, he said, take all the experienced crews to his new *Geschwader*. Schnaufer's adjutant with NJG 4 was *Oberleutnant* Eberhard Koltermann . A friendship had developed between Schnaufer and Fengler, but at that time neither man could possibly foresee, or even imagine, how very close their lives were to become in the future.

The mention of Hermann Greiner recalls an incident in the officers' mess at about this time that illustrates the importance of the *Funker* in a German night-fighter. It also indicates the loyalty that Schnaufer had towards his crew. Greiner made a somewhat disparaging remark about radio operators: Schnaufer interrupted him sharply and said, 'I owe at least eighty of my kills to my *Funker!*'

Ludwig Meister also recalls this period, and he draws attention to Heinz Schnaufer's approachability as a *Gruppenkommandeur* and his readiness to help a friend. He writes:

At the beginning of October 1944 Heinz proved to me that for him friendship was not just a word. By that time the Allies had advanced very near to our operational airfields in the West. I./NJG 4 at Florennes, to which I had been posted on August 1944 as Acting *Kommandeur* after

recovering from severe wounds, was ordered to withdraw to Frankfurt/Main in Germany, and I had been made responsible for the evacuation. I did not have nearly enough vehicles to transport the personnel and equipment of the *Gruppe*, so in my hour of need I telephoned Heinz. Although he himself was under similar pressure he sent me a number of vehicles, and I able to carry out the evacuation despite the short notice.

Schnaufer's final kills flying from Dortmund with IV./NJG 1 took place on the night of the 6th of November, when a force of 235 Lancasters from No. 5 Group attacked the junction of the Dortmund-Ems Canal with the Mittelland Canal near to Gravenhorst, losing ten Lancasters in the process. Schnaufer claimed three of them between 1926 and 1941 hours. In doing so he overtook Helmut Lent's score of 102 *Nachtjagd* victories and became the pilot with the highest tally ever of victories by night, although he still lagged seven behind Lent's overall score, made

*An early photograph of
Hermann Greiner, taken
about 1941, before the
night-fighters were
equipped with radar.
Greiner took over from
Heinz Schnaufer as*
Kommandeur
*IV./NJG 1 in October
1944.* (Greiner)

by day as well as night, of 110. Fritz Rumpelhardt points out, however, that this was in no way a race. Schnaufer had no ambition to be the
best for the sake of being the best, and was in fact extremely modest
about his achievements and accomplishments. Such ambition as he had
– and a burning one at that – was confined to doing his utmost in the
defence of his country and its citizens. Speaking of this period in 1995,
Georg Fengler had this to say:

> By that time, of course, we all knew that the war was over and that we
> could not win. That was very clear to us, but we were still defending our
> *Heimat*[1], not our government. And Heinz knew that as well, and he
> acknowledged it. When he got his *Brillanten*, which was just before he
> became *Geschwaderkommodore*, he made a speech to all the officers of the
> *Gruppe* in which he tacitly acknowledged the fact. He told us that he
> expected us to do our duty in the defence of the Fatherland, but it was
> clear to all of that we could not longer hope to win the war. It might be
> thought that it was dangerous for Heinz to say things like that, but you

[1] '*Heimat*' translates simply as 'home' or 'homeland', but neither English word is a true equivalent. *Heimat* is a deeper, more sentimental concept.

must understand the spirit on a night-fighter unit like ours. We were
almost like a secret society, and no one would report on anyone else –
we were too close. We trusted each other. We aircrew always lived off
camp and we were taken to the airfield when there was flying on by car
or by bus, and we used to 'fiddle' petrol for our own vehicles, which was
probably even more dangerous than not believing in victory, and we
were never caught. That is how it was. There was a lot of covering each
others' backs.

Nachtjagdgeschwader 4, Schnaufer's new command, had been operational
since 1942. Its principal responsibility since then had been the defence
of targets in Southern Germany against Bomber Command, and its aircraft had mainly operated from bases in the area around Frankfurt am
Main. In the invasion period some of its units had been moved up into
France and had operated in the front line both as night fighters and in
a ground-attack rôle. Now they were back in Germany, with the
Geschwader Staff Headquarters at Mainz-Finthen, but simultaneously
with Schnaufer taking up his appointment as *Kommodore* the *Stab* moved
north to Paderborn, and then, presumably almost immediately, to
Gütersloh, about twenty miles to the north-west of Paderborn., where
II./NJG 4 was located. Gütersloh was a fully-equipped, permanent airfield that had been purpose-built for the *Luftwaffe* before the war, and
it was from there, with very few exceptions, that Schnaufer flew his
operational missions with NJG 4 during the final six months of the war,
possibly commuting between there and Paderborn, where the administrative offices of the *Geschwader* were located.

Before he could fly operationally from Gütersloh there would be, it
seemed, an adjustment that Schnaufer had to make. Whereas IV./NJG
1 had been equipped with the Bf 110, on which Schnaufer had done
all his operational flying, II./NJG 4 flew the heavier Ju 88. Fritz
Rumpelhardt takes up the story:

When we first went to NJG 4 they were flying the Ju 88. At first
Schnaufer said it made no difference. 'As night fighters we fly by ourselves no matter what the aeroplane is. We don't fly in formation. And
as *Kommodore* I should fly the same aircraft as my men.' And we got a
new aircraft, a Ju 88, and we did a few daytime familiarisation trips in
it, not operations. That was in November 1944. Then we did a few night
take-offs, and we had a few problems. Schnaufer didn't feel happy with
it, and after the final night take-off he landed it, parked it, and we didn't
fly in the Ju 88 again for a time. He decided we would stick with the Bf
110, and we never flew the Ju 88 operationally. I think there was more
to it that just that he didn't get on with the machine. I think it was another example of Schnaufer's superstition.

Not only did Schnaufer stay with the type of machine that he had done
all his operational flying on, and in which he had scored his impressive
series of kills, but he also kept the Bf 110, G9+FE, that he had used
with IV./NJG 1, and in addition retained the callsign that he had used

during almost the whole of his time with NJG 1, '*Adler 133.*' Perhaps once more superstition had something to do with that decision: on the other hand, there were several highly placed pilots who for various reasons kept their own individual callsigns. In the exclusive circle that was the *Nachtjagd* other crews were stimulated, and possibly encouraged to greater effort, when they were flying on an operation and they heard 'Adler 133' (*Adler einhundert-drei-und-dreissig*), for example, call up '*Sieg Heil!*' or '*Horrido*' on the R/T to announce that he had scored yet another kill.

One of Heinz Schnaufer's first duties on being appointed *Kommodore* was to attend a high-level conference at the Air War Academy at

Gatow, Berlin. Nowadays one would probably describe *Areopag*[1] as a 'think tank'. The conference, and its title, were the brain-children of Hermann Göring, who loved high-sounding names. Participants were asked – somewhat belatedly, one might think – to put forward new ideas for waging the war in the air, no matter how revolutionary, and to suggest ways in which the structure of the *Luftwaffe*, particularly from the point of view of personnel, might be modernised. Both the bomber arm and the fighter arm were represented. Those taking part were mostly young but high-ranking officers, and the chairmen were *Generalmajor* Dietrich Peltz, a bomber man born in 1914 and, when he was promoted, the youngest officer in the *Wehrmacht* to hold that rank and, on the fighter side, 'Beppo' Schmid, General Commanding the First Fighter Corps. The emphasis was on youth. Thirty-eight officers took part, and Schnaufer was both the youngest and, as a *Hauptmann*, the junior in rank. For him, a newly appointed senior commander and a very young man at that, this must have been a somewhat daunting prospect.

It was not long after he took up his appointment that Heinz Schnaufer was in action again. Indeed, Fritz Rumpelhardt stresses that his senior appointment in no way diminished his operational readiness: whereas it was not unknown for officers elevated to command positions

The Schnaufer crew.
(Fengler)

[1] Aeropagus, a hill outside Athens where, in Ancient Greece, the city council and the law courts were located.

to find their time too full of administrative duties for them to fly as often as before, Schnaufer was always the first off when a scramble came. On 21 November, flying his first operation from Gütersloh, he destroyed two four-engined bombers on a night when Arthur Harris sent out 1,345 sorties to a number of separate targets for the loss of fourteen air-craft, including two Mosquitoes. The Dortmund Ems Canal and the Mittelland Canal were again among the targets, as were synthetic oil refineries at Castrop-Rauxel and Sterkrade, both in the Ruhr. It was in this latter area – map square KP – that Schnaufer's kills were logged, and it seems probable that his victims were the two Halifaxes lost from the Sterkrade raid. Both went down within two minutes. Later that month, on the 27th, Schnaufer flew to Berlin in a Ju 88, 3C+AA, to be decorated with the *Brillanten* by the *Führer*. He was promoted to the rank of *Major* on the first day of December 1944, the youngest man of that rank in the *Luftwaffe*. Four days afterwards he suffered a great shock. To describe it we must first go back in time.

Schnaufer, it will be recalled, came from a very close family and had three siblings, two brothers and a sister; the elder of the two brothers, Manfred[1], was born in 1925 and was therefore liable to service in the armed forces. In 1940 their father, Alfred, had died suddenly of a stroke. It is believed in the family that the stroke was the result of the Party requisitioning his private car, the only vehicle left with which to run the family wine-distribution business, which had suffered greatly as a result of war-time conditions. Whether that belief is correct can of course never be proved, but the fact is that the death of Alfred coincided with the loss of his car. Martha, Alfred's wife, had been left to bring up the family and run the business, which she did with great fortitude despite the rigours of life those days. Manfred had been called up for military service in 1943 and Schnaufer had promised their mother that he would 'look after' Manfred to the best of his ability.

Manfred Schnaufer was put into the Technical Branch (*Technischer Dienst*) of the *Luftwaffe* and was later posted to Wireless Operator's School at Erfurt to train as a *Bordfunker*. Apparently Heinz Schnaufer, at the time *Kommandeur* IV./NJG 1 and already an influential officer, contacted the commanding officer of the school and arranged that Manfred should be posted to Saint-Trond. Rumpelhardt recalls that on the 28th of July 1944 he had to fly to Berlin with *Hauptmann* Matzak to collect an aircraft with new radar equipment, and that they were ordered to divert to Erfurt on the way back in order to collect Manfred and take him to Saint-Trond. With IV./NJG 1 Manfred did not fly operationally, but worked as a ground radio operator.

When Heinz Schnaufer went to Gütersloh with NJG 4, his brother Manfred went with him. Manfred was put into the crew of *Leutnant* Falck von Tettenborn, the *Geschwader* Technical Officer. They flew in the Ju 88, which had a four-man crew, with Manfred as the Second *Funker*. Fritz Rumpelhardt takes up the story:

---

[1] Dr Manfred Schnaufer died in Calw on 7 March 1997.

Heinz Schnaufer with his sister Waltraut and his brother Eckart on a skiing holiday in the Arlberg in Winter 1944/45. (Schnaufer)

Hauptmann Breves and Leutnant Matzak, IV./NJG 1. (Hinchliffe)

On 5 December 1944 [when Bomber Command attacked Soest with a force of 485 heavies] we taxied out and took off, and just after we got airborne we saw a ball of fire in the sky. Someone had been shot down. Schnaufer said, 'God! Manfred is with von Tettenborn. They took off just after us!'

After the operation – we didn't have any kills that night – we landed at Frankfurt, where I./NJG 4 was stationed. Schnaufer immediately telephoned Gütersloh. It was confirmed that it was von Tettenborn who had been shot down, probably by a Mosquito. Nothing was known about what had happened to the crew.

Quite understandably, Schnaufer was distraught. They put a room at our disposal, where we could be alone. Schnaufer was completely beside himself. He was sure that his brother had died. 'Why? Why? It's my fault. I'm to blame. What am I going to tell my mother?' Those were two terrible hours. And then, after two hours, a telephone call came through. All four of the crew had reported in and were safe.

That was Manfred Schnaufer's one and only operational flight. I've never heard of anyone else who only flew one operational flight and was shot down and baled out! Heinz Schnaufer didn't allow him to fly again!

Georg Fengler also remembers Schnaufer's brother Manfred joining IV./NJG 1:

I remember Manfred coming to Saint-Trond in 1944. I was the Adjutant of IV./NJG 1, Heinz Schnaufer's *Gruppe*. I remember him arriving and checking in at the Orderly Room at Saint-Trond. His rank was *Gefreiter*. He was not given any special privileges as his Commanding Officer's brother – everything was done according to the book, and he had to do his duty just like any other soldier. Manfred flew with me in the Bf 110 once or twice, just practising making radio contact with the ground stations. Then he joined a crew, and he went with his brother to NJG 4. On his first operational trip he was shot down by a British intruder. He escaped by parachute with superficial injuries.

Manfred was quite different from his elder brother. You might say he was a reluctant soldier. In the family after the war he was often referred to as '*der Gefreiter des Zweiten Weltkrieges*' – the 'Lance Corporal of the Second World War'. The '*Gefreiter* of the First World War' was, of course, Adolf Hitler.

Heinz Schnaufer remained at Frankfurt Rhine/Main the day after his brother Manfred's lucky escape, and took off that evening against Bomber Command. Engine trouble meant that he had to return to Frankfurt after just over an hour in the air without making contact with the enemy. Schnaufer took the opportunity of an enforced short break from flying – his aircraft needed repair – to travel that very night by car to Kassel/Rothwesten, where II./NJG 4, one of *Gruppen* of his *Geschwader*, was stationed. Rumpelhardt travelled with him. That visit completed, he and Rumpelhardt drove back to Gütersloh, arriving there on the 8th of December to learn that Schnaufer was summoned to Vechta for high-level discussions on an operation that was in the

planning stages, '*Gisela*': *Gisela*, which will be referred to later, was said to be Schnaufer's own idea. They flew to Vechta immediately in a Ju 88. From Vechta, the conference concluded, they travelled on the 12th of December to Frankfurt, where their Bf 110 had been repaired and pronounced clear for operations. From Frankfurt they scrambled at 1855 hours and shot down a British bomber at 2000 hours. They landed at Dortmund at 2025 hours and returned to their base at Gütersloh the following day.

Heinz Schnaufer's kill on the night of 12 December was one of only six Lancasters lost from the force of 512 heavy bombers carrying out the last major attack by night on the steel-town of Essen. The use of '*Musical*' marking by Pathfinder Mosquitoes – so called because it was carried out by means of *Oboe* – meant that the vast and important Krupp works in the city, which in the early years of the war had seemed invulnerable to the attentions of Bomber Command, could now regularly be struck with awesome precision on the darkest of nights. When interrogated shortly after the war the Minister of War Production, Albert Speer, commented on the accuracy of the bombing during this specific raid.

Four days after Schnaufer's one December success, the Germans launched their massive ground offensive in the snow-covered low mountains of the Belgian Ardennes: it was the beginning of what came to be known as the Battle of the Bulge, and the Germans' aim was to drive through the comparatively lightly defended American front and capture their main supply port, Antwerp. It was a last-throw gamble, and it did not come off, although the Germans advanced well into Belgium before

A more serious photo of the crew. Left to right: *Rumpelhardt; Schnaufer; Gänsler*. (Diener)

*Pre-flight briefing,
probably early 1945.
Major Schnaufer in the
centre.*

they were halted and forced on to the retreat. *Reichsmarschall* Hermann
Göring had promised Hitler 1,000 ground-attack aircraft to support the
Ardennes offensive. They were to have struck simultaneously with the
attackers on the ground, but it was not until New Year's Day 1945 that
the weather conditions were good enough for the action to start. The
operation was code-named *Bodenplatte*, and its targets were Allied airfields in Belgium, France and the south of Holland. Just like the
Ardennes offensive itself, *Bodenplatte* was a surprise and achieved not
inconsiderable success. Precise records are not available, but it is probable that just over a thousand German fighters and ground-attack aircraft took off and destroyed something like two hundred Allied
machines[1], mostly on the ground, but at high cost to both aircraft and
crews. Approximately three hundred German aircraft were shot down,
many by their own flak over the battle front, and a large number of
experienced aircrew were lost. Several *Staffeln* of night fighters acted as
pathfinders for the day fighters, and they too had their losses. As
Kommodore NJG 4 Heinz Schnaufer had been involved in the planning
of *Bodenplatte*, and aircraft from his *Geschwader* were among those

[1] Figures vary considerable. Gebhard Aders (*Geschichte der deutschen Nachtjagd*) says, for example,
that the attackers destroyed 465 enemy aircraft but themselves lost 400.

pathfinding for the day fighters. He himself was forbidden by fly on the operation, as indeed were all night-fighter pilots with more than ten victories. An indirect adverse effect on the night fighters' capabilities in defence of the homeland came from the large amount of aviation fuel used up, fuel that could ill be afforded.

Despite the fact that Bomber Command was sending increasing numbers of bombers to Germany at this period, kills by night fighters were dropping significantly. From mid-1944 onwards overall losses of bombers fell to around the one-percent mark. From January to August of 1944 inclusive the *Nachtjagd* claimed 1,931 bombers, an average of 241 per month. From September to December the total was 304 and the average per month only 76. There were many reasons for this: the increasing confusion caused by, for example, No. 100 Group's diversion, deception and jamming activities; the deadly activities of the Mosquito intruders that made even taking off and landing a considerable hazard; the increasing attention being paid to night-fighter fields by marauding fighter-bombers and later heavy bombers in the hours of daylight; the need for the night fighters to switch, sometimes on an almost daily basis, from airfield to airfield because the one they had been using was out of action as a result of Allied strikes; and the unsatisfactory state of training of new crews arriving on the operational units, who had to be flung into the battle without adequate 'on-the-job' training. Fuel shortage, too was beginning to be felt. But by far the most serious factor in the decreasing effectiveness of the *Nachtjagd* lay in the loss of early warning of the coming of the bombers. Hermann Greiner comments:

> When we were forced to give up Saint-Trond and go to Dortmund-Brakel [in September 1944] we shared the airfield with day fighters, but it wasn't overcrowded, as far as operations went, because of course we flew at night. At about that time it was quite clear to us that it was the beginning of the end. To operate night fighters efficiently it is necessary for there to be a *Vorfeld* – a large area of country over which the approaching enemy must fly before you can intercept him. For us to have a good chance of success the controllers had to be able to decide when to order us off by calculating the time it would take the bombers to reach us and how long it would take us to reach their operational height. Or, put more simply, our airfield had to be far enough back from the early-warning radars for us to reach the bombers' height. We only had a slight overtaking speed, and if we were below and behind the bombers it was impossible for us to catch up. Our big radars along the North Sea and Atlantic coasts that told us in good time when the bombers were coming had been lost after the invasion as the Allies advanced, and so had our forward airfields. To maintain the necessary *Vorfeld* we should have moved back further into the Reich, but that was not possible.

The loss of the long-range radars on the coast meant that the radio monitoring service was now the only means the Germans had of knowing in advance when an attack was likely, but they still had no way of telling the route the bombers would be taking or their target. Only when echoes began to appear on their long-range radars in Germany could they begin to attempt positive assessments. The controllers were faced with a dilemma: if they scrambled their fighters too early, the possibility was that the bombers would either not come or that, if they did, they would head in a direction that would put them out reach. If they did not scramble them until the bombers appeared on the long-range radars they might miss them completely. In practical terms, this meant that the niceties of the three different methods of fighter control, *Himmelbett, Wilde Sau* and *Zahme Sau*, had become theoretical only. *Nachtjagd* crews could be sent up into the air, they could listen in to the *Zahme Sau* running commentaries – if they could hear what was being said through the overwhelming RAF jamming – but in the end effect each pilot was on his own and had to use his initiative, experience and skill to find the bombers on the way to the target, over the target or on the way home. As far as infiltrating the stream went, the first up into the air would have a clear advantage, and Schnaufer, who always led from the front, made it his business to be one of those.

On the 15th of January 1945 the local branch of the National Socialist Party in Calw arranged a reception in honour of their local hero, the *Brillantenträger* Heinz Schnaufer. The reception took place in the People's Theatre, with the guests of honour foregathering afterwards for a celebratory meal in a local inn, the *Zum Hirsch*, the owner of which was an ardent member of the Party. It was announced that 'the grateful citizens of Calw' – in reality the Party – were presenting Heinz with

The invitation to the reception given by the local Nazi Party in Calw to mark Heinz Schnaufer's Brillanten, *January 1945.* (Schnaufer)

DIE NSDAP. ORTSGRUPPE CALW

ladet Sie zu der am 15. Januar 1945, 18.30 Uhr, im Volkstheater Calw stattfindenden

EHRUNG DES BRILLANTENTRÄGERS MAJOR SCHNAUFER

höflichst ein.

Der Ortsgruppenleiter:

gez. N i c k

Obergemeinschaftsleiter der NSDAP.

Im Anschluß an die Ehrung treffen sich um 20 Uhr die Ehrengäste im Gasthaus z. „Hirsch" in Calw.

a writing desk in recognition of his achievements: the desk was never delivered. He was also awarded a building plot, but when he came to make enquiries about it after the war he was told that it had never been paid for.

That January Schnaufer failed to shoot down a single British bomber: it was his first month without a success since April 1943. His score now stood at 106.

He would more than make up for it in the following month, February, his first kill of the year coming on the night of the 3rd/4th, when attacks on oil targets at Bottrop and Dortmund in the Ruhr area cost Bomber Command twelve Lancasters from the 341 sent out. Schnaufer claimed just one of them in the map square LO, south-west of Essen, at about ten minutes past eight in the evening of the 3rd.

On the 16th of February 1945 *Major* Heinz Schnaufer, *Kommodore* NJG 4, celebrated his twenty-third birthday. It is reputed that the British clandestine propaganda radio station *Soldatensender West*[1] congratulated him on the occasion. Unlike, for example, the 'Night Ghost of Saint-Trond' myth, with which it is often coupled, that, in itself, would seem to be within the bounds of possibility. The radio station in question had been set up in November 1943 with the name '*Soldatensender Calais*', and the name had been changed after the Allies' post-invasion advances. Purporting to be from an official German station, and including subtle and well-researched propaganda, programmes included 'news from the forces' material, based on well-collated intelligence information and intended to persuade listeners of the genuineness of the broadcasts. It is known that a very thorough card index of personal and operational information on *Luftwaffe* officers was maintained. Records from those days seem, however, not to have survived, so it has proved impossible to confirm or repudiate the story. The writer of a chapter on Schnaufer in a German publication, '*Husaren des Himmels*'[2] however, opens his piece with this quotation, purporting to be from a BBC broadcast:

> You know, *Herr Major*, that our bomber crews have given you the honorary title of 'Night Ghost'. We respect our enemies. And because we know that you operate fairly, we hold you in high esteem. Today, your birthday, the BBC Dance Orchestra is playing the hit song 'The Night Ghost' for you.

The accompanying text is, to put it charitably, a gross distortion of historical fact, and it is a fair assumption that the quotation, too, comes into that same category.

For some reason no longer recalled *Major* Heinz Schnaufer, *Kommodore* NJG 4, did not take off operationally on the night of the 19th/20th February 1945, but Ludwig Meister remembers the date:

> Heinz Schnaufer had become my *Kommodore* in November 1944, and in

---

[1] 'Soldier's Radio Station West', originally 'Soldiers' Radio Station Calais'.
[2] *Husaren des Himmels*, published by Erich-Pabel Verlag, Stuttgart, 1964.

the middle of February 1945 my *Gruppe*, III./NJG 4, moved from Paderborn to Gütersloh, both to carry out routine night-fighter operations and to prepare for Operation *Gisela*. On 20 February 1945 my Ju 88 was unserviceable, and Schnaufer lent me his own Messerschmitt 110 to make an operational flight. I must admit that I flew it with a certain amount of trepidation, because every night-fighter pilot normally looked upon his own machine as the apple of his eye.

Schnaufer, now with 107 victories to his name, had many times scored more than one kill in a single sortie. Only once so far, however, had he shot down more than four in a night. The highest single-night tally in the *Nachtjagd* was eight, and the holder of that record was the then *Hauptmann* Herget of I./NJG 4, who had achieved the feat in December 1943. Two night-fighter pilots could claim seven RAF bombers shot down in one sortie: *Hauptmann* Martin 'Tino' Becker (I./NJG 6) on 30/31 March 1944, when nearly 100 bombers were destroyed in the course of the infamous Nuremberg mission; and *Hauptmann* Helmut Bergmann (III./NJG 4 – killed in action in August 1944), who did so on 11/12 April 1944, when Aachen was the target. Heinz Schnaufer was now about to live the most successful twenty-four hours of his illustrious and unique career.

At this period of the war Sir Arthur Harris had at his disposal in the region of 1,500 heavy bombers – Lancasters and Halifaxes – and their crews operationally available at any time. This fell far short of the 4,000 that Harris had originally envisaged as a desirable front-line strength for his Command[1], but it did mean that he could now send well over 1,000 bombers out by day or night almost whenever he chose to do so and still have a comfortable operational reserve of machines and crews in hand. During the night of 20/21 February, for example, he despatched 1,140 heavies, plus about 200 Mosquitoes, in attacks on four main targets and on support operations. The city of Dortmund was bombed, as were oil refineries in Düsseldorf and Monheim. Once again the Mittelland Canal near Gravenhorst was a target, but the area was cloud-covered and the Master Bomber cancelled the attack. Schnaufer's 'own' aircraft was unserviceable, and he flew a spare one, Bf 110 G9+MD.[2] He took off at 0105 hours and at 0153 hours he shot down a Lancaster in the general area of the border with Holland to the west of Düsseldorf and Cologne. Then, five minutes later, he shot down another in the same vicinity. His victims were from the force attacking Dortmund. Schnaufer landed back at Gütersloh at 0314 hours. At 1815 hours that evening he took off on a short test flight in his regular aircraft, found it fit for operations, and landed after being in the air for twenty-one minutes.

About an hour after Schnaufer landed after air-testing his Bf 110G, the first of approximately one thousand four-engined bombers took off from bases in England to continue their work of destruction. Two forces

[1] *Bomber Offensive*, Page 76.
[2] Like Schnaufer's 'own' machine at this period, G9+EF, this was also a Bf 110 from NJG1.

were briefed for simple area attacks: 362 Lancasters headed for
Duisburg, a city that had already suffered enormous damage in the
many raids that had been directed against it: 288 Halifaxes and thirty-
six Lancasters had the town of Worms, on the Rhine north of
Ludwigshafen, as their target. Unlike Duisburg, Worms had never
before suffered the attentions of Bomber Command, but on that night
approximately forty percent of its built-up area was destroyed. In comparative terms, the casualties suffered by Bomber Command on these
two raids, at three percent, were moderate. The third major attack that
night proved to be much more expensive.

Two of the most important elements of the comprehensive inland
waterway system of the Third Reich were long, broad and deep canals,
the Dortmund-Ems and the Mittelland. The former was the most
important transport route between the North Sea and the vast industrial, coal-mining and steel-producing area of the Ruhr Valley. The
Mittelland canal, one of the components of the water link between the
rivers Elbe and Rhine, joins the Dortmund-Ems Canal at Gravenhorst,
north of Münster in Westphalia, coming from the east past Wolfsburg,
Brunswick and Hanover. The Dortmund-Ems canal had been recog-

*Schnaufer adjusts
Gänsler's* Ritterkreuz.

nised early in the war as a prime target – knock the canal out, and you would deprive the Ruhr complex of vast quantities of materials vital to Germany's war potential. In the unrealistic days of 1940 unsuccessful attempts had been made using twin-engined light bombers, Blenheims, in attempts to breach the canal: Hampden medium bombers had been sent there in August 1940 in a daring and, by the standards of those days, successful low-level attack on aqueducts on the canal near Münster, in the course of which Flight Lieutenant R A B Learoyd of No. 49 Squadron, pressing home his attack in the face of withering and accurate anti-aircraft fire, had won the first VC to go to Bomber Command. In September 1944 there began a new, and infinitely more effective, series of attacks on the canals, particularly at the junction of the two at Gravenhorst. In his post-war debriefing, Albert Speer would comment on the accuracy of these later attacks and the enormous effect they had had on the supply of raw materials to the factories of the Ruhr, including the Krupp works. Although the canals were still heavily defended by flak guns, night fighters now represented the main hazard to the Bomber Command crews, and Schnaufer had been one of the factors in the equation. It is likely that the four bombers that he had shot down on the 23rd September 1944 were from the force attacking the Dortmund-Ems canal at Ladbergen, and it is virtually certain that the three that fell to him on the evening of 6 November were No. 5 Group Lancasters also briefed to attack the Ladbergen junction.

The attack on the canals planned for the night of the $20^{th}/21^{st}$ February 1945 having been aborted, a similar force – again from No. 5 Group – set out for the same target once more in the early evening of the 21st. This time visibility was good, and the bombing was devastatingly accurate. The raid was a success, but the cost was high. Thirteen Lancasters were lost from the 165 that took part in the attack, almost eight percent. Fritz Rumpelhardt described that day, and his graphic account merits inclusion in this book in full:

So far *Major* Heinz Wolfgang Schnaufer had made 107 kills by night, of which the first had taken place on the 2nd June 1942 near to Liège in Belgium. The 21st of February 1945 was the most successful day of his two-and-a-half years' operational career. He took off at 0115 hours together with his tried and trusted crew, *Leutnant* Fritz Rumpelhardt and *Oberfeldwebel* Wilhelm Gänsler as observer, in a spare aircraft for the Dortmund area. Flying at 3,500 metres he succeeded in shooting down two Lancasters flying at about 3,700 metres. His greatest success, however, came on the same day, about twenty hours later.

Schnaufer had taken over as *Geschwaderkommodore* of NJG 4 in November 1944. For him it was a matter of honour that whenever the order was received for operational take-off he would always be first in the air so that he could give his unit any available information about the whereabouts of the enemy in good time. Now, when it came to this second operation on the 21st of February, Fate played her part. I, as radio/radar operator, was sitting all alone in the *Geschwader* Staff readiness room gathering strength for the expected operation by partaking of the generous evening meal that was provided. The order to come to immediate readiness did not reach me. Then '*Sitzbereitschaft*' – 'Cockpit Readiness' – and the order to scramble came in rapid succession and the *Kommodore*, who was already at full operational readiness, found his surprised *Funker* completely unprepared. What he had to say was not exactly friendly.

Now everything went full speed ahead, but all to no avail. Our unit's other aircraft had been in the air quite a long time and were on the way to the Dortmund area, where they had been sent to, before our machine – this time it was our own trusty and proven EF[1], which had in the meanwhile been passed clear for operations – lifted off from the airfield at 2008 hours. Later I was to look upon this mishap, as it seemed to be at the time, as extremely significant. We flew on far behind on the heading that the ground station had given us and on which, we presumed, the *Geschwader* had already reached the area under attack by the British bombers. We couldn't understand why we could see neither enemy activity nor defensive *Flak* fire. Schnaufer was just on the point of debating whether he should stay on the course we had been given, when off on one side to the north strong fire by light flak broke out – it must have been in the Münster area. As I later found out, it was the Dortmund-Ems Canal. There must be something wrong here, I thought. Light flak, which only fires up to a maximum height of 2,000 metres, against British bombers that usually fly over the Reich at between 3,500 and 6,000 metres. But there was no point in stopping to think. Schnaufer began to lose height and headed towards the north-west so that he could cut off any bombers that might be on the way back home. In doing so we passed through a thin layer of cloud at about 2,500 metres. There were a number of targets on my SN-2, and we were now in a '*Leichentuch*'[2] situation. Above us there was a thin sheet of cloud and above it was the moon shining palely through, making the cloud look like a white tablecloth, and immediately we could see beneath it, as black silhouettes, a number of homeward-bound bombers a relatively long distance away.

Schnaufer picked out one Lancaster, which was flying calmly along on our right-hand side at about 1,700 metres. In all probability its crew were flying along not suspecting what was about to happen. We had only been in the air a little over half an hour when our *Kommodore* made the first attack from below. As always, whenever he could, he aimed with his vertical guns – '*Schräge Musik*' in the jargon – between the two starboard engines. That is where the fuel tanks were located, which made for the greatest, and above all the most rapid, effect. And what was important as regards this method of attack was that the enemy crew had a chance of survival, in that they were usually able to jump out by parachute.[3]

This attack had taken place at 2044 hours. The starboard wing was badly damaged by an explosion. A huge banner of flame lit up the night

---

[1] This was the Bf 110G that carried the markings G9+EF, which Schnaufer had brought with him from IV./NJG 1. He did not have the lettering altered to 3C (NJG 4), possible out of superstition.

[2] *Leichentuch*: shroud. A codeword introduced in connection with '*Wild Boar*', when searchlights sometimes illuminated clouds from below to provide a background against which bombers could be seen.

[3] This was a belief commonly held by German night-fighter pilots. In fact there was always only a small chance of escaping from a stricken bomber. See the account later in this chapter of the destruction of Lancaster NG329, JO-Z.

Heinz Schnaufer before a Bf 110. 'Willem' Gänsler is in the centre. (Diener)

sky for a considerable distance. After flying straight ahead for a short time, long enough to give the crew ample time to leave the doomed bomber by parachute, it tipped forward vertically onto its nose, and very shortly afterwards there was a huge explosion as it hit the ground in, as was later established, map-square HQ-HP.

Now things began to occur one after the other. Every time Schnaufer was able to pick out one specific target from several. In doing so he demonstrated his unique night-fighting capabilities. The bomber pilots were alerted and tried by means of defensive manoeuvres – the so-called 'corkscrew' tactic – to get away from the attacking fighter. So that he wouldn't get into the field of fire of the enemy bomber, Schnaufer had to fly the same 'roller coaster' as the bombers. That was the only way it was possible to remain in the 'dead area' under the wing that couldn't be covered by the gunners. Schnaufer was especially skilful at choosing precisely the right moment for his attack. In doing so he had to act as rapidly as possible. In one case he had no choice but to open fire with his cannon, which were built in to the fuselage just to the rear of the crew cabin, in a 'knife-edge' flying position, practically standing on one wing tip and hitting the enemy from a position that seemed almost impossible. It was unavoidable that in the course of doing it cannon shells hit the bomber's fuselage. I will come back to this later.

Our situation was made more difficult by the fact that as we were crossing the front line the American flak brought us under heavy fire. Schnaufer succeeded in setting seven enemy bombers on fire within exactly nineteen minutes, without our own machine having been hit a single time by enemy defensive fire. That shows that the *Major* had nerves of steel and that he gave careful thought to every attack, shooting down the enemy with a relatively short burst of fire from very close range. Each time his daring and his rapid reactions enabled him to escape from the danger area within a matter of seconds.

In the wild turmoil of battle there was scarcely the time for me to note down the details of each kill. On the other hand, because of the '*Leichentuch*' I mentioned earlier, I did not need to lead the pilot in on the bombers by means of radar, which was so important on dark nights. Once again Wilhelm Gänsler was the steadying influence in the crew. As so often before he was able to give the pilot good pieces of advice. We attempted two further attacks, however, but even Gänsler couldn't help. When we were making our eighth attack our *Schräge Musik* gave up the ghost at the decisive moment. There wasn't a single round left, and it took Schnaufer all his skill to get away from the heavy fire coming from the bomber. We still had the horizontal guns fixed in the nose of the Bf 110, but these too refused to fire a single shot when we made out ninth attack. So with that our pursuit of the homeward-bound bomber stream was finished. On our way back home we once more had to fly through the American flak in the front line.

Both the physical and metal powers of our *Kommodore* were almost at breaking point. I contacted our former base at Dortmund by radio and asked them to provide all possible flight-safety measures for the last leg of our flight to Gütersloh. Searchlights waving in the direction we should fly and Very lights fired into the air showed us the way, so that Schnaufer was able to land our trusty G9+EF with a final effort of concentration at our operational base, Gütersloh. When the machine had taxied to its dispersal and the engines were switched off, a deep silence prevailed among the crew. Head on breast, each one of us tried to gather his thoughts. And we thought too of the crews of the Lancasters, and above all we hoped that their parachutes had been the element that had saved their life.

Schnaufer's seven kills were logged at 2044, 2048, 2051, 2055, 2058, 2100, and 2103 hours. They stretched along a straight line starting (kill No. 110) roughly in the area of the target and finishing (kill No. 116) in the general vicinity of Eindhoven, Holland. The grid reference system used in Schnaufer's *Leistungsbuch* makes it impossible to be more precise. A point of not inconsiderable interest is that Schnaufer also claimed a probable kill, also in the Eindhoven area, logged in his *Leistungsbuch* as having taken place at 2110 hours. Rumpelhardt men-

Schnaufer helps to wheel his aircraft into the hangar.

tioned an eighth attack with *Schräge Musik*, but says that the cannon failed to fire 'at the decisive moment'. There is however a report by a British Lancaster crew that makes it seem likely that in reality Schnaufer shot down eight that night, making a total of ten within the twenty-four hours of the 21st of February rather than the nine with which he is formally credited.

Speaking in 1996, Fritz Rumpelhardt described Schnaufer's feelings after his seven victories:

> When we had finished shooting down Lancasters Schnaufer was so uptight that he could hardly hold the stick. We couldn't contact Gütersloh on the R/T for some reason, so I called up Dortmund, where our previous unit, IV./NJG 1, was stationed. We were still using our old callsign, *Adler 133*, so they knew who we were. We told them we had seven kills – *siebenmal Sieg Heil* – and we asked for all possible assistance from the flight-safety organisation to get back to Gütersloh. And they pulled out all the stops for us, and they switched the searchlights on and pointed us to Gütersloh, but when we landed Schnaufer was completely exhausted.

As was normal practice, the survivors from Lancaster JO-Z of No. 463 (Australian) Squadron, RAF Waddington, Lincolnshire, shot down over Holland on 21 February, were interrogated on their return to England,

---

[1] Report No. 5G/K.4, Air 27/1923, held in the Public Record Office, Kew.

Lfd. Nr. des Fluges	Führer	Begleiter	Muster	Zulassungs-Nr.	Zweck des Fluges	Abflug / Ort
611	Schnaufer	Rumpelhardt + Gänsler	Bf 110	MJ	*Rückverlegung*	*Fortenrath*
612	"	" Schnaufer Ju 88		AA	*Kommando*	*Gütersloh*
613	"	" " "	"	AA	*Platzflug*	*Berlin-Gatow*
614	"	" Schnaufer Bf 110	MJ		*Welsfling*	*Gütersloh*
615	"	" " "		EF	*Ft.-flug*	"
616	"	" " "		MJ		
617	"	" + Gänsler "		MJ	*Einsatz*	"
618	"	" " "		EF	*Welsflug*	"
619	"	" " "		EF	*Einsatz*	"
620	"	" Schnaufer "		EF	*Welsflug*	"
621	"	" Gänsler "		EF	*Einsatz*	"
622	"	" " "		EF	*Einsatz*	"

and a report on their debriefing issued[1]. The report is dated 9 March 1945. Most unusually, all the crew escaped from their aircraft, although the flight engineer was wounded in the legs and taken to hospital in Helmond. The captain, Flying Officer G H Farrow, was Australian, as were the wireless operator, Warrant Officer W D Wiltshire, and the bomb aimer, Warrant Officer R D Bermingham; the other members of the crew were British. They were Flying Officer P A Harris (navigator), Sergeant S B Bridgman (flight engineer), Sergeant F Bone (mid-upper gunner) and Sergeant F Clay, the rear gunner. The circumstances make it probable that JO-Z was Schnaufer's 'probable'. The interrogation report contains the following passages:

> Aircraft 463/Z was homeward bound from a successful attack on the Mittelland Canal on the night 21/22 February, 1945, when, at position 5132N 0554E, 2111 hours, 7800 feet, in bright moonlight and complete absence of cloud, on track strictly adhering to route and heights laid down, and making banking search, aircraft was hit by cannon fire from an unseen aircraft, firing from behind and below. No member of the crew can state definitely the source of the firing of the cannon, although the Mid Upper gunner did have a fleeting glimpse one minute before the attack of an unidentified aircraft passing underneath own aircraft from Port to Starboard.
>
> Strikes were received from stem to stern in the fuselage, damaging the Navigator's table, and also in the vicinity of the Accumulators, and the Electrical Panel, and also in the Rad. Flap of Starboard Engine and Starboard Engine. The Flight Engineer received damage to the legs from

Above and opposite:
An extract from Fritz Rumpelhardt's log book for February 1945, detailing his 611th to 622nd flights, of which 117 were operational missions (see numbers at bottom right-hand side). Fourteen kills are noted: two on the morning of 21st Feb., seven the same night, two on the 3rd March and three on the 7th March.
(Rumpelhardt)

Flug		Landung			Flugdauer	Kilometer	Bemerkungen
Tag	Tageszeit	Ort	Tag	Tageszeit			
8.2.45	0754	Gütersloh	8.2.	0807	13		
8.2.	1635	Berlin-Gatow	8.2.	1735	60		
10.2.	1300	"	10.2.	1310	10		
11.2.	1737	Gütersloh	11.2.	1748	11		
16.2.	1759	"	16.2.	1815	16		
19.2.	1200	"	19.2.	1221	21		
21.2.	0105	"	21.2.	0314	129		2 Abschüsse 11
21.2.	1815	"	21.2.	1836	21		
21.2.	2008	"	21.2.	2155	107		7 Abschüsse 61 feindlich 115
26.2.	1757	"	26.2.	1806	09		
3.3.	2130	"	3.3.	2251	81		2 Abschüsse 116
7.3.	1957	Brieg b. Magdeburg	7.3.	2230	153		3 Abschüsse 61 feindlich 117

shell splinters and had difficulty in standing.

Fire broke out almost immediately in the vicinity of the Rad. Flap and near the lower portion of the power plant assembly of the Starboard Engine, and almost over the entire wing. The Captain states that he turned off petrol cock and then tried to feather starboard Inner three times without avail. After the attack the aircraft dived to Starboard in a thirty-degree bank, and when the pilot applied Ailerons they reacted momentarily, then immediately became inoperative.

Almost immediately after the attack the Captain realized the seriousness of the situation and ordered the whole crew to 'Put on parachutes' – the order was acknowledged by all. About half a minute later when it was apparent that the fire would not diminish the order 'Jump, Jump' was given. Rear Gunner, Mid Upper Gunner and W/Operator abandoned aircraft through rear door without trouble. Rear Gunner was wearing seat type parachute but did not fancy leaving direct from Rear Turret as he had never received instruction to do so. Rest of crew abandoned aircraft through front hatch. Bomb Aimer had two attempts at opening front hatch before he finally freed it, no trouble was experienced in jettisoning. Rear Gunner injured right arm on landing, and Flight Engineer sprained his left ankle. The Captain is not certain prior to his jump whether he applied rudder trim, but was able to free himself from the front hatch while the aircraft was nearly upside down at approximately 2,000 feet.

There are still minor discrepancies between Rumpelhardt's account of that night's happenings and the version in the report, but the significant factors – time and location of the kill – tally as nearly as one could wish

*The Schnaufer crew.
Left to right Gänsler,
Schnaufer, Rumpelhardt.
(Rumpelhardt)*

– there is one minute's difference in the respective times and the general location logged by the night-fighter crew agrees with the bomber crew's report. The main differences between the two reports are that Rumpelhardt implies – but does not state positively – that his cannon failed completely to fire when they made their eighth attack and that he refers to heavy defensive fire from the bomber. It must, however, be born in mind that it was many years after the event when Fritz Rumpelhardt wrote his account, and it would be too much to hope for precise accuracy in the recollection of what was, at the time, an extremely rapid jumble of events. Fritz finished his memoir with a further paragraph that bears quoting:

> Many years later I had a letter from an Englishman – Stan Bridgman – from Welwyn Garden City. He was a member of a bomber crew in Lancaster JO-Z from No. 463 Squadron, shot down at 2002 hours[1] on 21 February 1945 over Holland. In this way crews of bombers and night fighters have come to know each other. Through the exchange of letters and gifts and a meeting in London in 1980 a friendship between former enemies has developed. It is unfortunate that *Major* Schnaufer could not share in it.

Heinz Schnaufer had claimed ten victories within the space of twenty-four hours, nine of which were subsequently confirmed. He had devel-

---

[1] This time differs by nine minutes from the time given in the PRO report quoted immediately above, which agrees to within one minute with Schnaufer's 'probable'.

Hauptmann *Martin*
'Tino' Becker

oped to a fine art the task of infiltrating the bomber stream, selecting
and destroying his quarry, and getting away unscathed. There were
other pilots in the *Nachtjagd*, too, who had the same abilities, but none
who demonstrated them so consistently over such a long period, with
the possible exception of Helmut Lent. Some would claim that *Prinz* zu
Sayn- Wittgenstein was comparable to Schnaufer and Lent, but they
tend possibly to overlook the fact that many of Wittgenstein's kills were
obtained on the eastern front, where the enemy were far less sophisticated and far easier to shoot down. But even Schnaufer's nine in a day
did not represent a record – although his ten would have done so, had
his 'probable' been confirmed. That record went a short time later to
Hauptmann Martin Becker, whose crew shot down nine bombers in a single sortie on the night of the 14th/15th March 1945. 'Tino' Becker was
the *Nachtjagd's* most successful exponent of the multiple kill, with, in
addition to his nine in a night, separate scores of six and seven in
March 1944. The second-highest score in one night, eight, was achieved
very late in the war by *Oberleutnant* Erich Jung of II./NJG 2 on 16/17
March 1945. Jung scored these successes against a Bomber Command
force attacking Nuremberg on what might be described as the last high-
loss raid of the bomber offensive.

Three other pilots made multiple kills on the night when Schnaufer
scored seven, although not against the force attacking the Mittelland
Canal. *Leutnant* Günther Bahr of I./NJG 6 also scored seven, while

Hauptmann Hager of II./NJG 1 and *Leutnant* Rökker of I./NJG 2 got six each. But after his day's work on 21 February, Heinz Schnaufer had increased his overall score to 116, and no one could match that, or was ever likely to.

By the beginning of March 1945 the Americans were standing on the Rhine and Soviet troops were well established in East Prussia, yet still the Germans would not accept the inevitable. In what can only be categorised as an act of desperation the *Nachtjagd*, essentially a defensive force, went over to the offensive on the night of the 3rd of the month, sending almost 150 Ju 88s – accurate figures are not available – over the North Sea towards and over England to attack RAF bombers on their way back from raids against Germany. Bomber Command had been out in some force that night, visiting a synthetic oil plant at Kamen in the Ruhr and, once more, the Dortmund-Ems Canal. None of the 222 heavies that went to Kamen was lost over Germany, but seven of the Lancasters from No. 5 Group attacking the canal failed to return: in addition the German intruder force shot down twenty heavy bombers over England. This was operation *Gisela* and, as mentioned earlier, Schnaufer had been involved in its planning and was believed to have been the originator of the idea. For example, Gebhard Aders[1]:

> It is said that the actual father of the idea was Schnaufer, who in the course of pursuing homeward-bound bombers had noticed that once across the front line one could fly as if it were peacetime, because windowing and jamming stopped abruptly. He had suggested to the *Division* that the night fighters should follow the bomber stream on its way back until they were over the North Sea and only then attack the unsuspecting enemy. But the Commander of the Third Fighter Division, *Generalmajor* Grabmann, wanted to take the idea a step further forward and not attack the bombers until they were coming in to land on their airfields in England with their landing lights switched on.

Unconfirmed reports also say that Schnaufer had wanted to participate in the operation personally, but had been refused permission to do so by higher authority in the same way that he had been forbidden to take part in *Bodenplatte*. If he had taken part he would have had to fly a Ju 88, which he did not like, because the Bf 110 did not have the range for such an undertaking. Aircraft from the three *Gruppen* of Schnaufer's *Geschwader*, NJG 4, participated in *Gisela*, and thirteen of them were among the total of twenty-six machines that either failed to return from the operation or were written off in crashes or crash-landings on return. *Gisela* was a failure, by any standards, and must have been a great disappointment to those who conceived and implemented it. Indeed it is hard to visualise what the Germans hoped it would achieve, with defeat so clearly staring them in the face.

Although he did not personally take part in *Gisela*, Schnaufer did fly

---

[1] *Die Geschichte der deutschen Nachtjagd*, published by Motorbuch Verlag, Stuttgart and the English translation, *The History of the German Night Fighter Force*, by Crécy Books, 1992.

that night. He shot down two of the Lancasters attacking the Dortmund-Ems Canal at 2155 and 2204 hours respectively. His friend and successor as *Kommandeur IV./*NJG 1, Hermann Greiner, accounted for a further three Lancasters, but it is not clear whether they were from the force attacking the same target.

Arthur Harris chose two oil refineries in North Germany, at Hemmingsted and Hamburg/Harburg, and one in city in Eastern Germany, Dessau, as the principal targets for a force of more than twelve hundred bombers four nights later. The raid against Dessau was area bombing pure and simple. Harris had seemingly still not abandoned his belief in the bombing of cities: in his memoirs he categorised Dessau as an 'important industrial centre'. Losses to the RAF that night were heavy for the period, amounting to forty-one machines, mostly shot down by night fighters. Heinz Schnaufer claimed three Lancasters from the Dessau force, two coming down in the Sauerland between Düsseldorf and Kassel and the third, his final kill of the war, in the Magdeburg area, some long distance to the east of his base at Gütersloh.

CHAPTER TWELVE

March to May 1945

Retreat further north. Imprisonment, Hospitalisation and release.

On the 6th of March 1945, the day before Heinz Schnaufer scored his 121st and final victory, the Americans had entered Cologne, where they hoped to be able to cross the formidable barrier to their continued advance, the Rhine. Their way was barred, because the vital bridges over the river there had been demolished in accordance with one of Hitler's many 'last-ditch' orders. The Americans found, however, that the Ludendorff rail bridge at Remagen some thirty miles to the south was intact, despite German efforts to demolish it. The story of the action that resulted in the capture of the bridge on the 7th of March and the opening of the way into Germany has been told many times.

At about the time that the Americans crossed the Rhine at Remagen – the exact date is not recorded – Schnaufer's friend and former adjutant *Oberleutnant* Georg Fengler, now *Staffelkapitän* of 11./NJG 1, was scrambled in the early hours of the morning from Dortmund to orbit a nearby radio beacon at 6,000 metres and await further instructions. He had flown just once around the beacon when his aircraft was hit without warning by cannon fire, probably from an intruder. Fengler was badly wounded near one eye by a splinter and the machine began to burn fiercely. His *Funker* had a bullet wound in one hand and his Third Man suffered facial burns from the flames. Fengler gave the order to abandon the aircraft, which was going down out of control in a steep dive. When he himself came to bale out the seat-type parachute that he was wearing caught on a projection in the cockpit and he had difficulty in freeing it, so that by the time he got clear of the Messerschmitt he was so near the ground that even as he pulled the cord the aircraft exploded beneath him on impact. Georg Fengler came down a mere fifty metres away from his machine in a meadow near to the Sorpe Dam, which had been one of the targets of No. 617 'Dambuster' Squadron in May 1943. Both the other members of his crew also survived, but for all of them it was their last operational mission. Fengler went into hospital and when he came out after a short stay he was transferred permanently to administrative duties. 'Permanently' turned out to be for the few weeks remaining until the war came to an end.

Opposite and following page: *In March 1945 Fritz Rumpelhardt was recommended to receive the* Eichenlaub *to the Knight's Cross. The war ended before the decoration could be awarded.*
(Rumpelhardt)

Nachtjagdgeschwader 4
(Vorschlagender Truppenteil)

Entwurf

Vorschlagsliste Nr. 2

für die Verleihung

~~xxKriegsverdienstkreuzesxxxKlassexmxSchxx~~

„ ~~xxEisernenxKreuzesxxxKlassexxxxxxxxxxxxxxxx~~

„ ~~xxEhrenpokalsxfxhesxLeistungenximxLuftkrieg~~

„ ~~xxDeutschenxKreuzesxinxxxxxxxxxxxxxxxxxxxx~~

Eichenlaubs zum
„ Ritterkreuzes d. Eisernen Kreuzes

(Nichtzutreffendes ist zu streichen)

Gefechtsstand , den 8.3. 1945

Schmaulg.

(Unterschrift des vorschlagenden Vorgesetzten)
(Dienstgrad u. Truppenteil)

Major und Geschwaderkommodore
m.d.W.d.G.b.

den Herrn Chef des
Oberkommandos der Wehrmacht
(Verleihende Dienststelle a. d. Dienstweg)

) neu. Din A 4 doppelt. Heidelberger Gutenberg-Druckerei GmbH. X. 42

Kurze Begründung und Stellungnahme der Zwischenvorgesetzten
Befürwortungen und Bemerkungen jeder Art sind nicht auf besondere angehängte Blätter,
sondern auf die 3. und 4. Seite dieser Liste zu schreiben.)

9

Leutnant R u m p e l h a r d t steht seit dem 1.11.1941 als
Nachtjagdbordfunker im Einsatz gegen den Feind. Nachdem er an
53 Nachtjagdabschüssen mit mir beteiligt war, wurde er zum
Ritterkreuz des Eisernen Kreuzes eingereicht, das ihm an 8.8.1944
verliehen wurde. In der Folgezeit war er an weiteren 47 Nachtjagdabschüssen massgeblich beteiligt und ist jetzt mit 100 Nachtjagd-
abschussbeteiligungen bei insgesamt 115 Nachtjagdeinsätzen der
weiterfolgreichste Nachtjagdbordfunker.

Diese einmaligen Erfolge konnten nur durch unbändigen Einsatz-
willen und hervorragendes funkerisches und technisches Können erzielt werden. Die ausserordentlichen Leistungen des Lt. R. zeigten
sich besonders, als der Feind seit dem Herbst des vergangenen Jahres
durch einen enormen Störmitteleinsatz die Bordfunkmessgeräte praktisch
ausschaltete. Durch eine als virtuos zu bezeichnende Beherrschung
seiner Geräte gelang es Lt. R. trotzdem immer wieder, den Gegner
zu finden und mich zum Erfolg zu bringen. Er wird dann gerade zum
anfeuernden Beispiel kämpferischen Einsatzwillens, wenn er, der
gesundheitlich sehr Angegriffene, nach einem harten Einsatz, der
ihn vollkommen geschwächt hat, unerschüttert zum sofortigen 2.Einsatz
drängt. Trotz des nervösen Augenleidens, das er sich durch den
Umgang mit dem Nachtjagdsuchgerät zugezogen hat, besitzt er eine
zähe Energie, die mir durch ihre Unerschütterlichkeit oft das Leben
gerettet hat.

Neben seinen vorzüglichen kämpferischen Qualitäten ist Lt.R.
der belehrende und erziehende Kamerad aller Bordfunker des
Verbandes, der ihnen in nimmermüdem Eifer seine Erfahrungen ver-
mittelt und sie mit der ständig variierenden Materie des Bordfunk -
messwesens vertraut macht.

Auf Grund der ausgezeichneten bisher einmaligen Leistungen als
Nachtjagdbordfunker wird Lt.R. der Auszeichnung mit dem Eichenlaub
zum Ritterkreuz des Eisernen Kreuzes für uneingeschränkt würdig
erachtet.

Major und Geschwaderkommodore
m.d.W.d.G.b.

Although numerically still strong, the *Nachtjagd* was in disarray and, after their comparatively rewarding night on 16/17 March 1945, when they scored about forty victories against 502 heavy bombers attacking Nuremberg and Würzburg, they enjoyed little success. In the remainder of the month of March they shot down an estimated twenty Lancasters and Halifaxes from the 1,253 that attacked Germany by night – at this period the major Bomber Command effort was in daytime – and in April only thirty or so from a total of almost 4,500 attackers. The area of the *Heimat* remaining for them to defend was shrinking daily as the Western Allies advanced into Germany from the west and the Soviets from the east, and airfield after airfield had to be evacuated as the invading troops grew near.

On 30 March 1945 the *Luftwaffe* abandoned the Gütersloh base and Schnaufer and his crew flew the short distance north-east to Wunstorf, taking off in darkness at 0229 hours. Subsequently – the exact date in not recorded, but events suggest that it was very soon afterwards – they moved yet again, this time to Fassberg. On 9 April they took off operationally from Fassberg when the RAF attacked Kiel, but they did not make contact with the bombers. On 11 April they headed north to Eggebek in Schleswig-Holstein, about fifteen miles south of the border with Denmark, which was destined to be their last base. There was little enemy activity by night in their area, and it was not until the 19th of April that they were scrambled operationally. They took off at 2310 hours and landed fifty-five minutes later. Again they had no success, because the only British bombers operating that night were 122 Mosquitoes, which flew well above the operational ceiling of the Bf 110. There were also, as was usual, a number of RCM aircraft active, but they, of course, did not fly in a stream, nor did they normally venture where they could be easily be intercepted by night fighters. In this way the operational flying career of Heinz Schnaufer, Fritz Rumpelhardt and Wilhelm Gänsler, the most successful night-fighter team ever, ended, not with a bang but a whimper. They would make one more flight together. On 21 April 1945 they took off from Eggebek and carried out an eighteen-minute air-test.

On the 4th of May 1945, in a tent on Lüneburg Heath, German generals signed the instrument of surrender of all German troops in Northwest Germany, the Netherlands and Denmark. Three days later the unconditional surrender was extended to the remaining German forces, including those on the eastern front. On the 8th Heinz Schnaufer issued a final order to his *Geschwader*:

Nachtjagdgeschwader 4. Kommodore.   Operations Room, 8 May 1945.

<u>Final Order to my tried and trusted NJG 4</u>

Men of my *Geschwader*!

The enemy is in our land and our proud aircraft have been handed over, Germany is occupied and has surrendered unconditionally.

Comrades, this devastating fact brings tears to our eyes. The future lies obscure and pitiless before us – it can only bring us grief and suffering.

But there is something that will remain forever with us, men – the tradition of our *Geschwader* and the glory of what our dead achieved. That tradition will always give us the necessary fortitude if we should be humiliated, will put new heart into us and enable us to look to the uncertainties of the future clearly and with pride.

I should like to remind you once more of the history of our glorious *Geschwader*, so feared by the enemy. NJG 4 was formed exactly three years ago, on the 1st of May 1942, originally with the task of defending Southern Germany from the mass night attacks that were beginning at that time. Our first bases were Mainz-Finthen, Laupheim, Jouvincourt and Laon-Athies. Then, in 1943, were added Florennes, St-Dizier and Coulommiers.

But we do not need to use empty words to vouch for what we have been and done – where we went aloft night after night the soil of France and Southern Germany is marked with many small scars made by the fires where the heavy bombers we shot down came to earth.

579 heavy bombers,

or three whole Bomber Divisions, were shot down by NJG 4 in bitter aerial combat and under the most difficult of conditions.

Successful ground-attack missions by night in every kind of weather on Avranches and Nijmegen, against road convoys and railway traffic behind the front, cost the enemy hundreds of vehicles and locomotives. For us, therefore, the words '*Wildvogel*' (Game Bird) and '*Wirbel*' (Turmoil), etc.[1] have a fine ring to them.

The last blows struck by our *Geschwader* were in the course of intruder operations over England.

The destruction of the pontoon bridges at Wesel formed a glorious finale to our hard nightly struggle.

Comrades, these great successes were achieved by your steadfast behaviour, your diligence and your belief in our Germany.

In addition to the severe blows we suffered from the enemy air force our unit was crushed by the overwhelming material steam-roller, but we always rose again after every blow and struck back with dogged determination.

This unequal battle called for the most bitter sacrifice.

One-hundred-and-two crews, totalling four-hundred officers, non-commissioned officers and men, did not come back. Fifty officers, NCOs and men died doing their duty, some in ground combat and some defending against enemy air attack.

They gave their all for Germany and our *Geschwader*, and they have the right to ask of us at this moment that we do not cease to be honourable and upright German men.

With a feeling of sadness, but also with a feeling of pride, I take leave today from my *Geschwader* and thank you for the trust that you have given to me in time of crisis.

When, in a different Germany, you are called upon to work hard, you can carry within you, men of NJG 4, the knowledge that you did everything humanly possible to win this war for Germany.

Long live our beloved Fatherland!

Signed: Schnaufer, *Geschwaderkommodore*.
Holder of the Diamonds to the Oak Leaves with
Swords to the Knight's Cross of the Iron Cross.

Later in May a team of twelve specialist officers from the DAT (Department of Air Technical Intelligence), Air Ministry, travelled to Schleswig to interrogate members of the defeated *Luftwaffe* on their night-fighting organisation. The team was led by Roderick 'Roddy' Chisholm[2], who had been one of the most successful night-fighter pilots in the RAF. From their base at Schleswig the team drove in 'liberated'

Opposite and following page: *8 May 1945*. Major *Schnaufer's Final Order to his* Geschwader. (Schnaufer)

---

[1] Presumably these were codewords for ground-attack missions in the post-invasion period.
[2] Air Commodore Roderick Chisholm, CBE, DSO, DFC.

Nachtjagdgeschwader 4   Gefechtsstand, den 8.Mai 1945
   K o m m o d o r e

<u>Letzter Befehl an mein bewährtes NJG 4.</u>

Männer meines Geschwaders !

Der Feind ist in unserem Land, unsere stolzen Flugzeuge
sind übergeben, Deutschland ist besetzt und hat bedingungslos
kapituliert – .

Kameraden, diese niederschmetternde Tatsache treibt uns
die Tränen in die Augen. Die Zukunft liegt undurchsichtig
und unerbittlich vor uns – sie kann uns nur Kummer und
Schmerz bringen.

Etwas aber wird in uns, meine Männer, ewig fortleben –
die Tradition unseres Geschwaders und unserer Toten Tatenruhm.
Diese Tradition wird uns dann das nötige Rückgrat geben,
wenn wir erniedrigt werden sollen, sie wird uns aufrichten
und lässt uns klaren und stolzen Blickes in die Wirrnis der
Zukunft blicken.

Noch einmal will ich Euch den Werdegang unseres ruhmreichen und vom Feinde gefürchteten Geschwaders ins Gedächtnis
zurückrufen. Genau vor 3 Jahren am 1.5.1942 Aufstellung des
NJG 4 mit der Aufgabe, zunächst Süddeutschland vor den begin-
nenden Nachtgrossangriffen zu schützen. Mainz-Finthen,
Laupheim, Juvincourt und Laon-Athies waren zunächst unsere
Stützpunkte. Dazu kamen 1943 noch Florennes, St.-Dizier
und Coulommiers.

Doch wir brauchen unseren Werdegang nicht durch leere
Namen festlegen – dort, wo wir Nacht für Nacht aufstiegen
ist der Boden Frankreichs und auch der Süddeutschlands mit
vielen kleinen Narben bedeckt, – den Aufschlagbränden der
von uns abgeschossenen Grossbomber.

<u>5 7 9   B o m b e r</u>

also drei vollständige Bomberdivisionen wurden vom NJG 4
in harten Luftkämpfen und unter den allerschwierigsten Be-
dingungen abgeschossen.

Erfolgreiche Nachtschlachteinsätze bei jedem Wetter auf
Avranches, auf Nymwegen, auf Kraftfahrzeugkolonnen und auf
Eisenbahnwege im Hinterland haben dem Feinde Hunderte von Kraft-
fahrzeugen und Lokomotiven gekostet. Deshalb haben die Namen
"Wildvogel" und "Wirbel" für uns einen guten Klang.

Fernnachtjagd über England war einer der letzten Schläge
des Geschwaders.

Die Zerstörung der Pontonbrücken bei Wesel bedeutet für
uns einen ruhmreichen Abschluss unseres harten, nächtlichen
Kampfes.

Kameraden, diese grossen Erfolge sind nur durch Eure uner-
schütterliche Haltung, durch Euren Fleiss und durch Euren
Glauben an unser Deutschland erzielt worden.

Es hat durch die harten Schläge der gegnerischen Luftwaffe oft nicht viel daran gefehlt, dass auch unser Verband
unter der erdrückenden Materialwalze zermalmt worden wäre,
aber wir haben uns nach allen Schlägen immer wieder aufge-
richtet und haben mit einer verbissenen Wut bis zuletzt
zurückgeschlagen.

Dieser ungleiche Kampf hat von uns schwerste Opfer
gefordert.

1o2 fliegende Besatzungen mit 4oo Offizieren,
Unteroffizieren und Mannschaften kehrten nicht
mehr zurück. 5o Offiziere, Unteroffiziere und
Mannschaften fielen in treuer Pflichterfüllung
teils im Erdkampf, teils bei der Abwehr feind-
licher Luftangriffe.

Sie haben für Deutschland und unser Geschwader alles
gegeben und haben das Recht von uns in diesem Augenblick zu
fordern, dass wir anständige und gerade deutsche Männer
bleiben.

Mit einem Gefühl der Wehmut aber auch mit einem Gefühl
des Stolzes verabschiede ich mich heute von meinem Geschwader und danke Euch für das Vertrauen, das Ihr mir besonders
in der Krisenzeit der letzten Monate entgegengebracht habt.

Wenn Ihr nun wieder in einem anderen Deutschland schwere
Arbeit leisten müsst, so könnt Ihr, meine Männer vom NJG 4,
das Gefühl in Euch tragen, dass Ihr alles Menschenmögliche
getan habt, um für Deutschland diesen Krieg zu gewinnen.

Es lebe unser geliebtes Vaterland.

                    Geschwaderkommodore

        Träger der Brillanten zum Eichenlaub
        mit Schwertern zum Ritterkreuz des
                Eisernen Kreuzes

Nachtjagdgeschwader 4   O.U.,10.5.1!45

B e s c h e i n i g u n g .

Der Leutnant Rumpelhardt ist im Besitz folgender Auszeichnungen:

1. Fliegerschützenabzeichen   5.2.42
2. Eisernes Kreuz 2.Klasse   5.6.42
3. Frontflugspange in Bronze   31.8.42
4. Eisernes Kreuz 1.Klasse   1.10.42
5. Frontflugspange in Silber   18.2.44
6. Ehrenpokal   20.3.44
7. Deutsches Kreuz in Gold   16.4.44
8. Ritterkreuz zum Eis. Kr.   8.8.44
9. Frontflugspange in Gold   4.2.45

Major und Geschwaderkommodore.

May 1945. A certificate, signed by Heinz Schnaufer, of the honours and awards held by Fritz Rumpelhardt. (Rumpelhardt)

German staff cars to Eggebek, only a short distance away, where they conducted a number of interviews with members of the former *Nachtjagd*, including Heinz Schnaufer. Chisholm refers to this visit in his book *Cover of Darkness*.[1]

In our inspections we came across a Messerschmitt 110 night-fighter, the rudder of which was covered with insignia to mark the destruction of British bombers, each a tiny RAF roundel and an aircraft in plan view. There were 121 such signs, and on each the type and date were meticulously painted in small letters. A German appeared, and we questioned him about this aircraft. It was, he said, that flown by the *Geschwader Kommodore*, a *Major* Schnauffer [sic]. He was here, the ace Schnauffer, waiting to be interrogated.

We settled down on the afternoon to interrogate the aircrews, starting with the redoubtable Major Schnauffer, who then claimed to have destroyed 124 bombers. He came in, saluted smartly and was told to sit down. He was a fine, sensitive-looking man, and round his neck he was wearing the highest order of the Iron Cross, a beautiful bit of jewellery studded with diamonds. As from the next day the wearing of decorations would be banned. I felt sorry for him. He had done well for his country

---

[1] First published 1953 by Chatto and Windus, London.

and, having been elevated on a pedestal of public adulation that would
have turned anyone's head, here he was, beaten down, now to be denied
the wearing of his decorations. What, I wondered, would happen to him
after release from the prisoners' cage? He would at least have a memen-
to of his great adventure when he had been living on the peaks, an individual above himself. These were the unavoidable sentimental trends of
my thoughts, and to redress the balance it was necessary to remember
the indescribable conditions of the Russian prisoners in a camp within
the precincts of the station, for which the ex-commander of the station
was being held responsible. We were the victors and these, the van-
quished, were all partly responsible for these horrors, excuse themselves
as they might. And so my feelings hardened and I listened to what Major
Schnauffer had to say.

He led off with an expression of regret that he had been responsible
for the deaths of so many fine men – he was shedding crocodile tears –
and in that atmosphere it hardly rang true. He insinuated that the con-
test was unequal and that once the fighter had made contact the conclusion was foregone. (He claimed to have destroyed seven and seen
many more bombers in one night.) He admitted, though, that the
corkscrew evasive action, recommended to all but unfortunately not used
enough by all, was entirely effective as evasion on a dark night, and he
recalled a forty-five minute chase which he had had to abandon. He
showed a profound knowledge of our equipment and tactics, and it was
plain that he was a master in his own sphere. His reluctance to be entirely frank on certain plans led to his abrupt dismissal with orders to appear
before the Allied Camp Commandant at the end of the interrogation.
Here he was ordered to produce a written report and all squadron documents within twenty-four hours. He was dealt with roughly; our interrogator minced no words and he was dismissed seemingly scared and
crestfallen. This was a strange situation, and the cross currents in one's
feelings were confusing. But these were the hated Nazis; so why be polite
to them? One knew that politeness, to put it generally, would triumph
ultimately; but why be fussy about it now? Why forget the responsibility
of each of these men for the prisoners' camp at the gateway of the aero-
drome?

Chisholm's conflicting sentiments despite his obvious sympathy for
Schnaufer are readily understandable. Schnaufer represented, in simple
terms, all that Britain and her allies had been fighting against for
approaching six years. The dreadful, almost unbelievable, horror of the
German concentration camps that were discovered as the allied armies
penetrated into the Third Reich – and obliquely reflected here in
Chisholm's account of the questioning of Schnaufer – was fresh in
memory. The question of corporate guilt is a vexed and insoluble one.

Roderick Chisholm describes Heinz Schnaufer's 'abrupt dismissal'
from the interrogation room. Ludwig Meister, at the time *Kommandeur
II./*NJG 4, remembers the same incident:

Our first meeting with the interrogation team took place in a barrack hut
on the airfield at Eggebek. This was a high-level team led by a British
General named 'Anderson' or something like that and was made up of

about twenty officers and a German-speaking interrogator. Heinz Schnaufer was the first to be called into the hut. After about forty minutes he came out again, pale-faced and with raised arms. He told us that he had been asked about all sorts of things – tactics, radar equipment, kills and so on – and at first the British had listened to him attentively. Then suddenly the interrogating officer had become excited for some trivial reason and had shouted at him to stand up and leave the room immediately. We, the three *Kommandeure*, Krause, Rauh[1] and Meister, were forewarned, but we though that the meeting with the most successful German night-fighter pilot must have caused some sort of shock and that we would be treated more leniently. We were wrong. After a certain time each of was 'chucked out' in turn. The image of the English fair play had suffered greatly!

There exists another report[2] of this visit that mirrors the atmosphere of the time even more clearly than does that of Chisholm. Just who wrote the report is not recorded, but one might fairly describe his style as atmospheric if not very objective. A few extracts give the tone:

This report aims to deal in the broadest outline from the aircrew's point of view with the successes and failures of the Hun Night Fighter. We spent ten days interrogating various types of Hun.

The first day started in a rather John Buchan way with 4 vast Mercedes with Hun chauffeurs rolling up to the door. Luckier than most British women the drivers were heavily scented and they drove us out to a nearby pine forest where 'LUFTFLOTTEREICH'[3] (Fighter Command approx.) were living in caravans having fled from Berlin before the Russian advance. Here we were met by a tall Hun officer looking like any old Austrian Count out of any rather second rate musical comedy, The Chief of Staff was a typical film Hun called *Oberst Leutnant* Kessel with a pink and white pomaded face and coarse hands with shaped and polished nails. He had commanded one of the famous bomber squadrons in the Blitz days and was still clanking with the decorations of a grateful Germany. Apart from him, his staff consisted of a motley crew more conspicuous for their suave Staff work than for their Nordic ancestry.

It was not however till we reached the aircrew themselves that we met people who seemed to know their job. The first station we visited was Eggebeck [sic]. Even here the type of man was somewhat different from his English counterpart. In enthusiasm and skill they were outstanding, but their flashy arrogant attitude was unattractive and very unfamiliar. *Major* Schnauffer the ace top scorer, with 121 four engined bombers to his credit, was a thin tall 'dago' looking pilot of about 27 with a swarthy complexion and rather long hair. He wore a high Hun peaked cap suitably thumbed and twisted in true aircrew style and a mass of medals including the *Ritterkreuz* with oak leaves, swords and diamonds – a magnificent affair that any dowager would be proud to wear on her corsage. There were other types of course, including scruffy Huns and lazy Huns, clean Huns and dreary Huns and on the whole a comparable Hun for

---

[1] Hans Krause (28 kills) and Hubert Rauh (31 kills).
[2] 'Report on GAF Night Fighting from the Interrogation of Prisoners', Public Record Office.
[3] Correctly '*Luftflotte Reich*'.

most of the well known British types.

Heinz Schnaufer comes in for occasional mention in the remainder of
the nineteen-page report, sometimes rather disparagingly. There is one
nice example of this: speaking of Schnaufer's seven victories in a night
on the 21ˢᵗ February 1945 and describing how Schnaufer turned off the
heading he had been given by the controller and went for the bombers
attacking the Dortmund-Ems Canal, the author says that Schnaufer
'thought he knew better' than the controller. He did, however, have the
grace to add parenthetically 'as in fact he did', but the tone of the comment remains rather snide.

Following on from a discussion of *Gisela*, which Schnaufer confirmed
was originally an idea of his, there is an interesting passage in the
report. Schnaufer had, he claimed, also suggested a variation on *Gisela*.
He had been ready to initiate the proposed operation, which was given
the code-name *Feuersee*[1], in January 1944, but permission from higher
authority was slow in coming through, and it had in fact not reached
him when the war came to an end. For *Feuersee* Schnaufer suggested
using all the available aircraft from his *Geschwader*, a total of about sixty
machines. The aircraft would have steered a westerly course over the
North Sea at very low level, using radio altimeters, homing towards a
radio beacon near Orfordness on the British coast, a beacon which, said
Schnaufer, was often used by *Nachtjagd* crews to help with their navigation: had they had any difficulties with the beacon they would have
resorted to dead-reckoning navigation. The plan was that when the
fighters arrived within about fifteen miles from England they would turn
around and head in the direction of Ostend to meet the oncoming
bomber stream: from long experience the Germans knew that that was
the way home most regularly used by Bomber Command. The fact that
the night fighters were flying over the sea would ensure that their *SN-
2* radar was not cluttered up with ground returns, and with luck some
of the British bombers might have become careless and switched their
navigation lights on. Schnaufer, according to the report, thought that
up to one hundred RAF bombers might have been destroyed in this
way.

If the way in which the visiting interrogators had acted had disillu-
sioned the three *Kommandeure* of NJG 4, a subsequent RAF visit went
some way towards restoring their faith. Ludwig Meister:

> A short time later we had the opportunity to revise our first impressions
> of the British. The Commanding Officer of the British intruder base
> Little Snoring, a Colonel with red hair and dark sunglasses, and the
> radar operator of the successful British night fighter 'Durbridge'[2] or
> something like that, visited us. We met outside on the edge of the air-

[1] '*Feuersee*' is not a word in common usage. The nearest English equivalent might be 'sea of fire',
and it is not difficult to imagine the thought process that inspired the codeword.

[2] This was Wing Commander Branse Burbridge, DSO, DFC, whose radar navigator was Bill
Skelton, DSO, DFC. Burbridge, with 21 kills, was the highest-scoring RAF night-fighter pilot.

field for a relaxed discussion of subjects of interest to night fighters, no matter what side they were on. The British took a fancy to our aircrew watches, and we swapped ours for theirs. The radar operator told me that a few days previously he had interviewed my former *Kommandeur*, *Major* Herget, in a prisoner-of-war camp in England. In the course of the meeting he had shown Herget a cine-camera film of his, Herget's, aircraft being shot down by his pilot [i.e. by Burbridge]. Herget had been shot down in the later afternoon at very low level by a British intruder when making an operational take-off from Florennes, and had only just managed to escape from his aircraft by parachute. When we had finished our conversation the two officers wanted to see Schnaufer's aircraft, and we went to the dispersal where it was parked. When the Colonel saw the machine with the 121 kills marked on the fins he remarked spontaneously, 'Was that Dr Goebbels' aircraft!?'

There were millions of former German servicemen who were now technically prisoners of war, and vast logistical problems concerning their detention, screening and eventually dispersal faced the occupying powers. Each power dealt with the problems in its own way. The British prisoners were concentrated in the Schleswig-Holstein peninsula, the last part of Germany in the British area of responsibility to be occupied by the victors. It has been said that Schleswig-Holstein became one vast PoW camp. Hermann Greiner gives a picture of what it was like there:

In the course of our retreat further into Schleswig-Holstein we eventually found somewhere we could settle, a former Labour Corps camp near Husum, 'the grey town on the sea'[1]. A short time later, thank God, came the capitulation of the Third Reich, which psychopaths and neurotics had called the 'Thousand-Year Reich' but which had lasted barely twelve years. We soon had to vacate these quarters, which were required for refugees from Silesia and East Prussia, and we PoWs had to move back behind the River Eider. There were simply too many people for the available accommodation, and we were forced to camp out as best we could with the cattle in meadows and pastures. But this was no great problem for us. The English, clever and resourceful as they are, let all of us, together with all our vehicles, into a huge area on the banks of the Eider and designated it a PoW camp, and our gifted and ingenious technicians converted all the lorries they could get hold of into comfortable living vans. In this way they [the British] were in a position to tow away any of the vehicles at any time, if they wanted to, and they also ensured that vehicles weren't pushed into a canal some dark night before they could use them themselves.

Schleswig-Holstein absorbed over 1,500,000 soldiers and more than four million refugees from the east who had escaped from the Russians. But things didn't go badly for us, and life with the cows in the fields, surrounded by cattle fences, was not entirely without its romantic side. On one occasion I had done some washing and hung it to dry, but when I came to take it in my 'grandfather-look' nightshirt had disappeared. As

[1] Husum is on the west coast of Schleswig-Holstein. It was the home of the poet Theodor Storm (1817-1888) who immortalised it in verse as *Die graue Stadt am Meer*.

there were only trustworthy people living in my neighbourhood I was puzzled as to who the culprit might be. It was in fact a calf, and one arm of my garment – which was very precious at that time – was dangling unchewed from its mouth. I could not bring myself to be angry with the animal. I realized that calves are inquisitive gourmets, and of course, as is well known, one shouldn't argue about matters of personal taste.

Fritz Rumpelhardt's recollections, if perhaps less 'romantic', contribute to the Schnaufer story. After all the German aircraft remaining at Eggebek had been immobilised by the simple expedient of removing their airscrews and parts of their tail-unit the personnel, with the exception of the *Geschwaderstab*, were moved across the peninsula to the vicinity of Eiderstede, the general area spoken of by Hermann Greiner. The Staff remained behind, quartered at Bollingsted, a short distance from the airfield. The British set Schnaufer and Rumpelhardt the task of writing a paper, which had to be at least thirty type-written pages in length, entitled, 'Future Plans and Further Development of the German Night-Fighter Force'. In composing the paper the two 'gave their fantasy free rein'. Then one day Heinz Schnaufer was called in to the administration office and told that he was to go to England. As Fritz Rumpelhardt says, 'Our leave-taking was painful. We asked ourselves what would happen to us now.' Within three days Schnaufer was back. He described how he had been taken to some camp or other and there questioned by a series of senior officers, some of them from Air Ministry, and then, to his great surprise, summarily sent back to Bollingsted.

There was very little to do a Bollingsted, and so to counter the boredom Rumpelhardt occasionally helped out on a local farm. In about the middle of July news filtered through that there was a mobile release centre operating at Rendsburg, forty miles or so to the south, and that priority was being given to prisoners with farming and technical qualifications. Heinz Schnaufer instructed Rumpelhardt to go there and get further details, and Rumpelhardt set out on foot, but before doing so he got a letter from the farmer he had been helping out that certified that he was a farm labourer. On the outskirts of Rendsburg he left his officer's jacket with a helpful family and then went and reported at the release centre, omitting to inform them that he was a highly decorated officer and still under the orders of the British commandant at Eggebek. As he puts it, he went through the sausage machine and two days later was, on paper at least, a free man.

Having picked up his uniform jacket Fritz Rumpelhardt set out on the road back to Bollingsted. On the way a car overtook him and he thumbed a lift. The car was driven by a British officer, but his passenger, by a great coincidence, was someone he had met before, albeit fleetingly, *Oberleutnant* Kurt Welter, a very well-known *Wilde Sau* pilot credited with destroying a number of RAF Mosquitoes in the Focke-Wulf 190 and the Messerschmitt 262 jet-propelled fighter.

Back at Bollingsted Fritz Rumpelhardt hid his release papers. Then, he says, things began to go wrong. He used a British telephone to ring up a former school friend in his home town to find out how things were there, which was contrary to British regulations. Shortly afterwards he was called back to the telephone: an officer from the British Security authorities in Kiel told him, 'You made an unauthorised call on the British telephone network, and in addition you have been reported for behaving arrogantly to a British officer.' Rumpelhardt was ordered to report to a Captain Hutchinson at Eggebek. When he did so Hutchinson demanded that he should hand over his aircrew watch, which Rumpelhardt did. There followed a long argument, with Rumpelhardt protesting that the British officer had no right to take the watch, and in the end it was returned to him. Hutchinson, however, said that he had had 'many bad reports' about Schnaufer and his men and that he proposed to make an example of Rumpelhardt. He sent for a military policeman and instructed him to lock Rumpelhardt up, which he did. The guardroom staff, however, gave him cigarettes and match-es, and the Orderly Officer, having inspected the meal that was pro-vided, declared it unfit for consumption and invited the German officer to eat with him and the duty guards: the meal was served by British defaulters.

After a few days Rumpelhardt was released from detention. He showed Schnaufer the official release papers he had obtained at Rendsburg and asked his advice. Schnaufer said he would fix things for him to go home, contacted the British Camp Commandant and obtained the necessary permission. On 4 August 1945 Fritz Rumpelhardt set out on the journey to his parents' home near Konstanz. Travel in Germany at that period was fraught with delays and difficulties, and it was not until two weeks later that he reached his destination.

Very many incorrect statements about Schnaufer have been made and repeated over the years, and one of them is that he was brought to England for interrogation. That is not so. Soon after Rumpelhardt left for home Schnaufer was admitted to hospital in Flensburg danger-ously ill with a combination of diphtheria and scarlet fever. Many years later Fritz Rumpelhardt was to have a chance meeting with a German doctor who had treated Schnaufer at Flensburg and who said that Schnaufer had been on the critical list for some time before recovering. After his discharge from hospital Schnaufer was released and allowed to go home to Calw.

Before passing on from happenings in Schleswig-Holstein immedi-ately after the end of hostilities in Europe there is one more individual whose experiences in the immediate post-war Germany we might look at, because he will feature again in the Heinz Schnaufer chronicle, and that is Georg Fengler. It will be remembered that Fengler had been Heinz Schnaufer's adjutant with IV./NJG 1 and had been shot down near the Eder Dam in March 1945.

After he was injured in his encounter with a British intruder Georg Fengler was transferred to the Staff of NJG 1 for administrative duties:

NACHTJAGDGESCHWADER

Dem letzten Kommandeur
der III./N.J.G. 1
MAJOR DREWES
zugeeignet

OBERSTLT. U. GESCHW. KOMMODORE

his responsibilities there were largely to do with the logistics of the rapid retreat northwards of his *Gruppe* until its final stopping place in Schleswig-Holstein. Fengler remembers

We were in a small village, some of us living in the school and some of in houses in the village itself. Then the British soldiers came. They were the first we saw, and it must have been about ten or fifteen days after the surrender. We were interned in a big camp not far from Husum – all our *Gruppe* went there together with our equipment, our vehicles, everything. The British questioned us in their military headquarters. That didn't last long, and we were surprised how soon we were released. First of all, about the end of May, they began to discharge the other ranks, then came the NCOs, and finally the officers.

As my home was in the East, I couldn't go there. I had myself discharged to an address in Schleswig-Holstein and I lived there a short time and then registered at the Labour Office. I was conscripted for the mines and sent to Recklinghausen in the Ruhr. We were mining at a depth of about nine hundred metres. I didn't want to be a miner, I wanted to go to university and train to be a vet, and I told them so. They were unsympathetic and told me I could train to be a foreman in the pit. I said that I hadn't gone to school for as long as I had just to be a miner, and they told me that if I didn't volunteer I would be directed. And as I didn't have any influential friends or family they conscripted me. They said, 'You were an officer on the active list, you were in the *Hitler Jugend*, you aren't married and you haven't any responsibilities, so you will have to go where you are directed.'

After about three weeks we were given a room in a large barracks, in which there were forty men to the one room, and we had to sleep on straw palliasses. I had never had a louse or flea throughout the whole war, but I got fleas there. And on the third day I had an infection from the toilet, and that is how I began life as a civilian.

1945 to 1950

Adjustment to civilian life.
A business recruitment and a marriage.

Before the end of 1945 – the exact date is not available – Heinz Schnaufer was released and returned to the Black Forest, where, as eldest son, he took over the reins of the wine business in Calw that his mother had been running since the death of her husband in 1940. The business was to all intents and purposes defunct, and Schnaufer had virtually to build it up from nothing. Heinz Schnaufer's father, who had never been fully contented in trade, had not intended his eldest son to go into the family business, nor had Heinz himself wanted to. His early ambition had been to pursue a career as an officer in the *Luftwaffe*, which was one of the reasons for his enthusiasm for a *Napola* education. But now there was no *Luftwaffe* and, as an eldest son who had inherited the business on his father's death in 1940, it was his responsibility to take over the reins from his mother. To this task he brought to bear the characteristics of leadership and initiative that had stood him in such good stead during his eventful five-and-a-half years as a pilot and officer in the *Nachtjagd*, in which he had achieved such high responsibility and acquitted himself with such high distinction. He was still only twenty-three years of age.

Three tasks, in broad terms, faced Heinz Schnaufer: firstly he had to re-establish the business links to suppliers and buyers that his father had built up before the war and to consolidate and develop them; secondly he had to expand the business by making and cultivating new contacts; and thirdly – and possibly most difficult of all – he had to build up a sound infra-structure on which to base the expansion of the company. In all these things Schnaufer succeeded more than might have been forecast.

Germany was in chaos, its cities and factories devastated to an extent that beggars description; its industry in a state of disintegration; a vast proportion of its civilian population homeless, displaced, disorientated and demoralised; its transport system in a condition of almost complete disruption; and such quite inadequate food supplies as there were impossible to distribute and share out fairly. Inevitably the black market burgeoned, and there were few Germans – or, it must be said, officers and men of the occupying forces – who did not succumb to the temptation to trade illegally. But there was a basic difference. For the majority of Germans black-marketing was a necessity of survival, whereas for the occupiers the black market was a source of profit, sometimes of considerable magnitude. There were, of course, those Germans, too, who took ruthless advantage of the desperate situation into which the war had led their country, the ruthless exploiters, the Harry Limes, but Heinz Schnaufer did not come into this category. Without exception, those who knew him personally and closely speak of him as an honourable man, a man of high moral standards who stemmed from a family that itself exemplified traditional integrity. Overlapping with the black-market sector, however, was the less clearly defined grey area of barter, and Schnaufer was fortunate in that the commodity to which he had access, wine, was eminently barterable. That, combined with a natural flair for business, provided a good basis for success. Hermann Greiner draws attention to the natural characteristics that predestined Heinz Schnaufer to make his mark in whatever field of endeavour he moved:

> He was completely social, yet at the same time the typical individualist. He possessed the distinctive, healthy and fundamentally decent self-confidence of those who are born highly gifted. At the same time he was modestly and politely reserved by nature, but he had a charisma that no-one could resist. He was universally gifted, and he could well have met the requirements necessary to be a leading captain of industry today. And whatever he produced would have sold well, not because of its intrinsic qualities, but because of his managerial strategy.

Fate, however, had decreed that Schnaufer would find himself in charge of a comparatively small family business, and it was as a family business that he set about developing and expanding it. Under Heinz Schnaufer's leadership the firm began to diversify, and had soon branched out into other areas of the wine trade. In addition to the original *Weinkellerei* (wine bottling and distribution) the Hermann Schnaufer KG[1] were now increasingly importing and selling wines from abroad; they had begun to produce *Sekt*, German, sparkling wine; they were distilling brandy and producing liqueurs; and they were setting up agencies and sales offices throughout Western Germany. Yet Schnaufer's watchword was 'Quality before Quantity' and this tradition survives in the company to this day.

Despite the considerable success he achieved as leader of the business, however, there is some evidence that Heinz Schnaufer did not become a businessman entirely willingly and without giving thought to alternative possibilities. One venture in the search for other employment brought him into conflict with the French occupying power and resulted in his spending several months in prison. Told in its entirety it makes

---

[1] KG – *Kommandit-Gesellschaft* (more usually written as one word) – Limited Partnership Company.

a fascinating story, but an outline of what happened must suffice here.

It was very natural that men who had flown during the war, and particularly those who had done so as pilots, should consider the possibilities of pursuing a career in aviation in peacetime. Schnaufer's ambition from an early age had been to fly, and he had realised that ambition during the war in spectacular fashion. He was in love with flying, and it was a love that could not easily be discarded or forgotten. He and Hermann Greiner were two of the many who took active steps to see if they could find employment in civilian aviation. The outcome was not encouraging.

The chances of obtaining a flying job in Europe or the United States were clearly very remote – the victorious powers themselves had a surplus of trained aircrew. There were, however, opportunities in South America, particularly in the Argentine, Brazil and Chile, where vast schemes to halt the deterioration of the rain forests were under way and there were said to be openings for, for example, pilots of spraying aircraft. Greiner and Schnaufer, who had remained in contact with each other, decided to find out what the prospects were, and they agreed to make an exploratory visit to Berne and make enquiries at the relevant Embassies. They met in Weil-am-Rhein, on the opposite bank of that river from Basel. Greiner was in favour of applying for official permission to enter Switzerland, but Schnaufer pleaded pressure of business and said he could only spare two days. He suggested that they should cross the border illegally. This they did, and were successful in reach-

The Schnaufer firm today. Its success was largely due to Heinz Schnaufer, who built it up after the end of the war and so ensured its continuing prosperity. Schnaufer's former adjutant, Georg Fengler, also played his part. (Hinchliffe)

ing Berne and speaking with South American diplomats there. The results were disappointing, and the two former night-fighter aces set off on their way back. Crossing the border illegally again, this time into French-occupied Germany, they were arrested by Swiss border guards and handed over to the French occupation authorities. They were imprisoned in the gaol at Lörrach, where they remained, living in unpleasant conditions, for the best part of six months without being charged of any offence. Eventually, through the good offices of a co-operative German warder, Schnaufer was able to pass a message of complaint about their treatment to a French general whom he knew through the wine business, and a short time later he and Greiner were released without explanation. Heinz Schnaufer's impatience meant that the two days he had been prepared to be absent from his business had turned out to be half a year.

Also in 1946 Georg Fengler, working much against his will in the Ruhr mines and still cherishing his ambition to be a vet, had applied again for permission to go to university. One of the obstacles in his way was that his education records, including his *Abitur* certificate, were still in the Soviet Zone and could not be produced in support of his application. Fengler got into touch with a former *Luftwaffe* colleague:

> I approached a wartime colleague in Hamburg, *Major* Sutor, and he helped me. He suggested I should go to Hamburg, where he held a senior teaching position. I didn't have any references or my *Abitur* certificate, but there were special night-school classes in Hamburg for people who had served in the war, and Sutor helped me so much that I passed my *Abitur* again in six months.

To make ends meet while carrying out his studies Fengler worked at a local veterinary clinic. His friendship with Heinz Schnaufer was renewed when the latter visited Hamburg. Schnaufer was travelling widely within Germany at that time, looking up old comrades to see whether they might be able to help in the build-up of *Schnaufer KG*, and he recruited Fengler informally as sort of local agent for the company. Eventually Schnaufer suggested that his former adjutant should give up his ideas of a university education and join the firm on a permanent basis, and Fengler accepted and in 1947 he moved down to Calw: 'Heinz made me an offer. He said, "Come to me in Calw; we're trying to build up the business." So I moved to Calw, and as it worked out he directed operations and I carried out his instructions: you might say that I became his executive officer.'

In 1949 Wilhelm Gänsler, the 'Third Man' in Schnaufer's Bf 110, also joined the firm. He had returned to his home in Thuringia, in the Soviet Zone of Germany, after the war ended, but had been unable to settle there. Heinz Schnaufer, who had stayed in touch with him through the mail, offered him employment, which he accepted, and then arranged for him and his family to travel – illegally from the point of view of the authorities of the German Democratic Republic – to Calw where the firm provided them with a flat and, eventually, built a

house for them. Gänsler, an engineer by training, worked on the technical side of the expanding business until his retirement, and he died of
a heart attack in November 1985.

There was another significant development. Georg Fengler takes up
the story:

> There are times when Fate comes in to human lives: things happen that
> are hard to explain. I knew that Heinz had a sister, and in fact I had
> spoken to her on the telephone on a number of occasions when I was
> Heinz's adjutant in IV./NJG 1. Heinz was always very close to his fam-
> ily, particularly his mother, and he used to telephone very frequently,
> usually after operational flights, to let her know he was well, and some-
> times Waltraut would answer the phone when I was ringing up his home
> for him either to pass on a message or to put him through personally.
> But I had never met her. She was still at school at that time.
>
> I had no ties, although I had had girl friends – that is quite normal.
> And I worked for the firm, did my duty, and lived with the family. And
> of course, we got to know each other. She was a very nice, friendly young
> woman – a *Kumpeltyp*[1]. She had grown up in a family with three broth-
> ers, and was fully at ease with men. We got to know each other very
> well, and the time came when we had to make a decision. It was in 1949,
> when Heinz was still alive, that we got around to discussing marriage.
>
> Of course, I had to go about the whole business very carefully, because
> she, as a member of the Schnaufer family, was strictly my employer, and
> so it wasn't so simple! There was a big Christmas party, and I was
> Heinz's right-hand man, and we had built the new office building in the

---

[1] *Kumpeltyp* – 'A *Kumpel*-type'. A *Kumpel* in this context is a close friend, a chum, what the
Americans would possibly call a 'buddy'. It is usually applied to males and suggests very close,
mutually supportive, friendship.

town, and there was a *Richtfest*[1], and we combined it with the Christmas festivities. And Heinz laid on the party. It was very fine. All the firm's employees were invited – at that time we already had between sixty and eighty working for us. We had a very good time, and of course everyone had something to drink. I gave four or five people from the firm a lift back home after the party, and on the way my car was in collision with a Volkswagen jeep, and I hurt my head and ended up in hospital. And somehow or other Waltraut and I became engaged! It's funny how life turns out!

Heinz was very agreeable, and his mother liked me as well – she did everything for us. That was important, because there could have been difficulties. It all turned out well – it couldn't have been better.

Heinz Schnaufer himself never married. He got on well with the opposite sex, but never allowed friendships to develop into anything more serious. During the war his one dedication, to the exclusion of all else, was his duty as an officer and a night fighter. The war was no time to form closer or more intimate attachments such as marriage: that would have been irresponsible. Then, with hostilities over, there was the matter of establishing himself and his family, for whom he felt himself responsible in the absence of his father, in civilian life, a task to which he dedicated himself just as he had done to his arduous duties in the *Luftwaffe*.

Fritz Rumpelhardt remembers one occasion when, it seemed, Heinz Schnaufer might have been smitten. In January 1945 Schnaufer's crew were on a rehabilitation leave in the ski-resort of Kitzbühl: Rumpelhardt and Gänsler were accommodated in a modest sports hotel and Schnaufer, as befitted a senior officer, in the Grand Hotel, where a number of displaced former diplomats and senior politicians were living, including the wife of the one-time Foreign Minister of Yugoslavia, Stojadinovic or something similar. The lady had two very pretty daughters, and Heinz became very friendly with the younger of the two. In Summer 1946 Heinz had a sudden summons to Kitzbühl, presumably from the Stojadinovic family, but when he arrived there it was to find that they had left and could no longer be contacted.

Another former German night-fighter ace, Wilhelm 'Wim' Johnen, had been attached to Schnaufer's *Gruppe* at Saint-Trond for a short period during the war but did not get to know him well at that time. At the time Heinz Schnaufer was already a *Hauptmann*, *Gruppenkommandeur* and holder of the Oak Leaves, while Johnen was still an *Oberleutnant*. Schnaufer made a strong impression on Johnen by reason of his unassuming nature and friendliness – many *Luftwaffe* officers of his status and with his reputation tended to arrogance and would have distanced themselves from an outsider. After the war Johnen studied building engineering in Munich, and then, on qualification, moved to Ulm to begin work. Schnaufer got into touch with him:

[1] A '*Richtfest*' is a topping-out ceremony when the roof of a new building is completed, traditionally the occasion for a convivial celebration

Hauptmann *Wilhelm 'Wim' Johnen was a member of 3./NJG 1 and later became* Kommandeur *of III./NJG 6.*

Schnaufer came to Ulm with a pick-up truck. He had built up his *Weinkellerei* and he was trying to set up branches all over the place, including Ulm. He stayed the night in my flat, and we had a party – we were young people in those days – and there was a doctor's daughter from Neu Ulm, on the Bavarian side, and they made friends with each other, and obviously got on very well. Heinz had brought me wine, and he went back to Calw with his lorry full of building materials, because at that period everything was in short supply. I can't remember whether it was bricks or cement or wood, but in any case I got wine in exchange. He came and visited me two or three times in this way, and stayed overnight. He met the doctor's daughter each time. I was expecting him to come to see me again when we got the dreadful news of his death. I might have read it in the newspapers – I can't remember. It was unbelievable, terrible, that this should happen to a man with over a hundred night victories, someone who had never even been wounded. It was tragic.

His successes never went to his head. He never acted in a superior manner to his subordinates or to outsiders like me, when I visited Saint-Trond. And later he was always a good friend who gave good advice. He was, in truth, a comrade. And now, suddenly, he was gone.

It was at about this time that Schnaufer visited another of his former night-fighter colleagues, Ludwig Meister, who after his release had begun to study architecture in Munich in 1946.

One day, only a few months before his tragic death, he came to see me in my student lodgings. As you can imagine, our meeting was an occasion for celebration. Heinz wanted me to give up my studies in bombed-out lecture halls and cold apartments and join him in his firm. I weakened, and I asked for time to think his proposition over. His death relieved me of the necessity to make a decision.

CHAPTER FOURTEEN

July 1950

Schnaufer's death. 'Those whom the Gods love.'

Heinz Schnaufer had celebrated his twenty-eighth birthday on the 16th of February 1950, and on the 15th of April he had given his younger sister Waltraut away in marriage to his close friend and business-colleague Georg Fengler: strictly one might refer to Fengler as Schnaufer's employee, but the relationship was much closer than that term would suggest. Fengler was looked upon as a member of the Schnaufer family. The Schnaufer firm was thriving, and its increasing prosperity was in considerable measure due to the dynamism and natural business acumen of the glittering star of the *Nachtjagd*, assisted by his former *Luftwaffe* friend and adjutant. The future of the company, and of Heinz Schnaufer himself, seemed assured.

In July 1950 Schnaufer was in France on a wine-buying visit, and during the late afternoon of the 13th of the month he was heading south on the N10 (*Route Nationale No. 10*) just to the south of Bordeaux, travelling in the direction of Biarritz. It was a pleasant summer's evening, and Schnaufer was driving his soft-top Mercedes *cabriolet*, registration number AWW 44-3435, with the top folded back.

About twenty kilometres south of Bordeaux a minor road, the D211 (it was designated the D1 at the period in question) crosses the N10 at right angles at the hamlet of Jauge. Both roads are perfectly straight for some distance on either side of this point, and the terrain is quite flat, although trees tend to obscure the crossroad itself. Visibility was excellent and the roads were dry. Schnaufer was driving fast, but there is no suggestion that his speed was excessive and, of course, he was on the major road. A French workman, Jean Antoine Gasc, was approaching the crossroad from Schnaufer's right, driving his firm's Renault 22 lorry, which was carrying a six-ton load of empty but heavy gas cylinders. It was shortly before seven o'clock.

Jean Gasc, approaching the major road at what witnesses were later to describe as 'high speed', sounded his horn as he approached the crossing but failed to give way and came on to the major road – again according to witnesses – without slowing down. Despite braking hard and pulling to the left, Schnaufer was too late to avoid the collision.

Opposite: *The notice of Schnaufer's death in a local French newspaper, July 1950.*

The two vehicles impacted side-on, the right-hand side of Schnaufer's Mercedes against the front left-hand side of the lorry. Schnaufer's car, badly damaged, veered across the main road and came to a stop on the right-hand side of the D1, at the far side of the crossing, and Gasc's lorry finished up nearby, partly in a roadside ditch. Schnaufer's car had left skid-marks just under twenty metres in length, showing that he had applied his brakes, but there were no sign of skid-marks from the lorry. The fuel tank of the Mercedes, which was located above the engine, was ruptured and petrol flowed on to the hot engine and ignited, but local people quickly extinguished the flames. Schnaufer was bleeding profusely from a wound at the back of his head, and a witness to the accident, *Mme* Alice Ducourneau, gave him such first-aid assistance as she could. It was not until 1930 hours that the police appeared on the scene, by which time Schnaufer had been taken from the car and put on to a makeshift stretcher. Soon afterwards an ambulance arrived and took him to the St-André Hospital in Bordeaux.

Jean Gasc was unhurt, and severe though the impact of the two vehicles had been it seems unlikely that the collision itself was the direct cause of Schnaufer's injuries. When the lorry and car had come into violent contact some thirty of the empty gas cylinders that the lorry was carrying – possibly not properly secured – were flung off the vehicle, and the probability is that at least one of them had struck Schnaufer.

The significance of what had just happened was not immediately reflected in the local newspaper report:

> M Walfgang Schnaufer, 28 years old, a commercial traveller for a Bordeaux firm, was driving along the Cestas road at about 1830 hours when he was struck by a lorry coming from one side at a crossing on the Pierroton road. The impact was extremely violent, and the unfortunate driver was immediately taken with a fractured skull to the Saint-André Hospital, where his condition was said to be very serious.

Schnaufer never regained consciousness, and two days later, on the 15th July 1950, the most successful night-fighter pilot the world has ever known, the never-defeated victor of more than a hundred night-time combats who had faced a violent death on countless occasions, ended his life in a hospital bed.

At a hearing before a *juge d'instruction* at Jauge on the 29th July 1950 the driver of the Renault truck, Jean Antoine Gasc, was charged with manslaughter and breach of the traffic regulations. In mitigation he claimed that the speed at which he was travelling as he approached the cross-roads was between 30 and 35 kilometres per hour, and that he had sounded his horn continuously as he approached the cross-roads: this latter point was confirmed by witnesses. He was, he said, unfamiliar with the road on which he was driving, not having driven that way before, and he had failed to see the give-way sign. The crossing itself was partly masked by a restaurant and by trees. An inspection of the site of the accident by the *juge d'instruction* himself and others did indeed confirm that the approach to the crossing on the D1 was obscured, and also that the give-way sign was 'entirely neglected and could escape the notice of a driver passing there for the first time.' The official report of the hearing, dated 16 November 1950, sums up as follows:

> That Gasc was at fault cannot be in doubt. He did not yield right of way, and his speed was too high. It is found that as a result of not observing the law, imprudence or negligence, he involuntarily caused the death of Schnauffer [sic].
>
> He is referred for confirmation of the findings and for sentencing to the correctional tribunal at Toulouse in accordance with the law.

To describe the effect of the shock of Schnaufer's untimely death on the family – or even, indeed, fully to imagine it – would be impossible. A bright star had been eclipsed, a young life already far more full of high endeavour, experience and success than most had been abruptly cut short, a family deprived of its deeply loved and respected leader. The German nation – indeed the world – had lost a great aviator and hero.

Schnaufer's death in France gave rise to widespread rumours to the effect that he had been assassinated by members of the former *Résistance*: the manner of his passing was neatly fitted into the conspiracy theory – the accident, it was claimed, was simply a cover-up by the French authorities. So persistent were these rumours that when Schnaufer's

Calw, den 24. Juli 1950.

Gott der Allmächtige hat unseren innigst geliebten, treusorgenden Sohn, Bruder und Schwager

Heinz Schnaufer

auf einer Geschäftsreise in Frankreich durch einen tragischen Unglücksfall im 29. Lebensjahre zu sich gerufen.

In tiefem Schmerz

Martha Schnaufer geb. Frey
Manfred Schnaufer
Ekart Schnaufer
Georg Fengler und Frau Waltraut
geb. Schnaufer

Beerdigung: Donnerstag, den 27. Juli, 15 Uhr

body was returned to Germany the family arranged to have a second post-mortem carried out privately, which action displeased the French occupation authorities. The findings of the examination, however, confirmed those of the French, and the emergence of another possible Schnaufer myth was prevented.

CHAPTER FIFTEEN

Schnaufer's Place in History

A question unanswered.

At one level it is simple to define Heinz Schnaufer's place in history. He was the pilot who shot down more enemy bombers by night than did any other man. It is a fact worthy of note that of the many hundreds of pilots who flew night fighters only Helmut Lent came within twenty of his total score, and only Heinrich Wittgenstein within fifty. In the course of climbing to the pinnacle of his success Schnaufer achieved senior rank and high distinction at a remarkably early age. In all probability his record of kills will remain unsurpassed, if only because opportunities for others to emulate his attainments are unlikely to arise.

It is, however, worth looking at the Schnaufer phenomenon from another, less clear-cut and certainly more controversial, viewpoint; to consider Schnaufer not as a unique example of a Second World War pilot, but as a German soldier fighting for a country governed by a

Heinz-Schnaufer-Strasse in Calw. The naming of the street caused controversy. (Hinchliffe)

régime fundamentally evil. Since the end of the war and the revelations of the atrocities committed by the Nazis – an appellation, incidentally, that is very difficult to define precisely – a great deal of accusation and condemnation has been directed in at wartime members of the *Wehrmacht*, much of it, sadly, justified.

There is a street in the Heumaden district of Schnaufer's home-town, Calw, that is named after him. In August 1994, as part of a series about roads named in honour of local personalities, the *Calwer Tagblatt* published an article about Schnaufer entitled, 'The British called him the Night-Ghost'. It was not a very good article, in that, as the headline reveals, it perpetuated old Schnaufer myths. It generated a lively response. The first letter published was from a reader named Heinrich Drummer:

> This is just the sort of stuff that radicals who scheme and lie about the past of our nation feed on: a 'Night Ghost' who put fear in the hearts of his enemies.
>
> It comes as no surprise today that Jewish cemeteries are vandalized, non-Germans are attacked on the street and foreigners' houses are reduced to ashes, when so-called deeds of heroism from Nazi Greater Germany are rewarded with the honour of a street-name after a time of shame that has lasted less than fifty years. No matter how successful a Second World War flyer might have been, he is not fitted to be an example for us today.

Herr Drummer's letter moved Gerhard Jäger, a retired parish priest, to respond. He began, 'I will try to do something that *Herr* Drummer did not attempt to do, that is to put himself in the position we were in at that time,' and he went on:

> The way in which our loyalty and the fulfilment of our duty towards our Fatherland in those days are viewed and judged today is quite shameful. We soldiers who took part in the war are dogmatically categorized as Nazis and, therefore, criminals.
>
> I didn't hear any protest from *Herr* Drummer when the Queen-Mam [sic] unveiled the memorial to Bomber Harris in England. He ordered the German towns, including Dresden, to be bombed. Did you experience Dresden, *Herr* Drummer? It has been proved that the bombing strategy did not shorten the war. On the contrary, people who were against the war joined together in solidarity to save what could still be saved of the Fatherland. They were not Nazis, they were Germans, just like you and me.
>
> In this phalanx of solidarity was a young airman called Heinz Schnaufer. He was faced with a task and he, without being a Nazi, loyally carried it out, to an even greater degree than he could reasonably have been expected to.
>
> We who took part in the war are unhappy with being lumped together with the Nazi criminals just because we did not leave our Fatherland in the lurch in its darkest hour.

Eugen Lebzelter, whose school-time recollections of Heinz Schnaufer appear earlier in this book, also contributed:

> Heinz Schnaufer flew in the defence against the enemy bombers flying in to attack German towns. With every one of the more than 120 bombers that he shot down and hence prevented from dropping their bombs, he saved the lives of countless innocent and defenceless human beings. Every time he flew on these operations he knew he was risking his life. That we should honour and remember Heinz Schnaufer is no more than he deserves.

The conflict of opinion manifest in these few letters epitomises a vastly greater controversy that has long exercised philosophers, pundits, politicians, soldiers and laymen – the latter frequently the most vociferous – not only in post-war, guilt-ridden Germany, but whenever and wherever wars have been fought, lost and won; which, if one accepts that Man is inherently a belligerent animal, means since the dawn of rationality – or, the more cynical might say, irrationality – in the species. The controversy has to do with collective responsibility and with collective guilt; with the definitions of guilt and of innocence; with patriotism, with nationalism; with self-defence and the defence of family and home; with duty; with military tradition; with loyalty; with soldiers' oaths; with treason and with 'resistance' – the catalogue is virtually endless: the very factors, one might wryly observe, that themselves contain the potential to contribute to the outbreak of wars. It is a perennial argument and, as the letters quoted above clearly illustrate, it provokes emotive, glib and dogmatic points of view. And it is a problem to which there can be no solution, one on which each individual who considers it will make up his own mind. Fortunately, in considering Schnaufer's place in history we are faced with a very much less complex dilemma.

The question is whether Heinz Schnaufer may justly be remembered as a great soldier and a valiant enemy – just as, for example Manfred von Richthofen, Erwin Rommel and Adolf Galland are popularly perceived in some circles – or whether he should be seen as a faithful servant of an evil régime and therefore himself evil. Was Heinz Schnaufer a great German or a 'Nazi'? After all, he was one of the young men selected straight from school to be trained in the ideology of National Socialism. As with the greater controversy, individuals will form their own opinion, but comments by some of his contemporaries might help in the process. These commentators' formative years, like Schnaufer's, were spent in the exciting and heady environment of the burgeoning Third Reich, and they knew him and like him they fought for the Hitler dictatorship. Regrettably Schnaufer himself cannot be questioned: perhaps it might be that the experiences and varied opinions of these men can help to explain him and to put him in historical context.

Georg Fengler, who served as Schnaufer 's adjutant and later joined the Schnaufer firm and married Heinz's sister Waltraut:

> I can only speak from my own experience, my own youth. At the begin-

ning, when National Socialism came in, things were very bad. We had nine million unemployed. And in two years the unemployed were off the streets.

Of course, no one can condone Hitler's treatment of the Jews. It was an unspeakable disgrace. It makes no difference whether there were six million or only a hundred. That is a fact, and of course those of us who survived are supposed to accept responsibility for it. But in any dictator state such things are possible. It is there in English history, French history, Spanish history. Wherever you choose to look you can find evil things. It cannot be excused, but at the same time one can't go on for ever accepting the blame.

I'm not trying to say that all of us in the *Luftwaffe* weren't Nazis. It would be easy to say that, but it wouldn't be true. In 1933 I was twelve, and I had just started *Oberschule*. And I was in a Christian organisation – the Scouts or something like that. But that didn't last very long. Less than a year passed and we were transferred compulsorily into the *Jungvolk*. I later became a *Jungvolkführer* and went into the *Hitlerjugend*. You must remember that the majority of our education came not from the home but from the State, and the youth of the country were under continuous pressure. But I was never a member of the Party, because I joined the *Luftwaffe*. I was lucky. It was simply a matter of luck. If you went about your work, followed your profession, you didn't need the Party. That's how it is in life: one needs a bit of luck. No nation is fundamentally bad. It's largely to do with education. If, as a child, you are educated in a certain direction – and Hitler concentrated on the young people.

When we were commissioned as *Leutnant*, we were in the *Deutschlandhalle* in Berlin. That would be in 1942. We were all young officers. And Goebbels came marching in. And he made a speech, and so on. And then Hitler came in; and it's hard to believe now, but we all shouted, '*Heil, mein Führer!*' – and we didn't think about it: it was completely automatic. And later, after the war, my mother-in-law and my wife, although they were Protestants, went to Rome to see the Pope. And they had an audience with the Pope. And my wife said it was so overwhelming, so impressive, that they found themselves crying out, '*Heil Papa!*' And as a human being there is nothing you can do about it.

On the 20th July we were at Saint-Trond. I was Adjutant, and a teleprinter message arrived on my desk – top secret, and so on. And I carried out the orders that came from above. On has to do one's duty – that goes without saying. There were many – hundreds of thousands – of foreign workers, conscripts, prisoners of war and so on, living in barracks. And the order came through that if, as a result of the attempt on Hitler's life, there should be an uprising among the workers, then we had to take off and open fire on them. Think about it! If it had come to that, do you think we could have refused to take off? That is unrealistic, as long as the régime was in place. We would have had no alternative.

I spoke with Heinz about this. He was, of course, affected, depressed, because he said to me later, 'Thank God it didn't happen.' Because if the order had come through to take off and suppress the uprising, we would have had no alternative but to take off. That's why I say it's all a matter of luck. If you are a soldier, or one who carried responsibility, if the order comes, you do as you are told: that is the dangerous side of being a soldier.

Kurt Meyer, contemporary of Heinz Schnaufer at *Napola* and later a distinguished bomber pilot on the Eastern Front:

The German people in general don't want to want to hear anything about that period, although at the time most of them supported National Socialism. This is primarily to do with the frightful cruelties and murders that were perpetrated on the Jews by the 'Nazis' – not by the National Socialists – in the name of Germany. Everything good, everything fine, everything positive and attractive in this world philosophy, all the fine, proud years before the war, are suppressed and never spoken of.

This, in its turn, is a success of the Allies' 'Re-education', which made everything that was in any way connected with the time of Adolf Hitler bad and despicable. When I was a young man and training to be an officer I met this man at very close quarters, and you would not believe the charisma that this 'genius' – later this 'Satan' – radiated, the way in which it affected those around him. It is not surprising that in 1938/1939 all the European diplomats and the Papal Nuncio bowed and scraped to him.

So Heinz Schnaufer was also an enthusiastic supporter of National Socialism, as indeed were virtually all young men born between 1920 and 1928, brought up as they were in the Hitler Youth and indoctrinated into the ideas of the NSDAP. It is not a matter for surprise that this applied to an even greater extent to us élite *Napola* pupils, who enjoyed an outstanding education, similar to the hard methods of the Scottish Salem School.

We Germans knew that concentration camps existed, but we did not know what was happening in them, so perfidious were the 'Nazis'. We did not know the darker side of the brown-shirted system of government. But we ought to have realised what was going on, had we not blindly followed the pipe-music of this Pied Piper, Hitler. No one can accuse him of having made a secret of his aims, because in every one of his speeches he spoke of eradicating the Jewish race. What we did not have at that time was the ability to take his words to their logical conclusion.

After the war the revelation of the ghastly murders of the Jews in Auschwitz, Treblinka and Theresienstadt – and above all the photographs that the Allies showed us – shocked us average Germans deeply. They also came as a great shock, particularly, to those who had until then supported the National Socialists on ideological grounds, to the intellectuals and to their supporters. It was then that the German 'Shame' began, and I, as a one-time convinced National Socialist, have no hesitation in confessing that today I am ashamed of the misdeeds that the Nazis committed in the name of Germany.

Heinz Schnaufer quite certainly felt the same way as I do, because we both had exactly the same way of thinking. It is said of my friend Heinz that when the *Führer* decorated him with the *Brillanten* he asked Hitler whether the war was lost. Whether this story is true or not, it is quite on the cards that *Major* Schnaufer could have put such a question, because he was dedicated to National Socialism and could not in any way have been considered an opponent of the régime.

There is a documented instance of an altercation that Heinz Schnaufer, at the time still a junior officer at Saint-Trond, had with his Commanding Officer, *Hauptmann* Ehle. Ehle had said that in his opinion

With no obvious changes to the exterior, over the last seventy years, the 'Schnaufer Haus' as it appears today. (The word 'Haus' in German does not necessarily mean a residential property, but a building). (Hinchliffe)

the Germans could no longer win the war, and Heinz, a convinced National Socialist, contradicted him violently. This took place in 1943 at a table in the Operations Room No. 6 of II./NJG 1 in front of the Cadet College on the Liège Road.

You ask me about my own thoughts and my attitude to National Socialism during the war. I will give you a clear and unequivocal reply: 'To the bitter end of the war I was a convinced supporter of National Socialism.'

I can imagine that after the war Heinz Schnaufer was also deeply shocked when he heard of the unending cruelties, and quite certainly he will have asked himself whether he had served the wrong masters.

Like myself and those other *Napola* pupils still alive he will often have been very depressed when he learned of the crimes of the Nazis. But until the end of the war he believed in his *Führer*, as millions of Germans did, and in the Nazi propaganda of Dr Goebbels, who right until the final days of the war spoke of 'miracle weapons': it is a good thing that in fact we did not have them (atomic bombs).

For people who did not experience those times it is difficult to comprehend what happened. And if we Germans had enjoyed the degree of knowledge that we have today, a great deal that has so stigmatized us in the world would not have occurred.

Peter Spoden did not know Schnaufer personally during the war, although, of course, he knew of him by reputation. Spoden finished the war as *Kommandeur* I./NJG 6 and had 24 confirmed victories to his credit:

Schnaufer has become a legend, a figure like Richthofen, a gallant, devil-may-care German officer full of idealism, in some ways a tragic representative of his generation, because he fought for the wrong ideas and on the losing side.

My early life ran parallel to that of Schnaufer. We both joined the *Jungvolk* in 1933 and went to *Oberschule* at the age of 10. I stayed at *Oberschule* for eight years, he stayed for six. We were both enthused of the new ideas, and the *Führerprinzip*[1] made a great impression on us. Prior to 1933 democracy in Germany had been unsuccessful. And as boys we were also very impressed by Hitler's successes – the occupation of the Rhineland, the annexation of Austria, the successful Olympic Games, the Sudetenland, there were no longer seven million unemployed, the economy and the armaments industry were flourishing, and so on.

Our parents were more sceptical, and some of the teachers at *Oberschule* didn't fall into line. The Principal of the *Oberschule* was, of course, a member of the Party, but at least a third – possibly more – of the teachers showed some latent resistance. I remember that when the synagogue was burning in Essen my teacher, Doctor Schwebke, a member of the Party, came into the classroom and said, 'One doesn't burn churches and synagogues down. Now let's get on with the lesson.' I would think that Schnaufer had a similar education. In the *Oberschulen* at that time we still

---

[1] The 'Leader-Principle' was in theory the executive basis of the National Socialist Party. It specified that at all levels of the Party organization power of final decision reposed in one individual, the leader of that sector, and not in the membership or in committees.

had teachers who supported the old Humboldt spirit of free science and free thinking. 'Thoughts are free.' Thank God that we had teachers like that.

I don't know why Schnaufer joined a *Napola*. Probably he wanted to become an officer as quickly as possible, in which case a *Napola* was obviously the right way.

It could, however, well be that Schnaufer was full of enthusiasm for the ideas of that time, and he wanted to go to such a school for that reason. I had a close friend in my class, Hans Adelhütte, who went to such an institution just before he took his *Abitur*, and who subsequently became a night fighter and went missing as an *Oberleutnant* over the North Sea after shooting down twenty bombers. It was a matter of defending our country, and we wanted to be a part of it, but it's also quite certain that the spirit of adventure and the thought of escape from the parental home played their part. There was nothing bad about going to a *Napola*: at that period millions of young men were fascinated by Hitler's ideas. Let's not forget that Chamberlain and Daladier visited Munich and shook Hitler's hand.

I cannot believe that Schnaufer was influenced by such concepts as racial ideology or the repression of other human beings. Admittedly the *Napolas* were national-socialist élite schools, but two years at one of them is not the same as ten years of Nazi indoctrination. The parental home and the first schools that one attended were far more important in forming character. At these élite schools considerable emphasis was put on discipline, obedience, patriotism, sport and physical education which are, after all, not bad qualities. You British built up you Empire on them, didn't you? But there was less instruction – or none at all – in the humanities, and criticism was not tolerated. People who had been to a *Napola* were in general rather too cool and career-conscious. I prefer people with heart and with feeling.

I believe that Schnaufer wanted to be a flyer from very early in life. In those days flying and helping in the building-up of a Greater Germany were more important than Nazi ideology with its racial stupidity and the repression of other peoples, which we knew nothing about when we volunteered for the *Luftwaffe* in 1939/40.

In the *Luftwaffe*, in which, it must be noted, Schnaufer spent six years of the Hitler era, there were no political or ethnological discussions. We flew, we shot bombers down, and we died! I don't remember ever having talked about Party, Parliament or Democracy. We knew nothing about the fate of the Jews or the people in the East. Sometimes we flew over the concentration camp at Dachau, which was usually lit up. As far as we knew criminals, dissidents and traitors were imprisoned there. And in the devastated cities we saw dead mothers with burned babies in their arms, and for us that was reason enough to continue the fight.

In the *Luftwaffe* there were many flyers who had heart and human feelings, and I got to know some of them – Commanders with the *Ritterkreuz* – very well. And there were the 'cool types', whom I also got to know. These men were hard to get close to know: they knew nothing except shooting-down, *Ritterkreuz* and *Eichenlaub*. But I never came across real 'Nazis' – officers who were inhuman and brutal – in the *Nachtjagd*. What is a 'Nazi' – a National Socialist? There is, I suggest, nothing wrong in a man who thinks in national terms and believes in Socialism – a more just distribution of the world's goods.

Schnaufer's gravestone in the Calw Cemetery. Was the verse intentionally left incomplete? (Güse)

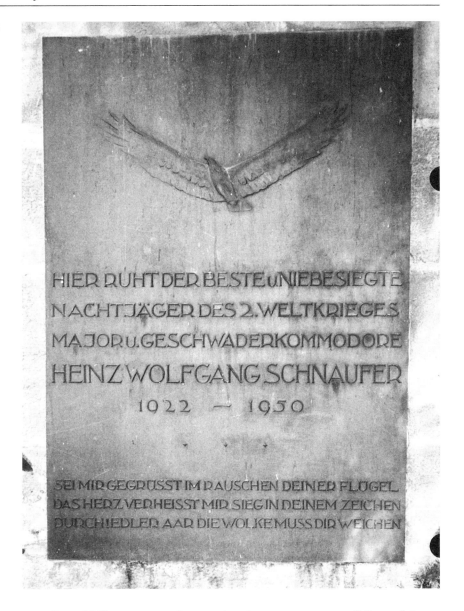

HIER RUHT DER BESTE u.NIEBESIEGTE
NACHTJÄGER DES 2.WELTKRIEGES
MAJOR u.GESCHWADERKOMMODORE
HEINZ WOLFGANG SCHNAUFER
1922 — 1950

SEI MIR GEGRÜSST IM RAUSCHEN DEINER FLÜGEL
DAS HERZ VERHEISST MIR SIEG IN DEINEM ZEICHEN
DURCH JEDER AAR DIE WOLKE MUSS DIR WEICHEN

I would like to repeat the question that you put to me: 'Many of the Germans I have consulted maintain that Heinz Schnaufer was not an adherent of the National-Socialist régime. In your view is that possible or likely, given that before his entry into the *Luftwaffe* in 1939 he was a pupil at a *Napola*?' Let me try to answer it.

We were all adherents of the National Socialist régime. We believed in the concept of self-determination for all Germans in Alsace-Lorraine, the South Tyrol, Austria, the Sudetenland, Upper Silesia, Danzig and the Memelland, areas that were taken away from us under the unjust Treaty of Versailles. We believed in the *Führerprinzip*, because democracy before 1933 had failed. We supported family values, such as marriage, children, respect for one's elders. We loved our German *Vaterland*, we admired nature, farming, the old customs of Germany. We wanted a strong army and air force, not just the 100,000 troops, no military aircraft and no tanks that the Versailles Treaty had allocated to us. We wanted the pride and honour back that our country had lost in 1914/1918.

All those who knew Schnaufer well say that he did not support the Nazi régime. I can fully believe that, insofar as he did not support the terrible cruelties of the concentration camps nor the inhuman treatment of the Poles and Russians. That applied to great majority of the German people. But without a belief in the sort of ideals that I have mentioned above one could not fight and be prepared to give one's life.

From 1942 onwards in Germany all Hell was let loose. It didn't happen suddenly; it began with a 'phoney war' and developed into a ghastly blood bath of mutual genocide. The terrible partisan war in the Balkans and Russia led to excesses on both sides, comparable with the frightful partisan war in Vietnam. The RAF and the USAF waged a pitiless bombing war against our cities, our women and our children. Total war dominated us. The whole world was fighting against Germany. It was a case of sheer survival. The National Socialist leadership reacted self-destructively instead of striving for a negotiated peace, but, at the same time, the Allies were also unwilling to negotiate. This idiotic talk of 'unconditional surrender' on the part of the Allies made any reasonable solution impossible, and the result was that the National Socialist leadership revealed its true face with the frightful war of annihilation in the East.

We were all part of the régime, Heinz Schnaufer as well.'

These are the views of men who shared Schnaufer's experience of youth and war. Because each man is an individual, their separate opinions differ in perception and in emphasis. Because each of us, too, is different, each of us will assess Heinz Schnaufer in our own way. There can be no definitive judgement.

The English translation of a piece of verse that appears on Schnaufer's gravestone was quoted at the beginning of this biography:

> Thee would I salute in the threshing of thy wings,
>   My heart foretells me triumph in thy name.
> Onward, proud eagle, to thee the cloud must yield.

The lines were penned in 1813, shortly before the death in battle of the poet, Theodor Körner, a resistance fighter against the forces of Napoleon, whose domination of Europe took in Austria and Prussia. They are the first three of the fourteen lines of a sonnet entitled '*Der preußischer Grenzadler*'[1], and the omission of the line that follows the three quoted above is striking:

> *Fleuch rächend auf von deiner Toten Hügel!*

The three lines of verse engraved on the gravestone do not give the impression of being a complete stanza – reading them, one is left wondering what might come next. That in its turn provokes a question –

[1] 'The Prussian Border-Eagle'.

why was the line omitted? Was it perhaps because it was considered inappropriate, or possibly because it was thought that it would be unwise to include it? The epitaph personifies Heinz Schnaufer as the Prussian Eagle, and the missing lines, had they been included, would have exhorted him to take to the air again and avenge his dead, which would have meant, in the context, the war-dead of Germany. To have expressed so provocative a sentiment as that in 1950 would have been unwise, to say the very least. Even today to do so would be controversial. But did those who chose the epitaph foresee, or possibly even hope, that other Germans familiar with the poem would understand its hidden significance? Was it a note of defiance, of national pride, even in defeat? Again, you will no doubt make up your own mind. And if, in your view, that should be the case, could you, in your innermost heart, blame those whose idea it was? The missing line translates as:

'Fly vengeful up from the burial-mound of thy dead!'

APPENDIX A

Another Schnaufer myth

The fins in the Museums – and elsewhere – and the Messerschmitt in Hyde Park – and Another Schnaufer Myth?

Schnaufer flew a number of Bf 110s operationally, of course, but there was one that has been described as his favourite. Fritz Rumpelhardt confirms this latter point, referring to it as, 'Our trusted EF.' Its identification letters were G9+EF, and in it the Schnaufer crew shot down at least 34 British bombers. Their first victory in this machine was on the night of 21 July 1944, when they destroyed two bombers, and their last – Schnaufer's final kill overall – on 7 March 1945. It was in G9+EF that Schnaufer shot down seven – probably eight – Lancasters on the night of 21 February 1945. Already there would seem to be an anomaly: in July 1944 Schnaufer was flying with *Nachtjagdgeschwader* 1, while in 1945 he was the Commanding Officer of *Nachtjagdgeschwader* 4, and in the *Luftwaffe* – as, indeed, in the Royal Air Force – the first two letters of the aircraft code indicated the unit to which it belonged. G9 meant NJG 1, but the correct code for NJG 4 was 3C. There seems to be another discrepancy, too. The letters after the German imperial cross were intended to show the position of the aircraft and its pilot in the hierarchy of the *Geschwader*. As *Kommandeur* of IV./NJG 1, Schnaufer should have been flying a machine coded G9+AE ('A' for *Kommandeur*, 'E' for *Stab IV. Gruppe*), while when he was *Kommodore* of NJG 4 his personal aircraft should, one might think, have been 3C+AA.

There are two principal matters concerning Schnaufer's aircraft – one a matter fact, the other possibly yet another Schnaufer legend – that invite examination and, if possible, clarification. The first has to do with certain surviving relics that are said to be from Schnaufer's machine. In the Imperial War Museum in London and the Australian War Memorial Museum in Canberra there are fins[1] from a Bf 110, port and starboard respectively, each embellished with 121 icons representing the 121 confirmed kills that Schnaufer made during the war. They

---

[1] These artefacts are more often than not referred to as 'rudders', which is strictly incorrect. The rudder was the moveable control surface by means of which the aircraft was steered, while the fin was the fixed vertical component of the tail unit on which the rudder was mounted.

are exhibited as being from 'a Me 110 flown by Schnaufer'. In Germany, however, there is another port fin, in the possession of a collector, which also carries the 121 'kill' symbols and which is, it is also claimed, the fin from Schnaufer's aircraft. These are facts.

The other aspect of the theme is this: it is widely believed, and maintained in various publications, that in September 1945, immediately following the end of the war, Schnaufer's aircraft was put on display in an exhibition of captured enemy equipment in Hyde Park, London. The aeroplane, it is said, was lettered G9+AA and was fitted with fins and rudders showing all Schnaufer's 121 kills. So strong is this belief that one is tempted to accept it as fact, yet it has proved impossible, in the course of the research for this book, to confirm or positively to refute it. One indication of the persistence of this story is that some plastic aircraft-model kits, usually noted for their attention to detail, reproduce 'Schnaufer's Messerschmitt' with the coding G9+AA and with the kills shown on the fins: the truth is that, as will be explained below, Schnaufer never flew an aircraft with such markings[1].

The events associated with these two puzzles are not uncomplicated. Let us go back in time. Schnaufer took over the command of NJG 4 in October 1944, and his new unit was equipped mainly with the Junkers 88. At first it was Schnaufer's intention to convert to the Ju 88 himself, and he made a few local flights in one. He felt uncomfortable with the aircraft, however, and decided that he would revert to the Bf 110, the type on which he had so far done all his operational flying. He had flown in to Gütersloh in G9+EF, and he decided to retain the aircraft for his operational flying. Why he did not have the coding altered from G9 to the correct one for NJG 4, 3C, is unclear. Probably this was another example of Schnaufer's superstition, because he also retained his IV./NJG 1 personal callsign, '*Adler 133*'. Heinz Schnaufer did sometimes fly the Ju 88 for non-operational purposes. When he was awarded the *Brillanten*, for example, and went to Berlin to be decorated by Hitler, he flew a Ju 88 carrying the correct identification coding for *Kommodore NJG 4*, 3C+AA.

On 7 March 1945, as already mentioned, Schnaufer shot down his final British bomber, and he did so in EF. He is recorded as having flown an air test in the same aircraft on 28th March, his last flight in EF. In the interim he had also flown locally in another Bf 110, 3C+BA. Then, on 30 March, the airfield at Gütersloh was abandoned before the advancing Allies, and Schnaufer took off in the very early hours of the morning for Wunstorf, some way to the north-east. The aircraft he made the journey in was 3C+BA, and we do not know why he did not take his 'favourite' C9+EF. At this late stage of the war the *Luftwaffe* was in headlong retreat, and very soon afterwards Schnaufer left Wunstorf for Fassberg: when exactly is not known, and Fritz Rumpelhardt's logbook does not show a flight. Possibly Schnaufer flew

---

[1] It goes without saying that any further information readers might have on this matter would be most gratefully received.

Schnaufer's last aircraft, in which he only flew once operationally without success, was 3C+BA, Werknummer 180560 (check). Here it is seen at Eggebek at the end of the war. In accordance with official instructions its airscrews and rudders have been removed to prevent it being flown.

the aircraft without a crew and the others went by road – it is only a short distance from Wunstorf to Fassberg – or possibly another crew flew it. On 9 April the Schnaufer crew made an operational flight from Fassberg in BA, but did not make contact with the enemy. Then, on 11 April, they flew BA to their final destination, Eggebek in Schleswig-Holstein.

At this stage, according to Rumpelhardt's logbook, another aircraft appeared on the scene, Bf 110 'DX', in which Schnaufer and his crew flew an air test on the 14th April. Rumpelhardt comments;

> Very soon after we arrived at Eggebek the airfield was attacked by low-flying Allied fighter-bombers, Typhoons or Thunderbolts or something like that, and all the aircraft, including ours, were set on fire. And our aircraft, 3C+BA, was completely destroyed. It was the only 110 on the airfield, and Schnaufer rang up Jabs and asked him if he could let us have another, and Jabs sent us one right away.
>
> We were very short of petrol, and we could hardly fly at all. We knew the English would soon be coming. Schnaufer had all his victories painted on the tail-unit of the machine that Jabs had let us have. We only flew one operation in it, on the 19th of April, and we didn't make contact with the enemy. That was the very last operational flight made by the *Geschwader*, and then all our petrol was used up. The British must have come about the 25th or 26th. Schnaufer put the aeroplane, complete with its kill markings, on display in front of the air traffic control building to make a point to the British.

Achim Jabs was *Kommodore* NJG 1. 'DX', therefore was G9+DX, the Messerschmitt he had provided as a replacement for BA, destroyed in an Allied strafing attack on Eggebek. We may presume that when Schnaufer had his kills painted on the tail-unit of the aircraft he also had the identification letters altered to 3C+BA, because Rumpelhardt's logbook shows that they were scrambled operationally in 'BA' on 19 April 1945, taking off from Eggebek at 2310 hours and landing at 0005 hours on the 20th without having made contact with the enemy. Their final flight overall took place on 21 April, an air test, again in BA.

GERMAN AIRCRAFT SELECTED FOR FERRYING
TO U.K.

LOCATION.	AIR MIN. NUMBER	TYPE	MARKINGS & WORKS NO.	REMARKS.
Schleswig	A.M. 1	Ju.88 G-6	4R+RB. 622983.	FuG 218V.R., NAXOS HALBE.
"	A.M.+2	Ju.88 G-6	4R+CB 620560	FuG 220. SN2., V.R. Naxos ZCR.
Flensburg	A.M. 3	Ju.88 G-6	3C+AN 622838	FuG 224. FuG217
"	A.M. 4	Si. 204 D-1	BU+PP. 322127	Night Fighter trainer. FuG217. 218 V.R.
"	A.M. 5	Si. 204 D-1	321523	
"	A.M. 6	Ju. 290 A-7	A3+OB. 110/186	Engines BMW 801 P-2.
"	A.M. 7	Do. 217M.	KF+JN.	Engines DB.605.
"	A.M. 8	Ju.352	KT+VJ. 010	Engines BMW.323.
Leck.	A.M. 9	Ju.88 G-6	4R+DR 621965	FuG 220VR. " 350ZC/R.
"	A.M.10	FW.190 A-6. R-6.	PN+LU 550214	Night Fighter. FuG 217
"	A.M.11	Ta.152+1-0	6.+ 150004	
"	A.M.12	Si.204 D-3	351547	
"	A.M.13	Si.204 D-1	251922	
Eggebeck	A.M.14	Ju.88 G-6	C9+AA 620788	FuG.220. Up, down Naxos. ZC.
"	A.M.15	Me.110 G4/R8	3C+BA 180560	FuG 218.
"	A.M.16	Ju.88 G-6	3C+DA. 622311	FuG 220.
"	A.M.17	Arado 232	A3+R.	Engines four BMW 323.
"	A.M.18	Ju.352	G6+WX.	Engines three BMW 323.
Leck	A.M.19	Ju.352	G6+YX	Engines three BMW 323.
Grove, Denmark.	A.M.20	He.219	D5+BL. 290126	FuG. 220 VR.

/Over ....

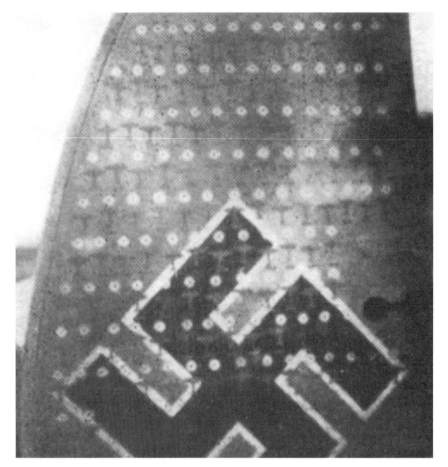

Previous page: *Report No. Air 40/2022 (Public Record Office) lists Schnaufer's last Messerschmitt, under A.M. 15.*

The port fin of 3C+BA. Its unfamiliar shape is because the rudder has been removed. The positions of the 'kill' symbols coincide exactly with those on the fin in the Imperial War Museum, London, proving beyond doubt that the two are identical. The symbols were painted on the fin on Schnaufer's instructions at the very end of the war.

3C+BA, with RAF roundels, photographed staging at Knokke-le-Zoute during its flight to the UK. (Photo check)

Another view of 3C+BA at Knokke. Almost certainly replacement fins and rudders were fitted. Note that the rearward-facing machine-gun has been removed. Schnaufer dispensed with his machine-gun in the interests of performance.

The port fin of 3C+BA
on display in the
Imperial War Museum.
(IWM).

The starboard fin of 3C+BA, on exhibition in the Australian War Memorial museum, Canberra. (Photo Fincher)

Bf.110G-4. Flown by Major Heinz-Wolfgang Schnaufer, Kommodore, NJG 4, Nov. 1944 with 105 victories. Fini the war with a total of 121 vict

Propellers, Dark Green
Wheel Hubs, Gloss Black

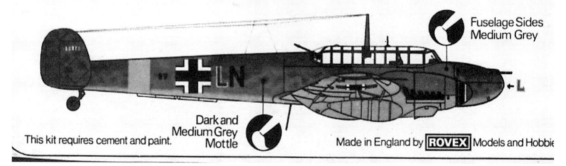

Bf.110G-2. 5 Staffel / II Gruppe Nachtjagdgeschwader 200, used for daylight operations, Russian Front, 1943-

Fuselage Sides
Medium Grey

Dark and
Medium Grey
Mottle

This kit requires cement and paint.

Made in England by **ROVEX** Models and Hobbi

The British occupied the airfield at Eggebek on about the 25th or 26th of April, and they found the new 3C+BA standing there proudly with 121 kill symbols on the fins. It is said – probably apocryphally – that the officer leading the British troops struck the fin on the Bf 110 with his riding whip and shouted, 'Impossible! Propaganda!'[1] The same officer then interviewed Schnaufer, Rumpelhardt and Gänsler, at first refusing to believe that any single crew could have shot down so many bombers. Eventually, however, he seems to have been persuaded of the truth. Rumpelhardt continues:

The fins of 3C+BA were just possibly fitted to another Bf 110 for the display of enemy equipment in Hyde Park in September 1945. The exhibit was lettered G9+AA, which was never flown by Schnaufer. Yet the myth persists, even on plastic aircraft models.

As I understand it, this aircraft was then flown to England. Schnaufer had to brief the British pilot on the controls and so on – only on the ground: he didn't fly with him. I don't know whether there was anyone else in the aeroplane when it went to England. They didn't tell us when it was going, but we told the ground staff to let us know, and so we were able to watch it taking off. There was very nearly a tragedy. The British pilot took off, but instead of retracting his undercarriage he raised his flaps, and the aeroplane cleared the airfield fence by what looked like a matter of centimetres. It was a very bad moment for us. We had a panic attack because if anything had gone wrong we would have got the blame. They would have said we had sabotaged the aircraft. But he managed to correct, and presumably he got to England OK.

[1] There is another, more believable, story that is told by Ludwig Meister, who was *Kommandeur* III./NJG 4. He recalls a senior officer commenting, 'This must be Dr Goebbels' machine!'.

The port fin from G9+EF, Schnaufer's 'favourite' Bf 110, shot down by day on Good Friday 1945. The fin is now in the possession of a German collector. Note the cannon-shell holes.

The selection of German aircraft to be flown to England for specialist examination was made by a team led by Group Captain G M Buxton, the Chief Technical Officer of the Central Fighter Establishment. Each machine chosen was given an Air Ministry serial number, and among the aircraft selected at Eggebek was listed[1] 'Air Ministry 15, Bf 110G4/R8 3C+BA, *Werknummer* 180560'[2]. This was clearly the aircraft in which the Schnaufer crew had made their final flights. Photos of the aircraft were published in Roderick Chisholm's book *Cover of Darkness*. When they were taken the airscrews and rudders had been removed from the machine in accordance with Air Ministry instructions as a precautionary measure to prevent the aircraft being flown without permission. A photograph of the port fin shows the 121 'kill' symbols.

[1] AIR 40/2022, Public Record Office.
[2] The *Werknummer* was the factory number of the aircraft.

For the purposes of the flight to the UK the German markings were painted out, RAF roundels painted on the wings and the Air Ministry number painted on the fuselage. 3C+BA became 'A.M. 15'. It seems likely that from Eggebek she went to Schleswig on the 14th of June and then flew onward to England a short time afterwards, staging at the Belgian airfield of Knokke-le-Zoute, where she was again photographed. It is likely that the fins with the kills marked on them were replaced before the trip and the fins brought separately to England. It is quite certain that the port fin that is in the possession of the Imperial War Museum is that from BC+A: comparison of the position of the individual kill icons on that fin with those shown on the photograph in Chisholm's book leaves no room for doubt on that point. The fin in the Imperial War Museum, when on display, is described as being from 'A Messerschmitt 110 flown by *Major* Heinz-Wolfgang Schnaufer', which is, of course, strictly correct, but it most certainly did not come from an aircraft in which he had scored any victories.

What, then, happened to Schnaufer's favourite operational aircraft, G9+EF? In the Bielefeld edition of the newspaper '*Neue Westfälische*' on 2 June 1973 there was an article headlined, '70,000 DM offered to collector for unique trophy of World War Two'. The Bielefeld citizen to whom the money had reportedly been offered by a collector in the USA was Wolfgang Lohmann, and he had come into possession of what seems certainly to be the port fin from Schnaufer's operational Messerschmitt, complete with all 121 'kill' icons. According to the article the artefact had been discovered being used as a patch on a roof in the village of Hillegossen and came from an aircraft that had been shot down at nearby Lämmershagen 'a few days before Easter 1945', killing two members of the crew and gravely injuring the third. G9+EF, it seems, came to an inglorious end in the hills of Westphalia.

Wolfgang Lohmann, an acknowledged expert on *Luftwaffe* aircraft and an enthusiastic military-air historian, tells how the rudder came into his possession:

Major Schnaufer's Me 110-G crashed on Good Friday 1945 [30th March] between 1400 and 1500 hours (local time) on the *Autobahn* from Hanover to Dortmund (today the A2). It came down in a flat trajectory on hard ground about 150 metres below the crest and about 250 metres from the Bielefeld side of the motorway. The wings and tail unit were torn off the fuselage by trees and undergrowth, but the fuselage itself was relatively undamaged. The remains of the machine were taken away by a local scrap dealer during Summer 1945 after American soldiers had helped themselves to souvenirs. The rudder that is now in my possession was taken by a chimneysweep immediately after the crash and kept in his workshop until I came on the scene and bought it from him — he was a pensioner by then.

   Shortly before the crash the aircraft had taken off from Gütersloh together with a number of Fw 190s. The aircraft were to be taken to safety from the advancing enemy troops. All the 190s were shot down by P-47s (?), two crashing in Werther and the remainder in the Verl-Kaunitz area. All the

The genuine G9+AA,
Oberstleutnant Jabs'
machine, was flown to
Sweden by another crew
at the end of the war
and crashed on landing.

pilots lost their life. It is said that they were all inexperienced pilots, possibly even mechanics. Another 110 crashed in the Senne Heath near the military exercise area, and it is said to be still buried in the ground there.

The crew of Schnaufer's machine were wounded, but they survived. They were taken to the Bethel Hospital near Bielefeld, which has been confirmed. At a later date they are said to have been moved to a hospital at Bad Lippspringe. Their papers went with them, so that it has proved impossible to find out who they were. The hospital at Bad Lippspringe is a sanatorium today, and old records are no longer available.

One thing should be noted. The dates of the kills on my rudder differ in one or two details from those published nowadays.

It is probable that the Bf 110 was heading for Wunstorf, for which airfield Schnaufer himself had taken off in 3C+BA in the early hours of the morning. Schnaufer flew in the hours of darkness and reached his destination: the crew flying G9+EF, whoever they were, flew in daylight and did not.

There still remains the mystery of the Bf 110 'G9+AA' reportedly exhibited in Hyde Park the following September. Assuming the story to be factual, – although the balance of probability is heavily against it – the aircraft was certainly a 'ringer', presumably specially painted by those arranging the exhibition in order to attract interest. Schnaufer never flew a G9+AA: that was the number of the aircraft flown exclusively by the *Kommodore* of NJG 1, who at the end of the war was Hans-Joachim Jabs. To make matters even more certain, the genuine G9/AA was hijacked at the end of the war by an NCO-pilot, *Unteroffizier* Alexander Siegfried König, and his radio operator, *Feldwebel* Fritz

Hrachowina. Reportedly[1] König and Hrachowina originated from Czechoslovakia and Estonia respectively and feared that they might be taken prisoner by the Russians. On 1 May 1945 they were ordered to fly G9+AA from Lüneburg to Schleswig: instead they went to Hammerlöv airfield near Trelleborg in Sweden, where they crashed on landing.

If it is true that a Bf 110 purporting to be that of Schnaufer was displayed in Hyde Park, and if it had the 121 symbols on the fins, it is possible that the fins were later removed and ultimately found their way into the Imperial War Museum and the Australian War Memorial respectively. But that is speculation.

---

[1] According to *The Luftwaffe in Sweden*, by Bo Widfeldt, published by Monogram Aviation Publications, Massachusetts.

Schnaufer's Victories

This is an attempt to identify as many as possible of Schnaufer's victories. The identifications cannot, by and large, be definitive, but some are more positive than others. Kills achieved when he was flying from Saint-Trond (II./NJG 1), Leeuwarden and Quakenbrück (IV./NJG) and Saint-Trond again (IV/NJG 1) respectively are easier to identify than those when he was flying towards then end of the war, mainly from Gütersloh, with NJG 4. There are a number of reasons for this: Saint-Trond and Leeuwarden were in occupied territory, Belgium and Holland respectively, and located on the approach routes of RAF bombers, so that kills tended to take place near to the airfield. In both those countries there have been, since the war, assiduous researchers whose work has been invaluable in attempting to reconcile crashes with the entries in Schnaufer's *Leistungsbuch*. Understandably there has been a lack of such enthusiasts in Germany. As the war progressed and the pressures on the night-fighter crews and the *Luftwaffe* administration increased, there was less time – and, probably, less incentive – to record and check precise details of the geographical location of kills. Schnaufer moved to Dortmund with IV./NJG 1 in late 1944 and then took over command of NJG 4, operating mostly from Gütersloh: from that period on many of his victories were achieved over territory occupied by the Allies, and his kills were logged by grid reference (*Planquadrat*) rather than by place-name, which makes it impossible to identify the victims.

Dates, times and locations are taken directly from Schnaufer's *Leistungsbuch*, and the spelling of names of places has been corrected as necessary. Schnaufer and his crew frequently misidentified their victims – Lancasters and Halifaxes (particularly Halifaxes Mark III) were very easy to mistake for one another – and the type given below is the correct type, except when I have been unable to identify the victim, in which case it is as given in the *Leistungsbuch*. I have graded the identifications A, B or C in the right-hand column, with A meaning 'virtually certain', B meaning 'probable' and C meaning 'possible'.

No.	Date	Time	Location	Unit.	Aircraft Type	Serial No./ Sqn No.
1	2.6.42	0155	Grez-Doiceau, 15 km south of Louvain, Belgium.	76 Sqn.	Halifax II	W1064//MP-J (B)
2	1.8.42	0247	1 km. SW of Loon op Zand, near Tilburg, Holland.	25 OTU.	Wellington IC	DV439/-H (B)
3	1.8.42	0317	Huldenberg, Belgium.	27 OTU.	Wellington IC	DV552/UJ-N (A)
4	1.8.42	0345	Gilly, Charleroi, Belgium.	24 OTU.	Whitley V	BD347 (B)
5	25.8.42	0254	Near Loonbeek, Belgium.	150 Sqn.	Wellington III	BJ651/JN-M (B)
6	29.8.42	0116	Tombeek, Belgium, 16 km SE of Brussels.	78 Sqn.	Halifax II	W7809/EY-
7	21.12.42	2353	Poelkapelle, Belgium.	106 Sqn.	Lancaster I	R5914/ZN- (A)
8	14.5.43	0214	Heerlen, Holland, east of Maastricht.	214 Sqn.	Stirling I	R9242/BU-O (B)
9	14.5.43	0307	Near Blanden, SE of Louvain, Belgium.	78 Sqn.	Halifax II	JB873/EY-J (A)
10	30.5.43	0048	South of Baelen, east	218 Sqn.	Stirling III	BF565/HA-H (A)
11	30.5.43	0143	Budingen, 7 km. NW of Saint-Trond, Belgium.	35 Sqn.	Halifax II	DT804/TL-C (A)
12	30.5.43	0222	Schaffen airfield, 22 km north of Saint-Trond, Belgium.	218 Sqn.	Stirling III	BK688/HA-A (A)
13	22.6.43	0113	Langdorp, near Aarschot, Belgium.	218 Sqn	Stirling III	BK712/HA-D (A)
14	25.6.43	0258	Hamme-Mille, south of Louvain, Belgium.		Wellington	
15	29.6.43	0125	Solwaster, south-east of Verviers, Belgium.	97 Sqn.	Lancaster III	LM323/OF-U (A)
16	29.6.43	0145	Wandre. north-east of Liège, Belgium.	76 Sqn.	Halifax V	DK137/NP-R (A)
17	29.6.43	0155	Near Vottem, north of Liège, Belgium.	35 Sqn.	Halifax II	HR812/TL-F (A)
18	4.7.43	0048	Averbode, 7 km. north-west of of Diest, Belgium.	196 Sqn.	Wellington X	HE980/ZO- (A)
19	4.7.43	0101	Near Geetbets, 9 km. north-west of Saint-Trond, Belgium.	149 Sqn.	Stirling III	BF530/OJ-B (A)
20	9.7.43	0233	Near Grobbendonk, 23 km. ESE of Antwerp, Belgium.	49 Sqn.	Lancaster III	ED663/EA- (A)
21	11.8.43	0032	Hähnlein, 25 km. SSW of Darmstadt.		Lancaster	
22	28.8.43	0359	Jemeppe sur Sambre, 15 km west of Namur,	102 Sqn.	Halifax II	JB835/DY-X (A)

			Belgium.			
23	31.8.43	2241	2 km. south-east of Kuinre, Zuider Zee.	35 Sqn.	Halifax II	HR878/TL-J (A)
24	31.8.43	0353	Near Lozen, north of Bree, Belgium.	166 Sqn.	Wellington X	HE988/AS-U (B)
25	24.8.43	0009	Near Eschede, 20 km. NNE of Celle, Germany.	77 Sqn.	Halifax II	JD379/KN-M (B)
26	23.9.43	2300	5 km. south of Kirchheimbolanden.	218 Sqn.	Stirling III	EJ104/HA-G (A)
27	27.9.43	2331	Near Stemmen, west of Stadthagen, Germany.		Halifax	
28	3.10.43	2150	Near Lande, 8 km. north of Minden.	51 Sqn	Halifax II	HR728/LK-D (C)
29	9.10.43	0113	Near Schwaförden, 9 km. N of Sulingen, Germany.	158 Sqn.	Halifax II	HR945/NP-Y (B)
30	9.10.43	0142	Near Holtensen, SW of Hanover, Germany.		Halifax	
31	18.10.43	2025	Near Negenborn, NNW of Hanover	101 Sqn.	Lancaster III	DV230/SR-T (B)
32	20.10.43	1913	Near Gieten, east of Assen, Holland	7 Sqn.	Lancaster III	JB175/MG-A (A)
33	20.10.43	1925	Near Harrenstätte, NW of Wertle, Germany.	405 Sqn.	Lancaster III	JB348/LQ-R (A)
34	22.10.43	2140	Near Dransfeld, Hanover, Germany.	57 Sqn.	Lancaster III	JB320/DX-X (B)
35	23.11.43	1850	2 km. from Ter Apel, near Emmen, Holland.	405 Sqn.	Lancaster III	JA939 LQ-C (A)
36	23.11.43	1900	Lorup, NNW Cloppenburg, Germany.	12 Sqn.	Lancaster III	JB 537/PH-N (C)
37	16.12.43	1801	Near Follega, Holland.	7 Sqn.	Lancaster III	JA853/MG-L (A)
38	16.12.43	1812	Near Lemmer, Holland.	101 Sqn.	Lancaster I	DV300/SR-W (A)
39	16.12.43	1823	South-west of Wolvega, Holland.	49 Sqn.	Lancaster III	JB545/EA-O (A)
40	16.12.43	1841	2 km. south-west of Wirdum, Holland.	432 Sqn.	Lancaster II	DS831/QO-N (A)
41	29.12.43	1850	5 km. north-east of Meppel, Holland.	10 Sqn.	Halifax II	JD314/ZA-X (A)
42	29.12.43	1915	Near Wietmarschen, west of Lingen, Germany.	408 Sqn.	Lancaster II	DS718/EQ-R (A)
43	27.1.44	1945	Near Essen, 4 km. NW Quakenbrück, Germany.	12 Sqn.	Lancaster III	JB283/PH-W (C)
44	30.1.44	2215	In GK5, west of Amsterdam, Holland.		Lancaster	
45	15.2.44	2258	In the sea, DJ93.	103 Sqn.	Lancaster III	ND363/PM-A (A)
46	15.2.44	2319	Near Hoorn, Holland.	115 Sqn.	Lancaster II	LL689/KO-P (A)
47	15.2.44	2333	EL78 in the Wattenmeer, Holland.	622 Sqn.	Lancaster I	W4272/GJ-C (A)

48	22.3.44	2310	Halle, near Lembeek, 18 km. south of Brussels.	9 Sqn.	Lancaster III	LM430/WS-B (A)
49	25.3.44	0021	Neuwarendorf, east of Münster, Germany.	626 Sqn.	Lancaster I	HK539/UM-A2 (B)
50	25.3.44	0012	East of Dortmund, Germany.		Four-engined bomber	
51	25.3.44	0041	Nr Varsseveld, Holland, NE Emmerich, Germany.		Four-engined bomber	
52	11.4.44	2315	Near Beerse, 6 km. west of Turnhout, Belgium.	83 Sqn	Lancaster III	ND389/OL-A (A)
53	11.4.44	2325	2 km. north of Saint-Lenaerts, Belgium.	49 Sqn.	Lancaster I	LL899/EA-P (A)
54	25.4.44	0203	Near Alken, Belgium	115 Sqn.	Lancaster I	HK542/KO-J (B)
55	25.4.44	0228	3 km. north of Mechelen, Belgium	115 Sqn.	Lancaster II	DS734/KO-Y (A)
56	25.4.44	0230	1 km. west of Haasdonk, Belgium.	192 Sqn.	Halifax III	LW622/DT-R (B)
57	25.4.44	0240	In the sea at LG3		Halifax	
58	27.4.44	0205	1 km. south of Achtmaal, Holland.	156 Sqn.	Lancaster III	JB307/GT-H (A)
59	27.4.44	0218	Over the sea, LG38	408 Sqn.	Lancaster II	DS719/LQ-U (B)
60	28.4.44	0130	8 km. north of Aubel, Belgium, 15 km SW of Aachen, Germany.	434 Sqn.	Halifax V	LL258/WL-W (A)
61	28.4.44	0140	Town area, Verviers, Belgium.	432 Sqn	Halifax III	MZ588/QO-W (A)
62	9.5.44	0334	Nr Grand-Reng, 30km. SW of Charleroi, Belgium.	432 Sqn.	Halifax III	LW594/QO-G (A)
63	13.5.44	0044	Londerzeel, 8 km. west of Mechelen, Belgium.	426 Sqn.	Halifax III	LK883/OW-E (B)
64	13.5.44	0036	5 km. ENE Hasselt, Belgium.	158 Sqn.	Halifax III	HX334/NP-C (C)
65	13.5.44	0048	Hoogstraaten, 16 km. NW of Turnhout, Belgium.	466 Sqn.	Halifax III	LV919/HD-O (A)
66	22.5.44	0134	3 km. south of Mol, Belgium.		Lancaster	
67	22.5.44	0151	10 km. south of Herentals, Belgium.		Lancaster	
68	23.5.44	0123	Near Neerpelt, Belgium.	75 Sqn.	Lancaster I	ME690/AA-Z (A)
69	23.5.44	0136	Near Brecht, 22 km. NE of Antwerp, Belgium.	100 Sqn.	Lancaster I	ME670/HW-Q (B)
70	25.5.44	0115	3 km. NW of Eindhoven, Holland.	51 Sqn.	Halifax III	LK885/MH-Z (A)
71	25.5.44	0118	2 km. NNW of Tilburg, Holland.	158 Sqn.	Halifax III	LW653/NP-T (C)
72	25.5.44	0122	1.5 km. west of Goirle, SSW of Tilburg, Holland.	76 Sqn.	Halifax III	MZ622/MP-L (B)
73	25.5.44	0125	Between Dongen and	429 Sqn.	Halifax III	LW124/AL-N

			Tilburg, Holland.			(C)
74	25.5.44	0129	7 km. SW of Tilburg, Holland.		Lancaster	
75	13.6.44	0027	Avennes les Auvert, Belgium.	408 Sqn.	Lancaster II	DS772/EQ-T (A)
76	13.6.44	0031	Cambrai airfield.	408 Sqn.	Lancaster II	DS726/EQ-Y (B)
77	13.6.44	0034	Tilloy, 2 km. north of Cambrai.	408 Sqn.	Lancaster II	DS688/EQ-R (A)
78	16.6.44	0100	North of Arras		Lancaster	
79	17.6.44	0154	Dreumel, north of s'Hertogenbosch, Holland.		Four-engined bomber	
80	17.6.44	0204	Berkel, Holland.	77 Sqn.	Halifax III	NA524/KN-F (A)
81	22.6.44	0125	Valkenswaard, Holland.	44 Sqn.	Lancaster III	LM582/KM-Q (B)
82	22.6.44	0130	2 km. south of Meeuven, Belgium.	207 Sqn.	Lancaster I	ME683/EM-W (B)
83	22.6.44	0136	5 km. south of Opoerteren, Belgium.	44 Sqn	Lancaster III	LM434/KM-F (C)
84	22.6.44	0204	6 km. south of Hamont, Belgium.	630 Sqn.	Lancaster 1	ME843/LE-U (B)
85	21.7.44	0140	1.5 km. north of Boxtel, Holland.	90 Sqn.	Lancaster I	LM183/WP-L (C)
86	21.7.44	0151	8 km. north of Breda, Holland.		Four-engined bomber	
87	29.7.44	0138	Cemetery at Pforzheim, Germany.	467 Sqn.	Lancaster 1	ME856/PO-T (C)
88	29.7.44	0150	Eutingen, near Pforzheim, Germany.		Four-engined bomber	
89	29.7.44	0157	Malmsheim, 20 km. west of Stuttgart, Germany.	106 Sqn.	Lancaster 1	ME778/ZN-O (C)
90	13.8.44	0048	Wasserliesch, Germany.		Four-engined bomber	
91	13.8.44	0115	Gouvy, 28 km. SSW of Malmédy, Belgium.		Four-engined bomber	
92	13.8.44	0109	Werbomont, SSE of Liège, Belgium.	635 Sqn.	Lancaster III	ND694/F2-R (B)
93	13.8.44	0119	3 km. west of Mons, near Liège, Belgium.		Four-engined bomber	
94	12.9.44	2307	RQ – RP		Four-engined bomber	
95	23.9.44	2253	JP – HP		Four-engined bomber	
96	23.9.44	2310	JO		Four-engined bomber	
97	23.9. 44	2315	HO -JO		Four-engined bomber	
98	23.9.44	2325	JN – HN		Four-engined bomber	
99	9.10.44	2032	South of Bochum,		Four-engined	

				Germany.		bomber	
100	9.10.44	2055	JO			Four-engined bomber	
101	6.11.44	1926	KP – IP			Four-engined bomber	
102	6.11.44	1934	KP – IP			Four-engined bomber	
103	6.11.44	1941	KP – IP			Four-engined bomber	
104	21.11.44	1905	KP			Lancaster	
105	21.11.44	1907	KP			Four-engined bomber	
106	12.12.44	2000	MO – LO			Four-engined bomber	
107	3.2.45	2109	LO			Four-engined bomber	
108	212 45	0153	MM – MN			Lancaster	
109	21.2.45	0158	MM			Lancaster	
110	21.2.45	2044	HQ – HP			Lancaster	
111	21.2.45	2048	HP – HO			Lancaster	
112	21.2.45	2051	HP – HO			Lancaster	
113	21.2.45	2055	HP – HO			Lancaster	
114	21.2.45	2058	IO – JN			Lancaster	
115	21.2.45	2100	JN – KM			Lancaster	
116	21.2.45	2103	KM – KL			Lancaster	
*	21.2.45	2110	KM – KL	463 Sqn	Lancaster I		NG329/JO-Z (B)
117	3.3.45	2155	HQ			Lancaster	
118	3.3.45	2204	HQ			Lancaster	
119	7.3.45	2041	LR – MR			Lancaster	
120	7.3.45	2047	LS – MS			Lancaster	
121	7.3.45	2156	GC – HC			Lancaster	

* Schnaufer did not claim this kill as his cannon failed during the attack and his crew did not witness the fate of the enemy machine.

Selected Bibliography

ADERS, Gerhard, *Die Geschichte der Deutschen Nachtjagd* (Motorbuch Verlag Stuttgart, 1978). Published in English as *The History of the German Night Fighter Force* (Crécy Books, 1992)

BENNETT, D C T, *Pathfinder* (Frederick Muller Ltd., 1958).

BUTLER, Philip H, *Air Min* (Merseyside Aviation Society, 1977).

BUTLER, Philip H, *War Prizes* (Midland Counties Publications, 1994).

CHISHOLM, Roderick, *Cover of Darkness* (Chatto & Windus, 1953).

CHORLEY, William R, *Bomber Command Losses of the Second World War* (Three volumes, 1942, 1943 and 1944 respectively. Midland Counties Publications).

DUNMORE, Spencer, & CARTER, William, *Reap the Whirlwind* (Crécy Books, 1992)

ENGAU, Fritz, *Nachtjäger, Bomber, Wolken und Sterne* (Hoppe, Graz, 1983).

HAGEN, H P, *Husaren des Himmels* (Erich-Pabel Verlag, Stuttgart, 1964).

HARRIS, Sir Arthur, *Bomber Offensive* (Collins 1947).

HELD, Werner, & NAUROTH, Holger, *Die deutsche Nachtjagd* (Motorbuch Verlag Stuttgart).

JANSEN, A, *Wespennest Leeuwarden* (Hollandia B.V., 1976)

JOHNEN, Wilhelm, *Duel Under The Stars* (Crécy Books, 1994)

MIDDLEBROOK, Martin, & EVERITT, Chris, *The Bomber Command War Diaries* (Viking Press, 1985)

MIDDLEBROOK, Martin, *The Berlin Raids* (Viking Press, 1988)

PRICE, Alfred, *Instruments of Darkness* (Peninsula Publishing, 1987)

PRICE, Alfred, *Luftschlacht über Deutschland* (Motorbuch Verlag Stuttgart, 1973) Translation of *Battle over the Reich*.

TOLIVER, Raymond F, & CONSTABLE, Trevor J, *Das waren die Deutschen Jagdfliegerasse 1939–1945* (Motorbuch Verlag Stuttgart 1976). Translation of 'Horrido'.

ÜBERHORST, Horst, *Elite für die Diktatur* (Droste, Düsseldorf, 1969)

WEBSTER, Sir Charles, & FRANKLAND, Noble, *The Strategic Air Offensive against Germany 1939–1945* (HMSO, 1961)

WEST, Kenneth S, *The Captive Luftwaffe* (Putnam, London, 1978)

Alphabetical Index of Names